Multiple Objective and Goal Programming

Advances in Soft Computing

Editor-in-chief
Prof. Janusz Kacprzyk
Systems Research Institute
Polish Academy of Sciences
ul. Newelska 6
01-447 Warsaw, Poland
E-mail: kacprzyk@ibspan.waw.pl
http://www.springer.de/cgi-bin/search-bock.pl?series=4240

Tadeusz Trzaskalik
Jerzy Michnik
Editors

Multiple Objective and Goal Programming

Recent Developments

With 75 Figures
and 76 Tables

Physica-Verlag

A Springer-Verlag Company

Professor Dr. Tadeusz Trzaskalik
Dr. Jerzy Michnik
The Karol Adamiecki University of Economics in Katowice
Operations Research Department
ul. Bogucicka 14
40-226 Katowice
Poland
ttrzaska@ae.katowice.pl
jmichnik@ae.katowice.pl

ISSN 1615-3871
ISBN 3-7908-1409-1 Physica-Verlag Heidelberg New York

Cataloging-in-Publication Data applied for
Die Deutsche Bibliothek – CIP-Einheitsaufnahme
Multiple objective and goal programming: recent developments; with 76 tables / Tadeusz Trzaskalik; Jerzy
Michnik, ed. – Heidelberg; New York: Physica-Verl., 2002
   (Advances in soft computing)
   ISBN 3-7908-1409-1

Physica-Verlag Heidelberg New York
a member of BertelsmannSpringer Science+Business Media GmbH

© Physica-Verlag Heidelberg 2002
Printed in Germany

Hardcover Design: Erich Kirchner, Heidelberg

SPIN 10831102   88/2202-5 4 3 2 1 0 – Printed on acid-free paper

Preface

This volume constitutes the proceedings of the Fourth International Conference on Multi-objective Programming and Goal Programming. Theory & Applications (MOPGP'00) held in Ustroń, Poland on May 29 – June 1, 2000. Sixty six people from 15 countries attended the conference and 53 papers were presented.

MOPGP'00 was organized by the Department of Operations Research, The Karol Adamiecki University of Economics in Katowice, Poland and chaired by Tadeusz Trzaskalik. The members of the International Committee were: James Ignizio, Dylan Jones, Pekka Korhonen, Carlos Romero, Ralph Steuer and Mehrdad Tamiz. The Local Organizing Committee consisted of Ewa Konarzewska-Gubała, Ignacy Kaliszewski, Jaroslav Ramik, Andrzej Skulimowski, Roman Słowiński and Tadeusz Trzaskalik.

The volume is divided into two parts: Theory and Applications. 15 papers from Part direct at theoretical topics, in Part II there are 18 papers on innovative applications, implementation and practice of multi-objective programming and goal programming. Thanks to the efforts made by the referees, readers will enjoy turning the pages.

MOPGP'00 was made possible by the support of the State Committee for Scientific Research (KBN) and The Karol Adamiecki University of Economics in Katowice. I would like to thank to the all people who helped to organize the conference, have made the success of MOPGP'00 possible.

Those in attendance at MOPGP'00 were: Alejandro Balbas, Rafael Caballero, Stefan Chanas, Yuh-Wen Chen, Sydney Chu, Bogdan Ciupek, Szabolcs Csikai, Hoa Do Thien, Ludmila Domeova, Cezary Dominiak, Renata Dudzińska, Petr Fiala, Paweł Gąsiorowski, Barbara Gołąbowska, Trinidad Gomez, Jacinto Gonzalez-Pachon, Karen Z. Hairapetyan, Pirja Heiskanen, Edwin Hinloopen, Miguel Angel Hinojosa, Josef Jablonsky, Andrzej Jaszkiewicz, Pedro Jimenez Guerra, Dylan Jones, Ignacy Kaliszewski, Gregory Kersten, Ewa Konarzewska-Gubala, Pekka J. Korhonen, Michael Kostreva, Margit Kovacs, Lech Kruś, Dorota Kuchta, Moussa Larbani, Simon J. Mardle, Miguel Martinez Panero, Wojtek Michałowski, Jerzy Michnik, Keyvan Mirrazavi, Dorota Miszczyńska, Marek Miszczyński, Pavel Mosorin, Hirotaka Nakayama, Maciej Nowak, Agnieszka Osiecka, Jaroslav Ramik, Maria Victoria Rodriguez Uria, Carlos Romero, Francisco Ruiz, Sebastian Sitarz, Andrzej M.J. Skulimowski, Ralph E. Steuer, Tomas Subrt, Tomasz Szapiro, Mehrdad Tamiz, Richard Treloar, Tadeusz Trzaskalik, Grażyna Trzpiot, Anna Urbanek, Tomasz Wachowicz, Petra Weidner, Ye Boon Yun, Kazimierz Zaraś, Michał Zawisza, Zdenek Zmeskal.

Tadeusz Trzaskalik
Jerzy Michnik

Katowice, August 2001

Contents

I I APPLICATIONS

I
THEORY

Measuring the Balance Space Sensitivity in Vector Optimization*

Alejandro Balbás[†]and Pedro Jiménez Guerra[‡]

Abstract

Recent literature has shown that the balance space approach may be a significant alternative to address several topics concerning vector optimization. Although this new look also leads to the efficient set and, consequently, is equivalent to the classical viewpoint, it yields new results and algorithms, as well as new economic interpretations, that may be very useful in theoretical frameworks and practical applications. The present paper focuses on the sensitivity of the balance set. We prove a general envelope theorem that yields the sensitivity with respect to any parameter considered in the problem. Furthermore, we provide a dual problem that characterizes the primal balance space and its sensitivity. Finally, we also give the implications of our results with respect to the sensitivity of the efficient set.

1   Introduction

Since the concepts of balance point and balance set were introduced in [6] for vector optimization problems, several authors have analyzed their significant properties and have developed some algorithms to compute them in practice (see [5], [6], [7], [8] and [9] for further details).

Mainly, this approach yields a very general alternative method in vector optimization because multiobjective problems may be deeply analyzed by means of their ideal points rather than scalarized problems. It is not necessary to seek appropriate weights to compute a balance point. Instead, one has to choose a direction of preferential deviations from the ideal point in order to reach an optimal point.

*We would like to thank Professor Efim A. Galperin for very helpful comments and suggestions.

[†]Universidad Carlos III. Departamento de Economía de la Empresa. C/ Madrid 126. 28903 Getafe, Madrid (Spain). balbas@emp.uc3m.es

[‡]U.N.E.D. Departamento de Matemáticas Fundamentales. C/ Senda del Rey s/n. 28040 Madrid (Spain). pjimenez@mat.uned.es

Consequently, an interesting economic meaning is possible since the ideal point may be considered an adequate reference for the decision maker. Given an arbitrary balance point $b = (b_1, b_2, ..., b_n)$, b_i is the difference between the final level attained in the ith objective and its "ideal level", and thus, the decision maker can choose another balance point when these differences are not very successful. Furthermore, b is proportional to the direction used to leave the ideal point and, therefore, each quotient b_i/b_j provides the number of units lost in the ith objective per unit lost in the jth one. When the problem is scalarized, the meaning of the weights is not so clear.

This nonscalarized procedure provides new algorithms which, as said above, are very general. When we are choosing a concrete direction to detect a balance point we are also choosing ratios of losses among the conflicting objectives.

As pointed out in [5], the set of Pareto solutions and the balance set are equivalent from a theoretical viewpoint, in the sense that there exists a simple relationship between both sets. Thus, balance set techniques also apply to study the Pareto solutions.

Both advantages, new nonscalarized algorithms and economic interpretations, justify the interest of extending the discussion in order to address another important issues of vector optimization. So, this paper focuses on duality and sensitivity since these topics still present many open questions when dealing with vector problems.

Regarding duality and sensitivity, scalar problems have many deep properties whose extension for vector problems is not straightforward. This fact is clearly pointed out in [10] and [15], where interesting, general and classical treatments are presented. Although significant advances have been achieved and useful developments have been provided from both theoretical and practical viewpoints, in general, the dual objective is given by multifunctions[1], and this situation makes it rather difficult to establish saddle point conditions or sensitivity results. In fact, statements are far more complicated than the corresponding results for scalar problems, and their practical applications present larger difficulties too. Linear vector problems are much easier but, as pointed out in [1] and [4], even this case becomes complex when using flexible criteria to choose an optimal solution in the efficient set.[2]

In order to overcome these difficulties the recent literature (see for instance [2], [3], [11] or [12]) has developed new ideas and methods, and we will try to show here that the balance space approach may be an useful alternative and can broaden possible techniques. Most of the classical caveats disappear

---

[1]*i.e.*, if λ represents the dual objective and y is a dual feasible element, then $\lambda(y)$ is not a vector but a set of vectors.

[2]For instance, in order to guarantee that dual solutions measure the primal sensitivity with respect to the vector in the right side, one has to impose restrictive assumptions with regard to the weights used when composing an efficient solution as a linear convex combination of extreme points.

when dealing with the ideal point sensitivity[3] (see for instance [16] for a complete analysis that holds in a very general framework) and, therefore, since the efficient set equals the ideal point plus the balance set (see [5]), the sensitivity of this set would allow us to obtain the primal sensitivity by adding two terms.

The remainder of the paper is as follows. Section 2 presents the basic concepts, notations and hypotheses. Section 3 deals with the primal sensitivity. First of all we establish Theorem 1, that yields a scalar programming problem whose solution leads to the balance point proportional to the direction of preferential deviations.[4] Later, we draw on the sensitivity of this scalar problem, along with the sensitivity of the ideal point, and prove a general envelope theorem (Theorem 2) that provides the sensitivity of a general vector problem with respect to any parameter considered in the problem. Theorem 2 gives the sensitivity by means of a far simpler analytic expression than those provided by previous literature (see for instance [2]). Accordingly, the sensitivity may be easily computed in practical applications. Corollary 3 presents the sensitivity with respect to the vector of the right side.

The duality theory for convex problems is addressed in Section 4. Theorem 1 allows us to introduce a dual problem for which several properties are proved. So, the dual objective is never greater than the primal one, the absence of duality gap may by stated, dual and primal solutions are characterized by saddle points and complementary slackness conditions and, finally, the dual problem is linear if so is the primal one. Furthermore, the dual solutions coincide with the Lagrange multipliers and, according to our general envelope theorem, provide the primal sensitivity. Theorem 6 might merit particular attention since it provides special saddle points and slackness conditions that are given by means of vector inequalities and, consequently, may be easily applied in practical applications.[5]

The last section concludes and summarizes the article.

2 Preliminaries and Notations

Let k, l, m and n be entire numbers, W and P subsets of $\mathbb{R}^n$ and $\mathbb{R}^l$ respectively, $d = (d_1, d_2, ..., d_k) \in \mathbf{R}^k$ with $d_i \geq 0$ for $i = 1, 2, ..., k$ and $d \neq 0$, and $f : W \longrightarrow \mathbf{R}^k$ and $g : W \times P \longrightarrow \mathbb{R}^m$ two vector functions whose real components will be denoted by f_i, $i = 1, 2, ..., k$, and g_j, $j = 1, 2, ..., m$, respectively.

---

[3]Consequently, if there are no conflicts among the objectives and all of them attain the optimal value at the same feasible point, then the main properties of the scalar programming may be extended without introducing more complex statements and stronger assumptions.

[4]As said above, the direction of preferential deviations may be easily interpreted because it provides ratios of losses in each objective.

[5]In fact, in the statement of Theorem 6 we will use the symbol $\leq$ instead of $\not\geq$. However, previous literature often uses $\not\geq$ unless the author deals with non-conflicting objectives.

6

Let us focus on the following vector optimization problem

$$Min\ f(x)\quad \left\{ \begin{array}{l} x \in W \\ g(x, p) \leq 0 \end{array} \right. \tag{1}$$

being $p \in P$ an arbitrary element. Assume the following assumption:

(A1) For any $p \in P$ and $i = 1, 2, ..., k$, there exists $x(i, p) \in W$ such that $g(x(i, p), p) \leq 0$ and $f_i(x(i, p)) \leq f_i(x)$ for every $x \in W$ with $g(x, p) \leq 0$.

Assumption (A1) just means that the scalar problem

$$Min\{f_i(x) : x \in W,\ g(x, p) \leq 0\} \tag{2}$$

attains an optimal value at $x(i, p) \in W$ ($i = 1, 2, ..., k$) and, therefore, the ideal point (or the set of partial minima)

$$J(p) = [f_1(x(1, p)), f_2(x(2, p)), ..., f_k(x(k, p))] \in \mathbf{R}^k$$

does exist. In order to achieve an easier notation, we will denote $J_i(p) = f_i(x(i, p))$, $i = 1, 2, ..., k$.

Following the approach of [8] or [9], an element $b \in \mathbb{R}^k$, $b \geq 0$, is said to be a balance point of (1) if $\{f(x) : x \in W, g(x, p) \leq 0\} \cap [J(p), J(p) + b] \neq \emptyset$ and $\{f(x) : x \in W, g(x, p) \leq 0\} \cap [J(p), J(p) + b^*] = \emptyset$ for every $b^* \in \mathbb{R}^k$ such that $0 \leq b^* \leq b$, $b^* \neq b$.[6] As pointed out in [5], $b \in \mathbf{R}^k$ is a balance point of (1) if and only if $J(p) + b$ belongs to the efficient line of (1).

In order to guarantee the existence of balance points in the direction of preferential deviations, we also impose the following assumption:

(A2) For every $p \in P$ there exists a balance point proportional to d.

3   The Envelope Theorem

Let us introduce the following scalar problem whose decision variables are $\tau \in \mathbf{R}$ and $x \in W$

$$Min\ \tau\quad \left\{ \begin{array}{l} x \in W \\ g(x, p) \leq 0 \\ f(x) - \tau d \leq J(p) \end{array} \right. \tag{3}$$

Assumptions (A1) and (A2) allows us to establish the statement below

---

[6]If $u, v \in \mathbf{R}^k$ with $u \leq v$, then $[u, v]$ denotes the set $\{x \in \mathbf{R}^k : u \leq x \leq v\}$.

Theorem 1 *Assume that $p \in P$ and $\tau_p \geq 0$. Then, $\tau_p d$ is a balance point of Problem (1) if and only if there exists $x(p) \in W$ such that $(x(p), \tau_p)$ solves (3).[7] In the affirmative case, $x(p) \in W$ is a Pareto solution of (1) such that $f(x(p)) = J(p) + \tau_p d$.[8]*

Proof. Suppose that $\tau_p d$ is a balance point of (1). Then $J(p) + \tau_p d$ is an efficient point and there exists $x(p) \in W$, Pareto solution of (1), such that $f(x(p)) = J(p) + \tau_p d$. Thus, $f(x(p)) - \tau_p d = J(p)$ and $(x(p), \tau_p)$ verifies the constraints of (3). Moreover, if $(x(p), \tau_p)$ does not solve (3) we have that there exists a feasible couple (x, τ) such that $\tau < \tau_p$. Since (x, τ) is feasible we have that $f(x) - J(p) \leq \tau d < \tau_p d$. Hence $f(x) \in [J(p), J(p) + \tau d]$ and this is a contradiction because $\tau_p d$ is a balance point of (1) and $\tau < \tau_p$.

Conversely, let us suppose that $(x(p), \tau_p)$ solves (3) but $\tau_p d$ is not a balance point of (1). (A2) guarantees the existence of a balance point $\tau^* d$. Assume at the moment that $\tau^* > \tau_p$. Since $(x(p), \tau_p)$ solves (3) it must be (3)$-$feasible and, therefore, $f(x(p)) - J(p) \leq \tau_p d < \tau^* d$. Thus $f(x(p)) \in [J(p), J(p) + \tau_p d]$ and this is a contradiction because $\tau^* d$ is a balance point. Assume now that $\tau^* < \tau_p$. Since $\tau^* d$ is a balance point there exists $x \in W$ such that x is a Pareto solution of (1) and $J(p) + \tau^* d = f(x)$. Therefore, (x, τ^*) is (3)$-$feasible and $\tau^* < \tau_p$ which contradicts the hypothesis because τ_p must be the minimum value of (3). $\blacksquare$

The latter theorem allows us to compute the balance point associated with the direction of preferential deviations. In fact, in a first step the ideal point $J(p)$ may be computed by solving k scalar problems and, later, once $J(p)$ is known, Problem (3) leads to the balance point $\tau_p d$.

As a consequence, the sensitivity of Problem (1) with respect to the parameter p depends on the sensitivity of $k + 1$ scalar problems. Theorem 2 establishes this property with precision and extends the classical envelope theorem, well-known in the scalar programming case.

Theorem 2 *Let us assume that W and P are open sets and f and g are continuously differentiable functions. Denote by*

$$\lambda(i, p) = (\lambda_1(i, p), \lambda_2(i, p), ..., \lambda_m(i, p)) \in \mathbf{R}^m$$

the Kuhn-Tucker multiplier of (2) associated to $x(i, p)$ $(i = 1, 2, ..., k$, $p \in P)$. Suppose that $(\mu(p), \nu(p)) = (\mu_1(p), ..., \mu_m(p), \nu_1(p), ..., \nu_k(p)) \in \mathbf{R}^{m+k}$ represents the Kuhn-Tucker multiplier of (3) for each $p \in P$. Consider finally that all of the Kuhn-Tucker multipliers continuously depend on $p \in P$ and

---

[7]If $\tau_0 d$ is a balance point for Problem (1) then the existence of $x(p)$ may be proved without imposing Assumption (A2).

[8](A2) and Theorem 1 guarantee the existence of solutions of (3). Henceforth $\tau_p \geq 0$ will represent the optimal value of (3), and $x(p)$ will represent the corresponding Pareto solution of (1).

define the function $P \ni p \longrightarrow F(p) = J(p) + \tau_p d = f(x(p))$. *Then,*

$$
\begin{aligned}
\frac{\partial F_r}{\partial p_s} \;=\;& \sum_{j=1}^{m} \lambda_j(r,p) \frac{\partial g_j}{\partial p_s}(x(r,p),p) \\[2mm]
&+ d_r \sum_{j=1}^{m} \mu_j(p) \frac{\partial g_j}{\partial p_s}(x(p),p) \\[2mm]
&- d_r \sum_{i=1}^{k} \sum_{j=1}^{m} \nu_i(p) \lambda_j(i,p) \frac{\partial g_j}{\partial p_s}(x(i,p),p)
\end{aligned}
\tag{4}
$$

holds for $r = 1, 2, ..., k$, $s = 1, 2, ..., l$ *and every* $p \in P$.[9]

Proof. The envelope theorem of scalar programming guarantees that

$$
\frac{\partial J_r}{\partial p_s} = \sum_{j=1}^{m} \lambda_j(r,p) \frac{\partial g_j}{\partial p_s}(x(r,p),p)
\tag{5}
$$

Thus, the proof will be completed if we show that the function $P \ni p \longrightarrow h(p) = \tau_p \in \mathbf{R}$ verifies the equality

$$
\frac{\partial h}{\partial p_s} = \sum_{j=1}^{m} \mu_j(p) \frac{\partial g_j}{\partial p_s}(x(p),p) - \sum_{i=1}^{k} \nu_i(p) \left[\sum_{j=1}^{m} \lambda_j(i,p) \frac{\partial g_j}{\partial p_s}(x(i,p),p) \right]
\tag{6}
$$

The Lagrangian function of (3) is given by

$$
L(\tau, x, p, \mu, \nu) = \tau + \sum_{j=1}^{m} [\mu_j g_j(x,p)] + \sum_{i=1}^{k} \nu_i [f_i(x) - \tau d_i - J_i(p)]
$$

being $\mu = (\mu_1, \mu_2, ..., \mu_m) \in \mathbf{R}^m$ and $\nu = (\nu_1, \nu_2, ..., \nu_k) \in \mathbf{R}^k$. Therefore, the envelope theorem of scalar programming ensures that

$$
\frac{\partial h}{\partial p_s} = \frac{\partial L}{\partial p_s} = \sum_{j=1}^{m} \left[\mu_j \frac{\partial g_j}{\partial p_s}(x(p),p) \right] - \sum_{i=1}^{k} \nu_i \left[\frac{\partial J_i}{\partial p_s} \right],
$$

and (6) trivially follows from (5). ∎

The latter theorem can be particularized in order to obtain the sensitivity of F with respect to the term of the right side. In this case (4) may be significantly simplified.

---

[9]Let us remark that the partial derivative $\dfrac{\partial g_j}{\partial p_s}$ is evaluated at $k+1$ different points $((x(i,p),p),\ i = 1, 2, ..., k,$ and $(x(p),p))$.

Corollary 3 *Assume that $l = m$ and $g(x,p) = \bar{g}(x) - p$, being $\bar{g} : W \longrightarrow \mathbb{R}^m$ an arbitrary function. Then, under the assumptions of Theorem 2, the following expression*

$$\frac{\partial F_r}{\partial p_s} = - \left[\lambda_s(r,p) + \mu_s(p)d_r - d_r \sum_{i=1}^{k} \nu_i(p)\lambda_s(i,p) \right] \tag{7}$$

holds for $r = 1, 2, ..., k$, $s = 1, 2, ..., m$ and every $p \in P$. ∎

4 Convex Problems and Duality Theory

Throughout this section we will assume that W is a convex set, f_i is a convex function $(i = 1, 2, ..., k)$, $l = m$ and $g(x,p) = \bar{g}(x) - p$ being $\bar{g} : W \longrightarrow \mathbb{R}^m$ an arbitrary convex function (*i.e.*, its components $\bar{g}_j : W \longrightarrow \mathbb{R}$, $j = 1, 2, ..., m$, are convex functions). Therefore, (1) is a convex vector problem and (2) and (3) are convex scalar problems.

Consider an arbitrary matrix $\Lambda = (\lambda_{i,j})_{i=1,2,...,k}^{j=1,2,...,m}$ and two elements $\mu = (\mu_1, ..., \mu_m) \in \mathbb{R}^m$ and $\nu = (\nu_1, ..., \nu_k) \in \mathbb{R}^k$. Suppose that all the components of these matrices are nonnegative. Then, (Λ, μ, ν) is said to be dual-feasible if the sets $\{f(x) + (\bar{g}(x) - p)\Lambda^T : x \in W\}$ and $\{\tau + (\bar{g}(x) - p)\mu^T + (f(x) - \tau d - J(p))\nu^T : x \in W, \tau \in \mathbb{R}\}$ are bounded from below in $\mathbb{R}^k$ and $\mathbb{R}$, respectively,[10] in which case we will define the dual objectives by[11]

$$\varphi(\Lambda) = Inf \{f(x) + (\bar{g}(x) - p)\Lambda^T : x \in W\} \in \mathbb{R}^k \tag{8}$$

and

$$\psi(\mu, \nu) = Inf \{\tau + (\bar{g}(x) - p)\mu^T + (f(x) - \tau d - J(p))\nu^T : x \in W, \tau \in \mathbb{R}\} \in \mathbb{R} \tag{9}$$

The dual problem of (1) is given by

$$Max \ (\varphi(\Lambda), \psi(\mu, \nu)) \ \{(\Lambda, \mu, \nu) \in \Gamma \tag{10}$$

being Γ the set of dual-feasible elements.[12]

It is clear that (10) is a vector problem with $k + 1$ objectives, but there exists a simple relationship between the primal and the dual objectives.

Lemma 4 *If $(\Lambda, \mu, \nu) \in \Gamma$, then the following assertions are fulfilled:*
a) $\varphi(\Lambda) \leq J(p)$ and $\psi(\mu, \nu) \leq \tau_p$
b) If $\bar{x} \in W$ verifies $\bar{g}(\bar{x}) \leq p$, then expressions $f(\bar{x}) \leq \varphi(\Lambda) + \psi(\mu, \nu)d$ and $f(\bar{x}) \neq \varphi(\Lambda) + \psi(\mu, \nu)d$ cannot simultaneously hold.

---

[10] As usual, if M is an arbitrary matrix, M^T will denote the transpose matrix.

[11] Recall that $\mathbb{R}^k$ is an order complete Banach lattice (see, for instance, [14]) and, consequently, bounded from below subsets have an infimum element. Besides, notice that (8) and (9) are related to usual expressions of previous literature when dealing with dual functions (see, for example, [13] for scalar problems or [3] for vector problems).

[12] Notice that Γ does not depend on $p \in P$.

Proof. Since $\lambda_{i,j} \geq 0$ for $i = 1, 2, ..., k$ and $j = 1, 2, ..., m$, it is obvious that $\varphi(\Lambda) \leq Inf\{f(x) + (\bar{g}(x) - p)\Lambda^T : x \in W, \bar{g}(x) - p \leq 0\} \leq Inf\{f(x) : x \in W, \bar{g}(x) - p \leq 0\} = J(p)$.

Analogously, $\psi(\mu, \nu) \leq Inf \{\tau + (\bar{g}(x) - p)\mu^T + (f(x) - \tau d - J(p))\nu^T : x \in W, \bar{g}(x) - p \leq 0, \tau \in \mathbb{R}, f(x) - \tau d - J(p) \leq 0\} \leq Inf \{\tau : x \in W, \bar{g}(x) - p \leq 0, \tau \in \mathbb{R}, f(x) - \tau d - J(p) \leq 0\} = \tau_p$.

Moreover, bearing in mind a), if $f(\bar{x}) \leq \varphi(\Lambda) + \psi(\mu, \nu)d$ then $f(\bar{x}) \leq J(p) + \tau_p d = f(x(p))$. Thus, $f(\bar{x}) = f(x(p))$ since $x(p)$ is a Pareto solution of (1). ∎

Hereafter the following Slater qualification is imposed:

($A3$) The vector of preferential deviations satisfies the inequality $d_i > 0$ for $i = 1, 2, ..., k$, and for any $p \in P$ there exists $x^p \in W$ such that $\bar{g}_j(x^p) - p_j < 0$, $j = 1, 2, ..., m$.

As will immediately be shown, the Slater qualification guarantees the existence of strong dual solutions and the absence of duality gap.

Theorem 5 *Given an arbitrary $p \in P$, there exists $(\Lambda(p), \mu(p), \nu(p)) \in \Gamma$ such that:*

a) $\varphi(\Lambda(p)) \geq \varphi(\Lambda)$ and $\psi(\mu(p), \nu(p)) \geq \psi(\mu, \nu)$ for every $(\Lambda, \mu, \nu) \in \Gamma$.[13]

b) $\varphi(\Lambda(p)) = J(p)$, $\psi(\mu(p), \nu(p)) = \tau_p$, and $\varphi(\Lambda(p)) + \psi(\mu(p), \nu(p))d = f(x(p))$

Proof. Assertion a) trivially follows from b) and Lemma 4, so let us prove b). Let $i \in \{1, 2, ..., k\}$ and consider the convex and scalar Problem (2). The saddle point theorem of [13] (Chapter IX) guarantees the existence of

$$\lambda_i(p) = (\lambda_{i,1}(p), \lambda_{i,2}(p), ..., \lambda_{i,m}(p))$$

such that $\lambda_{i,j}(p) \geq 0$, $j = 1, 2, ..., m$, and

$$Inf\{f_i(x) + (\bar{g}(x) - p)\lambda_i(p)^T : x \in W\} \geq J_i(p)$$

Now, it is clear that $\Lambda(p) = (\lambda_{i,j}(p))_{i=1,2,...,k}^{j=1,2,...,m}$ satisfies the required condition. Furthermore, since (3) is also a scalar convex problem that verifies the Slater qualification, analogous arguments lead to the existence of $\mu(p)$ and $\nu(p)$. ∎

The absence of duality gap and the existence of strong dual solutions allow us to characterize dual solutions and balance points by means of saddle points and complementary slackness conditions. Furthermore, the saddle point condition is stated by means of a vector inequality instead of the failure to hold the opposite inequality, as usual in the vector programming case.

---

[13]*i.e., $(\Lambda(p), \mu(p), \nu(p)) \in \Gamma$ is a strong solution of (10)*

Theorem 6 *Consider an arbitrary (3)—feasible* $(\bar{x}, \bar{\tau}) \in W \times \mathbf{R}$ *and* (Λ, μ, ν) $\in \Gamma$. *Then* $(\bar{x}, \bar{\tau})$ *solves (3)* [14] *and* (Λ, μ, ν) *solves (10) if and only if*

$$f(\bar{x}) + (\bar{g}(\bar{x}) - p)\Lambda^T \leq f(x) + (\bar{g}(x) - p)\Lambda^T \tag{11}$$

for every $x \in W$,

$$\bar{\tau} + (\bar{g}(\bar{x}) - p)\mu^T + (f(\bar{x}) - \bar{\tau}d - \varphi(\Lambda))\nu^T$$
$$\leq \tau + (\bar{g}(x) - p)\mu^T + (f(x) - \tau d - \varphi(\Lambda))\nu^T \tag{12}$$

for every $x \in W$ *and every* $\tau \in \mathbb{R}$, *and the complementary slackness conditions*

$$(\bar{g}(\bar{x}) - p)\Lambda^T = 0 \tag{13}$$

$$(\bar{g}(\bar{x}) - p)\mu^T = 0 \tag{14}$$

and

$$(f(\bar{x}) - \bar{\tau}d - \varphi(\Lambda))\nu^T = 0 \tag{15}$$

hold.

Proof. Suppose that $(\bar{x}, \bar{\tau})$ solves (3) and (Λ, μ, ν) solves (10). Theorem 1 guarantees that $\bar{x}$ solves (1) and, therefore, the results of [13] (Chapter IX) apply on Problems (2) $(i = 1, 2, ..., k)$ and (3) and show that (11), (13) and (14) hold and (12) and (15) also hold if $\varphi(\Lambda)$ is substituted by $J(p)$. Hence, the conclusion trivially follows from the equality $\varphi(\Lambda) = J(p)$ already established in the previous theorem.

Conversely, assume (11), (12) (13), (14) and (15). Then, (8) and (11) show that $\varphi(\Lambda) = f(\bar{x}) + (\bar{g}(\bar{x}) - p)\Lambda^T$ and, consequently, (13) leads to $\varphi(\Lambda) = f(\bar{x}) \geq J(p)$. Now, Lemma 4 proves that $\varphi(\Lambda) = J(p)$. Analogous arguments lead to $\psi(\mu, \nu) = \tau_p$ and the latter theorem proves that (Λ, μ, ν) is a dual solution. Moreover, $\varphi(\Lambda) = J(p)$ implies that (12) and (15) hold if $\varphi(\Lambda)$ is substituted by $J(p)$, and these conditions, along with (14) and the results of [13], permit us to ensure that $(\bar{x}, \bar{\tau})$ solves (3). ■Once the complementary slackness conditions have been provided, standard arguments permit us to establish the equivalence between dual solutions and Lagrange multipliers when dealing with convex and differentiable problems. Thus, Theorem 2 and Corollary 3 may be adapted so that one can measure the primal sensitivity by means of dual solutions. For instance, the following result, whose proof is omitted, may be easily obtained.

Corollary 7 *Let* P *be an open (and convex) set. Denote by* $(\Lambda(p), \mu(p), \nu(p))$ $\in \Gamma$ *the strong dual solution of (10) (for every* $p \in P$*) whose existence is guaranteed by Theorem 5. Suppose that the function* $P \ni p \longrightarrow (\Lambda(p), \mu(p), \nu(p))$

---

[14]Recall that Theorem 1 ensures that $(\bar{x}, \bar{\tau})$ solves (3) if and only if $\bar{x}$ is a Pareto solution of (1) and $\bar{\tau}d$ is a balance point such that $J(p) + \bar{\tau}d = f(\bar{x})$.

is continuous. Then, the function $P \ni p \longrightarrow F(p) = \varphi(\Lambda(p)) + \psi(\mu(p), \nu(p))d \in$ $\mathbb{R}^k$ *is continuously differentiable and*

$$\frac{\partial F_r}{\partial p_s} = - \left[\lambda_{r,s}(p) + \mu_s(p)d_r - d_r \sum_{i=1}^{k} \nu_i(p)\lambda_{i,s}(p) \right]$$

for $r = 1, 2, ..., k$, $s = 1, 2, ..., m$ *and every* $p \in P$. ∎

Remark 8 *Notice that (3) is linear if (1) is linear, in which case it may be proved that (10) is also linear because* Γ *may be given by linear constraints and* φ *and* ψ *have a linear expression (see [1] or [3] for further details on this point in a very general setting). Hence, in the important linear case, the balance space approach yields a linear dual problem with a strong solution that avoids the duality gap, characterizes the balance points by means of complementary slackness conditions (no saddle point conditions are required in this case) and measures the primal sensitivity with respect to any parameter appeared in the problem. These properties are identical to those observed in the scalar programming and usually fail when dealing with classical duals in vector optimization.*

5 Conclusions

This paper has shown how the theory of global optimization and the balance space approach may apply in order to develope a general theory of duality and sensitivity for vector optimization problems. This general theory points out that the balance space approach is an interesting alternative and complements the classical Pareto approach. The theory overcomes several caveats usual in the literature. For instance, it yields a general envelope theorem that easily applies in practical situations and measures the sensitivity with respect to any parameter of the problem. Regarding the duality theory for convex (and linear) problems, the balance set and the set of dual solutions may be characterized by means of saddle point conditions whose statements may be given in terms of vector inequalities. Consequently, our saddle point conditions seem to be more effective than those obtained by previous literature, and they lead, along with some complementary slackness conditions, to a system of equations providing us with the efficient line, the set of dual solutions and the sensitivity with respect to any parameter.

References

[1] Balbás, A., Ballvé, M. and P.J. Guerra, 1999, "Sensitivity analysis in multiobjective programming under homogeneity assumptions." *Journal of Multi-Criteria Decision Analysis*, 8, 133-138.

[2] Balbás, A., Fernández, F.J. and P.J. Guerra, 1995, "On the envolvent theorem in multiobjective programming." *Indian Journal of Pure and Applied Mathematics*, 26, 11, 1035-1047.

[3] Balbás, A. and P.J. Guerra, 1996, "Sensitivity analysis for convex multiobjective programming in abstract spaces." *Journal of Mathematical Analysis and Applications*, 202, 645-658.

[4] Balbás, A. and A. Heras, 1993, "Duality theory for infinite-dimensional multiobjective linear programming." *European Journal of Operational Research*, 68, 379-388.

[5] Ehrgott, M., Hamacher, H.W., Klamroth, K., Nickel, S., Schobel, A. and M.M. Wiecek, 1997, "A Note on the equivalence of balance points and Pareto solutions in multiple objective programming." *Journal of Optimization. Theory and Applications*, 92, 209-212.

[6] Galperin, E.A., 1990, " The Cubic Algorithm for Optimization and Control." NP Research Publication. Montreal, Québec, Canada.

[7] Galperin, E.A., 1992, "Nonscalarized multiobjective global optimization." *Journal of Optimization. Theory and Applications*, 75, 69-85.

[8] Galperin, E.A., 1997, "Pareto analysis vis-à-vis balance space approach in multiobjective global optimization," *Journal of Optimization. Theory and Applications*, 93, 3, 533-545.

[9] Galperin, E.A. and M.M. Wiecek, 1999, "Retrieval and use of the balance set in multiobjective global optimization," *Computers and Mathematics with Applications*, 37, 111- 123.

[10] Jahn, J., 1986, "Mathematical vector optimization in partially ordered linear spaces." Verlag Peter Lang, Frankfurt am Main.

[11] Klose, J., 1992, "Sensitivity analysis using the tangent derivative." *Numerical Functional Analysis and Optimization*, 13, 143-153.

[12] Kuk, H., Tanino, J. and M. Tanaka, 1996, "Sensitivity analysis in vector optimization. " *Journal of Optimization. Theory and Applications*, 89, 713-730.

[13] Luenberger, D.G., 1969, "Optimization by vector space methods." Wiley. New York.

[14] Meyer-Nieberg, P., 1991, "Banach lattices." Springer-Verlag. New York.

[15] Sawaragi, Y., H. Nakayama and T. Tanino, 1985, "Theory of multiobjective optimization." Academic Press.

[16] Zowe, S., 1977, "The saddle point theorem of Kuhn and Tucker in ordered vector spaces." *Journal of Mathematical Analysis and Applications*, 57, 41-55.

On a Certain Approach to Fuzzy Goal Programming[*]

Stefan Chanas
Institute of Industrial Engineering and Management, Technical
University of Wrocław,
ul. Smoluchowskiego 25, 50-371 WROCŁAW, POLAND
chanas@ioz.pwr.wroc.pl

Dorota Kuchta
*Institute of Industrial Engineering and Management, Technical
University of Wrocław,
ul. Smoluchowskiego 25, 50-371 WROCŁAW, POLAND
and
Wroclaw College of Management and Finance
ul. Pabianicka 2, 53-339 WROCŁAW, POLAND
kuchta@ioz.pwr.wroc.pl*

Abstract: Two goal programming problems are considered in which the goals are given in the form of a fuzzy number. In the first problem the decision maker can set the exact values of the goals and searches for the best values of them, trying at the same time to minimise the deviations from the goals. In the second problem the decision maker cannot influence the exact values of the goals, but wants to have some knowledge about the possibility distribution of the total deviation from the goals. For both problems a solution procedure is proposed and a computational example is solved.

Key words: goal programming, fuzzy programming, fuzzy number

1. Introduction

Goal programming is a well-known and widely used approach to solving various optimisation and decision problems. First of all, it is used to model

---

[*] This work was partially supported by the 7T11F02120 grant of the Polish State Commitee for Scientific Research (KBN).

multicriterial problems, in which there are several objectives that cannot be achieved simultaneously. The goal programming approach allows the decision maker to define satisfying levels of the value of each objective (the goals) and then to find a solution which optimises unfavourable (negative) deviations from those goals. On the other hand, goal programming can also be used to soften some constraints in the model, when in fact the constraints are not quite rigid and a small violation of some of them allows finding a better solution.

There have been various attempts in the literature to generalise the goal programming approach to the fuzzy case. Those attempts differ considerably among themselves (in the fuzzy goals interpretation and in the way they measure the goal satisfaction) and it is not our aim to make a review of them. In [7] there is a wide review of various fuzzy goal programming models and methods. We have proposed a new approach (together with a corresponding solution procedure) in [3]. In this paper we propose two more interpretations and applications of fuzzy goal programming. The basic difference between our approach to fuzzy goal programming and that proposed usually in the literature can be formulated as follows: In most fuzzy goal programming models the decision maker formulates the goals in a fuzzy form. In our case the decision maker formulates the goals as crisp numbers, but he either searches for these crisp numbers (having some preferences in mind) or there are two decision makers and one does not know what crisp goals the other has formulated.

The first interpretation of fuzzy goals we propose corresponds thus to the situation when the decision maker can set the goals himself and he searches for the best values of them. His satisfaction with each individual goal is known (generally, he wants the goals to be rather ambitious) and the aim is to determine such set of goal values that would be most satisfying to him and at the same time not too ambitious, not too "frightening" for people who have to carry out the undertaking that gave rise to the decision situation in question.

The other interpretation corresponds to the situation when the decision maker cannot set the goals himself, he only knows the possibility distribution of their values. In such a case he wants to know what he should expect in the future and searches for the possibility distribution of the minimal value of the total deviation from the goals that will be set by someone else.

The paper is organised as follows: in the 2. section we describe the goal programming approach in its classical version. In the 3. section basic notions from the theory of fuzzy numbers is presented. The 4. section contains the results of the research: the two applications of fuzzy goal programming approach. The 5. section presents a computational example, illustrating the proposed approaches. We finish with some conclusions in section 6.

2. Classical Goal Programming Approach

In the classical linear programming approach the model is usually formulated as follows:

$$\mathbf{C}_i\mathbf{x} \stackrel{<}{=} d_i, \quad i=1,...,k_1$$
$$\mathbf{C}_i\mathbf{x} \stackrel{\wedge}{=} d_i, \quad i=k_1+1,...,k_2 \tag{1}$$
$$\mathbf{C}_i\mathbf{x} \stackrel{>}{=} d_i, \quad i=k_2+1,...,k_3$$
$$\mathbf{A}_i\mathbf{x} = b_i, \quad i=1,...,m \tag{2}$$
$$\mathbf{x} \geq 0$$

in which $\mathbf{x}=\left(x_j\right)_{j=1}^n$ is the vector of positive decision variables, $\mathbf{A}_i=\left(a_{ij}\right)_{j=1}^n$ and $\mathbf{C}_i=\left(c_j\right)_{j=1}^n$ are vectors of coefficients, the constraints, numbered with $i=1,...,k_3$, correspond to the three kinds of goals and (2) is the canonical form of the classical constraints which define the feasible sets of solutions. Numbers d_i, $i=1,...,k_3$, are the target values (the goals) given by the decision maker.

The constraints (1), which we call goal constraints, differ from the crisp ones (2) in the sense that they are not so rigorous and may be violated within some ranges (but not too much, as far as possible). We could read the relations $\stackrel{<}{=}(\stackrel{\wedge}{=},\stackrel{>}{=})$ as "approximately $\leq(=,\geq)$". Of course, such a formulation of goal constraints is imprecise and their meaning must be formally defined.

In the goal programming approach the general model (1)-(2), which is somewhat imprecise, is concretised in the following way:

Let us denote the deviations from the target values d_i, $i=1,...,k_3$, in the following way:

$$d_i^+ = \max\{\mathbf{C}_i\mathbf{x}-d_i,0\}, \qquad d_i^- = \max\{d_i-\mathbf{C}_i\mathbf{x},0\} \tag{3}$$

d_i^+ represent deviations over the target value, d_i^- deviations under the target value. In all the three types of goals (1) we admit all of them, but some of them are undesired:

– for $i=1,...,k_1$ d_i^+ are undesired

– for $i=k_1+1,...,k_2$ both d_i^+ and d_i^- are undesired

– for $i=k_2+1,...,k_3$ d_i^- are undesired.

Our aim is to minimise the undesired deviations. But in view of the fact that there are $k_3+k_2-k_1$ of them, we do not minimise them individually, but put all of them, multiplied with positive weights w_i chosen by the decision maker, into one objective function:

$$\sum_{i=1}^{k_1} w_i d_i^+ + \sum_{i=k_1+1}^{k_2}\left(w_i d_i^+ + w_i d_i^-\right)+ \sum_{i=k_2+1}^{k_3} w_i d_i^- \to \min \tag{4}$$

Thus, we solve the problem defined by (2), (3) and (4). Because of (3), it is not a linear programming problem. However, it can be formulated as such. Here is the equivalent formulation (and in fact, the most widely spread one), which is a classical linear programming problem with $n + 2k_3$ positive decision variables. The equivalency between both problems can be proved very easily.

$$\sum_{i=1}^{k_1} w_i d_i^+ + \sum_{i=k_1+1}^{k_2} \left(w_i d_i^+ + w_i' d_i^- \right) + \sum_{i=k_2+1}^{k_3} w_i d_i^- \rightarrow \min$$

$$C_i x - d_i^+ + d_i^- = d_i, \quad i = 1,...,k_3 \qquad (5)$$

$$A_i x = b_i, \quad i = 1,...,m$$

$$x \geq 0, d_i^+, d_i^- \geq 0, \quad i = 1,...,k_3$$

w_i, $i = 1,...,k_3$, and w_i', $i = k_1 + 1,...,k_2$, are positive weights.

Example 1:
Let us consider the following example: A company manufactures three types of products. The total amount of products manufactured in the considered period cannot exceed 1000 (this a strict restriction, no values over 1000 are accepted). Each product passes through three different plants. The following table gives the amount of labour needed in each plant for one piece of each product:

	Product 1	Product 2	Product 3
Plant 1	3	7	5
Plant 2	6	5	7
Plant 3	3	6	5

The total usage of labour in plant one should be about 2100, in plant two about 2800, and in plant three about 25. Deviations in both directions are undesirable (if too much labour is required, there may be not enough resources, if too little labour is required, the workers may feel unneeded). The aim is to determine an optimal production plan.

If x_1, x_2, x_3 denote, respectively, the number of pieces of each product that will be manufactured, the problem can be stated in the following way (it is a general formulation of the problem corresponding to (1)-(2)):

$$3x_1 + 7x_2 + 5x_3 \cong 2100$$
$$6x_1 + 5x_2 + 7x_3 \cong 2800$$
$$3x_1 + 6x_2 + 5x_3 \cong 25 \qquad (6)$$
$$x_1 + x_2 + x_3 \leq 1000$$
$$x_1, x_2, x_3 \geq 0$$

Assuming the weights corresponding to undesired deviations equal to one, the problem (6) can be rewritten as the following linear programming problem (see (5)):

$$d_1^+ + d_1^- + d_2^+ + d_2^- + d_3^+ + d_3^- \rightarrow \min$$

$$3x_1 + 7x_2 + 5x_3 + d_1^- - d_1^+ = 2100$$

$$6x_1 + 5x_2 + 7x_3 + d_2^- - d_2^+ = 2800$$

$$3x_1 + 6x_2 + 5x_3 + d_3^- - d_3^+ = 25 \tag{7}$$

$$x_1 + x_2 + x_3 \leq 1000$$

$$x_1, x_2, x_3, d_1^+, d_1^-, d_2^+, d_2^-, d_3^+, d_3^- \geq 0$$

An optimal solution of (7) is as follows:

$x_1 = 337$, $x_2 = 155.6$, $x_3 = 0$, $d_1^+ = d_1^- = d_2^+ = d_2^- = d_3^- = 0$, $d_3^+ = 1919{,}4$

Such a big deviation from the third goal is of course likely to be unacceptable and some weights should be introduced in the objective function of the above problem, but this would depend on the decision maker. He may be satisfied with the solution if it is more important to him that the deviations in the other two plants are equal to 0 and if he is able to find extra workers for the third plant fairly easily.

The aim of our paper is to consider the case when the target values d_i, $i = 1, \ldots, k_3$, will be known exactly only in the future, but for the moment they are given only in an imprecise form. Let us thus start by reminding some basic definitions that help to model this imperfection of information about the goals.

3. Basic notions from the area of fuzzy numbers

A concept of a fuzzy number of the L-R type, introduced by Dubois and Prade [4], is very popular and convenient in many applications. Also here we will confine ourselves to such fuzzy numbers.

Definition 1: A fuzzy number of the L-R type is a fuzzy number A whose membership function μ_A, $\mu_A : \Re \rightarrow [0,1]$, has the following form:

$$\mu_A(z) = \begin{cases} 1 & for \quad z \in [\underline{a}, \overline{a}] \\ L\left(\dfrac{a-z}{\alpha_A}\right) & for \quad z \leq \underline{a} \\ R\left(\dfrac{z-\overline{a}}{\beta_A}\right) & for \quad z \geq \overline{a} \end{cases} \tag{8}$$

where L and R are so called shape functions defined on $[0, +\infty)$. They are continuous non-increasing functions, strictly decreasing to zero in those subintervals of the interval $[0, +\infty)$ in which they are positive, and fulfilling the conditions $L(0) = R(0) = 1$. The parameters α_A and β_A are non-negative real numbers.

The shape functions L and R usually take one of the following forms:
a) **linear:** $S(y) = \max\{0, 1-y\}$
b) **exponential:** $S(y) = \exp(-py)$, $p \geq 1$
c) **power:** $S(y) = \max\{0, 1-y^p\}$, $p \geq 1$ (9)
d) **rational:** $S(y) = 1/(1+y^p)$, $p \geq 1$

A fuzzy number A of L-R type is denoted as $A = \left(\underline{a}, \overline{a}, \alpha_A, \beta_A\right)_{L-R}$.

Definition 2: Let A be a fuzzy number. The interval
$$A^\lambda = \left[\underline{a}(\lambda), \overline{a}(\lambda)\right] = \left\{x \in \Re \mid \mu_A(x) \geq \lambda\right\}, \text{ for } \lambda \in (0,1], \qquad (10)$$
and
$$A^0 = \left[\underline{a}(0), \overline{a}(0)\right] = \mathrm{supp}(A), \text{ for } \lambda = 0, \qquad (11)$$
where
$$\underline{a}(0) = \inf\left\{x \mid \mu_A(x) > 0\right\} = a \quad \text{and} \quad \overline{a}(0) = \sup\left\{x \mid \mu_A(x) > 0\right\} = b$$
is called λ-cut of A.

For a fuzzy number A of L-R type, the λ-cut A^λ, $\lambda \in [0,1]$, has the following form:
$$A^\lambda = \left[\underline{a} - L^{-1}(\lambda)\alpha_A, \overline{a} + R^{-1}(\lambda)\beta_A\right], \qquad (12)$$
where L^{-1} (similarly R^{-1}) denotes the reverse function to L in this part of its domain in which it is positive.

A fuzzy number A can be used in decision making models to describe two basic situations (see e.g. [6]). In both the exact value of a certain magnitude a is not known exactly for the moment and will be known only in the future. The only thing that is known is that this value will be "about something". But in the first situation (the possibility case) the decision maker cannot influence what value a will take and the only thing he can say is that for each real number x the possibility of a being x is equal to $\mu_A(x)$. Here the membership function μ_A is, in a certain sense, an equivalent of the probability measure. However, it is not the same. It expresses only the degree of the potential (subjective) possibility of a certain event, i.e. of a being x (see [9]). In the second situation (the preference case) the decision maker is able to choose the exact value of a, but some values are more satisfactory to him and some less. In this case, for each real number x, $\mu_A(x)$ measures the satisfaction of the decision maker with the equality $a = x$.

4. Two Fuzzy Goal Programming Problems

Let us assume that the target values d_i, $1,...,k_3$, are not known exactly. The only thing that is imposed is that they have to be "about something", so are given in the form of fuzzy numbers D_i, $1,...,k_3$. In such a case formulation (1)-(2) becomes:

$$\mathbf{C}_i\mathbf{x} \mathrel{\hat{\leq}} D_i, \quad i = 1,...,k_1$$
$$\mathbf{C}_i\mathbf{x} \mathrel{\hat{=}} D_i, \quad i = k_1 + 1,...,k_2$$
$$\mathbf{C}_i\mathbf{x} \mathrel{\hat{\geq}} D_i, \quad i = k_2 + 1,...,k_3 \qquad (13)$$
$$\mathbf{A}_i\mathbf{x} = b_i, \quad i = 1,...,m$$
$$\mathbf{x} \geq 0$$

We assume in further considerations that all the fuzzy goals D_i, $i = 1,...,k_3$, are fuzzy numbers of the same L-L type, $D_i = \left(\underline{d}_i, \overline{d}_i, \alpha_i, \beta_i\right)_{L-L}$, where L is one of the shape functions listed in (9). It seems that in many real situations the linear shape function will be the proper choice, which is equivalent to the assumption that all D_i are trapezoidal fuzzy numbers. We assume the same shape function for each goal, because only in this case it is possible to use linear programming methods. This will be clear in the passage between (16) and (17).

Of course, formulation (13) is not precise. It requires an interpretation, and this interpretation will depend on the way of understanding the fuzzy numbers D_i, $i = 1,...,k_3$, and on the adopted solution concept. In our paper we will understand (13) in two ways. Each of the two interpretations will correspond to one of the two situations that can be modelled by fuzzy numbers – the possibility case and the preference case (see section 3).

Let us start with the first decision situation (13) may represent. This first situation corresponds to the preference case. Let us assume that the decision maker can choose the exact value d_i of each goal D_i, $i = 1,...,k_3$, and the value $\mu_{D_i}(d_i)$ expresses, for each real number d_i, the satisfaction of decision maker with the fact that $D_i = d_i$. He wants to find such values d_i, $i = 1,...,k_3$, that would give him the maximal overall satisfaction with the selected goals and he also wants to determine the solution vector $\mathbf{x}$ that corresponds to this "best" choice of goals, i.e. it minimises the total sum of deviations with respect to these goals.

In this place it is necessary to state precisely what "the overall satisfaction with the goals" means. We propose the following natural definition corresponding to the Bellman-Zadeh concept of decision making in fuzzy environment ([1]):

Definition 3: Let us consider an arbitrary selection of exact values of goals $d = (d_i)_{i=1}^{k_3}$. The satisfaction of the decision maker with this selection, denoted with $SAT(d)$, is defined as:

$$SAT(d) = \min_{i=1,...,k_3} \mu_{D_i}(d_i) \qquad (14)$$

The following easy to prove lemma will be helpful in reformulating (13) in a convenient way:

Lemma 1: The following equality holds true:

$$SAT(d) = \max\left\{\lambda \mid d_i \in D_i^\lambda \text{ for all } i = 1,...,k_3\right\} \tag{15}$$

The proof is straightforward from (10) and (14).

In view of the fact that the decision maker wants to maximise his satisfaction with the selected goals, we can reformulate (13) in the following way (taking into account Lemma 1 and the form of the λ-cuts of L-L fuzzy numbers):

$\lambda \to \max$

$$\begin{aligned}
&\mathbf{C}_i\mathbf{x} \hat{\leq} d_i, \quad i = 1,...,k_1 \\
&\mathbf{C}_i\mathbf{x} \hat{=} d_i, \quad i = k_1 + 1,...,k_2 \\
&\mathbf{C}_i\mathbf{x} \hat{\geq} d_i, \quad i = k_2 + 1,...,k_3 \\
&\mathbf{A}_i\mathbf{x} = b_i, \quad i = 1,...,m \\
&\underline{d}_i - \alpha_i L^{-1}(\lambda) \leq d_i \leq \overline{d}_i + \beta_i L^{-1}(\lambda), \quad i = 1,...,k_3 \\
&0 \leq \lambda \leq 1 \\
&\mathbf{x} \geq 0
\end{aligned} \tag{16}$$

Formulation (16) assures that such goals d_i, $i = 1,...,k_3$, will be determined that give the highest satisfaction of the decision maker. However, this formulation is still imprecise, but now we can interpret the constraints in the same way as it is usually done in goal programming – by incorporating the deviations from the goals into the objective function. Doing this and, additionally, substituting $L^{-1}(\lambda) = \theta$ we obtain the following bicriterial linear programming problem:

$\theta \to \min$

$$\begin{aligned}
&\sum_{i=1}^{k_1} w_i d_i^+ + \sum_{i=k_1+1}^{k_2} \left(w_i d_i^+ + w_i' d_i^-\right) + \sum_{i=k_2+1}^{k_3} w_i d_i^- \to \min \\
&\mathbf{C}_i\mathbf{x} - d_i^+ + d_i^- = d_i, \quad i = 1,...,k_3 \\
&\underline{d}_i - \alpha_i\theta \leq d_i \leq \overline{d}_i + \beta_i\theta, \quad i = 1,...,k_3 \\
&\underline{\theta} \leq \theta \leq \overline{\theta} \\
&\mathbf{A}_i\mathbf{x} = b_i, \quad i = 1,...,m \\
&\mathbf{x} \geq 0, d_i^+, d_i^- \geq 0, \quad i = 1,...,k_3
\end{aligned} \tag{17}$$

where w_i, $i = 1,...,k_3$, and w_i', $i = k_1 + 1,...,k_2$, are positive weights, $\underline{\theta} = L^{-1}(1)$ and $\overline{\theta} = L^{-1}(0)$.

It is easy to see that the two objectives of the above bicriterial problem are contradictory: for a given $\mathbf{x}$, the greater the value of θ, i.e. the lower the value of λ (deterioration of the first objective), the wider the domain of the decision variables d_i, $i = 1,...,k_3$, thus the values of these target variables can be selected in such a way that the deviations d_i^+, d_i^-, $i = 1,...,k_3$, will be smaller (improvement of the second objective).

In which situations the decision maker may be interested in a trade-off solution of problem (17)? On one hand, he may want to maximise his satisfaction with the selected target values d_i, $i = 1,...,k_3$, i.e. the value of the first objective, if he thinks that ambitious objectives are good even if they cannot be attained completely, because negative deviations from the goals motivate people to work better, to try to improve the efficiency and productivity. On the other hand, he may not want the negative deviations (the second objective) to be very big, if he thinks that goals that seem unreachable do not motivate people any more, but, on the contrary, discourage them and make them think that they are not capable anyway, that there is no point in making efforts.

There exist many approaches to solving bicriterial problems. A very widely used one consists in determining all efficient (or Pareto optimal) solutions, i.e. such solutions, for which the improvement of one objective necessarily implies the deterioration of the other one. Then it is left to the decision maker to select one solution from the set of efficient ones. We will apply this approach to problem (17).

It is well known that solution of the following parametrical problem will give the set of all Pareto optimal solutions of problem (17):

$$p\theta + (1-p)\left(\sum_{i=1}^{k_1} w_i d_i^+ + \sum_{i=k_1+1}^{k_2} \left(w_i d_i^+ + w_i' d_i^- \right) + \sum_{i=k_2+1}^{k_3} w_i d_i^- \right) \to \min$$

$$\mathbf{C}_i\mathbf{x} - d_i^+ + d_i^- = d_i, \quad i = 1,...,k_3$$

$$\underline{d}_i - \alpha_i\theta \le d_i \le \overline{d}_i + \beta_i\theta, \quad i = 1,...,k_3 \tag{18}$$

$$\underline{\theta} \le \theta \le \overline{\theta}$$

$$\mathbf{A}_i\mathbf{x} = b_i, \quad i = 1,...,m$$

$$\mathbf{x} \ge 0, d_i^+, d_i^- \ge 0, \quad i = 1,...,k_3$$

where p is a parameter: $p \in [0,1]$.

Solving problem (18) by means of the parametric simplex method we obtain only the basic Pareto optimal solutions. The values of both functions for those solutions determine in the criteria space the vertex points of a curve containing all the Pareto optimal solutions (in this space). Hence, all the other solutions in the criteria space can be found as points of intervals linking adjacent vertices. If we wanted to find in the solution space the solutions corresponding to those points, we would have to take convex combinations of the corresponding adjacent basic solutions. As we will see later on, the full set of Pareto optimal solutions, both in the solution space and in the criteria one, can be found in a direct way, by solving a corresponding parametric linear programming problem with a parameter in the constraints (see problem (22)).

As the above approach gives the decision maker usually several solutions, out of which he has to select one, it is sometimes more convenient to apply an approach that would lead to just one solution of the bicriterial problem. The compromise programming (see [5]) constitutes such an approach. In the compromise programming one objective function K is formulated that best expresses the attitude of the decision maker with respect to the objectives. In our case we would get the following formulation:

$$K\left(\theta, \sum_{i=1}^{k_1} w_i d_i^+ + \sum_{i=k_1+1}^{k_2} \left(w_i d_i^+ + w_i' d_i^-\right) + \sum_{i=k_2+1}^{k_3} w_i d_i^-\right) \rightarrow \min(\max)$$

$$\mathbf{C}_i \mathbf{x} - d_i^+ + d_i^- = d_i, \quad i = 1, \ldots, k_3$$

$$\underline{d}_i - \alpha_i \theta \le d_i \le \overline{d}_i + \beta_i \theta, \quad i = 1, \ldots, k_3 \tag{19}$$

$$\underline{\theta} \le \theta \le \overline{\theta}$$

$$\mathbf{A}_i \mathbf{x} = b_i, \quad i = 1, \ldots, m$$

$$\mathbf{x} \ge 0, d_i^+, d_i^- \ge 0, \quad i = 1, \ldots, k_3$$

Of course, the above formulation is not precise, as function K is not defined. In practice, various forms of this function are considered. For example, we can define K as follows:

$$K\left(\theta, \sum_{i=1}^{k_1} w_i d_i^+ + \sum_{i=k_1+1}^{k_2} \left(w_i d_i^+ + w_i' d_i^-\right) + \sum_{i=k_2+1}^{k_3} w_i d_i^-\right) =$$

$$p_1 \theta + p_2 \left(\sum_{i=1}^{k_1} w_i d_i^+ + \sum_{i=k_1+1}^{k_2} \left(w_i d_i^+ + w_i' d_i^-\right) + \sum_{i=k_2+1}^{k_3} w_i d_i^-\right) \rightarrow \min \tag{20}$$

where p_1, p_2 are positive weights assigned to each of the objectives.

The weights p_1, p_2 are usually chosen in such a way the two goals become comparable. For example, in the problem that is considered in this paper the values of the first objective functions are included in the interval $[\underline{\theta}, \overline{\theta}]$, which is equal to the interval $[0,1]$ in the case of linear and power shape functions L, and the values of the second objective may be very big. In such a case, in order to avoid the dominance of the second objective, we can assign a big value to p_1. The weights can also express the importance of the individual goals to the decision maker.

In the following section we will present a computational example illustrating the described decision situation and its solution. But now, as announced before, we will pass on to the second interpretation of (13). This interpretation will correspond, as far as the interpretation of fuzzy numbers is concerned, to the possibility case (see section 3). Now the decision maker is not able to choose the exact value of each goal, because the goals will be fixed by someone, on whom the decision maker has no influence. However, the decision maker possesses some knowledge about the goals: he knows the possibility distributions of all the crisp values of the goals that are possible. We assume that these possibility distributions are given in the form of L-L fuzzy numbers D_i, $i = 1,...,k_3$. The value $\mu_{D_i}(d_i)$ expresses, for each real number d_i, the possibility of d_i of being the final value of the i-th goal.

In this case of little manoeuvre possibilities the decision maker might just be interested in the possibility distributions of the deviations from the (for the moment unknown) exact goal values. In other words, he might want to know what deviations may occur and how possible they are, in order to be able to evaluate his risk of the deviations being too big. In particular, the information about the possibility distribution of the <u>minimal</u> value of the total deviation may be of use to him.

The minimal value of the total deviation from the goals, i.e. the minimal value of the objective function in problem (5), is of course a function of goals $d = (d_i)_{i=1}^{k_3}$. Let us denote this function by $MTD(d)$. According to the extension principle of Zadeh ([8]) applied to this function, the possibility distribution μ_{MTD} of the total deviation from the fuzzy goals $D = (D)_{i=1}^{k_3}$, i.e. the membership function of $MTD(D)$, generated by the possibility distributions of D_i, can be defined in the following way:

$$\mu_{MTD}(z) = \sup_{\substack{d \text{ such that } z \text{ is optimal value} \\ \text{of objective function in problem (5)} \\ \text{with values of goals equal to } d}} \min_{i=1,...,k_3} \mu_{D_i}(d_i) \qquad (21)$$

The function μ_{MTD} can be found by solving the following parametric linear programming problem (similarly as it is done in [2] for the general case of the fuzzy linear programming problem):

$$\sum_{i=1}^{k_1} w_i d_i^+ + \sum_{i=k_1+1}^{k_2} \left(w_i d_i^+ + w_i' d_i^- \right) + \sum_{i=k_2+1}^{k_3} w_i d_i^- \to \min$$

$$\mathbf{C}_i \mathbf{x} - d_i^+ + d_i^- = d_i, \quad i = 1,...,k_3$$

$$\underline{d}_i - \alpha_i \theta \le d_i \le \overline{d}_i + \beta_i \theta, \quad i = 1,...,k_3 \qquad (22)$$

$$\mathbf{A}_i \mathbf{x} = b_i, \quad i = 1,...,m$$

$$\mathbf{x} \ge 0, d_i^+, d_i^- \ge 0, \quad i = 1,...,k_3$$

where $\theta \in \left[\underline{\theta}, \overline{\theta}\right]$ is now a parameter (and not a decision variable) with $\underline{\theta}$ and $\overline{\theta}$ defined as in (17).

Let us denote the optimal value of the objective function from (22) for each $\theta \in \left[\underline{\theta}, \overline{\theta}\right]$ by $z(\theta)$. Then $\mu_{MTD}(z(\theta)) = L(\theta)$.

By solving (22), the decision maker would know more exactly what expects him in the future and with what possibility degree, even if he cannot influence the choice of the goals.

Before passing to the computational example illustrating both interpretations of (13), let us notice that by solving (22) we obtain more than what we require for the second interpretation of (13) that we are discussing. Apart from the various minimal values of the total deviation together with the corresponding possibility degrees, we also obtain the corresponding values of d_i, $i = 1, ..., k_3$. In the second interpretation of (13) they are practically useless, because the decision maker cannot influence the way the goals are set. However, it can be shown that in this way we obtain at the same time all the Pareto optimal solutions of (17), not just the basic ones. This means that (22) allows to solve (13) in both decision situations we have discussed.

5. Computational example

Let us consider Example 1 in a modified form, with the goals being imprecise. Here is formulation (13) for this example:

$$3x_1 + 7x_2 + 5x_3 \triangleq (2100, 2100, 1000, 1000)_{L-L}$$

$$6x_1 + 5x_2 + 7x_3 \triangleq (2800, 2800, 5, 5)_{L-L}$$

$$3x_1 + 6x_2 + 5x_3 \triangleq (25, 25, 20, 20)_{L-L} \qquad (23)$$

$$x_1 + x_2 + x_3 \leq 1000$$

$$x_1, x_2, x_3 \geq 0$$

Let us consider the first interpretation of (23) (preference case): the goals for the amount of labour in the plants are not fixed yet, but the decision maker is able to fix them and is looking for the best ones. He would be most satisfied if they are as close as possible to, respectively, 2100, 2800, 25, but they can also differ from these values (decreasing the decision maker satisfaction) if, in exchange, the total deviation from the goals is smaller (which increases the satisfaction of those who are responsible for the work organisation in each individual plant). The right-hand values of the first three constraints of (23) express the decision maker satisfaction with the goals. This problem can be formulated as the following bicriterial linear programming problem (see (17)); the weights related to the undeserved deviations are assumed to be equal to 1:

$\theta \to \min$

$d_1^+ + d_1^- + d_2^+ + d_2^- + d_3^+ + d_3^- \to \min$

$3x_1 + 7x_2 + 5x_3 + d_1^- - d_1^+ = d_1$

$6x_1 + 5x_2 + 7x_3 + d_2^- - d_2^+ = d_2$

$3x_1 + 6x_2 + 5x_3 + d_3^- - d_3^+ = d_3$

$2100 - 1000\theta \le d_1 \le 2100 + 1000\theta$ $\qquad\qquad$ (24)

$2800 - 5\theta \le d_2 \le 2800 + 5\theta$

$25 - 20\theta \le d_3 \le 25 + 20\theta$

$0 \le \theta \le 1$

$x_1 + x_2 + x_3 \le 1000$

$x_1, x_2, x_3, d_1^+, d_1^-, d_2^+, d_2^-, d_3^+, d_3^-, d_1, d_2, d_3 \ge 0;$

where $\theta = L^{-1}(\lambda) = 1 - \lambda$. Of course here $\underline{\theta} = L^{-1}(1) = 0$ and $\overline{\theta} = L^{-1}(0) = 1$.

Solving the following parametric linear programming problem (see (18)):

$p\theta + (1 - p)\left(d_1^+ + d_1^- + d_2^+ + d_2^- + d_3^+ + d_3^-\right) \to \min$

$3x_1 + 7x_2 + 5x_3 + d_1^- - d_1^+ = d_1$

$6x_1 + 5x_2 + 7x_3 + d_2^- - d_2^+ = d_2$

$3x_1 + 6x_2 + 5x_3 + d_3^- - d_3^+ = d_3$

$2100 - 1000\theta \le d_1 \le 2100 + 1000\theta$ $\qquad\qquad$ (25)

$2800 - 5\theta \le d_2 \le 2800 + 5\theta$

$25 - 20\theta \le d_3 \le 25 + 20\theta$

$0 \le \theta \le 1$

$x_1 + x_2 + x_3 \le 1000$

$x_1, x_2, x_3, d_1^+, d_1^-, d_2^+, d_2^-, d_3^+, d_3^-, d_1, d_2, d_3 \ge 0$

where $p \in [0,1]$ is a parameter, we obtain the set of all the basic Pareto optimal solutions (it has 3 elements):

a) for $p \in (0, 0.18]$:

$x_1 = 465.8; x_2 = 0; x_3 = 0; d_1 = 1397.5; d_2 = 2795; d_3 = 45;$

total deviation $= d_3^+ = 1352.5;$ $\theta = 1;$

b) for $p \in (0.18, 0.89]$:

$x_1 = 466.01; x_2 = 0; x_3 = 0; d_1 = 1398.2; d_2 = 2796.5; d_3 = 39;$

total deviation $= d_3^+ = 1359.2;$ $\theta = 0.7;$

c)   for $p \in (0.89,1)$:

$x_1 = 337; x_2 = 155.6; x_3 = 0; d_1 = 2100; d_2 = 2800; d_3 = 25;$

total deviation $= d_3^+ = 1919.4; \; \theta = 0$.

Thus, if the decision maker wants to have ambitious goals (his satisfaction degree with the goals $\lambda = 1$ ($\theta = 0$), he will have to accept a bit bigger deviation value (1919,4) than the one that would occur if he accepted his smaller satisfaction with the goals (0,3). If the decision maker wants to know the expected deviations for his satisfaction degree λ with the goals being between 0.3 and 1, he can find this out by determining all the linear convex combinations of the points (0.7, 1359,2) and (0,1919.4).

In this example, the trading is being done between the main decision maker and the person who is responsible for the 3. plant, because the negative deviations in the other two plants can be equal to 0.

If we apply the compromise programming (19), with the objective function being equal e.g. to (20) and if we assume $p_1 = 100$ and $p_2 = 1$, we get the following solution:

$x_1 = 466,01; x_2 = 0; x_3 = 0; d_1 = 1398,2; d_2 = 2796,5; d_3 = 39;$ total deviation $=$

$d_3^+ = 1359,2; \; \theta = 0.7 \; (\lambda = 0,3)$.

Let us now pass to the second interpretation of (13), and in our example of (23) (the possibility case). Now the decision maker cannot choose the goals, he only knows the possibility distributions of its values (right-hand side of the constraints in (23)). He is interested in the possibility distribution of the values of the minimal total deviation from the goals, i.e. in the membership function $\mu_{MTD}(z)$ (see (21)). This function will be found by solving the following problem (if we assume the corresponding weights to be equal to 1):

$d_1^+ + d_1^- + d_2^+ + d_2^- + d_3^+ + d_3^- \to \min$

$3x_1 + 7x_2 + 5x_3 + d_1^- - d_1^+ = d_1$

$6x_1 + 5x_2 + 7x_3 + d_2^- - d_2^+ = d_2$

$3x_1 + 6x_2 + 5x_3 + d_3^- - d_3^+ = d_3$

$2100 - 1000\theta \le d_1 \le 2100 + 1000\theta$ \hfill (26)

$2800 - 5\theta \le d_2 \le 2800 + 5\theta$

$25 - 20\theta \le d_3 \le 25 + 20\theta$

$x_1 + x_2 + x_3 \le 1000$

$x_1, x_2, x_3, d_1^+, d_1^-, d_2^+, d_2^-, d_3^+, d_3^-, d_1, d_2, d_3 \ge 0;$

where θ is a now a parameter from the interval $[0,1]$.

Here is the solution of the above problem:

a) $\theta \in [0.7,1]$

$x_1 = 466.63 - 0.83\theta; x_2 = 0; x_3 = 0;$

$d_1 = 1399.75 - 2.25\theta; d_2 = 2800 - 5\theta; d_3 = 25 + 20\theta;$

total deviation $= d_3^+ = 1375 - 22.5\theta$

b) $\theta \in [0, 0.7]$

$x_1 = 337.01 + 183.89\theta; x_2 = 155.6 - 221.7\theta; ; x_3 = 0;$

$d_1 = 2100 - 1000\theta; d_2 = 2800 - 5\theta; d_3 = 25 + 20\theta;$

total deviation $= d_3^+ = 1919,4 - 798,3\theta$;

The above solution can be interpreted as follows: the possibility that the minimal total deviation will be equal to $1375 - 22.5\theta$ is $1-\theta$ for $\theta \in [0.7, 1]$ and the possibility that the minimal total deviation will be equal to $1919,4 - 798,3\theta$ is $1-\theta$ for $\theta \in [0, 0.7]$.

What is more, the solutions of (26), corresponding to, respectively, $\theta=1$, $\theta=0.7$ and $\theta=0$ determine all the solutions of problem (24), thus of (23) in its "preference" interpretation discussed at the beginning of this section.

6. Conclusions

We have proposed two fuzzy goal programming methods, each one solving another decision situation. In both situations the goals are not known in an exact form, but only in that of a fuzzy number. In the first decision situation, however, the decision maker can set the goals himself and only searches for the set of such goal values that would be most satisfying to him. In the second decision situation the goals do not depend on the decision maker. He only knows the possibility distributions of their values and is interested in what total deviation from the goals he should expect in the future.

We proposed a solution method for both decision situations (using only linear programming methods) and illustrated both approaches with a computational example.

References:
[1] Bellman R.R., Zadeh L.A., Decision-making in a fuzzy environment, Management Science B17(1970) 203-218;
[2] Chanas S., Parametric techniques in fuzzy linear programming problems, in: J.L. Verdegay and M. Delgado (eds), The Interface between Artificial Intelligence and Operations Research in Fuzzy Environment, Verlag TÜ Rheinland, 1989, 105-116;
[3] Chanas S., Kuchta D. (1999), Fuzzy Goal Programming, Inst. of Ind. Eng. and Manag., Technical University of Wrocław, PRE No. 66 , 1999;
[4] Dubois D., Prade H., Operations on fuzzy numbers, Int. J. of Systems Science 6(1978), 613-626;

[5] Galas Z., Nykowski N., Żółkiewski Z., Programowanie wielokryterialne, PWE, Warszawa 1987;

[6] Lai Y.J., Hwang C.L., Fuzzy Mathematical Programming. Methods and Applications, Lecture Notes in Economics and Mathematical Systems 394, Springer-Verlag 1992;

[7] Lai Y.J., Hwang C.L., Fuzzy Multiple Objective Decision Making. Methods and Applications, Lecture Notes in Economics and Mathematical Systems 404, Springer-Verlag 1994;

[8] Zadeh L.A., The concept of linguistic variable and its application to approximate reasoning, Parts 1, 2 and 3, Inform. Sci., 8(1975), 199-294, 301-357; 9(1975), 43-80;

[9] Zadeh L.A., Fuzzy sets as a basis for a theory of possibility, Fuzzy Sets and Systems 1(1978), 3-28.

A Multiobjective Linear Programming Algorithm Based on the Dempster-Shafer Composition Rule

Szabolcs CSIKAI(csikasz@cs.elte.hu) and
Margit KOVÁCS(margo@cs.elte.hu)
Dept. of Operations Research, Eötvös Loránd University,
Budapest, Hungary

Abstract

In this paper a new algorithm is given to find an efficient solution with maximal commonality for multiobjective linear programming problems. The algorithm is based on the evidence theory.

Keywords: multiobjective linear programming, efficient point, basic probability assignment, Dempster-Shafer composition rule.

1. Introduction

Let us consider the multiobjective linear programming problems (MOLP) stated in the following

$$\max \{\langle c_1, x\rangle, ..., \langle c_k, x\rangle \} \qquad (1)$$

subject to

$$Ax \le b, \quad x \ge 0, \qquad (2)$$

where $x \in \mathbf{R}^n$, $c_i \in \mathbf{R}^n$ $(i = 1, ..., k)$, $b \in \mathbf{R}^m$, A is an $m \times n$ matrix and C denote the constraints set (2). In this paper we will assume that the set of constraints, C, is compact and the number of objective functions is at least 3, i.e. $k \ge 3$.

It is known that $x \in C$ is a Pareto-optimal solution or an efficient point of the problem (1)-(2) if there is no other feasible point $x' \in C$ such that $\langle c_i, x\rangle \le \langle c_i, x'\rangle$ for all $i = 1, ... k$ and at least one inequality fulfills strictly. Let C^p denote the set of the Pareto-optimal points of (1)-(2) and assume that we know a subset $X \subset C^p$, which is a face of C and it is not a singleton.

The aim of our investigation is to find the most preferred point with a given accuracy from the given Pareto-optimal subset X. X is not a singleton, therefore an additional criterion is necessary to define the most preferred solution from this efficient subset. Since the objective functions, in general, are conflicting, this additional criterion must resolve the conflicts, too, producing a compromised solution. There are different methods to find an efficient point with special properties (see e.g. in [1] or [4]).

In this paper the additional criterion will be the following: the most preferred efficient solution would have "maximal commonality" with respect to the objective functions, where the commonality will be understood in the sense of the theory of evidences [3].

2. Preliminaries from Dempster-Shafer theory

Let Θ be a finite nonempty set called universe.

The basic probability assignment is a function $m : 2^{\Theta} \rightarrow [0,1]$ such that:

$$m(\varnothing) = 0 \text{ and } \sum_{A \subset \Theta} m(A) = 1.$$

The basic probability function can be considered as an expert's evaluation of the given set from the point of view of the problem. The quantity $m(A)$ is to be understood as a measure of the belief that is committed exactly to the subset A. The basic probability number of a set is independent from the evaluation of its subsets. Therefore, in general, it gives a complete evaluation confined to subsets, even more to points.

To avoid these difficulties in evaluation the belief function $Bel: 2^{\Theta} \rightarrow [0,1]$ can be introduced in the following way:

$$Bel(A) = \sum_{B \subset A} m(B).$$

The quantity $Bel(A)$ measures the total belief committed to the subset A.
The commonality number

$$Q(A) = \sum_{A \subset B \subset \Theta} m(B)$$

measures the probability mass that is confined to A but can confined freely to every point of A. So, it evaluates all points of subset with the same quantity, independently from its further partitioning.

Belief functions are adapted to the representation of evidence because they admit a natural rule of combination. Given several belief functions over the same Θ but based on different bodies of evidence, the Dempster's rule of combination enables us to compute their orthogonal sum. Suppose that m_1 and m_2 are two different basic probability assignments given over Θ as two different experts's estimations. The Dempster's rule of composition is defined by

$$(m_1 \oplus m_2)(A) = K \sum_{B \cap C = A} m_1(B) m_2(C)$$

where K is the normalizing constant given by

$$K = \left(1 - \sum_{B \cap C = \varnothing} m_1(B) m_2(C)\right)^{-1}.$$

The composition rule can be extended to any number of basic probability assignments by iterating this form. It is known that

$$(Q_1 \oplus Q_2)(A) = K \cdot Q_1(A)Q_2(A).$$

If $|\Theta|=2$, (where $|\cdot|$ denote the cardinality of the given set), then this theory is much more simple, because the evidence functions express the same preference:

Proposition 2.1. Let $\Theta=\{A,B\}$ and let m, Bel and $Q : 2^\Theta \rightarrow [0,1]$ be the basic probability function, the belief function and the commonality function over Θ respectively. Then the following statements are equivalent:

1. $m(A) = m(B)$,
2. $Bel(A) = Bel(B)$,
3. $Q(A) = Q(B)$.

Proof: It is obvious from the definition of the used functions.

This simplified theory will be used in our investigation. Detailed discussion of evidence theory can be seen in [3].

3. Basic ideas of the algorithm

We can assume that each objective function is nonnegative over the set of constraints, otherwise, by introducing a slack variable v change the objective functions

$$\langle c_i, x \rangle, \quad (i = 1,...,k)$$

to

$$\langle c_i, x \rangle + v, \quad (i = 1,...,k), \tag{3}$$

where $v \geq -\min(f_i^* : f_i^* < 0)$ and f_i^* $(i = 1,...,k)$ are obtained by minimizing each of the objective functions individually subject to the constraints set.

Let $Y = C \cap X$ and let $(f_1^*(Y), ..., f_k^*(Y)) \in \mathbf{R}^k$ be the ideal criterion vector on Y the components of which are obtained by maximizing each objective function individually subject to the Y subset. Assume that none of these LP problems is degenerate. Let $x_i^*(Y)$ denote the solution of the ith individual maximization problem. Every $x_i^*(Y)$ is an efficient point and they will be called ideal efficient points.

3.1. Measuring the conflicts

Definition 3.1. The measure of conflict between the ith and jth objective function with respect to the constraints Y or between the ith and jth ideal efficient points of Y is defined by

$$\kappa_{ij}(Y) = \| x_i^*(Y) - x_j^*(Y) \|, \tag{4}$$

where $\|x\|$ is the Euclidean norm of a vector x. The total conflict measure κ of the set of all objective functions is defined by

$$\kappa(Y) = \max \{\kappa_{ij}(Y) : i,j \in \{1,...k\}\}. \tag{5}$$

The i-th and the j-th objective functions are the most conflicting objective functions on Y if $\kappa(Y) = \kappa_{ij}(Y)$.

It is obvious, that $\kappa_{ij}(Y) \geq 0$ and the farther the ideal efficient points are the greater conflict the measure is.

3.2. Definition of the universe and the basic probability assignments

Choose a covering set-system $\{C^t \subset C: t=1,...,q\}$ of the constraints set C satisfying the following conditions:

[C1] $q \geq 2$ and q does not exceed the number of different ideal efficient points;

[C2] $C = \bigcup_{t=1}^{q} C^t$;

[C4] $C^t \cap X \neq \varnothing \quad t = 1,...,q.$

[C3] $\bigcap_{t=1}^{q} \text{int}(C^t) = \varnothing$;

Let the universe Θ be defined as the set of the statements P_j written in the following form:

"The subset G_j contains the most preferred efficient point of Y",
where G_j is one of the sets $C^t \cap X = Y^t$ ($t=1,...,q$) or the union of finite number of them. So, between the subsets G_j ($j=1,...,2^{q-1}$) of Y and the statements P_j ($j=1,...,2^{q-1}$) there is a one-to-one mapping.

Every individual objective function evaluates the subsets G_j by its individual maximal value subject to $\text{cl}(G_j)$ ($\text{cl}(G)$ is the closure of G). Let consider these evaluations apart from a multiplying factor K_i as basic probability assignments to the propositions P_j ($j=1,...,2^{q-1}$). (The multiplying factor must be chosen such that the sum of the basic probability assignments be equal to 1.):

$$m_i(G_j) = K_i \cdot f_i^*(G_j), \quad j=1,\ldots, 2^{q-1}, \ i=1,\ldots,k. \tag{6}$$

Taking into consideration all objective functions by the Dempster's composition rule we obtain common basic probability assignments and commonality quantities for all subsets. Let $j^* \in \text{argmax} \{Q(G_j): j=1,\ldots,2^{q-1}\}$. Then G_i^* is the best approximation of the most preferred efficient set with the given partitioning. The decision maker can increase the accuracy of the approximation repeating the process after refining the partitioning inside G_{j^*}.

3.3. Rules of partitioning

For the simplicity we begin the process with dividing the set C into two parts (C^1 and C^2) by a cutting plane

$$\langle \alpha, x \rangle = \beta$$

such that the closure of the partitions be

$$\text{cl}\,(C^1) = C \cap \{\, x \in \mathbf{R}^n : \langle \alpha, x \rangle \le \beta \,\},$$
$$\text{cl}\,(C^2) = C \cap \{\, x \in \mathbf{R}^n : \langle \alpha, x \rangle \ge \beta \,\}, \tag{7}$$
$$Y^t = C^t \cap X \quad t=1,2.$$

Let i_1 and i_2 denote the indices of the most conflicted objective functions. Since in the first step we have no information which partition would be better, in order to derive the normal vector α and β of the cutting plane we follow the rules mentioned below:

[R1] The cutting plane is a hyperplane.

[R2] The cutting plane is orthogonal to the vector ($x_{i_1}^*(Y) - x_{i_2}^*(Y)$).

[R3] The cutting plane contains the point $\dfrac{1}{2}(x_{i_1}^*(Y) + x_{i_2}^*(Y))$.

The rules [R1]-[R3] satisfies the conditions [C1]-[C4] and the following propositions hold:

Proposition 3.1 There exists only one cutting plane satisfying the rules [R1]-[R3], and the equation of this cutting plane is

$$\langle \alpha, x \rangle = \beta, \tag{8}$$

where $\alpha = x_{i_1}^*(Y) - x_{i_2}^*(Y)$ and $\beta = \dfrac{1}{2}(\| x_{i_1}^*(Y) \|^2 - \| x_{i_2}^*(Y) \|^2)$.

Proof: It is easy to see that [R1] is satisfied and by choosing $\alpha = x_{i_1}^*(Y) - x_{i_2}^*(Y)$ [R2] is also satisfied. To prove [R3] we can consider the following equation:

$$\langle\, x_{i_1}^*(Y) - x_{i_2}^*(Y), \ \frac{1}{2}(x_{i_1}^*(Y) + x_{i_2}^*(Y)) \,\rangle =$$

$$= \frac{1}{2} \left(\langle x_{i1}^{*}(Y), x_{i1}^{*}(Y) \rangle - \langle x_{i1}^{*}(Y), x_{i2}^{*}(Y) \rangle + \langle x_{i2}^{*}(Y), x_{i1}^{*}(Y) \rangle - \langle x_{i2}^{*}(Y), x_{i2}^{*}(Y) \rangle \right) =$$

$$= \frac{1}{2} \left(\| x_{i1}^{*}(Y) \|^{2} - \| x_{i2}^{*}(Y) \|^{2} \right),$$

so [R3] is satisfied. The uniqueness follows from [R1].

Proposition 3.2. The hyperplane given by (8) separates the most conflicting ideal efficient points of Y.

Proof: This proposition is follows from [R2] and [R3]. Because the distance between the ideal points and the hyperplane is equal to $\frac{1}{2} \| x_{i1}^{*}(Y) - x_{i2}^{*}(Y) \|$ and we have assumed that the number of the ideal point is at least 2.

3.4 Computation of evidences

Let the partition be defined according to the section 3.3 and assume that the indices 1 and 2 are assigned to the most conflicted objective functions on Y. Let

$$m_i(Y^t) = K_i f_i^*(Y^t), \ i=1,\ldots,k, \ t=1,2,$$

where K_i, $i=1,\ldots,k$ are the factors of normalization with respect to the i-th objective function. Let $I \subset \{1,\ldots,k\}$ and let us denote by $m_I(Y)$, $m_I(Y^t)$, (t=1,2) the basic probability assignments to the corresponding sets calculated by the Dempster-Shafer composition rule. We have the following propositions:

Proposition 3.3. The following equations are true:

$$m_{1\ldots r}(Y) = K_{1\ldots r}(Y) \, m_{1\ldots r-1}(Y)) \, m_r(Y), \quad r \leq k,$$

$$m_{1\ldots r}(Y^t) = K_{1\ldots r}(Y) \, ((m_{1\ldots r-1}(Y^t) \, m_r(Y^t) + m_{1\ldots r-1}(Y^t) \, m_r(Y)) +$$
$$+ m_{1\ldots r-1}(Y)) \, m_r(Y^t)), \qquad t=1,2; \ r \leq k,$$

$$m_{12}(Y) = K_{12}(Y) \, m_1(Y) m_2(Y),$$

$$m_{12}(Y^1) = K_{12}(Y) \, m_1(Y) \, (2m_2(Y^1) + m_2(Y)),$$

$$m_{12}(Y^2) = K_{12}(Y) \, m_2(Y) \, (2m_1(Y^2) + m_1(Y)),$$

where $K_I(Y)$ denotes the joint normalization factor with respect to the objective functions corresponding to the index-set I.

Proof: The first and second equations follow directly from the Dempter-Shafer theory. We know that $m_t(Y^t) = m_t(Y))$ for $t=1,2$, so

$$m_{12}(Y^t) = K_{12}(Y) \, (m_1(Y^t) \, m_2(Y^t) + m_1(Y^t) m_2(Y) + m_1(Y) \, m_2(Y^t)) =$$
$$= K_{12}(Y) \, m_1(Y) \, (2m_2(Y^t) + m_2(Y)), \qquad t=1,2.$$

4. Algorithm

Step 1 Compute f_i^* $(i=1,...,k)$. If there exist an index i such that $f_i^* < 0$ then compute v and transform the problem into (4) by introducing a new slack variable. Let $s=0$ and $Y=X \cap C$.

Step 2 Compute the ideal criterion vector $(f_1^*(Y),..., f_k^*(Y))$ and the corresponding ideal efficient points $x_{i1}^*(Y),..., x_{ik}^*(Y)$.

Step 3 If the set of different ideal efficient points is a singleton, then STOP else go to Step 4.

Step 4 Derive the indices i_1 and i_2 of the most conflicting ideal efficient points by (3)

Step 5 Derive the cutting plane by (4).

Step 6 Define the partitions C^1, C^2 and Y^1, Y^2 by (7).

Step 7 Compute the communality numbers $Q_{1...k}(Y^1)$ and $Q_{1...k}(Y^2)$ by the formulas of Proposition 3.3.

Step 8 Let $s=s+1$ and $C_s^* = \begin{cases} C^1 & Q_{1...k}(Y^1) \geq Q_{1...k}(Y^2) \\ C^2 & otherwise \end{cases}$

Then C_s^* is the s-th approximation of the most preferred efficient point.

Step 9 If the accuracy is satisfactory then STOP, else repeat the process from Step 2 using the approximating set C_s^* instead of C.

The following theorem is hold:

Theorem 4.1. Let C_s^* denote the best approximation of the most preferred efficient point in the s-th iteration. Then $\kappa(X_s) \to 0$ if $s \to \infty$ where $X_s = C_s^* \cap X$.

Proof: Let us assume that the theorem is not true. It means that there exists a sequence of indices for which $\kappa(X_s) > \varepsilon$. The number of the objective function pairs is finite so there exists two objective function (without loss of generality we can assume that the first two) and an infinite sequence of indices such that $\kappa_{1,2}(X_s) > \varepsilon$ and $\kappa_{1,2}(X_s) = \kappa(X_s)$. Let us denote by $x_1^*(X_s)$ and $x_2^*(X_s)$ the corresponding ideal efficient points. X_s is compact so there exist subsequences of the $\{x_i^*(X_s)\}$, $i=1,2$, which tends to x_1^* and x_2^*, respectively. (We can assume that that these subsequences are denoted by $\{x_i^*(X_s)\}$, $i=1,2$)

Let I be an index such that

$$\|x_1^*(X_s) - x_1^*\| < \frac{\varepsilon}{4} \quad \text{and} \quad \|x_2^*(X_s) - x_2^*\| < \frac{\varepsilon}{4} \quad \forall i > I.$$

In the I-th step the cutting plane separates $x_1^*(X_I)$ and $x_2^*(X_I)$. Since

$$\| x_1^*(X_I) - x_2^*(X_I) \| > \varepsilon,$$

this cutting plane separates the balls $B(x_1^*(X_I), \frac{\varepsilon}{4})$ and $B(x_2^*(X_I), \frac{\varepsilon}{4})$, too, (where $B(x,a)$ denotes the ball with a radius and x center), Consequently, it separates x_1^* and x_2^* as well. But this is a contradiction, because both points are limit points and if $i > I$ then neither x_1^* nor x_2^* is in X_i.

5. Conclusion

The method given in this paper is an effective method to approximate the efficient point with maximal commonality. From computational point of view it is simple, because it can be based on simplex method, and in every iteration the simplex tableau differs from the previous one only in adding a new row.

The idea of our algorithm can also be applied when X is not a face but an arbitrary subset of the Pareto optimal set or the objective functions are nonnegative nonlinear functions. But in these cases there may occur some difficulties in the step 2 when we calculate the ideal criterion vectors.

Worthy to note that in this algorithm the commonality means commonality in function values. However we can use other values as basic probability numbers, and gather communality of these values on a set. So, a large number of different methods can be built by this technique. It means that we can derive efficient point with different additional criteria by the same technique.

Acknowledgment

This research mainly has been performed under the auspices of the Inter-University Centre of Telecommunications and Informatics (ETIK) which is a collaboration of five companies located in Hungary (namely, Ericsson Hungary Ltd., Hungarian Telecommunication Inc., KFKI Computer System Corp., Sun Microsystem Hungary Ltd. and WESTEL 900 GSM Inc.) and two universities (Budapest University of Technology and Economic and Eötvös Loránd University, Budapest).

The research has partially been supported by the grant of the Hungarian Higher Education Research and Development Program FKFP 157/2000.

References

[1] Chankong V., Haimes Y.Y., *Multiobjective Decision Making Theory and Methodology*, Elsevier, 1983.
[2] Carlsson C., Fuller R., Multiple Criteria Decision Making: The Case for Interdependence, *Computers & Operations Research* 22(1995) 251-260.
[3] Shafer G. A *Mathematical Theory of Evidence*, Princeton Press, 1976 .
[4] Yu P.L., *Multiple-Criteria Decision Making Concepts, Techniques and Extensions*, Plenum Press, 1985.

Data Envelopment Analysis by Multiobjective Linear Programming Methods

Petr Fiala

Department of Econometrics, University of Economics, W. Churchill Sq. 4, 13067 Prague 3, Czech Republic, pfiala@vse.cz

Abstract: The paper presents a brief introduction to possibility of application of multicriteria approaches to performance analysis of decision making units. The Data Envelopment Analysis (DEA) is an approach of performance evaluation of decision making units by multiple input and multiple output. Solving of a multiobjective linear programming problem by the Aspiration Level Oriented Procedure (ALOP) can be used for search of the efficient frontier in DEA.

Keywords: Performance measurement, Data Envelopment Analysis, Multiobjective Programming, Aspiration Level Oriented Procedure. Analytical Hierarchy Process

1. Introduction

Several frameworks for organisational performance measurement have been suggested. There are several principles that emerge from these suggested performance measurement frameworks. Different perspectives must be considered in contrast to a traditional single focus on financial performance. Many authors have suggested including non-financial measures, besides traditional cost measures, in production performance measurement systems, in order to control the correct implementation of the production strategy with respect to all competitive priorities. But the use of non-financial performance measures makes it difficult to assess and compare the overall effectiveness of each decision making unit in terms of support provided to the achievement of the production strategy. since to this aim is necessary to integrate performance measures expressed in heterogeneous measurement units.

Data Envelopment Analysis (DEA) encompasses a variety of models and methods to evaluating performance. The essential characteristic of the DEA model is the reduction of the multiple input and multiple output using weights to that of a single "virtual" input and a single "virtual" output (see [1]). The method searches for the set of weights which maximise the efficiency of the decision making unit. The DEA may be characterised as method of objective weight assessment.

For some reasons can be very useful to search the efficient frontier in the DEA model. Searching the efficient frontier in the DEA model can be formulated as a multiobjective linear programming problem. We propose an interactive procedure ALOP (Aspiration Levels Oriented Procedure) for multiobjective linear programming problems (see [3]). By changing aspiration levels it is possible to analyse an appropriate part of the efficient frontier.

The measures used in the DEA model can be located within the linked hierarchical structure to ensure that they capture the main elements of organisational performance. The performance pyramid represents a performance system that captures multiple perspectives (see [5]).

The Analytic Hierarchy Process (AHP) is the method for setting priorities (see [6]). A priority scale based on reference is the AHP way to standardise non-unique scales in order to combine multiple inputs and multiple outputs and aggregate the hierarchical structure of factors. The AHP can be characterised as method of subjective weights assessment and can be used to weight restrictions in DEA.

2. Data Envelopment Analysis

The first DEA model was developed by Charnes, Cooper and Rhodes (see [1]). Suppose there are n decision making units each consuming r inputs and producing s outputs and (r,n)-matrix X, (s,n)-matrix Y of observed input and output measures. The essential characteristic of the CCR ratio model is the reduction of the multiple input and multiple output to that of a single "virtual" input and a single "virtual" output. For a particular decision making unit the ratio of the single output to the single input provides a measure of efficiency that is a function of the weight multipliers (u,v). Instead of using an exogenously specified set of weights (u,v), the method searches for the set of weights which maximise the efficiency of the decision making unit P_0 . The relative efficiency of the decision making unit P_0 is given as maximisation of the ratio of single output to single input to the condition that the relative efficiency of every decision making unit is less than or equal to one. The formulation leads to a linear fractional programming problem.

$$\frac{\sum_{i=1}^{s} u_i y_{i0}}{\sum_{j=1}^{r} v_j x_{j0}} \to max$$

$$\frac{\displaystyle\sum_{i=1}^{s} u_i y_{ih}}{\displaystyle\sum_{j=1}^{r} v_j x_{jh}} \leq 1 \qquad h = 1,2,\ldots,n$$

$$u_i, v_j \geq \varepsilon \;,\; i = 1,2,\ldots,s \;,\; j = 1,2,\ldots,r.$$

If it is possible to find a set of weights for which the efficiency ratio of the decision making unit P_0 is equal to one, the decision making unit P_0 will be regarded as efficient, otherwise it will be regarded as inefficient.

Solving of this nonlinear nonconvex problem directly is not an efficient approach. The following linear programming problem with new variable weights (μ, v) that results from the Charnes - Cooper transformation gives optimal values that will also be optimal for the fractional programming problem.

$$\sum_{i=1}^{s} \mu_i y_{i0} \rightarrow \max$$

$$\sum_{j=1}^{r} v_j x_{j0} = 1$$

$$\sum_{i=1}^{s} \mu_i y_{ih} - \sum_{j=1}^{r} v_{jh} x_{jh} \leq 0 \qquad , \quad h = 1,2,\ldots,n$$

$$\mu_i, v_j \geq \varepsilon \;,\; i = 1,2,\ldots,s \;,\; j = 1,2,\ldots,r.$$

If it is possible to find a set of weights for which the value of the objective function is equal to one, the decision making unit P_0 will be regarded as efficient, otherwise it will be regarded as inefficient.

3. Searching the efficient frontier

The set of efficient decision making units is called the reference set. The set spanned by the reference set is called the efficient frontier. Searching the efficient frontier in the DEA model can be formulated as a multiobjective linear programming problem (see [4]).

The problem is defined as maximisation of linear combination of outputs and minimisation of linear combination of inputs.

$$Y\lambda \rightarrow \text{"max"}$$

$$X\lambda \rightarrow \text{"min"}$$

$$\lambda \geq 0$$

A solution λ_0 is efficient iff there does not exist another λ such that

$$Y\lambda \geq Y\lambda_0, \ X\lambda \leq X\lambda_0 \text{ and } (Y\lambda, X\lambda) \neq (Y\lambda_0, X\lambda_0).$$

Different multiobjective linear programming methods can be used for solving of the problem.

4. Aspiration Levels Oriented Procedure

We propose an interactive procedure ALOP (Aspiration Levels Oriented Procedure) for multiobjective linear programming problems (see [3]). In the DEA model the decision alternative $\lambda = (\lambda_1, \lambda_2, ..., \lambda_n)$ is a vector of n variable coefficients. The decision maker states aspiration levels $y^{(k)}$ and $x^{(k)}$ of outputs and inputs.

We verify three possibilities by solving the problem

$$z = \sum_{i=1}^{s} d_i^+ + \sum_{j=1}^{r} c_j^- \rightarrow \max$$

$$Y\lambda - d^+ = y^{(k)}$$

$$X\lambda + c^- = x^{(k)}$$

$$\lambda, d^+, c^- \geq 0. .$$

If it holds :

- $z > 0$, then the problem is feasible and d^+ and c^- are proposed changes $\Delta y^{(k)}$ and $\Delta x^{(k)}$ of aspiration levels which achieve an efficient solution in the next step,

- $z = 0$, then we obtained an efficient solution,

- the problem is infeasible, then we search the nearest solution to the aspiration levels by solving the goal programming problem

$$z = \sum_{i=1}^{s} (d_i^+ + d_i^-) + \sum_{j=1}^{r} (c_j^+ + c_j^-) \rightarrow \min$$

$$Y\lambda - d^+ + d^- = y^{(k)}$$

$$X\lambda - c^+ + c^- = x^{(k)}$$

$$\lambda, d^+, d^-, c^+, c^- \geq 0.$$

The solution of the problem is feasible with changes of the aspiration levels $\Delta y^{(k)} = d^+ - d^-$ and $\Delta x^{(k)} = c^+ - c^-$. For changes of efficient solutions the duality theory is applied. Dual variables to objective constraints in the problem are denoted q_i, $i=1,2,...,s$, and p_j, $j=1,2,...,r$.

If it holds

$$\sum_{i=1}^{s} q_i \Delta y_i^{(k)} + \sum_{j=1}^{r} p_j \Delta x_j^{(k)} = 0,$$

then for some changes $\Delta y^{(k)}$ and $\Delta x^{(k)}$ the value $z=0$ is not changed and we obtained another efficient solution. The decision maker can state $s + r - 1$ changes of the aspiration levels, then the change of the rest aspiration level is calculated from the previous equation.

The decision maker chooses a forward direction or backtracking. Results of the procedure ALOP are solutions on the efficient frontier.

5. Analytical Hierarchy Process

The performance pyramid (see [5]) represents a comprehensive, fully integrated performance system that captures multiple perspectives as internal, financial, customer and innovation. Each side of the pyramid represents a perspective as a hierarchical structure of success factors, managerial measures and process drivers. Not only are measures and process drivers linked to each side of pyramid, but linkages also exist to other sides of the pyramid as impact of process drivers on more than one key perspective .

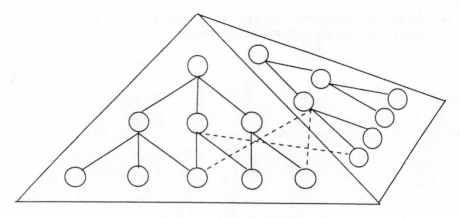

Fig. 1. The performance pyramid

The Analytical Hierarchy Process (see [6]) is appropriate method for assessing and comparing the overall performance of different decision making units. The AHP derives ratio scale priorities by making paired comparisons of elements on a common hierarchy level by using a 1 to 9 scale of absolute numbers. The absolute number from the scale is an approximation to the ratio w_j / w_k and then is possible to derive values of w_j and w_k. The AHP method uses the general model for synthesis of the performance measures in the hierarchical structure

$$u_i = \sum_{j=1}^{n} v_j w_{jk} .$$

The weights in the DEA can be restricted by the decision maker's judgements by the AHP. The comparison matrix $C = (c_{jk})$, where elements c_{jk} are judgements of w_j / w_k. It is known that the preference region W is structured by column vectors of the comparison matrix C. Any weight vector from W can be obtained as linear combination of column vectors

$$w = C\lambda ,$$

where λ is a nonnegative vector of coefficients, $\lambda = (\lambda_1, \lambda_2. ..., \lambda_n)$.

If the matrix C is consistent, the consistency index C.I. = 0, the preference region is a line through origin. If the matrix C is inconsistent, the consistency index C.I. > 0, the preference region is a convex cone, the greater consistency index, the greater preference cone.

6. Conclusion

The performance measurement is appropriate for applying some multicriteria methods for evaluation of decision making units and consequently to demonstrate usefulness of the methods for managers. Combination of the methods for searching the efficient frontier and methods for specific requirements (weight restrictions, aspiration level changes)   gives a powerful instrument to capture managerial problems.

A more informative view may be obtained by separating out measures of efficiency, effectiveness and economy (concept of the three "E`s"). Efficiency can be expressed in terms of the relationship between outputs and inputs, effectiveness in terms of the relationship between outputs and outcomes, economy in terms of the relationship between outcomes and inputs.

References

[1] Charnes, A., Cooper, W.W., Rhodes, E.: Measuring Efficiency of Decision Making Units. European Journal of Operational Research 1, 1978, 429-444.

[2] Cooper, W.W., Tone, K.: A Survey of Some Recent Developments in Data Envelopment Analysis. In: EURO XIV Conference, Jerusalem 1995, 149-168.

[3] Fiala, P.: Models of Cooperative Decision Making. In: . Gal and G. Fandel, eds: Multiple Criteria Decision Making, Hagen 1995, Springer, Berlin 1997, 128-136.

[4] Korhonen, P.: Searching the Efficient Frontier in Data Envelopment Analysis. IIASA Report IR-97-79, Laxemburg 1997.

[5] Rouse, P., Puterill, M., Ryan, D.: Towards a General Managerial Framework for Performance Measurement: A Comprehensive Highway Maintenance Application. Journal of Productivity Analysis 8, 1997, 127-149.

[6] Saaty, T.L.: The Analytic Hierarchy Process. RWS Publications, Pittsburgh 1990.

A Fuzzy Borda Count in Multi-person Decision Making[*]

José Luis García-Lapresta and Miguel Martínez-Panero

Departamento de Economía Aplicada (Matemáticas)
Facultad de Ciencias Económicas y Empresariales
Universidad de Valladolid
Avda. Valle de Esgueva 6, 47011 Valladolid, Spain
E-mail: lapresta@cpd.uva.es & panero@eco.uva.es

Abstract

Inspired by the Borda count, in this paper we introduce a "fuzzy Borda count". It is obtained by means of score graduation and normalization processes from its original pattern. The advantages of the Borda count hold, and are even improved, and its drawbacks are somehow corrected, providing an appropriate scheme in multi-person decision making. In addition, these Borda counts are related to approval voting, establishing a unified framework from distinct points of view.

1   Introduction

Among the great variety of methods in multi-person decision making[1], in this paper we focus our attention on the Borda count, which has been considered as an "optimal" procedure by Saari (1995, p. 12). Dummett (1998, p. 290) also argues that the Borda count is "the best tool for reaching the decision most likely to be correct when the object is to reconcile different judgements about effective means to a common aim, and the most equitable method of determining a resultant of divergent desires". Moreover, an institution called the *De Borda Institute*[2] exists, which shows its advantages and tries to shed light on it.

Despite works presented earlier[3], this method was proposed by Jean Charles de Borda, as indicated by its name. This engineer and navy officer denounced, in a Memory read in 1770 in the French Academy of Sciences, that the usual multi-person decision procedures only considered the most preferred alternative for each agent, ignoring the rest. Taking into account this partial information, the final output could not faithfully reflect the agents' preferences. Borda showed examples with this fault, and then advocated the following scheme: each agent arranges all the alternatives linearly, and gives integer marks to each of them: the highest score, which coincides with the number of alternatives, to the most preferred; one

---

[*] The authors want to acknowledge the financial support of *Consejería de Educación y Cultura de la Junta de Castilla y León* (project VA09/98).
[1] See Fishburn (1990), for example.
[2] http://members.tripod.co.uk/deBordaInstitute.
[3] McLean – Urken (1995 a, pp. 19 and ff.) indicated that Nicolaus Cusanus (XVth c.) foresaw the idea of the Borda count.

point less to the next alternative; and so on, in a descent manner, till the least preferred is reached, which is given only one point.

This Borda count was chosen by the French Academy of Sciences to select its members, and it was both critiziced and praised. Indeed, the Marquis of Condorcet censured its manipulability and pointed out the following fact: an alternative which defeats all others one by one in the majority of the cases[4] might not be selected if the Borda count is used (see Black (1958, pp. 156 and ff.)). On the other hand, the Spanish enlighted mathematician Morales (1797) considered it as the most appropriate and representative procedure. However, it was said that the Borda count did not respect the agents' freedom of scoring and did not reflect the candidates' merit with accuracy. In order to refute these arguments, Morales (1805, pp. 18 and ff.) showed that, if the scale of values 0,1,2..., is used instead of 1,2,3..., to score the alternatives from the least to the most preferred, then the total score of a fixed alternative is the number of alternatives evaluated worse than it. This fact had already been pointed out by Borda and commented by Condorcet to ensure that the range of values used by the Borda count was not arbitrary (see McLean – Urken (1995 a, pp. 81 – 89)). More recently, the unfulfillment of the independence of irrelevant alternatives principle considered by Arrow (1951, 2nd ed. 1963) has been added to the above-mentioned drawbacks[5].

In contrast, advantages of the Borda count which promote this method are the use of information from the entire preference rankings of all the voters, and its direct execution. In addition, Black (1958 and 1976), Mueller (1979) and Straffin Jr. (1980), among others, have noted that the Borda count chooses the alternative which stands highest on average in the agents' preference orderings.

The Borda rule has been re-considered many times, inspiring other collective decision making procedures. In 1882, Nanson (see McLean – Urken 1995 a, pp. 321 – 359) introduced a sort of Borda count with eliminations. Copeland (1951) considered Borda-type scores for each alternative, wich were the number of alternatives better than that marked minus the number of alternatives worse than it (see Saari – Merlin (1996)). Black (1958, p. 66) proposed a hybrid procedure consisting in the choice of the Condorcet winner, if it exists. Orherwise, Borda count should be used. Kemeny (1959) formuled a rule defined with arguments similar to those of the Borda rule (see Young (1995, pp. 61 and ff.) and Saari – Merlin (1997)). Later on, Sen (1977) considered the so-called narrow and broad Borda counts in connection with the independence of irrelevant alternatives principle. In addition, Dummett (1998) introduced the revised and adjusted Borda counts to penalize the manipulability of the classic Borda count.

From a theoretical point of view, several characterizations of the Borda count have been obtained by Young (1974), Debord (1992), Nitzan – Rubinstein (1981), among others. The last authors consider non-transitive preferences over the alternatives. In this paper, transitivity will be a coherence assumption needed to ensure "reasonable" Borda scores, as we shall show.

---

[4] This alternative, if it exists, is called the *Condorcet winner*.

[5] Again, McLean – Urken (1995 b) have shown how Condorcet anticipated Arrow's independence of irrelevant alternatives principle.

According to the De Borda Institute, no state political institutions are known to use the Borda count, but it has been used by the Green Party of Ireland. In another context, Parker (1995) has considered the Borda count as a synthesis decision method in recognition of hand-printed characters. The scores given in the European musical contest of Eurovision and in the championship of rallies races are also examples of Borda count, although in these cases the marks are not in arithmetic progression.

In this paper the classic Borda count is considered and extended in a natural way to non-linear orderings, where the agents can declare indifference among distinct alternatives. This method will even be generalized by considering fuzzy preferences for the agents and not necessarily integer[6] scores over the alternatives. In each case, special attention will be paid to the underlying rationality assumptions.

The paper is organized as follows. In Section 2 we formalize the classic (discrete) Borda count. In Section 3 a fuzzy Borda count is introduced. These Borda counts are connected with approval voting in Section 4. Finally, in Section 5, the results obtained are commented and a utilitarian view to the scores used is exposed.

2   The discrete Borda count

At first, the Borda count was designed to score the alternatives sequentially, assuming the agents' preferences to be linear orderings. This can be formalized and generalized in a natural way as follows. Let $P^1, P^2, ..., P^m$ be the preference relations (binary asymmetric relations) of m agents over n alternatives $x_1, x_2,..., x_n$. Each agent gives a mark to each alternative, according to the number of alternatives worse than it: $r_k(x_i) = \#\{x_j \mid x_i P^k x_j\}$ is the score given by agent k to the alternative x_i. The same result is obtained by considering, for each agent k, its preference matrix:

$$\begin{pmatrix} r_{11}^k & r_{12}^k & ... & r_{1n}^k \\ r_{21}^k & r_{22}^k & ... & r_{2n}^k \\ ... & ... & ... & ... \\ r_{n1}^k & r_{n2}^k & ... & r_{nn}^k \end{pmatrix},$$

where

$$r_{ij}^k = \begin{cases} 1, & \text{if } x_i P^k x_j, \\ 0, & \text{otherwise.} \end{cases}$$

[6] We have just pointed out the arguments of Morales and Borda to justify integer value scale of the Borda count as the number of times each alternative is preferred pairwise to each other. Laplace, on his own, obtained this spectrum of scores by means of probabilistic-type arguments based on the agents' "latent estimates", recently re-formulated by Tanguiane (1991, pp. 80 and ff.) and Tangian (2000), who already suggest the fuzzy counts considered in this paper, and also appearing in Marchant (1996, 2000).

In this way, the agent k gives the alternative x_i the following mark:

$$r_k(x_i) = \sum_{x_i P^k x_j}^{n} r_{ij}^k.$$

We note that the possible score range is contained in the set of values $\{0,1,...,n-1\}$. Some of the upper values might not be reached if there is indifference (absence of preference) among distinct alternatives. However, if the orderings were linear, the above-mentioned set would exactly ranged.

With these individual counts a collective one is obtained:

$$r(x_i) = \sum_{k=1}^{m} r_k(x_i).$$

So, the collective preference relation P^B is defined by:

$$x_i P^B x_j \Leftrightarrow r(x_i) > r(x_j),$$

which is always negatively transitive[7]. Thus, the highest scored alternatives (maximals for P^B) will be chosen.

Nevertheless, it is reasonable for the Borda count to require the fulfillment of the following property of monotonicity: when two alternatives are compared by an agent, the highest scored must be the preferred one.

Definition 1. The count r_k is *monotonic* if and only if:

$$x_i P^k x_j \Rightarrow r_k(x_i) > r_k(x_j)$$

for all pair of alternatives $x_i, x_j \in X$.

As we shall show, this demand is verified by assuming transitivity in individual preferences. This is the reason why we assume this rationality hypothesis in the following.

Proposition 1. If the preference relation P^k is transitive, then the count r_k is monotonic.

Proof: Suppose $x_i P^k x_j$. Being P^k transitive, if $x_j P^k x_l$, then $x_i P^k x_l$. So $\{x_l \mid x_j P^k x_l\} \subset \{x_l \mid x_i P^k x_l\}$. The inclusion is strict because the alternative x_j belongs to the second set and not to the first one. Consequently, $r_k(x_i) = \#\{x_l \mid x_i P^k x_l\} > r_k(x_j) = \#\{x_l \mid x_j P^k x_l\}$. $\square$

Remark 1. If P^k is not transitive, then the count r_k is not necessarily monotonic, as it is showed in the following example. Suppose a preference

---

[7] An ordinary preference relation P is negatively transitive if, not being verified $x_i P x_j$ nor $x_j P x_k$, then $x_i P x_k$ is not verified either. It is easy to prove that if P is negatively transitive, it is also transitive.

relation P^k over 4 alternatives, explicitly given by: $x_1 P^k x_2$, $x_2 P^k x_3$, $x_3 P^k x_4$, $x_2 P^k x_4$. Then $r_k(x_1) = 1 < r_k(x_2) = 2$, although, as pointed out, $x_1 P^k x_2$.

3 A fuzzy Borda count

Consider the following examples in decision making:

• Young (1995): "Suppose [...] that the common objective is to reduce crime, and the three proposed policies are: a) hire more police, b) increase prison sentences, and c) offer training programs for ex-convicts. Voters may agree on the objective, yet differ in their judgement about which of these policies is in fact more likely to reduce crime per dollar spent".

• Parker (1995): "This is most likely a FIVE, but could be a THREE, and is even less likely to be a FOUR" (in recognition of hand-printed characters).

The authors of these examples consider only discrete Borda counts to determine which alternatives are preferred to the others. It seems a natural transition for the agents to show numerically how much some alternatives are preferred to the others[8], evaluating their preference intensities from 0 to 1. This is possible by considering fuzzy binary relations. The following pre-requisites are introduced to formalize the fuzzy Borda counts.

We shall consider a finite set of alternatives, $X = \{x_1,...,x_n\}$, over each one of the m agents show their preferences by means of fuzzy binary relations $R^1,...,R^m$. Let $\mu_{R^k} : X \times X \to [0, 1]$ the membership function of R^k, $k = 1,...,m$. The number $r_{ij}^k = \mu_R(x_i, x_j) \in [0,1]$ indicates the level of preference intensity of agent k for x_i over x_j, as higher as closer to 1.

Because of normalization reasons, the total capacity to prefer between pairs of alternatives is considered to be unitary for each agent. It is also plausible to admit that however greater the intensity r_{ij} with wich x_i is preferred to x_j, the lower intensity r_{ji} with which x_j is preferred to x_i will be. These considerations are contemplated in the following axiom of reciprocity, which will be assumed in our arguments[9].

Definition 2. A fuzzy binary relation R over X is *reciprocal* if and only if it is verified $r_{ij} + r_{ji} = 1$ for all $i, j \in \{1,...,n\}$.

Definition 3. For each agent $k \in \{1,...,m\}$, the reciprocal fuzzy binary relation

---

[8] This idea appears implicitly in Morales (1797 and 1805) and in Condorcet's comments of to the Memory of Borda (see McLean – Urken (1995, pp. 81 – 89)).

[9] To justify the axiom of reciprocity see, among others, Bezdek - Spillman – Spillman (1978), Nurmi (1981) and García-Lapresta-Llamazares (2000).

R^k induces an ordinary preference relation over X defined by

$$x_i \succ_k x_j \Leftrightarrow r_{ij}^k > 0.5,$$

for all pair of alternatives $x_i, x_j \in X$.

Given R^k, the reciprocal fuzzy preference relation of the agent k over X, we can consider the matrix of preference intensities:

$$\begin{pmatrix} r_{11}^k & r_{12}^k & \cdots & r_{1n}^k \\ r_{21}^k & r_{22}^k & \cdots & r_{2n}^k \\ \cdots & \cdots & \cdots & \cdots \\ r_{n1}^k & r_{n2}^k & \cdots & r_{nn}^k \end{pmatrix},$$

where the symmetric entries respect the main diagonal add up to 1.

For each agent $k \in \{1, ..., m\}$, we shall define a new count to evaluate each alternative according to its preference intensities. In the discrete case, the value assigned by the individual count is the number of alternatives considered worse than it for an ordinary preference relation P^k. Now, analogously, this role will be played by the ordinary preference relation $\succ_k$ induced by the reciprocal fuzzy binary relation R^k. So, the introduced individual count will add up the preference intensities among the alternative and those considered worse according to $\succ_k$. Taking into account Definition 3, agent k gives the alternative x_i the value

$$r_k(x_i) = \sum_{x_i \succ_k x_j} r_{ij}^k,$$

which coincides with the sum of the entries greater than 0.5 in the row i.

Again, with these individual counts a collective one is obtained:

$$r(x_i) = \sum_{k=1}^{m} r_k(x_i).$$

So, the collective preference relation P^{FB} is defined by

$$x_i P^{FB} x_j \Leftrightarrow r(x_i) > r(x_j),$$

which is always negatively transitive. Thus, the highest scored alternatives (maximals for P^{FB}) will be chosen.

We have to point out that the discrete Borda count gives individual scores belonging to the set $\{0, 1, ..., n-1\}$, while the fuzzy Borda count takes its values in the interval $[0, n-1]$, all intermediate values being possible. In the last section we shall comment this fact.

In this fuzzy framework we also consider a monotoniciy property for an agent's individual counts, as in the discrete case: when two alternatives are compared by an agent, the highest score must be given to the preferred one according to $\succ_k$.

Definition 4. The count r_k is *monotonic* if and only if

$$r_{ij}^k > 0.5 \quad \Rightarrow \quad r_k(x_i) > r_k(x_j)$$

for all pair of alternatives $x_i, x_j \in X$.

One can believe that this request is verified if, keeping the analogy with the discrete case, the ordinary preference relation $\succ_k$ is transitive. However, as we shall show, this is not sufficient. All the hypotheses of fuzzy coherence related below ensure the transitivity of $\succ_k$, but only the so-called weak max-max transitivity in the agents' individual preferences implies the monotonicity of the count r_k.

Definition 5. Let $*$ be a binary operation in $[0, 1]$ with the following properties:

• Commutativity: $a*b = b*a$ for all $a,b \in [0,1]$.

• Non-decreasing in each component: $(a \leq a'$ and $b \leq b') \Rightarrow a*b \leq a'*b'$ for all $a,a',b,b' \in [0,1]$.

• Super-idempotency: $a*a \geq a$ for all $a \in [0,1]$.

A reciprocal fuzzy binary relation R^k over X is *weak max-* transitive* if and only if it is verified:

$$(r_{ij}^k > 0.5 \text{ and } r_{jl}^k > 0.5) \Rightarrow r_{il}^k \geq r_{ij}^k * r_{jl}^k$$

for all $x_i, x_j, x_l \in X$.

Among the operations $*$ used in the literature to modelize the agents' rationality, the following ones, proposed by Zadeh (1971) and Bezdek – Harris (1978), among others, are considered:

$$a *_1 b = \min\{a,b\}, \quad a *_2 b = \frac{a+b}{2}, \quad a *_3 b = \max\{a,b\}.$$

Definition 6. $T_i(X)$ denotes the set of reciprocal fuzzy binary relations verifying $*_i$ weak[10] transitivity, $i = 1,2,3$.

Remark 2. Taking into account that for all $a,b \in [0,1]$ it is verified

$$\min\{a,b\} \leq \frac{a+b}{2} \leq \max\{a,b\} \quad \text{and} \quad (a > 0.5, \ b > 0.5) \Rightarrow \min\{a,b\} > 0.5,$$

---

[10] Max- $*$ transitivity for R^k is initially defined by demanding $r_{il}^k \geq r_{ij}^k * r_{jl}^k$. "Weak" (or "restricted") conditions are considered by Tanino (1984) and Dasgupta – Deb (1996), among others, when certain additional hypotheses are required. In our case, these are to consider preference intensities in Definition 5 greater than 0.5.

then

$$R^k \in T_3(X) \implies R^k \in T_2(X) \implies R^k \in T_1(X) \implies \succ_k \text{ transitive.}$$

Proposition 2. If $R^k \in T_3(X)$, then the count r_k is monotonic.

Proof: For each $i \in \{1,...,n\}$ consider the set $P(i) = \{l \mid r_{il}^k > 0.5\} \subset \{1,...,n\}$. Thus $r_k(x_i) = \sum_{l \in P(i)} r_{il}^k$ and $r_k(x_j) = \sum_{l \in P(i)} r_{jl}^k$. Suppose $r_{ij}^k > 0.5$. Now $P(j) \subset P(i)$ is verified: if $l \in P(j)$, then $r_{jl}^k > 0.5$. By hypothesis, $r_{ij}^k > 0.5$; consequently $r_{il}^k \geq \max\{r_{ij}^k, r_{jl}^k\} > 0.5$ and so $l \in P(i)$. What is more, this inclusion is strict, because $r_{ij}^k > 0.5$ implies $j \in P(i)$, while $j \notin P(j)$, since by reciprocity $r_{jj} = 0.5$. In conclusion $r_k(x_i) > r_k(x_j)$. $\square$

Remark 3. If $R^k \in T_1(X)$ or $R^k \in T_2(X)$, then r_k is not necessarily monotonic, as is shown in the following example. Let R^k be the reciprocal fuzzy binary relation over $X = \{x_1, x_2, x_3, x_4, x_5\}$ whose matrix is:

$$\begin{pmatrix} 0.5 & 0.52 & 0.76 & 0.88 & 0.79 \\ 0.48 & 0.5 & 1 & 1 & 1 \\ 0.24 & 0 & 0.5 & 0.5 & 0.82 \\ 0.12 & 0 & 0.5 & 0.5 & 0.6 \\ 0.21 & 0 & 0.18 & 0.4 & 0.5 \end{pmatrix}.$$

It is easy to verify $R^k \in T_2(X)$ and, taking into account Remark 3, also $R^k \in T_1(X)$. Note that $x_1 \succ_k x_2$, because $r_{12}^k = 0.52 > 0.5$. Nevertheless,

$$r_k(x_1) = 0.52 + 0.76 + 0.88 + 0.79 = 2.95 < 1 + 1 + 1 = 3 = r_k(x_2).$$

The fuzzy Borda count shares the same drawbacks as the discret one: unfulfillment of the independence of irrelevant alternatives principle and manipulability. Nevertheless, a notable advantage with respect to the classic Borda count is the agents' possibility to show their preferences more faithfully.

4 Approval voting *versus* Borda count

Up to now the agents' scores given by means of Borda counts are a consequence of their pair-wise preferences (crisp or fuzzy) over the alternatives. Another way in multi-person decision making is that suggested by the voting procedure called *approval voting*. In this method, we consider the alternatives to be evaluated one by one by the agents, using what we call *approval counts*, in a binary or fuzzy manner. In the first one, each alternative is approved or disapproved absolutely by each agent. In the second manner, the individual decision is more precise, estimating the agent's level of resolution. In both cases the individual agent's results are added up together in order to obtain the final decision. These discrete and fuzzy approval counts are formalized below. Again, it is considered a finite set of alternatives $X = \{x_1,...,x_n\}$ to be evaluated by each of the m agents.

With the discrete approval count, each agent accepts each alternative or not, as many as wanted. This can be formalized by defining the binary index:

$$r_i^k = \begin{cases} 1, & \text{if the alternative } x_i \text{ is approved by the agent } k, \\ 0, & \text{if the alternative } x_i \text{ is disapproved by the agent } k. \end{cases}$$

Thus, the boolean matrix $\begin{pmatrix} r_1^1 & r_1^2 & \cdots & r_1^m \\ r_2^1 & r_2^2 & \cdots & r_2^m \\ \cdots & \cdots & \cdots & \cdots \\ r_n^1 & r_n^2 & \cdots & r_n^m \end{pmatrix}$ is defined, and each alternative is

given the sum of individual scores: $r(x_i) = \sum_{k=1}^{m} r_i^k$ is the total score obtained by the alternative x_i, which coincides with the sum of the entries of the i-th row. As in the Borda count, this scoring defines a collective preference relation $x_i P^A x_j \Leftrightarrow$, $r(x_i) > r(x_j)$, which is negatively transitive. The highest scored alternatives (maximals for P^A) will be chosen.

The fuzzy approval count is defined in a parallel manner. Each agent estimates the level of acceptance over each alternative as follows. Let $r_i^k \in [0, 1]$ be the approval estimation given by the agent k to the alternative x_i, and dispose these indexes as entries in the scoring matrix

$$\begin{pmatrix} r_1^1 & r_1^2 & \cdots & r_1^m \\ r_2^1 & r_2^2 & \cdots & r_2^m \\ \cdots & \cdots & \cdots & \cdots \\ r_n^1 & r_n^2 & \cdots & r_n^m \end{pmatrix}.$$

Again, we can define, for each alternative x_j, the sum of individual scores: $r(x_i) = \sum_{k=1}^{m} r_i^k$ is the total score obtained by x_i, which coincides with the sum of the values of the i-th row. Thus, a collective preference relation can be defined by $x_i P^{FA} x_j \Leftrightarrow r(x_i) > r(x_j)$, which is once more negatively transitive. The highest scored alternatives (maximals for P^{FA}) will be chosen.

We have to point out the following fact about the marks used. While the discrete approval count gives total scores belonging to the set $\{0,1,...,m\}$, the fuzzy approval count does so in the interval $[0,m]$, all the intermediate values being reachable. And then, the last mentioned decision making procedure provides more flexibility to the agents. As a result, the existence of ties is less likely in the maximum total scores (which are maximals according to the collective preference relation defined in each case) if fuzzy counts are used instead of the discrete ones. Nevertheless, if it happens, procedures to break the ties must be established. The mentioned comment is also applicable to the fuzzy Borda count with respect to the discrete Borda count.

5 Comparative examples

Example 1. Consider two agents, whose preferences over three alternatives are given by reciprocal fuzzy preference relations R^1, R^2, with the following associated matrices of preference intensities:

$$\begin{pmatrix} 0.5 & 1 & 1 \\ 0 & 0.5 & 0.6 \\ 0 & 0.4 & 0.5 \end{pmatrix}, \begin{pmatrix} 0.5 & 0.4 & 0.4 \\ 0.6 & 0.5 & 0.6 \\ 0.6 & 0.4 & 0.5 \end{pmatrix},$$

respectively. If these agents were compelled to show their pair-wise preferences in the usual way, it would be reasonable for them to decide for the alternatives with intensities of preference greater than 0.5. Formally, agent k should change the reciprocal fuzzy preference R^k into the associated ordinary preference $\succ_k$. Thus, their associated matrices of ordinary preference are obtained by changing in the matrices above each entry greater than 0.5 into 1, and the others into 0. In our example, the new matrices are:

$$\begin{pmatrix} 0 & 1 & 1 \\ 0 & 0 & 1 \\ 0 & 0 & 0 \end{pmatrix}, \begin{pmatrix} 0 & 0 & 0 \\ 1 & 0 & 1 \\ 1 & 0 & 0 \end{pmatrix}.$$

We can observe that, according to the classic Borda count, the total scores are:

$$r(x_1) = 2, \ r(x_2) = 3, \ r(x_3) = 1,$$

i.e., the second alternative is the winner. However, with the more complete information of the intensities of preference, taking into account the introduced fuzzy Borda count, the new scores are:

$$r(x_1) = 2, \ r(x_2) = 1.8, \ r(x_3) = 0.6,$$

and, consequently, the first alternative should be the winner.

Example 2. Consider again two agents, whose estimations about three alternatives are given by means of approval indices over each one, with the following associated scoring matrix:

$$\begin{pmatrix} 0.9 & 0.4 \\ 0.6 & 0.6 \\ 0.3 & 0.2 \end{pmatrix}.$$

If these agents had to accept (or not) each alternative in an absolute manner, it would be reasonable for them to consider *approval thresholds*, so that the approved alternatives were precisely those passing such limit values. Although there are several ways to select these approval thresholds[11], in our example we shall consider a common value for all the agents: the intermediate point between the minimum and the maximum possible individual scores, i.e., 0.5. Thus, the associated boolean matrix, which reflects the absolute approval or disapproval, is obtained again by changing in the matrix above each entry greater than 0.5 into 1, and the others into 0. In our example, the new matrix is:

$$\begin{pmatrix} 1 & 0 \\ 1 & 1 \\ 0 & 0 \end{pmatrix},$$

and we can observe that, according to the classic approval count, the total results are:

$$r(x_1) = 1, \ r(x_2) = 2, \ r(x_3) = 0,$$

i.e., the second alternative is the winner. However, with the accurate information of the scoring matrix above and using the fuzzy approval count, the marks for each alternative are:

$$r(x_1) = 1.3, \ r(x_2) = 1.2, \ r(x_3) = 0.5,$$

and, then, the first alternative should be the winner.

According to the previous examples we can state that however more simplified the information given by the agents is, the more distorted the multi-person decision will be. Thus, allowing the agents to express their sincere assessments over the alternatives, the collective decision will represent more faithfully their preferences than using binary information.

6   Concluding remarks

In the following table possible ranges of values appear, individual as well as total, of the considered counts.

Possible marks for n alternatives, m agents				
COUNT	**BORDA**		**APPROVAL**	
DISCRETE	Individual	$\{0,...,n-1\}$ step=1	Individual	$\{0,1\}$ step=1
	Total	$\{0,...,m(n-1)\}$ step=1	Total	$\{0,...,m\}$ step=1
FUZZY	Individual	$[0, n-1]$ no step	Individual	$[0, 1]$ no step
	Total	$[0, m(n-1)]$ no step	Total	$[0, m]$ no step

---

[11] Brams – Fishburn (1983), among others, have considered arithmetic mean and median-type approval thresholds.

It is possible to unify the amplitude of the individual scores in Borda and approval counts by dividing these individual scores by $n-1$. So, the scale changes, but not the ordering, and then the scores range from 0 to 1 with step $\frac{1}{n-1}$ in the discrete case, and continuously in the interval [0, 1] in the fuzzy one. When these normalized individual scores are added up, total possible values are obtained from 0 to m with the same step as in the discrete case, and again continuously in the interval [0, m] in the fuzzy one.

It is also feasible to unify the variation amplitude of the individual and total scores, so that both of them will vary from 0 to 1. To do this, we normalize again by dividing the total scores by the number of agents, m. That is to say, individual scores are aggregated in a total one as an arithmetic mean [12]. In this way, the following table is obtained:

Possible marks for n alternatives, m agents		
COUNT	**NORMALIZED BORDA**	**NORMALIZED APPROVAL**
DISCRETE	Individual $\{0,...,1\}$ step=$\frac{1}{m-1}$	Individual $\{0, 1\}$ step=1
	Total $\{0,...,1\}$ step=$\frac{1}{m(n-1)}$	Total $\{0,...,1\}$ step=$\frac{1}{m}$
FUZZY	Individual $[0, 1]$ no step	Individual $[0, 1]$ no step
	Total $[0, 1]$ no step	Total $[0, 1]$ no step

One can observe by examining the table above that discrete counts are particular cases of the fuzzy ones, where marks are scaled in the unit interval. As for the fuzzy Borda and approval counts, the marks obtained are the same, although corresponding to distinct conceptions in each case, as pointed out earlier.

The marks used in the counts appearing in this paper admit a utilitarian-cardinal perspective, as pointed out by Black (1976), Sugden (1981) and recently by Marchant (2000). The total score obtained by the alternatives can be understood as defined by a collective utility function $U : X \to [0,1]$, such that

$$U(x_i) = \frac{u_1(x_i) + u_2(x_i) + \cdots + u_m(x_i)}{m},$$

where $u_j(x_i) \in [0,1]$ are the normalized scores which are aggregated through of

---

[12] About the arithmetic mean as an aggregation procedure, see Chichilnisky – Heal (1983), Le Breton – Uriarte (1990), Candeal – Induráin – Uriarte (1992), Candeal – Induráin (1995) and García-Lapresta – Llamazares (2000).

the arithmetic mean, as indicated. The possible critique of interpersonal comparison of utilities is refuted[13], bearing in mind that all the agents use the same numerical scale to score the alternatives, that is, the interval $[0,1]$.

References

Arrow, K.J. (1951, 2nd ed. 1963): *Social Choice and Individual Values.* John Wiley & Sons, Inc., New York.

Bezdek, J.C. – Harris, J.D. (1978): "Fuzzy partitions and relations: an axiomatic basis for clustering". *Fuzzy Sets and Systems* 2, pp. 5 – 14.

Bezdek, J.C. – Spillman, B. – Spillman, R. (1978): "A fuzzy relation space for group decision theory". *Fuzzy Sets and Systems* 1, pp. 255 – 268.

Black, D. (1958): *The Theory of Committees and Elections.* Cambridge University Press, London.

Black, D. (1976): "Partial justification of the Borda count". *Public Choice* 28, pp. 1 – 15.

Brams, S.J. – Fishburn, P.C. (1983): *Approval Voting.* Birkhäuser, Boston.

Candeal, J.C. – Induráin, E. (1995): "Aggregation of preferences from algebraic models on groups". *Social Choice and Welfare* 12, pp. 165 – 173.

Candeal, J.C. – Induráin, E. – Uriarte, J.R. (1992): "Some issues related to the topological aggregation of preferences". *Social Choice and Welfare* 9, pp. 213 – 227.

Chichilnisky, G. – Heal, G. (1983): "Necessary and sufficient conditions for a resolution of the social choice paradox". *Journal of Economic Theory* 31, pp. 68 – 87.

Copeland, A.H. (1951): "A 'reasonable' social welfare function". Notes from a seminar on applications of mathematics to the social sciences (mimeo), University of Michigan.

Dasgupta, M. – Deb, R. (1996): "Transitivity and fuzzy preferences". *Social Choice and Welfare* 13, pp. 305 – 318.

Debord, B. (1992): "An axiomatic characterization of Borda's k-choice function". *Social Choice and Welfare* 9, pp. 337 – 343.

Dummett, M. (1998): "The Borda count and agenda manipulation". *Social Choice and Welfare* 15, pp. 289 – 296.

Fishburn, P.C. (1990): "Multiperson decision making: a selective review", in Kacprzyk, J. – Fedrizzi, M. (eds.): *Multiperson Decision Making Using Fuzzy Sets and Possibility Theory,* pp. 3 – 27. Kluwer Academic Publishers, Dordrecht.

García-Lapresta, J.L. – Llamazares, B. (2000): "Aggregation of fuzzy preferences: some rules of the mean". *Social Choice and Welfare* 17, pp. 673 – 690.

Kemeny, J. (1959): "Mathematics without numbers". *Daedalus* 88, pp. 571 – 591.

---

[13] With reference to the interpersonal comparison of utilities, see, for example, Münnich – Maksa – Mokken (1999, p. 221).

Le Breton, M. – Uriarte, J.R. (1990): "On the robustness of the impossibility result in the topological approach to Social Choice". *Social Choice and Welfare* 7, pp. 131 – 140.

Marchant, T (1996): *Agrégation de relations valuées par la méthode de Borda en vue d'un rangement. Considérations axiomatiques.* Ph. D. Thesis, Université Libre de Bruxelles.

Marchant, T. (2000): "Does the Borda Rule provide more than a ranking?". *Social Choice and Welfare*, forthcoming.

McLean, I. – Urken, A.B. (eds.) (1995 a): *Classics of Social Choice.* Ann Arbor – The University of Michigan Press.

McLean, I. – Urken, A.B. (1995 b): "Independence of irrelevant alternatives before Arrow". *Mathematical Social Sciences* 30, pp. 107-126.

Morales, J.I. (1797): *Memoria Matemática sobre el Cálculo de la Opinion en las Elecciones.* Imprenta Real. Madrid. English version in McLean – Urken (1995 a, pp. 197 – 235).

Morales, J.I. (1805): Apéndice á la Memoria Matemática sobre el Cálculo de la Opinion en las Elecciones. Imprenta de Sancha. Madrid.

Mueller, D.C. (1979): *Public Choice.* Cambridge University Press, London.

Münnich, A. – Maksa, G. – Mokken, R.J. (1999): "Collective judgement: combining individual value judgements". *Mathematical Social Sciences* 37, pp. 211 – 233.

Nitzan, S. – Rubinstein, A. (1981): "A further characterization of Borda ranking method". *Public Choice* 36, pp. 153 – 158.

Nurmi, H. (1981): "Approaches to collective decision making with fuzzy preference relations". *Fuzzy Sets and Systems* 6, pp. 249 – 259.

Parker, J.R. (1995): "Voting Methods for Multiple Autonomous Agents". ANZIIS '95, Perth, Australia. Nov. 27, 1995.

Saari, D.G. (1995): *Basic Geometry of Voting.* Springer – Verlag. Berlin.

Saari, D.G. – Merlin, V.R. (1996): "The Copeland method I: relationships and the dictionary. *Economic Theory* 8, pp. 51 – 76.

Saari, D.G. – Merlin, V.R. (1997): "A geometric examination of Kemeny's rule". Northwestern University, preprint.

Sen, A. (1977): "Social Choice Theory: a re-examination". *Econometrica* 45, pp. 53 – 89.

Straffin Jr., P.D. (1980): *Topics in the Theory of Voting.* Birkhäuser, Boston.

Sugden, R. (1981): *The Political Economy of Public Choice: An Introduction to Welfare Economics.* Oxford: Martin Robertson.

Tangian, A.S. (2000): "Unlikelihood of Condorcet's paradox in a large society". Social Choice and Welfare 17, pp. 337 – 365.

Tanguiane, A.S. (1991): *Aggregation and Representation of Preferences. Introduction to Mathematical Theory of Democracy.* Springer – Verlag, Berlin.

Tanino, T. (1984): "Fuzzy preference orderings in group decision making". *Fuzzy sets and Systems* 12, pp. 117-131.

Young, H.P. (1974): "An axiomatization of Borda's rule". *Journal of Economic Theory* 9, pp. 43 – 52.

Young, P. (1995): "Optimal voting rules". *Journal of Economic Perspectives* 9, pp. 51 – 64.

Zadeh, L.A. (1971): "Similarity relations and fuzzy orderings", *Information Sciences* 22, pp. 203 – 213.

Multiple Criteria Choice Models for Quantitative and Qualitative Data

Edwin Hinloopen, Department of Finance, Nederlandse Spoorwegen, PO Box 2025, NL 3500 HA Utrecht, e.hinloopen@reizigers.ns.nl,

Peter Nijkamp, Department of Economics, Free University, PO Box 7161, NL 1007 MC Amsterdam, pnijkamp@econ.vu.nl,

Piet Rietveld, Department of Economics, Free University, PO Box 7161, NL 1007 MC Amsterdam, prietveld@econ.vu.nl

Abstract

Suppose a decision-maker faces the problem of outranking a discrete number of choice-options, which are characterised by a number of judgement criteria. To solve this problem, many so called multiple criteria evaluation methods have been developed. The present paper describes a further development of one of these methods, the Regime Method.

The Regime Method is a weighting method, based on a paired comparison of choice-options. Originally, the Regime Method was developed to deal with the pure ordinal situation: only rankings are available with respect to the consequences of the choice-options related to the judgement criteria. In addition, the relative importance of the judgement criteria is a ranking of their weights.

In this paper, the situation of mixed data is addressed: as well cardinal as ordinal information may be available. Special attention is paid to the standardisation of the data. This standardisation is based on the concept of *value difference functions.*

Apart from the final outranking of choice-options, the basic result of many multiple criteria evaluation methods, the Regime Method also produces a sensitivity analysis that can be used to investigate the robustness of the final outranking.

As a case study, the choice of an automated people mover in the city of Nijmegen (Netherlands) was used.

1. Introduction

Suppose a decision-maker faces the problem of outranking I choice options or alternatives i (i = 1, . . . ,I) and J judgement criteria j (j = 1, . . . ,J). The information available is presented in a so-called consequence matrix S.

$$
S = \begin{pmatrix} S_{11} & \cdots & S_{1J} \\ \cdot & & \\ \cdot & & \\ \cdot & & \\ S_{I1} & \cdots & S_{IJ} \end{pmatrix}
\tag{1.1}
$$

The entry S_{ij} (i = 1, . . . ,I; j = 1, . . . ,J) may represent the (cardinal) consequence of alternative i according to criterion j (for instance the fuel consumption of a car) or may represent the (ordinal) rank order of alternative i with respect to criterion j (for instance the safety of a car).

In this paper, we assume that the rankings of the alternatives with respect to the individual criteria are not identical. This means that additional information is needed about the relative importance of the judgement criteria. In case of weighting methods, this information is given by means of preference weights attached to the judgement criteria. These preference weights are presented in a so-called weight vector λ.

$$
\lambda = (\lambda_1, \ldots, \lambda_J)
\tag{1.2}
$$

The entry λ_j (j = 1, . . . ,J) may represent the (cardinal) weight of criterion j or may represent the (ordinal) rank order of criterion j in relation to the other criteria.

Based on the information of the consequence matrix S and the weight vector λ, the Regime Method establishes a final outranking of the alternatives.

A fundamental attribute of the Regime Method is that it based on paired comparisons of alternatives in such a way that the mutual comparison of two alternatives is not influenced by the presence and effects of other alternatives. Based on this principle, the outranking procedure is constructed. It consists of three steps.

Step 1: standardisation

Step 2: aggregation

Step 3: outranking

The following of this paper describes these steps.

2. Standardisation (Step 1)

The first step is to make the information of the consequence matrix comparable with each other by means of a standardisation procedure. Various ways of standardisation have been developed (see Voogd, 1983). One of these standardisation methods is the value function (see Keeney and Raiffa, 1976). The Regime Method uses the concept of *value difference functions* to standardise the information.

Definition 1, value difference function. The value difference function of the consequences of two alternatives with respect to a certain criterion equals the difference of the value functions of the consequences of the two alternatives with respect to the criterion considered.

We discuss the use of value difference functions for cardinal and ordinal data separately.

2.1 Value difference functions for cardinal data

In this section, value difference functions for cardinal data are developed. Let

$V_j(\ .\ ) =$ The value function of the consequences with respect to criterion j
S_{ij} =   The consequence of alternative i with respect to criterion j

The Regime Method assumes that the consequences indicate either a benefit criterion or a cost criterion. In this section, we assume that all criteria are benefit criteria. This means that if $s_{ij} > s_{i'j}$, then, with respect to criterion j, alternative i is preferred to alternative i':

$$S_{ij} > S_{i'j} \Leftrightarrow V_j(S_{ij}) > V_j(S_{i'j}) \tag{2.1}$$

Additionally, in order to compare values of the consequences with respect to all criteria under consideration, all value functions must have the same range. Without loss of generality, the range is [0,1]. Therefore, all value functions are monotonically non-decreasing functions $R \rightarrow [0,1]$. In order to create a value function, the minimum of information required are two threshold values Smax and Smin. These threshold values are determined <u>independently</u> of the consequences S_{ij}. For example: the criterion "maximum velocity" of a car may have threshold values 120 km/h and 160 km/h. This means that the value of the consequences with respect to the criterion "maximum velocity" equals 0 for all cars with a maximum velocity less than 120 km/h and equals 1 for all cars with a maximum velocity more than 160 km/h. The lower bound threshold value can also be used as a selection criterion for alternatives to be considered.

As a "default situation", the Regime Method assumes that only the two threshold values are known and that no other information about the shape of the value function is available. In this situation, linear value functions are used:

$$V_j(S_{ij}) = \begin{cases} 0 & \text{if } S_{ij} < Smin_j \\ \dfrac{S_{ij} - Smin_j}{Smax_j - Smin_j} & \text{if } Smin_j \le S_{ij} \le Smax_j \\ 0 & \text{if } S_{ij} < Smin_j \end{cases} \qquad (2.2)$$

Or, in one formula:

$$V_j(S_{ij}) = \frac{\text{MAX}\{Smin_j, \text{MIN}\{Smax_j, S_{ij}\}\} - Smin_j}{Smax_j - Smin_j} \qquad (2.3)$$

If, however, there is additional information about the shape of the value function, this information can be used to derive a more appropriate value function than the linear value function, (see Keeney & Raiffa, 1976 and Beinat, 1995).

The value difference function can be formulated as follows.

$D_j(\,.\,,\,.\,) =$ The value difference function of the consequences of two alternatives with respect to criterion j

Then

$$D_j(S_{ij}, S_{i'j}) = V_j(S_{ij}) - V_j(S_{i'j}) \qquad (2.4)$$

In the situation of linear value functions, the following table gives the relation between D_j on one hand and S_{ij} and $S_{i'j}$ on the other hand.

$S_{i'j}$	$S_{i'j} < Smin_j$	$Smin_j \le S_{i'j} \le Smax_j$	$S_{i'j} > Smax_j$
$V_j(S_{i'j})$	0	$\dfrac{S_{i'j} - Smin_j}{Smax_j - Smin_j}$	1

$V_i(S_{ij})$	$D_j(S_{ij},S_{i'j})$			
0		0	$\dfrac{Smin_j - S_{i'j}}{Smax_j - Smin_j}$	-1
$\dfrac{S_{ij} - Smin_j}{Smax_j - Smin_j}$ 1		$\dfrac{S_{ij} - Smin_j}{Smax_j - Smin_j}$ 1	$\dfrac{S_{ij} - S_{i'j}}{Smax_j - Smin_j}$ $\dfrac{Smax_j - S_{i'j}}{Smax_j - Smin_j}$	$\dfrac{S_{ij} - Smax_j}{Smax_j - Smin_j}$ 0

This can also be formulated in one formula:

$$D_j(S_{ij},S_{i'j}) = \frac{\text{MAX}\{Smin_j, \text{MIN}\{Smax_j, S_{ij}\}\} - \text{MAX}\{Smin_j, \text{MIN}\{Smax_j, S_{i'j}\}\}}{Smax_j - Smin_j}$$

$$(2.5)$$

So the value difference function is a monotonically non-decreasing function in S_{ij} and a monotonically non-increasing function in $S_{i'j}$ with domain R^2 and range $[-1,1]$.

2.2 Value difference functions for ordinal data

Consider a criterion with ordinal data. These data represent the ranking of the alternatives with respect to criterion j. The aim of this subsection is to operationalise the concept of "value difference" for ordinal data, in such a way that it is compatible with the meaning it has in a cardinal context. This compatibility obviously enables one to use cardinal and ordinal data in a joint evaluation framework. Compatibility requires that value differences assume values between -1 and $+1$. Our solution to arrive at compatibility is to interpret the rankings of ordinal data as the corresponding order statistic to a random sample from a certain unknown probability distribution function. This distribution function plays the same role as the value function for cardinal data. Let

Fj(.) =   The probability distribution function of the consequence with respect to criterion j

s_{ij} =   The random variable representing the consequence of alternative i with respect to criterion j

This means that, with respect to criteria with ordinal data, the Regime Method uses the following value functions.

$$V_j(s_{ij}) = F_j(s_{ij}) \tag{2.6}$$

So, the value difference function in the situation of ordinal data can be formulated as follows:

$$D_j(S_{ij}, S_{i'j}) = F_j(S_{ij}) - F_j(S_{i'j}) \tag{2.7}$$

Since the value of the consequence is relevant and not the consequence it self, we are not interested in the distribution of s_{ij}, but in the distribution of $F_j(s_{ij}) - F_j(s_{i'j})$. This distribution is formulated in theorem 1.

Theorem 1

$$D_j(S_{ij}, S_{i'j}) = \begin{cases} z(2-z)I_{(0,1)}(z) & \text{if } S_{ij} > S_{i'j} \\ z(2+z)I_{(-1,0)}(z) & \text{if } S_{ij} < S_{i'j} \end{cases} \tag{2.8}$$

where $I_{(0,1)}$ is defined as an indicator function: $I_{(0,1)}(z) = \begin{cases} 1 \text{ if } 0 \leq z \leq 1 \\ 0 \text{ elsewhere} \end{cases} \tag{2.9}$

The proof is given in appendix I.

If we compare the value difference functions for cardinal data and the value difference functions for ordinal data, we see the following resemblance.

- The value difference function between two alternatives compared does not depend on the presence other alternatives that are involved in the outranking.
- The value difference functions have domain R^2 and range $[-1, 1]$

An alternative approach would have been to consider all ordinal rankings simultaneously. In this situation however, the value function between two alternatives depends on the presence of other alternatives, which makes is less compatible with the value difference functions of the cardinal data.

2.3 Extensions of value difference functions for ordinal data

Notice that the value difference function formulated in theorem 1 is a Beta function with parameters 1 and 2. This means that the expected value of the difference equals 1/3 and the variance equals 1/18. This result does not depend on the pair of alternatives considered and this result does not depend on the ordinal criterion considered.

The question is whether this is a desirable result. Generally, the average value of the value difference functions for the cardinal data may be unequal to 1/3. In addition, it is likely to depend on the pair of alternatives considered. Suppose, for instance, that the average value of the value difference functions for the cardinal data is for a certain pair of alternatives 1/4. Then, according to the aggregation function of the value differences $D(S_i , S_{i'}) = \Sigma \lambda_j * D_j(S_{ij} , S_{i'j})$ (see section 3), this causes an "extra weight" to the ordinal criteria. In order to ensure compatibility in the treatment of cardinal and ordinal criteria, it is desirable that the expected value of the value difference functions for the ordinal data is equal to the (not-weighted) average of the values of the difference functions for the cardinal data. Of course, if a priori information would be available that the value differences of a certain ordinal criterion are different from those of another criterion, a different approach has to be used. However, if such a priori information is lacking (the "default situation" assumed by the Regime Method) the most reasonable approach is to assume that the average differences are equal.

As for the average value, the variance of the value difference functions for the cardinal data may be unequal to /18 and is also likely to depend on the pair of alternatives considered. Suppose, for instance, that the variance of the values difference functions for the cardinal data is for a certain pair of alternatives 1/48. Then, this causes an "extra weight" to the variance of the value difference functions for the ordinal criteria. Hence, it is desirable that the variance of the value difference functions for ordinal data is equal to the (not-weighted) variance of the values of the difference functions for the cardinal data. Consequently, this variance will depend on the pair of alternatives considered.

The question is how to find a method that makes it possible to "balance" the average values of an ordinal value difference function with the average value of the cardinal value difference functions. The solution is to add a number of "virtual alternatives" to the two alternatives that are compared with each other. These virtual alternatives do not have any consequences on the cardinal criteria. They only have rankings on the ordinal criteria. These virtual alternatives appear every time a paired comparison of two (real) alternatives is made and they disappear as soon as a comparison is completed!

The distribution of the value difference function is as follows. Consider two (real) alternatives and add (N-2) virtual alternatives. Assume that the real alternatives have ranks α and β ($\alpha<\beta$). Let

$$D_j(S_{ij}, S_{i'j}) = F_j(S_{ij}) - F_j(S_{i'j}) \qquad (2.10)$$

Then we have the following theorem.

Theorem 2

$$D_j(S_{ij}, S_{i'j}) = \begin{cases} B(u;\beta-\alpha;N+1-\beta+\alpha)I_{(0,1)}(u) & \text{if } S_{ij} > S_{i'j} \\ \\ -B(-u;\beta-\alpha;N+1-\beta+\alpha)I_{(-1,0)}(u) & \text{if } S_{ij} < S_{i'j} \end{cases} \qquad (2.11)$$

with $B(x;a;b)$ the Beta distribution with parameters a and b.
The proof is given in appendix I.
In the example, the average value of the value difference functions for the cardinal data equals 1/4 and the corresponding variance equals 1/48. Then, $\beta-\alpha$ and N have to be given the values in such a way that $E[Z] = 1/4$ and $Var[Z] = 1/48$. This means, we have to invert $E[Z]$ and $Var[Z]$: let $\mu = E[Z]$ and $\sigma^2 = Var[Z]$. From the Beta distribution we know that

$$E[Z] = \frac{\beta-\alpha}{N+1} \qquad (2.12)$$

$$Var[Z] = \frac{(\beta-\alpha)(N+1-\beta+\alpha)}{(N+2)(N+1)^2} \qquad (2.13)$$

It follows that

$$\beta-\alpha = \mu\left[\frac{(1-\mu)\mu}{\sigma^2} - 1\right] \qquad (2.14)$$

$$N = \frac{(1-\mu)\mu}{\sigma^2} - 2 \qquad (2.15)$$

In the numerical example, μ has to be equal to 1/4 and σ^2 has to be equal to 1/48. This means that $\beta-\alpha$ has to be equal to 2 and N has to be equal to 7. The interpretation of this result is as follows: 5 virtual alternatives have to be added and the difference in ranking between the two real alternatives equals 2.
In general of course, the number of the virtual alternatives that have to be added and the difference in ranking between the two real alternatives that has to be met do not have a natural interpretation like in this example. For instance, if μ has to

be equal to 1/10 and σ^2 has to be equal to 1/50, 0,5 virtual alternatives have to be added and the difference in ranking between the two real alternatives equals 0,35. The central issue however is not the interpretation of the values of the parameters. The central issue is the fact that we can assign a probability distribution function to the value difference function, which has, under certain circumstances (β-α an N being natural numbers), a natural interpretation.

We conclude that the refinement added to the approach of subsection 2.2 indeed lead to outcomes for value differences of ordinal criteria that are compatible with those of cardinal criteria.

Two situations deserve special attention: the situation that all criteria are measured on an ordinal scale and the situation that all but one criteria are measured on an ordinal scale. In the first situation, there is no need to "balance" the average values of the ordinal value difference functions with the average values of the cardinal value difference functions. This means that we can simply use the value difference functions of section 2.2. In the second situation, σ^2 cannot be estimated. Unless external information about σ^2 is known, we only have information about μ. In this situation, the simplest solution is to fix β-α to 1 and to calibrate N by $(1-\mu)/\mu$.

2.4 Ties

In the situation of ties in the consequences of a criterion measured on an ordinal scale, the Regime Method needs to know how this tie must be interpreted. Does the tie mean that the rankings are equal or that the mutual ranking of the tied alternatives is unknown? In the first situation, the value difference function simply has the cardinal value 0. In the second situation, the Regime Method investigates all possible rankings that do not contradict the ties.

3 Aggregation (Step 2)

Since more than one criterion is considered, and usually the rankings of the alternatives with respect to the individual criteria are not identical, an aggregation over the criteria is necessary. This aggregation is the second step of the Regime method and it can be formulated as follows.

D(. , .) =   The linear aggregation function of the weighted value differences of two alternatives

λ_j =   The weight attached to criterion j (j=1, ... ,J)

Then

$$D(S_i , S_{i'}) = \sum_j \lambda_j * D_j(S_{ij} , S_{i'j}) \tag{3.1}$$

In the situation of at least one ordinal criterion or in the situation that the weights are measured on an ordinal scale, D(. , .) is a stochastic variable. The Regime Method uses the probability that alternative i wins a paired comparison from alternative i' as the measure of distinction between alternatives i and i'. In other words: the Regime method uses the probability that $D(S_i , S_{i'}) > 0$ as the measure of distinction between alternatives i and i'. Let

$$P_{ii'} = \text{Prob} (D(S_i , S_{i'}) > 0) \tag{3.2}$$

Then $P_{ii'}$ is the measure of distinction between alternatives i and i'.
In the situation that the weights are measured on an ordinal scale, the weights are interpreted as random variables, following a certain probability distribution function. If no additional information is available about the shape of this distribution (default assumption of the Regime Method), the decision-maker is faced with a decision under uncertainty. In this situation, according to the Laplace criterion, the Regime Method uses the uniform distribution (see Taha, 1976).

4 Outranking (Step 3)

As stated in section 3, the Pii' are the measure of distinction between alternatives i and i'. Based on the Pii', the final outranking of alternatives is established. The final outranking is determined by the average probability that an alternative wins a paired comparison from a (randomly chosen) other alternative. Let

$$P_i = 1/(I-1) * \sum_{i' \neq i} P_{ii'} \tag{4.1}$$

Then P_i is the average probability that an alternative wins a paired comparison from a (randomly chosen) other alternative. An interpretation of the $P_{ii'}$ and the P_i is the following. Suppose one wants to outrank a number of soccer teams based on a number of competitions played in the past. One can proceed as follows. First, consider all individual matches of two specific teams A and B. The percentage of matches won by A is the estimation of the probability $P_{ii'}$ that A beats B (draws are excluded). This probability is the measure of distinction between soccer teams. Secondly, the final outranking is determined by the probabilities that a team beats a (randomly chosen) other team.

An interesting quantity is the probability that a certain soccer team beats in a competition a certain number of other teams. Let

$$B_{ii'} = \left\{ \begin{array}{c} 1 \\ 0 \end{array} \right\} \quad \text{if} \quad D(S_i, S_{i'}) = \left\{ \begin{array}{c} > 0 \\ < 0 \end{array} \right\} \quad i,i'=1, \dots ,I \text{ and } i' \neq i \qquad (4.2)$$

$$P_i^k = \text{Prob} \left(\sum_{i' \neq i} B_{ii'} = k \right) \qquad (4.3)$$

Then Pik is the probability that an alternative wins k paired comparisons. In other words: Pik is the probability that a soccer team beats in a competition k other teams. Then, also on this quantity a final outranking of alternatives can be established. Let

$$E_i = \sum_{k=0}^{I-1} k * P_i^k \qquad (4.4)$$

Then E_i is the expected number of times that an alternative wins a paired comparison. In other words: E_i is the expected number of times a soccer teams beats an other team. An interesting result is that P_i and E_i establish the same final outranking! This is formulated in the following theorem.

Theorem 3

$$\text{Let} \quad P_i = 1/(I-1) * \sum_{i' \neq i} P_{ii'} \qquad (4.5)$$

$$\text{with} \quad P_{ii'} = \text{Prob} (B_{ii'} = 1) \qquad (4.6)$$

$$\text{Let} \quad E_i = \sum_{k=0}^{I-1} k * P_i^k \qquad (4.7)$$

$$\text{with} \quad P_i^k = \text{Prob} (\sum_{i' \neq i} B_{ii'} = k) \qquad (4.8)$$

Then: $E_i = \quad (I-1) * P_i$ \hfill (4.9)

Corollary P_i and E_i lead to the same final outranking.

The proof of this theorem is given in appendix II of this paper. The proof of corollary is rather trivial.

5. Case study: people mover Nijmegen (Netherlands)

Hague Consulting Group (a Dutch consulting company in the field of traffic and transportation) used the Regime Method in order to rank a number of people movers for the city of Nijmegen. Ten public transport techniques were evaluated:

1.	**Bus**
2.	**Skytrain: train-like automatic people mover ("steel on steel")**
3.	**SK: automatic people mover drawn by a cable**
4.	**SPM: Small sized automatic people mover ("rubber on concrete")**
5.	**"Traditional" monorail**
6.	**H-Bahn: hanging monorail**
7.	**Cable tram**
8.	**Bus with a 100% free lane**
9.	**Trolley bus with a 100% free lane**
10.	**Tram with a 100% free lane**

The criteria (and their corresponding weights) used in this case study are

1.	**Results of a cost-benefit-analysis**	47,2%
2.	**Passenger's probability of having a seat**	2,16%
3.	**Punctuality**	6,12%
4.	**Comfort in vehicle**	0,96%
5.	**Comfort at waiting location**	0,96%
6.	**Is it easy to enter or leave the vehicle?**	0,96%
7.	**Image of the transportation system**	3,96%
8.	**Accesibility by disabled passengers**	1,08%
9.	**Vehicles' safety**	1,80%
10.	**Social safety**	1,80%
11.	**Spatial impact I: land use**	3,06%
12.	**Spatial impact II: creation of a physical barrier**	3,06%
13.	**Spatial impact III: interference with other means of transport**	3,06%
14.	**Local emissions**	2,07%
15.	**Global emissions**	1,98%
16.	**Noise emission**	2,97%
17.	**Visual impact**	1,98%
18.	**Impact on local employability**	2,04%
19.	**Impact on local grond prices**	1,87%
20.	**Impact on population density**	1,87%
21.	**Technical complexity**	2,03%
22.	**Flexibility in upgrading the system**	0,98%
23.	**Flexibility in the level of service**	2,03%
24.	**Organisational complexity of operating the system**	0,98%
25.	**Flexibility in avoiding traffic jam**	0,98%
26.	**Impact on the environment during construction**	2,04%

The consequence matrix has the following information

People mover nr.									
	1	2	3	4	5	6	7	8	9	10
Criterion nr.										
1.	0	0,129	0,394	0,358	-0,16	0,241	1,457	1,889	1,427	1,043
2.	0	1	1	1	1	1	1	1	1	1
3.	0	2	2	2	2	2	2	1	1	1
4.	0	3	2	3	3	3	1	1	1	2
5.	0	1	1	1	1	1	1	1	1	1
6.	0	2	1	2	2	2	1	0	0	2
7.	0	3	2	3	3	3	2	1	1	2
8.	0	3	3	3	3	3	3	1	1	2
9.	0	3	3	3	3	3	3	1	1	2
10.	1	0	0	0	0	0	0	1	1	1
11.	3	1	1	1	1	1	2	0	0	0
12.	3	0	0	0	0	0	1	2	2	2
13.	0	2	2	2	2	2	2	1	1	1
14.	0	2	2	3	3	3	3	1	3	3
15.	0	1	1	2	2	2	3	3	3	3
16.	0	1	2	2	5	5	4	2	4	3
17.	5	1	2	2	0	1	3	4	4	4
18.	0	2	1	2	2	2	1	0	0	1
19.	0	2	1	2	2	2	1	0	0	1
20.	0	2	1	2	2	2	1	0	0	1
21.	2	0	1	0	0	0	1	2	2	2
22.	0	1	0	0	0	0	0	1	1	2
23.	0	2	2	2	2	2	2	0	0	1
24.	3	0	0	0	0	0	0	2	2	1
25.	3	0	0	0	0	0	0	2	1	0
26.	2	0	0	0	0	0	1	1	1	1

People mover nr. 1 (the traditional bus) is the reference option. Its net cost-benefit value is set at zero and the other net cost-benefit values are related to this. For instance, reduction of travelling time (one of the elements of the cost-benefit analysis) is related to the travelling time by bus. The upper bound of the cost-benefit value is set at 2 and the lower value at −1.

All ordinal information is formulated as "the higher, the better". Ties are treated like "equals".

The results of the Regime Method are given in the following three tables.

Table 1. Final outranking based on P_i (cardinal weights)

Nr.	Name	Estimated P_i	95% Confidence Interval		
			min.	max.	difference
7	Cable Tram	.946	.935	.957	.023
8	Bus Lane	.942	.930	.954	.023
9	Trolley	.770	.749	.791	.042
10	Tram	.674	.651	.697	.047
4	SPM	.552	.527	.577	.050
6	H-Bahn	.442	.417	.467	.050
3	SK	.329	.306	.353	.047
2	Sky train	.232	.211	.253	.042
5	Monorail	.105	.090	.121	.031
1	Bus	.008	.003	.012	.009

Table 2. Paired comparisons, based on $p_{ii'}$ (cardinal weights)

Nr.	7	8	9	10	4	6	3	2	5	1
7	****	.523	.991							
8	.477	****								
9	.009		****	.921						
10			.079	****	.994	.993				
4				.006	****	.960	.999			
6				.007	.040	****	.933			
3					.001	.067	****	.914	.983	
2							.086	****	.999	
5							.017	.001	****	.930
1									.070	****

Table 3. Relative frequency of number of paired victories, based on p_i^k (cardinal weights)

Number	9	8	7	6	5	4	3	2	1	0
Cable Tram	.519	.476	.005							
Bus Lane	.477	.523								
Trolley			.912	.079						
Tram			.079	.909	.012					
SPM				.006	.954	.040				
H-Bahn					.001	.042	.895	.063		
SK						.062	.843	.094	.001	
Sky train							.085	.914	.001	
Mono rail								.017	.914	.069
Bus									.070	.930

The entries left out in the upper right triangle of Table 2 have value 1.000. The entries left out in the lower left triangle have value .000.

The entries left out in Table 3 have value .000.

Table 1 shows that the Cable Tram is on top of the outranking, although the difference in final consequence with the Bus Lane is small. The paired comparison of those two choice options confirms that the Cable Tram is slightly better than the Bus Lane. Tables 3 however shows that the Bus Lane is a choice option that is less risky.

In order to investigate the sensitivity of the final outranking with respect to the cardinal values of the weights, the Regime Method is run while only taking account for the ranking information about the weights. This means, that Regime Method randomly draws numbers that are a monotonic transformation of the given set of weights. The results of the Regime Method are given in the tables below.

Table 4. Final outranking based on P_i (ordinal weights)

Nr.	Name	Estimated P_i	95% Confidence Interval		
			min.	max.	difference
7	Cable Tram	.971	.962	.979	.017
6	H-Bahn	.823	.804	.842	.038
4	SPM	.696	.673	.719	.046
5	Monorail	.644	.620	.668	.048
10	Tram	.508	.483	.533	.050
9	Trolley	.411	.386	.436	.049
2	Sky Train	.378	.354	.402	.048
3	SK	.313	.290	.337	.046
8	Bus Lane	.298	.226	.270	.043
1	Bus	.008	.004	.013	.009

We see that the people movers with a relatively low net cost-benefit value (H-Bahn and the Monorail) have climbed in the final outranking. Additionally, the people movers with a relatively high cost-benefit value (Bus Lane and Trolley) have fallen down. The explanation for this phenomena is that in the situation with cardinal weights, the weight of the cost benefit criterion is very high, almost 50%.

Table 5. Paired comparisons, based on $p_{ii'}$ (cardinal weights)

Nr.	7	6	4	5	10	9	2	3	8	1
7	****	.872	.986	.926	.972	.989	.996	1.00	.994	1.00
6	.128	****	.592	1.00	.950	.882	.999	.997	.874	.986
4	.014	.408	****	.656	.792	.610	1.00	.998	.788	.995
5	.074	.000	.344	****	.918	.804	.878	.986	.815	.977
10	.028	.050	.208	.082	****	.904	.448	.857	.997	.999
9	.011	.118	.390	.196	.096	****	.548	.503	.841	.997
2	.004	.001	.000	.122	.552	.452	****	.642	.645	.984
3	.000	.003	.002	.014	.143	.497	.358	****	.815	.988
8	.006	.126	.212	.185	.003	.159	.355	.185	****	1.00
1	.000	.014	.005	.023	.001	.003	.016	.012	.000	****

We see that, due to the fact that the information about the weights is only ordinal in stead of cardinal, the results of the paired comparisons are generally spoken less strict. On the other hand, the Cable Tram is now stronger at the first position: the probability that it is better than a randomly chosen other choice option is at least .872!

We like to draw special attention to the paired comparison of the Tram and the Sky Train. Although in the final outranking, the Tram has a higher place than the Sky Train, the paired comparison say that the Sky Train is better than the Tram. This intransitivity is a phenomenon we also meet in "real life": a soccer team can win a competition without having won all matches.

Table 6. Relative frequency of number of paired victories, based on p_i^k (ordinal weights)

Number	9	8	7	6	5	4	3	2	1	0
Cable Tram	.763	.213	.021	.002	.001					
H-Bahn	.055	.428	.398	.110	.009					
SPM	.001	.120	.291	.360	.188	.035	.005			
Monorail		.015	.208	.424	.272	.073	.007	.001		
Tram			.014	.133	.374	.372	.101	.005		
Trolley			.007	.051	.176	.322	.300	.130	.014	
Sky Train				.010	.142	.310	.342	.168	.027	
SK					.023	.200	.410	.310	.056	.001
Bus Lane				.004	.017	.081	.249	.402	.247	
Bus								.003	.067	.930

We see that, like in table 5, due to the fact that the information about the weights is only ordinal in stead of cardinal, the results of the relative frequencies of number of paired victories are generally spoken less strict. We also see that in this situation, the Cable Tram is also the less risky choice option.

The overall conclusion of this case study is that the Cable Tram is likely to be the most appropriate solution.

6. Some concluding remarks

Applications of multiple criteria analysis often relate to cases where part of the criteria is cardinal whereas the other part is ordinal. This calls for an approach where the two data types are treated in a compatible way. In the present paper we discussed such a method specifically designed for mixed quantitative/qualitative data, based on paired comparisons of choice options. The central concept used is a 'value difference' function. Based on a definition of this function for cardinal criteria, we apply a stochastic interpretation to the ordinal case to arrive at a compatible measure for value differences between ordinal data. The method described can also be used in the case of ordinal criterion weights. We indicate that there are various ways to arrive at final rankings based on paired comparison matrices. Consistency between some of these has been demonstrated.

The feasibility of our approach is tested by applying it to an empirical case on the choice of transport technology. We find that the multiple criteria analysis leads to a rather clear result on the two best alternatives. A sensitivity analysis based on ordinal weights shows that the final outcomes are rather robust.

References

Beinat, E.,(1995), "Multi Attribute Value Functions for Environmental Management", Phd., Vrije Universiteit, Amsterdam

Hague Consulting Group, (1997),"Beoordelingsinstrument people movers: case-studt Nijmegen", report nr. 6086-6, The Hague

Hinloopen, E., Nijkamp, P. & Rietveld, P. (1983), "Qualitative discrete multiple criteria choice models in regional planning", *Regional Science and Urban Economics* 13: 77-102.

Hinloopen, E., Nijkamp, P. (1986), "Regime Methode voor Ordinal Multi-criteria Analyse", *Kwantitatieve Methoden*, vol. 7, no. 22, 61-78

Hinloopen, E,, Nijkamp, P. (1990), "Qualitative multiple criteria choice analysis, The Dominant Regime Method", *Quality & Quantity* 24: 37-56

Keeney, R.L. and Raiffa, H. (1976), *"Decisions with Multiple Objectives, Preferences and Value Tradeoffs"*, Wiley, New York

Mood, A.M., F.A. Graybill & Boes, D.C. (1974), *"Introduction to the Theory of Statistics"*, McGraw-Hill, New York

Rietveld, P. (1980), *Multiple Objective Decision Methods and Regional Planning*, North Holland, Amsterdam

Rietveld, P., Ouwersloot, H. (1992), "Ordinal data in multicriteria decision making; a stochastic dominance approach to siting nuclear power plants", *EUR. J. Oper. Res.,* 56, 249-262

Taha, H.A. (1976), "*Operations Research"*, Macmillan, New York.

Voogd, H. (1983), *"Multicriteria Evaluation for Urban and Regional Planning"*, Pion Ltd, London

Appendix I

Consider two (real) alternatives and add (N-2) virtual alternatives. Consider a criterion j with consequences measured on an ordinal scale. Let $y_{1j} < y_{2j} < \ldots < y_{Nj}$ be the corresponding order statistic to $x_{1j}, x_{2j}, \ldots, x_{Nj}$ with $x_{nj} = F_j(s_{nj})$ and $s_{1j}, s_{2j}, \ldots, s_{Nj}$ a random sample from a probability distribution $F_j(\ . \ )$. Assume that the real alternatives have ranks α and β. Then

$$f_{Y_\alpha Y_\beta}(y_\alpha, y_\beta) =$$

$$\frac{N!}{(\alpha-1)!(\beta-\alpha-1)!(N-\beta)!} * [F(y_\alpha)]^{\alpha-1}[F(y_\beta) - F(y_\alpha)]^{\beta-\alpha-1}[1 - F(y_\beta)]^{N-\beta} f(y_\alpha)f(y_\beta)$$

with $0 \leq y_\alpha \leq y_\beta \leq 1$ (Mood Graybill Boes, 1974, page 254, Th. 12)   (I.1)

Notice that the joint probability density function of $x_1, x_2, \ldots, x_N$ is the uniform density. It follows that

$$f_{Y_\alpha Y_\beta}(y_\alpha, y_\beta) =$$

$$\frac{N!}{(\alpha-1)!(\beta-\alpha-1)!(N-\beta)!} * y_\alpha^{\alpha-1}(y_\beta - y_\alpha)^{\beta-\alpha-1}(1 - y_\beta)^{N-\beta}, \text{ with } 0 \leq y_\alpha \leq y_\beta \leq 1 \quad (I.2)$$

Let $z = y_\beta - y_\alpha$. Then

$$f_Z(z) = \int_{y_\beta} f_{Y_\alpha Y_\beta}(y_\beta - z, y_\beta) \, dy_\beta = \int_z^1 f_{Y_\alpha Y_\beta}(y_\beta - z, y_\beta) \, dy_\beta, \text{ with } 0 \leq z \leq 1 \quad (I.3)$$

(MGB, page 185, Th. 7)
Hence, in this situation

$$f_Z(z) = \int_z^1 \frac{N!}{(\alpha-1)!(\beta-\alpha-1)!(N-\beta)!} * (y_\beta - z)^{\alpha-1} z^{\beta-\alpha-1}(1 - y_\beta)^{N-\beta} \, dy_\beta, \text{ with } 0 \leq z \leq 1 \quad (I.4)$$

Integrating out y_β gives

$$f_Z(z) = \frac{N!}{(\alpha-1)!(\beta-\alpha-1)!(N-\beta)!} * z^{\beta-\alpha-1}(1 - z)^{N-\beta+\alpha}, \text{ with } 0 \leq z \leq 1 \quad (I.5)$$

This is a Beta distribution with parameters $\beta-\alpha$ and $N+1-\beta+\alpha$.

It follows that

$$F_j(S_{ij}) - F_j(S_{i'j}) = \begin{cases} B(u; \beta-\alpha; N+1-\beta+\alpha)I_{(0,1)}(u) & \text{if } S_{ij} > S_{i'j} \\[2mm] -B(-u; \beta-\alpha; N+1-\beta+\alpha)I_{(-1,0)}(u) & \text{if } S_{ij} < S_{i'j} \end{cases} \quad (I.6)$$

with $B(x;a;b)$ the Beta distribution with parameters a and b.

The proof of Theorem 1 is simply the observation that we have a Beta distribution with parameters 1 and 2.

Appendix II

Notice that $B_{ii'}$ is defined as follows (see section 3).

$$B_{ii'} = \left\{ \begin{array}{c} 1 \\ 0 \end{array} \right\} \text{ if } \sum_j \lambda_j * D_{ii'j} = \left\{ \begin{array}{c} > 0 \\ < 0 \end{array} \right\} \quad i,i'=1, \dots ,I \text{ and } i'\neq i \tag{II.1}$$

with $D_{ii'j} = D(S_{ij} , S_{i'j})$ \hfill (II.2)

Some elements of λ and $S_1 , \dots , S_I$ are measured on an ordinal scale. The Regime Method interprets these elements as stochastic variables (see section 2). Let Ω be the sample space of the stochastic variables of λ and $S_1 , \dots , S_I$. Then the following, almost trivial observation about $B_{ii'}$ can be done.

$$B_{ii'} = \left\{ \begin{array}{c} 1 \\ 0 \end{array} \right\} \quad \text{for all } (\lambda, S_i, S_{i'}) \in \Omega^{(*)} \tag{II.3}$$

Generally, the value of $B_{ii'}$ depends on the values of the stochastic elements of λ, S_i and $S_{i'}$. If the values of the stochastic elements of λ, $S_i, \dots , S_i$ vary, the value of $B_{ii'}$ may be altering between 1 and 0. In order to prove the theorem, the sample space Ω has to be partitioned in a number of subspaces. The subspaces will be constructed in such a way that for all values of the stochastic elements of λ, $S_1, \dots , S_I$ that are in a subspace, $B_{ii'}$ does not change its value.

The partition of the sample space Ω is as follows. The sample space Ω can be partitioned in two disjoint subspaces $\Omega_{i'}$ and $\Omega^c_{i'}$ ($\Omega^c_{i'}$ is the complement of $\Omega_{i'}$) in such a way that

$$B_{ii'} = 1 \text{ for all } (\lambda, S_i, S_{i'}) \in \Omega_{i'} \text{ and } B_{ii'} = 0 \text{ for all } (\lambda, S_i, S_{i'}) \in \Omega^c_{i'} \tag{II.4}$$

Notice that it is not necessary that both subspaces are non-empty.

This partition can also be done for alternatives i and i". The sample space Ω can be partitioned in two disjoint subspaces $\Omega_{i''}$ and $\Omega^c_{i''}$ in such a way that

$$B_{ii''} = 1 \text{ for all } (\lambda, S_i, S_{i''}) \in \Omega_{i''} \text{ and } B_{ii''} = 0 \text{ for all } (\lambda, S_i, S_{i''}) \in \Omega^c_{i''} \tag{II.5}$$

The combination of these two partitions lead to the partition of Ω in four disjoint subspaces $\Omega^1, \Omega^2, \Omega^3$ and Ω^4. Let

$$B^n_{ii'} = B_{ii'} \text{ with } (\lambda, S_1, \dots ,S_I) \in \Omega^n \tag{II.6}$$

Then this partition of Ω is in such a way that

$$B^n_{ii'} = \begin{cases} 1 \text{ for all } (\lambda, S_i, S_{i'}) \in \Omega^n \\ \text{or} \\ 0 \text{ for all } (\lambda, S_i, S_{i'}) \in \Omega^n \end{cases} \Bigg\} n = 1, \dots, 4 \qquad (II.7)$$

(*)"for all $(\lambda, S_i, S_{i'}) \in \Omega$" means: for all stochastical elements of $(\lambda, S_i, S_{i'})$ being a member of Ω.
Notice that is not necessary that all subspaces are non-empty.and also

$$B^n_{ii''} = \begin{cases} 1 \text{ for all } (\lambda, S_i, S_{i''}) \in \Omega^n \\ \text{or} \\ 0 \text{ for all } (\lambda, S_i, S_{i''}) \in \Omega^n \end{cases} \Bigg\} n = 1, \dots, 4 \qquad (II.8)$$

The above mentioned partitions can be realised for all alternatives $(1, \dots, I)$ that are to compared with alternative i. This leads to the following result.

$B_{i1} = 1$ for all $(\lambda, S_i, S_1) \in \Omega_1$ and $B_{i1} = 0$ for all $(\lambda, S_i, S_1) \in \Omega^c_1$
.
$B_{ii'} = 1$ for all $(\lambda, S_i, S_{i'}) \in \Omega_{i'}$ and $B_{ii'} = 0$ for all $(\lambda, S_i, S_{i'}) \in \Omega^c_{i'}$ \qquad (II.9)
.
$B_{iI} = 1$ for all $(\lambda, S_i, S_I) \in \Omega_I$ and $B_{iI} = 0$ for all $(\lambda, S_i, S_I) \in \Omega^c_I$

The combination of these I-1 partitions lead to the partition of Ω in N disjoint subspaces $\Omega^1, \dots, \Omega^N$ in such a way that

$$B^n_{ii'} = \begin{cases} 1 \text{ for all } (\lambda, S_1, \dots, S_I) \in \Omega^n \\ \text{or} \\ 0 \text{ for all } (\lambda, S_1, \dots, S_I) \in \Omega^n \end{cases} \Bigg\} i' = 1, \dots, I, i' \neq i, n = 1, \dots, N \qquad (II.10)$$

Notice that in the situation, that all I-1 partitions of Ω are different and that all partitions of Ω result in two non-empty sub-spaces, N equals $2^{(I-1)}$.
The result of this partitioning of the sample space of the stochastic elements of λ, $S_1, \dots, S_I$ is the following. Generally, the value of $B_{ii'}$ (1 or 0) depends on the values of the stochastic elements of $\lambda, S_1, \dots, S_I$. If the values of the stochastic elements of $\lambda, S_1, \dots, S_I$ vary, the value of $B_{ii'}$ may alternate between 1 and 0. The value of $B^n_{ii'}$ on the other hand (also 1 or 0) does not depend on the values of the stochastic elements of $\lambda, S_1, \dots, S_I$. The subspaces are constructed in such a way that for all values of the stochastic elements of $\lambda, S_1, \dots, S_I$ that are in subspace n, $B^n_{ii'}$ does not alternate between 1 and 0, see II.10. This result will be used in the following of this appendix.
In the first place, the outranking based on $P_{ii'}$ (see theorem 2) will be derived. This outranking is called method 1. Secondly, the outranking based on P_i^k (see theorem 2) will be derived, method 2. Finally, it will be derived that method 1 and method 2 lead to the same outranking.

The $B^n_{ii'}$ are presented in the following table. The rows indicate the paired comparisons of alternative i with alternative i' (i' = 1, ... , I; i' ≠ i) or the number op times alt i wins a paired comparison. The columns indicate the subspaces.

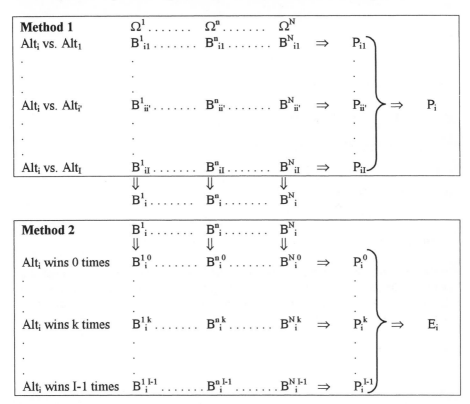

Method 1

In this method, the first step is an aggregation over the subspaces Ω^n, the $P_{ii'}$. The second step is an aggregation over the paired comparisons of alternatives.
Aggregation 1

$$P_{ii'} = \text{Prob} \ (\ B_{ii'} = 1 \ ) \tag{II.11}$$

The relation between $P_{ii'}$ and $D^n_{ii'}$ can be reformulated as follows.
Prob ($B_{ii'} = 1$) =

$$\sum_{n=1}^{N} \text{Prob}(\ B^n_{ii'} = 1|(\lambda, S_1, \ldots ,S_I)\in\Omega^n \ ) * \text{Prob} \ ((\lambda, S_1, \ldots ,S_I)\in\Omega^n \ ) \tag{II.12}$$

And, as a consequence of the definition of $B^n_{ii'}$, this can be written as

$$\text{Prob} \ (\ D_{ii'} = 1 \ ) = \sum_{n=1}^{N} B^n_{ii'} * \text{Prob}(\ (\lambda, S_1, \ldots ,S_I)\in\Omega^n \ ) \tag{II.13}$$

Let $V^n = \text{Prob}(\ (\lambda, S_1, \ldots, S_I) \in \Omega^n\ )$ \hfill (II.14)

Then the result of this first aggregation can be formulated as follows.

$$P_{ii'} = \sum_{n=1}^{N} B^n_{ii'} * V^n \hfill (II.15)$$

Aggregation 2

$$P_i = 1/(I-1) * \sum_{i' \neq i} P_{ii'} \text{ (see section 4)} \hfill (II.16)$$

The combination of (II.15) and (II.16) gives

$$P_i = 1/(I-1) * \sum_{n=1}^{N} V^n * \sum_{i' \neq i} B^n_{ii'} \hfill (II.17)$$

Method 2

In this method, the first step is, within a subspace Ω^n, an aggregation over the results of the paired comparisons ($B^n_{ii'}$). The second step is an aggregation over the subspaces. The third step is the calculation of the expected number of times that an alternative wins a paired comparison, which also gives a final outranking.

Aggregation 1

Let
$$B^n_i = \sum_{i' \neq i} B^n_{ii'} \hfill (II.18)$$

B^n_i gives the number of times alternative i wins a paired comparison from another alternative, with the restriction that $(\lambda, S_1, \ldots, S_I) \in \Omega^n$.

Aggregation 2

Let
$$B^{n\,k}_i = \begin{cases} 1 \text{ if } B^n_i = k \\ 0 \text{ if } B^n_i \neq k \end{cases} \hfill (II.19)$$

As defined in section 4,

$$P^k_i = \text{Prob} (\ \sum_{i' \neq i} B_{ii'} = k\ ) \hfill (II.20)$$

This can be rewritten as

$$P_i^k = \sum_{n=1}^{N} V^n * B_i^{n,k} \tag{II.21}$$

P_i^k gives the probability that alternative i wins k paired comparisons.

Aggregation 3

The third aggregation establishes the final outranking. As defined in section 4,

$$E_i = \sum_{k=0}^{I-1} k * P_i^k \tag{II.22}$$

The combination of (II.21) and (II.22) gives

$$E_i = \sum_{n=1}^{N} V^n * \sum_{k=0}^{I-1} k * B_i^{n,k} \tag{II.23}$$

Proof of the theorem

Finally, the theorem can be proven:

Multiplying and (II.17) with $(I - 1)$ gives

$$(I - 1) * P_i = \sum_{n=1}^{N} V^n * \sum_{i' \neq i} B_{ii'}^{n} \tag{II.24}$$

The combination of (II.19) and (II.23) gives

$$E_i = \sum_{n=1}^{N} V^n * \sum_{k=0}^{I-1} k * \begin{cases} 1 \text{ if } \sum_{i' \neq i} B_i^n = k \\ 0 \text{ if } \sum_{i' \neq i} B_i^n \neq k \end{cases} \tag{II.25}$$

Notice that

$$\sum_{i' \neq i} B_{ii'}^{n} = \sum_{k=0}^{I-1} k * \begin{cases} 1 \text{ if } \sum_{i' \neq i} B_i^n = k \\ 0 \text{ if } \sum_{i' \neq i} B_i^n \neq k \end{cases} \tag{II.26}$$

The combination of (II.24), (II.25) and (II.26) results in

$$E_i = \sum_{k=0}^{I-1} k * P_i^k = \sum_{i' \neq i} P_{ii'} = (I - 1) * P_i \tag{II.27}$$

Q.E.D.

On the Computational Effectiveness of Multiple Objective Metaheuristics

Andrzej Jaszkiewicz

Institute of Computing Science
Poznań University of Technology
ul. Piotrowo 3a, 60-965 Poznań, Poland
Jaszkiewicz@cs.put.poznan.pl
www-idss.cs.put.poznan.pl/~jaszkiewicz

Abstract
The paper describes a technique for comparison of computational effectiveness of two approaches to generation of approximately Pareto-optimal solutions with the use of metaheuristics. In the on-line generation approach the approximately Pareto-optimal solutions are generated during the interactive process, e.g. by optimization of some scalarizing functions. In the off-line generation approach, the solutions are generated prior to the interactive process with the use of multiple objective metaheuristics. The results of experiment on travelling salesperson instances indicate that in the case of some multiple objective metheuristics the off-line generation approach may be computationally effective alternative to the on-line generation of approximately Pareto-optimal solutions.
Keywords Multiple objective optimization, metaheuristics, scalarizing functions, interactive methods, computational effectiveness

Introduction

In recent years, one could observe growing interest in multiple objective analysis of computationally hard problems, e.g. multiple objective combinatorial optimization (MOCO) problems. In the case of such problems, the use of exact methods that guarantee generation of exact Pareto-optimal solutions may be not possible because of computational requirements of the methods. As single objective metaheuristics proved to be successful on many hard optimization problems, it seems natural to apply them to generation of approximately Pareto-optimal solutions in multiple objective context.

A number of authors proposed multiple objective metaheuristic algorithms that aim at effective generations of samples of approximately Pareto-optimal solutions being approximations of the whole Pareto set. The methods are usually based on classical single objective metaheuristics. For example, the methods of Schaffer [21], Fonseca and Fleming [4], Horn, Nafpliotis and Goldberg [9], Srinivas and Deb [24] are based on genetic algorithms, the methods of Serafini [22], Czyzak and Jaszkiewicz [2], Ulungu et al. [29] are based on simulated annealing, and the methods of Gandibleux et. al. [6] and Hansen [8] are based on tabu search.

Hwang et al. [11] proposed a classification of MOO methods taking into account the moment of collecting the preference information with respect to the exploration process. They classify the MOO methods as either methods with a priori or a posteriori, or progressive (interactive) articulation of preferences. According to this classification the multiple objective metaheuristic algorithms should be treated as techniques used within a posteriori articulation of preferences approach. Note, however, that generation of a set of approximately Pareto-optimal solutions does not necessarily allows easy selection of the best compromise by the DM. The set of approximately Pareto-optimal solutions may contain a large number of solutions. In the case of two objectives, the objective trade-offs may be visualized in a two-dimensional plot allowing the DM to select the best compromise. No such simple visualization is possible in the case of three or more objectives. Thus, the DM analyzing a generated a priori large set of approximately Pareto-optimal solutions may need some further support characteristic to interactive procedures in the search for the best compromise.

Several interactive procedures for analysis of finite sets of alternatives have been already proposed. This class of methods includes: Zionts method [32], Korhonen, Wallenius and Zionts method [16], Köksalan, Karwan and Zionts method [14], Korhonen method [15], Malakooti method [18], Taner and Köksalan method [27], AIM [17], Light Beam Search-Discrete [13] and Interquad [26]. Such methods could be used for interactive analysis of large sets of approximately Pareto-optimal solutions. The methods are usually based on well-known interactive procedures for continuous case. In fact, the DM may not be even aware if the solutions presented to him/her in decision phases were generated a priori or if the solutions are generated on-line in computational phases alternating with phases of decision. Clearly, in both cases we deal with progressive articulation of preferences.

In results, we propose to distinguish two versions of approaches with progressive articulation of preferences, taking into account the way of generation of the (approximately) Pareto-optimal solutions. In the *on-line* approach the solutions are generated during the interactive process, i.e. generation of solutions alternates with articulation of DM's preferences. In contrary, in the *off-line* approach the (approximately) Pareto-optimal solutions are generated prior to interactive analysis.

On-line generation of (approximately) Pareto-optimal solutions is assumed in most classical interactive procedures proposed for continuous case (see e.g. reviews in [9] and [23]). The methods usually generate Pareto-optimal solutions by optimization of some substitute problems which global optima correspond to Pareto-optimal solutions. For example, a number of methods use, so called, scalarizing functions that are optimized on the original set of feasible solutions. In particular, optimization of weighted Tchebycheff scalarizing functions allows generation of all Pareto-optimal solutions ([25], ch. 14.8; [31]). In the case of hard MOO problems a natural approach consist in optimization of the scalarizing functions with classical single objective metaheuristics.

Note that most of the mentioned above interactive procedures for analysis of finite sets of alternatives also select the solutions presented to the DM applying a scalarizing function. In this case, however, the best solution on a scalarizing function is selected from the set of explicitly known solutions without optimization. In the rest of the paper, we will concentrate on on-line and off-line approaches that use scalarizing functions for selection of the approximately Pareto-optimal solutions presented to the DM.

Off-line generation of approximately Pareto-optimal solutions has several advantages with respect to the on-line approach:

- It allows different types of statistical analysis, e.g. calculation of correlation between objectives, and graphical visualization of the explicitly known set of approximately Pareto-optimal solutions that may increase the DM's knowledge about the problem.
- It assures very fast interaction with the DM, as no optimization is performed during the interactive process.
- It guarantees that all solutions presented to the DM are mutually non-dominated. In contrary, approximate solutions generated by a heuristic used within the on-line approach may dominate each other.

In this paper, we focus, however, on the issue of computational effectiveness of generation of approximately Pareto-optimal solutions. We propose a technique that allows comparing quality of solutions generated by the on-line and off-line approaches. Then, we propose to compare computational requirements of the two approaches needed to achieve the same quality of approximately Pareto-optimal solutions.

The paper is organized in the following way. The next section contains problem statement and basic definitions. The technique for comparison of computational effectiveness of the on-line and off-line approaches to generation of approximately Pareto-optimal solutions is described in details in the third section. In the fourth section, computational experiments on travelling salesperson instances are described. The conclusions are presented in the last section.

Problem Statement and Basic Definitions

The general multiple objective optimization (MOO) problem is formulated as:
$$\max\{f_1(\mathbf{x}) = z_1,...,f_J(\mathbf{x}) = z_J\} \qquad \text{(P1)}$$
s.t. $\quad \mathbf{x} \in D$,

where *solution* $\mathbf{x} = [x_1,...,x_I]$ is a vector of *decision variables*, D is the set of feasible solutions.

A solution $\mathbf{x} \in D$ is *Pareto-optimal* (*efficient*) if there is no $\mathbf{x}' \in D$ such that $\forall_j f_j(\mathbf{x}') \geq f_j(\mathbf{x})$ and $f_j(\mathbf{x}') > f_j(\mathbf{x})$ for at least one j. The set of all Pareto-optimal solutions is called *Pareto set*.

The point $\mathbf{z}^*$ composed of the best attainable objective function values is called the *ideal point*:

$$z_j^* = \max\{z_j \mid \mathbf{z} \in Z\} \qquad j = 1,...,J.$$

Range equalization factors [25] are defined in the following way:

$$\pi_j = \frac{1}{R_j}, j=1, \ldots, J$$

where R_j is the (approximate) range of objective j in the set N or D. Objective function values multiplied by range equalization factors are called *normalized objective function values*.

Weighted Tchebycheff scalarizing functions are defined in the following way:

$$s_\infty(\mathbf{z}, \mathbf{z}^o, \Lambda) = \max_j \left\{ \lambda_i \left(z_j^o - z_j \right) \right\}.$$

In the rest of the paper we will assume that $\mathbf{z}^o = \mathbf{z}^*$. Each scalarizing function of this type has at least one global optimum (minimum) belonging to the set of Pareto-optimal solutions. For each Pareto-optimal solutions $\mathbf{x}$ there exists a weighted Tchebycheff scalarizing function s_∞ such that $\mathbf{x}$ is global optimum of s_∞ [25].

Augmented weighted Tchebycheff scalarizing functions are defined in the following way:

$$s_a(\mathbf{z}, \mathbf{z}^*, \Lambda) = \max_j \left\{ \lambda_i \left(z_j^* - z_j \right) \right\} + \varepsilon \sum_j \lambda_i \left(z_j^* - z_j \right),$$

where ε is a small number greater than zero.

Weight vectors than meet the following conditions:

$$\forall j\, \lambda_j \geq 0, \sum_{j=1}^{J} \lambda_j = 1,$$

are called normalized weight vectors.

Comparison of the Computational Effectiveness of On-line and Off-line Generation of Approximately Pareto-Optimal Solutions

Consider a scalarizing function s used in a given iteration of an interactive procedure. In the case of both on-line and off-line approaches, the solution presented to the DM is not guaranteed to be optimal on s. Denote solution obtained within the on-line approach, i.e. by optimization of s with a single objective metaheuristic, by $\mathbf{x}^s$. Denote the solution obtained within the off-line approach, i.e. by selection from the set of a priori generated approximately Pareto-optimal solutions, by $\mathbf{x}^m$. The values $s(\mathbf{x}^s)$ and $s(\mathbf{x}^m)$ allow comparison of the two solutions. For example, solution $\mathbf{x}^s$ is better than $\mathbf{x}^m$ if $s(\mathbf{x}^s) < s(\mathbf{x}^m)$.

Of course, comparison on a single scalarizing function is meaningless. We propose to compare the two kinds of approaches on a set $S = \{s_1, \ldots, s_L\}$ of randomly selected scalarizing functions. Let $\mathbf{x}^{s1}, \ldots, \mathbf{x}^{sL}$ be the best solutions obtained by optimization of $s_1, \ldots, s_L$, respectively, with a single objective metaheuristic. Let $\mathbf{x}^{m1}, \ldots, \mathbf{x}^{mL}$ be the best solutions on $s_1, \ldots, s_L$, respectively, selected from a set PE of potentially Pareto-optimal solutions generated by a multiple objective metaheuristic, i.e. $\forall \mathbf{x} \in PE \; s_l\left(\mathbf{x}^{ml}\right) \leq s_l(\mathbf{x})$, $l = 1,...,L$. We consider the multiple objective metaheuristic not worse than the single objective metaheuristic if:

$$\sum_{l=1}^{L}\left(s_l\left(\mathbf{x}^{ml}\right) - s_l\left(\mathbf{x}^{sl}\right)\right) \leq 0 . \qquad (*)$$

If $L \rightarrow \infty$ the above condition means that the set PE of potentially Pareto-optimal solutions gives the same average quality of approximation over all scalarizing functions that optimization of the functions with the single objective metaheuristic. In practice, we use, of course, finite values of L. The parameter plays the role of the size of statistical sample. The greater L the more significant the result given by (*).

If condition (*) is fulfilled, we may compare computational requirements of the single and multiple objective metaheuristics. Let CT_s be the average running time of the single objective method spent on optimization of $s_1,...,s_L$. Let CT_m be the running time of the multiple objective method needed to generate PE. We define then *effectiveness index EI*:

$$EI = \frac{CT_m}{CT_s} .$$

The lower EI the more effective the multiple objective metaheuristic with respect to the single objective method.

We propose to apply effectiveness index to comparison of single and multiple objective metaheuristics based on similar ideas. For example, multiple objective genetic algorithms could be compared to single objective GAs, multiple objective genetic local search could be compared to single objective genetic local search, etc. As most multiple objective metaheuristics are some extensions/modifications of single objective methods, the effectiveness index gives some information about quality of this extension. Of course, in this·case, it is natural to expect $EI > 1$.

The effectiveness index may be used to compare different multiple objective metaheuristics based on the same single objective method.

The effectiveness index has some clear interpretation from the point of view of interactive procedures. Assume that the interactive process requires generation of R approximately Pareto-optimal solutions of a given problem in order meet the stopping criteria or to reach the solution satisfying the DM. If $R > L$ then the overall computational requirements of the on-line generation of approximately Pareto-optimal solutions are higher than computational requirements of the off-line approach.

Computational Experiment

Overview of the Experiment

This section describes computational experiment performed on multiple objective travelling sales person instances. The pairs of methods compared are genetic algorithm vs. Pareto ranking based multiple objective genetic algorithm, and genetic local search vs. multiple objective genetic local search.

We use augmented Tchebycheff scalarizing functions with $\varepsilon = 0.1$. Parameter L - the number of scalarizing functions on which the pairs of methods are compared, is equal to 50. The scalarizing functions are defined by L normalized weight vector randomly generated with the algorithm presented in Figure 1. The algorithm assures that weight vectors are drawn with uniform probability distribution $p(\Lambda)$, i.e. a distribution for which:

$$\forall \Psi' \subseteq \Psi \quad \int_{\Lambda \in \Psi'} p(\Lambda) d\Lambda \Big/ \int_{\Lambda \in \Psi} p(\Lambda) d\Lambda = V(\Psi')/V(\Psi)$$

where Ψ and Ψ' denote the set of all normalized weights and a subset of it, respectively; $V(\Psi)$ and $V(\Psi')$ are Euclidean hyper-volumes of Ψ and Ψ', respectively. In other words, the probability of drawing a weight vector belonging to Ψ' is proportional to the hyper-volume of Ψ'.

$$\lambda_1 = 1 - \sqrt[J-1]{rand()}$$

$$\cdots$$

$$\lambda_j = \left(1 - \sum_{l=1}^{j-1} \lambda_l\right)\left(1 - \sqrt[J-1-j]{rand()}\right)$$

$$\cdots$$

$$\lambda_J = 1 - \sum_{l=1}^{J-1} \lambda_l$$

Figure 1. Algorithm of generation of random weight vectors.

For each instance the following experiment was performed. In the first phase 50 random scalarizing functions were optimized with a single objective method. Then, the multiple objective method was started. After specified number of iterations of the multiple objective method the quality of the current set of potentially Pareto-optimal solutions was compared to the quality of solutions generated by the single objective method with condition (*). When condition (*) was met the multiple objective method was stopped and the effectiveness index was calculated. Another stopping criterion of the multiple objective method was running time greater than 500 times the average running time of the single objective method. In the second case, we can state that the effectiveness index is $\geq$ 500.

Methods Used in the Experiment

Single objective genetic local search

Genetic local search (GLS) is a method that hybridizes recombination operators with local search. The version of GLS algorithm we use assumes complete elitism, i.e. the current population is always composed of a sample of best known solutions. The details of this algorithm are in Figure 2.

Parameters: K – size of the current population, stopping criterion
Initialization:
Current population $P:=\varnothing$
repeat K times
    Construct randomly a new feasible solution x
    Optimize locally the objective function starting from solution x obtaining x'
    Add x' to P.
Main loop:
repeat
    Draw at random with uniform probability two solutions x_1 and x_2 from P.
    Recombine x_1 and x_2 obtaining x_3
    Optimize locally the objective function starting from solution x_3 obtaining x_3'
    if x_3' is better than the worst solution in P and different in the decision space to all solutions in P **then**
        Add x_3' to P and delete from P the worst solution
until the stopping criterion is met

Figure 2.   Algorithm of the basic single objective genetic local search

In the experiments described in this paper, the optimization was stopped if in 20 successive iterations current population was not changed. This value was selected experimentally. It was observed that population that was not changed in 20 iterations gives little chance for further improvements.

Size of the current population K is the main parameter controlling the calculation time. Generally, the larger K the larger CPU time and the better quality of results.

In this algorithm, mutation operator is not explicitly used. The recombination operator may introduce, however, some elements of randomness. In other cases explicit mutation operators may be necessary.

Multiple objective genetic local search

One of the multiple objective metaheuristics used in the experiment is multiple objective genetic local search (MOGLS) proposed in [12] on the basis of the single objective algorithm presented in Figure 2. In each iteration, the method draws at random a scalarizing function s for optimization. Then, two of previously generated solutions being good on s are recombined and local search is applied to their offspring. We use augmented weighted Tchebycheff scalarizing functions with $\varepsilon = 0.1$ in this experiment.

Parameters: K – size of the temporary population, stopping criterion

Initialization:

The set of potentially Pareto-optimal solutions $PE := \varnothing$

The current set of solutions $CS := \varnothing$

repeat until CS meets stopping condition for generation of initial solutions

    Draw at random a scalarizing function s

    Construct randomly a new feasible solution **x**

    Optimize locally the scalarizing function s starting from solution **x** obtaining **x'**

    Add **x'** to the current set of solutions CS

    Update set PE with **x'**

Main loop:

repeat

    Draw at random a scalarizing function s

    From CS select K different solutions being the best on scalarizing function s forming temporary population TP

    Draw at random with uniform probability two solutions $\mathbf{x}_1$ and $\mathbf{x}_2$ from TP.

    Recombine $\mathbf{x}_1$ and $\mathbf{x}_2$ obtaining $\mathbf{x}_3$

    Optimize locally the scalarizing function s starting from solution $\mathbf{x}_3$ obtaining $\mathbf{x}_3\text{'}$

    if $\mathbf{x}_3\text{'}$ is better than the worst solution in TP and different in the decision space to all solutions in TP **then**

        Add $\mathbf{x}_3\text{'}$ to the current set of solutions CS

        Add $\mathbf{x}_3\text{'}$ to TP and delete from TP the worst solution

    Update set PE with $\mathbf{x}_3\text{'}$

until the stopping criterion is met

Figure 3. **Algorithm of the multiple objective genetic local search**

The generation of initial solutions is stopped when the average quality of K best solutions in CS over all scalarizing functions is the same as average quality of local optima of this function. Consider **x** being an initial solution obtained by local optimization of function scalarizing s_x. Note that **x** need not be the best solutions on s_x in current set of solutions CS. Let $B(K, CS, \mathbf{x}, s_x) \subseteq CS$ be the set of K best solutions of function s_x different than **x**. Let $\bar{s}(B(K, CS, \mathbf{x}, s_x))$ be the average value of s_x in $B(K, CS, \mathbf{x}, s_x)$. We stop generation of the initial solutions when the following condition is met:

$$\sum_{x \in S} \left(s(B(K, CS, \mathbf{x}, s_x)) - s_x(\mathbf{x}) \right) \geq 0$$

Of course, the above condition could only be tested when the number of solutions in CS is greater or equal to $K + 1$.

Set CS is organized as a queue of size $K \times S$, where S is the number of initial solutions. In each iteration, the newly generated solution is added to the beginning of the queue if it is better than the worst solution in the temporary population and different to all solutions in the temporary population. If the size of the queue is greater than $K \times S$ the last solution from the queue is removed.

The stopping criterion of the main loop is defined by maximum number of iterations.

Updating the set of potentially Pareto-optimal solutions PE with solution $\mathbf{x}$ consists of:

- adding $\mathbf{x}$ to PE if no solution in PE dominates $\mathbf{x}$,
- removing from PE all solutions dominated by $\mathbf{x}$.

Note that the set of potentially Pareto-optimal solutions is updated with local optima only. In general, other solutions generated during the local search may also be potentially Pareto-optimal. This approach allows, however, for significant reduction of running time. Furthermore, a data structure called quad tree allows for very effective implementation of this step [3], [7].

The random scalarizing functions are defined by random weight vectors constructed with the algorithm presented in Figure 1. The weights are applied to normalized objective function values.

Genetic algorithm

In our experiment, we used genetic algorithm presented in Figure 4.

Parameters: K – size of the genetic population, maximum number of generations, mutation probability

Initialization:

Generate K random solutions forming the initial population

Main loop:

repeat

    Select K pairs of solutions with roulette wheel selection

    Recombine each pair of solutions

    Mutate each of the offspring with mutation probability

    Replace previous population with the new one

until the maximum number of generations is reached

Figure 4.   Genetic algorihm

Pareto ranking based multiple objective genetic algorithm

In the experiment we used a Pareto ranking based multiple objective genetic algorithm (Pareto MOGA) proposed in [4] without mating restrictions. In addition, we maintain the set of potentially Pareto-optimal solutions updated with each newly constructed solution. The details are given in Figure 5.

> **Parameters:** K – size of the genetic population, maximum number of generations, mutation probability
> *Initialization:*
> The set of potentially Pareto-optimal solutions $PE:=\varnothing$
> Generate K random solutions forming the initial population
> Update set PE with each solution from the current population
> *Main loop:*
> **repeat**
> > Assign to each solution from the current population the fitness on the basis of Pareto ranking
> > Reduce fitness of close solutions by fitness sharing
> > Select K pairs of solutions with roulette wheel selection
> > Recombine each pair of solutions
> > Mutate each of the offspring with mutation probability
> > Replace previous population with the new one
> > Update set PE with each solution from the current population
> **until** the maximum number of generations is reached

Figure 5. **Pareto-ranking based multiple objective genetic algorithm**

Multiple Objective Symmetric Travelling Salesperson Problem

Single objective TSP is often used to test single objective metaheuristics. It is defined by a set of cities and cost (distance) of travel between each pair of cities. In symmetric TSP the cost does not depend on direction of travel between two cities. The goal is to find the lowest cost hamiltonian cycle.

In J-objective TSP, J different cost factors are defined between each pair of cities. In practical applications, the cost factors may for example corresponds to cost, length, travel time or tourist attractiveness. In our case, J-objective symmetric TSPs instances are constructed from J different single objective TSP instances. Thus, j-th cost factor, $j=1,...,J$, between a pair of cities comes from j-th single objective problem. Individual optima of particular objectives are equal to optima of corresponding single objective problems. In our case, the single objective problems are completely independent, so, also objectives are independent and therefore non-correlated. The same approach was used by [1] and [12].

Also following [1] and [12] we use multiple objective problem instances based on TSPLIB library [20]. For example, problem instance kroABC100 denotes a three-objective problem with cost factors corresponding to the first objective taken from kroA100, cost factors corresponding to the second objective taken from kroB100, and cost factors corresponding to the second objective taken from kroC100. In this way 10 different three-objective problem instance were created. We used also 10 three-objective instances and 5 four-objective instances with 50 leading cities taken from kroA100-kroE100 instances.

The recombination operator used by all the methods is the distance-preserving crossover introduced in [5]. An offspring is constructed in the following steps:

Step 1. Put in the offspring all arcs common to both parents
Step 2. Complete the hamiltonian cycle with randomly selected arcs.

Table 1.   **Results of GLS – MOGLS comparison**

(Tempo-rary) population size		Average running time of GLS (number of functions' evaluations)	Running time of MOGLS (number of functions' evaluations)	Effectiveness index	Number of potentially Pareto-optimal solutions generated by MOGLS
3 objectives, 50 cities					
10	Average	614 309	9 676 310	**15.69**	1003
	Standard dev.	32 877	3 043 922	**4.51**	235
20	Average	1 186 259	18 164 128	**15.12**	1573
	Standard dev.	57 406	13 115 967	**10.38**	406
30	Average	1 676 203	19 408 022	**11.64**	1790
	Standard dev.	106 760	2 314 632	**1.70**	219
3 objectives, 100 cities					
10	Average	4 912 063	187 879 890	**38.63**	2726
	Standard dev.	238 474	91 281 659	**19.42**	921
20	Average	10 111 330	357 766 821	**35.84**	4837
	Standard dev.	514 896	190 908 770	**20.29**	1886
30	Average	14 837 900	557 799 727	**37.89**	6547
	Standard dev.	790 362	165 688 406	**12.26**	1800
4 objectives, 50 cities					
10	Average	680 775	57 336 646	**84.55**	8785
	Standard dev.	25 605	11 756 380	**19.16**	2038
20	Average	1 183 152	96 166 142	**81.05**	14267
	Standard dev.	42 735	19 870 387	**15.16**	3199
30	Average	1 750 500	116 369 545	**66.44**	16602
	Standard dev.	78 749	12 193 400	**5.89**	1804

The local search used is based on standard 2-arcs exchange neighborhood. While constructing the initial population, greedy local search is used. After recombination, steepest local search is used. This combination was found to give the best results. As local search consumes most of the CPU time, we measure the running time in the number of functions' evaluations (number of evaluated solutions). In the case of 2-arcs exchange operator, neighbor solutions can be evaluated in very short time. In results about 1 000 000 functions' evaluations can be performed on 350 MHz Pentium PC in one second.

The mutation operator exchanges to randomly selected arcs.

Results

Table 1 contains results of the experiments with genetic local search and multiple objective genetic local search. The entries in the table contain averages and standard deviations of ten experiments on three objective instances and five experiments on four objective instances (one experiment for each instance). As could be expected the effectiveness index grows with the problem size and the number of objectives. In both cases, the growth of the effectiveness index is correlated to the growth of the size of the set of potentially Pareto-optimal solutions.

In our opinion, the results prove that generation of approximately Pareto-optimal solutions with the MOGLS is competitive from the computational effectiveness point of view to generation of the solutions with single objective GLS. Note that GLS is one of the best methods for single objective TSP [19].

Significantly different results were obtained in the case of comparison of GA and Pareto MOGA. In none of the experiments the set of potentially Pareto-optimal solutions generated by Pareto MOGA fulfilled the condition (*) in running time lower or equal to 500 times the average running time of GA. Thus, we conclude that the effectiveness index of Pareto MOGA in comparison to GA on the TSP instances used in the experiment is greater than 500.

Conclusions

We have introduced a measure call effectiveness index that relates computational requirements of single and multiple objective metaheuristic necessary to generate approximately Pareto-optimal solutions of the same average quality.

The results of experiments on the TSP instances indicate that off-line generation of approximately efficient solutions may be computationally competitive approach. In particular multiple objective genetic local search is able to generate high quality approximations to the whole Pareto-optimal set in running time 11.64 - 84.55 longer than the average time needed to generate single approximately Pareto-optimal solution with the same average quality using the single objective genetic local search. Note that GLS is known to be very effective method for single objective TSP. The results indicate also that the relative effectiveness of MOGLS decreases with the growth of the number of objectives.

In the experiments with genetic algorithm and Pareto ranking based multiple objective genetic algorithm the effectiveness index was found to be greater than

500. We conclude that from the computational point of view Pareto MOGA is not competitive tool for generation of approximately Pareto-optimal solution in comparison to GA on TSP instances.

Note that off-line generation of approximately Pareto-optimal solutions has a number of additional advantages over on-line approach (see introduction section). Thus, computational effectiveness is not the only reason for the use of this approach.

The two approaches for generation of approximately Pareto-optimal solutions, are in fact extreme possibilities. In the off-line approach we assume that a single run of a metaheuristic generates a sample of approximately Pareto-optimal solutions approximating the whole Pareto set. In the online, approach only a single Pareto-optimal solution by each run of a metaheuristic. It is also possible to generate in a single run of a metaheuristic a sample of approximately Pareto-optimal solutions approximating a promising subregion of the whole Pareto set. In fact, many multiple objective metaheuristics can be easily used in this way. For example in MOGLS algorithm, it is possible to draw at random scalarizing functions from a subset of all scalarizing functions. In this case, multiple objective metaheuristics may be computationally effective even in the case of many objectives. An approach of this kind is proposed e.g. in [4].

Acknowledgment

This research was supported by KBN grant no. 8T11F 006 19.

Bibliography

[1] Borges P.C., Hansen P.H. (1998), A basis for future successes in multiobjective combinatorial optimization. *Technical Report, Department of Mathematical Modelling, Technical University of Denmark*, IMM-REP-1998-8.

[2] Czyzak P., Jaszkiewicz A. (1998), Pareto simulated annealing - a metaheuristic technique for multiple-objective combinatorial optimization. *Journal of Multi-Criteria Decision Analysis*, 7, 34-47.

[3] Finkel R.A. and Bentley J.L. (1974), Quad Trees, A data structure for retrieval on composite keys. *Acta Informatica*, 4, 1-9.

[4] Fonseca C.M., Fleming P.J. (1993), Genetic algorithms for multiobjective optimization: Formulation, discussion and generalization. In S. Forrest (Ed.), *Genetic Algorithms: Proceedings of 5th International Conference*, San Mateo, CA, Morgan Kaufmann, 416-423.

[5] Freisleben B., Merz P. (1996), A genetic local search algorithm for travelling salesman problem. In H.-M. Voigt, W. Ebeling, I. Rechenberg, H.-P. Schwefel (eds.), *Proceedings of the 4th Conference on Parallel Problem Solving fram Nature- PPSN IV*, 890-900.

[6] Gandibleux, X., Mezdaoui N., Fréville A. (1996). A tabu search procedure to solve multiobjective combinatorial optimization problems, In R. Caballero, R. Steuer (Eds.), *Proceedings volume of MOPGP '96*, , Springer-Verlag.

[7] Habenicht W. (1982), Quad Trees, A datastructure for discrete vector optimization problems. *Lecture Notes in Economics and Mathematical Systems*, **209**, 136-145.

[8] Hansen M. (1997), Tabu search for multiobjective optimization: MOTS, presented at the 13th MCDM conference, Cape Town, South Africa, January 6-10.

[9] Horn. J., Nafpliotis N. (1994). A niched Pareto genetic algorithm for multiobjective optimization. *Proceedings of the First IEEE Conference on Evolutionary Computation, IEEE World Congress on Computational Intelligence*, vol. 1, IEEE, New York, 82-87.

[10] Hwang C.-L. and Masud A.S.M. (1979). *Mutiple Objective Decision Making - Methods and Applications*, Springer, Berlin.

[11] Hwang C.-L., Paidy S.R., Yoon K. and Masud A.S.M. (1980), Mathematical programming with multiple objectives: A tutorial. *Comput. Oper. Res.*, 7, 5-31.

[12] Jaszkiewicz A. (1998). Genetic local search for multiple objective combinatorial optimization. Research report, Institute of Computing Science, Poznań University of Technology, **RA-014/98**, pp.23.

[13] Jaszkiewicz A., Słowiński R. (1997). The LBS-Discrete Interactive Procedure for Multiple-Criteria Analysis of Decision Problems. In: J. Climaco (red.) *Multicriteria Analysis. Proceedings of the XIth International Conference on MCDM*, 1-6, August 1994, Coimbra, Portugal, Springer-Verlag, Berlin - Heidelberg, 320-330.

[14] Köksalan M., Karwan M.H. and Zionts S. (1988). An Approach for Solving Discrete Alternative Multiple Criteria Problems Involving Ordinal Criteria. *Naval Research Logistics*, **35**, 6, 625-642.

[15] Korhonen P. (1988). A Visual Reference Direction Approach to Solving Discrete Multiple Criteria Problems. *EJOR*, **34**, 2, 152-159.

[16] Korhonen P. Wallenius J. and Zionts S. (1984). Solving the Discrte Multiple Criteria Problem Using Convex Cones. *Management Science*, **30**, 11, 1336-1345.

[17] Lotfi V., Stewart T.J. and Zionts S. (1992). An aspiration-level interactive model for multiple criteria decision making. *Comput. Ops. Res.*, **19**, 677-681.

[18] Malakooti B. (1989). Theories and an Exact Interactive Paired-COmparison Approach for Discrete Multiple Criteria Problems. IEEE Transactions on Systems, Man, and Cybemetics, **19**, 2, 365-378.

[19] Merz P., Freisleben B., Genetic Local Search for the TSP: New Results, In *Proceedings of the 1997 IEEE International Conference on Evolutionary Computation*, IEEE Press, 159-164, 1997.

[20] Reinelt G. (1991). TSPLIB – a traveling salesman problem library. *ORSA Journal of Computing*, **3**, 4, 376-384.

[21] Schaffer J.D. (1985). Multiple objective optimization with vector evaluated genetic algorithms. In: J.J. Grefenstette (ed.), *Genetic Algorithms and Their Applications: Proceedings of the Third International Conference on Genetic Algorithms*, Lawrence Erlbaum, Hillsdale, NJ, 93-100.

[22] Serafini P. (1994). Simulated annealing for multiple objective optimization problems. In: Tzeng G.H., Wang H.F., Wen V.P., Yu P.L. (eds), *Multiple Criteria Decision Making. Expand and Enrich the Domains of Thinking and Application*, Springer Verlag, 283-292.

[23] Shin W.S. and Ravindran A. (1991). Interactive multiple objective optimization: survey I - continuous case, *Comput. Oper. Res.*, **18**, 97-114.

[24] Srinivas N., Deb K. (1994). Multiobjective optimization using nondominated sorting in genetic algorithms. *Evolutionary Computation*, 2, 2, 221-248.

[25] Steuer R.E. (1986). *Multiple Criteria Optimization - Theory, Computation and Application*, Wiley, New York.

[26] Sun M., Steuer R. E. (1996). InterQuad: An Interactive Quad Tree Based Procedure for Solving the Discrete Alternative Multiple Criteria Problem. *European Journal of Operational Research*, **89**, No. 3, 462-472.

[27] Taner O.V. and Köksalan M.M. (1991). Experiments and an Improved Method for Solving the Discrete Alternative Multiple-Criteria Problem. *Journal of the Operational Research Society*, **42**, 5, 383-392.

[28] Ulungu E.L. and Teghem J. (1994). Multiobjective Combinatorial Optimization Problems: A Survey. *Journal of Multi-Criteria Decision Analysis*, **3**, 83-101.

[29] Ulungu E.L., Teghem J., Fortemps Ph., Tuyttens (1999). MOSA method: a toll for solving multiobjective combinatorial optimization problems. *Journal of Multi-Criteria Decision Analysis*, 8, 221-236.

[30] Wierzbicki A.P. (1980), The use of reference objective in Multiobjective Optimization. In: Fandel G. and Gal T. (eds.) *Multiple Criteria Decision Making, Theory and Application*, Springer-Verlag, Berlin, 468-486.

[31] Wierzbicki A.P. (1986), On the completeness and constructiveness of parametric characterization to vector optimization problems. *OR Spektrum*, **8**, 73-87.

[32] Zionts S. (1981). A Multiple Criteria Method for Choosing among Discrete Alternatives. *EJOR*, 7, 1, 143-147

On Considering Flexible Constraints of Different Importance in Goal Programming Problems

Jiménez, M.[1];Rodríguez Uría, M. V.[2]; Arenas Parra, M.[2]; Bilbao Terol, A.[2] .

(1)Dpto. Econ. Aplicada I. Univ. del País Vasco. Spain.

e-mail: eupjilom@se.ehu.es.

(2) Dpto. Ec. Cuantitativa. Univ. de Oviedo. Spain.

e-mail:vrodri@.econo.uniovi.es.

Abstract:

In this paper we propose a method to solve a linear goal-programming problem whose parameters are crisp and where both the constraints and the achievement of goals are flexible.

Many Decision-Makers prefer to follow a satisfaction criterion rather than an optimization one; the satisfaction criterion leads to the concept of goal. When attributes, goals or relationships in a problem's formulation cannot be stated with precision, we work in fuzzy goal programming.

Also, the Decision Maker usually offers information that permits us to establish suitable values, in fuzzy terms, of the degree in which the goals and constraints are reached; then, we can construct an aggregate function of them giving a different weight to each, that will reflect DM's preferences.

Without distinction between goals and constraints, we will accept that a solution may verify each one with a certain degree of achievement and the membership function of each fuzzy set describing them represents this degree. Then, we propose as problem solution the decision vectors x that maximize a global measure for the degree of achievement of goals and constraints.

Using linear membership functions and aggregate function as the weighted mean, the initial problem was converted into a new one, monoobjective and lineal, that we solve in an interactive way. Our proposal will be illustrated by an example.

Keywords: Multiobjective Programming, Decision Making, Fuzzy Programming.

1. Introduction

Decision-Makers (DM) usually consider criteria of a diverse nature in their decision process and in general some of them clash. Then it is possible to describe a lot of real decision problems through multiobjective programming models and sometimes it is necessary to formulate them with elements of imprecision or uncertainty.

The simultaneous optimization of all objectives is usually impossible, so the Decision-Maker should be willing to make the attainment of objectives and the satisfaction of constraints flexible. Therefore, it is reasonable to construct a model reflecting imprecise data or flexibility in terms of fuzzy sets and a lot of fuzzy approaches to multiobjective programming have been developed.

Many Decision-Makers prefer to follow a satisfaction criterion rather than an optimization one; the satisfaction criterion leads to the concept of goal. Goal programming (GP) is the method that expresses this kind of approach to the problem and GP has been proven to be one of the most powerful methods to solve multiobjective programming problems. When attributes, goals or relationships in a problem's formulation cannot be stated with precision, we work in fuzzy goal programming.

The fuzzy programming approach to multiobjective programming problems was first introduced by Zimmerman [14] and further developed by other authors: i.e. [2, 6, 12]. It is possible also to find in literature diverse formulation of GP models reflecting imprecision in problem formulation, see [1, 4, 5, 6, 8, 9, 10, 13].

The first step in the formulation of a general GP model is to establish a set of target values i.e., the achievement level desired for each attribute considered in the problem situation, which transforms the objective functions into goals. Usually the DM is the one who provides those numerical values in order to set an acceptable level of achievement for any of the attributes considered. Then, deviations not desired with respect to those values must be minimized.

In this paper we propose a method to solve a linear goal-programming problem whose parameters are crisp and where both the constraints and the achievement of goals are flexible, i.e. it is accepted that they may be unfulfilled in some way.

2. Flexible MOLP

A classic model of the Multi-Objective Linear Programming (MOLP) can be presented as the following system:

$$\begin{aligned} & \text{maximize} \left[c_1 x, c_2 x, \ldots, c_k x \right] \\ & \text{subject to } a_i x \leq b_i \qquad i = 1, 2, \ldots, m \\ & \qquad x \geq 0 \end{aligned} \tag{1}$$

where $c_j, a_i, x \in R^n$, $b_i \in R$.

To convert problem (1) into a GP one, the Decision-Maker (DM) is requested to fix precise aspiration levels for each objective. But the solution obtained through a classical GP approach may deviate excessively from some of proposed targets, or it may excessively violate some constraints, so it could be unacceptable to the Decision-Maker.

In a flexible approach to the GP problem, the Decision-Maker initially, besides the aspiration level, provides the maximum deviation that he is willing to accept for each one of them, so that the goals and the restrictions become flexible.

This approach better represents real situations in which DM is not able to exactly establish the target value associated with each objective and he can only say that $c_j x$ should be *"essentially greater than or equal to target g_j"* or *"approximately equal to h_j"*, or $a_i x$ should be *"essentially smaller than or equal to b_i"*.

From now on, we will not distinguish between goals and constraints and we will accept that a solution of the problem may verify each one with a degree of achievement; then model (1) can be written as follows [15]:

$$
\begin{aligned}
&\textit{Find } x \\
&\text{s.t. } c_i x \stackrel{\sim}{\geq} g_i \qquad i = 1,...,q \\
&\quad\ \ c_i x \cong h_i \qquad i = q+1,...,k \\
&\quad\ \ a_i x \stackrel{\sim}{\leq} b_i \qquad i = 1,...,m \\
&\quad\ \ x \geq 0
\end{aligned}
\tag{2}
$$

where symbols $\stackrel{\sim}{\geq}, \stackrel{\sim}{\leq}, \cong$ indicate that the inequalities or equalities are flexible. They may be described by fuzzy sets whose membership function, $\alpha_i = \mu_i(x)$, represents the degree in which each relationship is attained.

To solve (2) is to find a solution x^* that maximizes a global measure $F(\alpha_1, \alpha_2, ..., \alpha_{k+m})$ of the degree of fulfillment of constraints [13]. But all constraints may not be considered of equal importance. The most simple aggregation function that considers the different importance of constraints is the weighted mean: $F(\alpha_1, \alpha_2, ..., \alpha_{k+m}) = \sum_i w_i \alpha_i$, where the weighted vector w is defined as $w_i \geq 0$ and $\sum_i w_i = 1$.

Then the model (2) can be written as follows:

$$
\begin{aligned}
&\text{Max } F(\alpha_1, \alpha_2, ..., \alpha_{k+m}) = w_1 \alpha_1 + w_2 \alpha_2 + ... + w_{k+m} \alpha_{k+m} \\
&\text{s.t. } \mu_i(x) = \alpha_i \\
&\quad\ \ 0 < \alpha_i \leq 1 \quad \sum_i w_i = 1 \quad i = 1,2,...,k+m \\
&\quad\ \ x \geq 0 \quad w_i \geq 0
\end{aligned}
\tag{3}
$$

In order to define the membership function $\mu_i(x)$ for the *i-th* inequality due to goals or constraints, we will have to know the tolerance margin with respect to the right-hand side that DM is willing to accept.

So $\mu_i(x)$ should be 0 if the *i-th* constraint is strongly unfulfilled, and 1 if it is completely satisfied. Then, for flexible inequalities of type $\widetilde{\geq}$, $\mu_i(x)$ should increase monotonously from 0 to 1 over the tolerance interval, and for inequalities of type $\widetilde{\leq}$, $\mu_i(x)$ should decrease monotonously from 1 to 0 over the same interval.

Then, if we suppose that membership function $\mu_i(x)$ is linear, we can write:

For flexible inequalities of type $\widetilde{\geq}$ (see fig. 1):

$$\alpha_i = \mu_i(x) = \begin{cases} 1 & \text{if } c_i x \geq g_i \\ 1 - \dfrac{g_i - c_i x}{d_i} & \text{if } g_i - d_i \leq c_i x < g_i \\ 0 & \text{if } c_i x < g_i - d_i \end{cases} \tag{4}$$

where tolerance margin is $d_i \geq 0$

For flexible inequalities of type $\widetilde{\leq}$ (see fig. 2):

$$\alpha_i = \mu_i(x) = \begin{cases} 1 & \text{if } a_i x \leq b_i \\ 1 - \dfrac{a_i x - b_i}{t_i} & \text{if } b_i < a_i x \leq b_i + t_i \\ 0 & \text{if } a_i x < b_i + t_i \end{cases} \tag{5}$$

where tolerance margin is represented by $t_i \geq 0$

For flexible equalities $\cong$ (see fig. 3), representing $d_i \geq 0$ and $t_i \geq 0$ one for each tolerance margins, we have:

$$\alpha_i = \mu_i(x) = \begin{cases} 0 & \text{if } c_i x < h_i - d_i \\ 1 - \dfrac{h_i - c_i x}{d_i} & \text{if } h_i - d_i \leq c_i x < h_i \\ 1 - \dfrac{c_i x - h_i}{t_i} & \text{if } g_i \leq c_i x \leq h_i + t_i \\ 0 & \text{if } c_i x > h_i + t_i \end{cases} \tag{6}$$

3. Flexible goal programming: a solution approach

To solve the model (3) we observe that:
In case of inequalities $\widetilde{\geq}$, from eq. (4) (see fig. 1):

$$\mu_i(x) = 1 \Leftrightarrow c_i x - p_i = g_i, \text{ where } p_i \geq 0$$
$$\mu_i(x) = \alpha_i \in (0,1] \Leftrightarrow c_i x + n_i = g_i, \text{ where } n_i = (1 - \alpha_i) d_i \qquad (7)$$
$$\mu_i(x) = 0 \Leftrightarrow n_i \geq d_i \Leftrightarrow c_i x + d_i + r_i = g_i, \text{ where } r_i \geq 0$$

where $n_i = g_i - c_i x > 0$ is the target negative deviation and $p_i = c_i x - g_i \geq 0$ is the target positive deviation and r_i is the amount by which the constraint is strongly unfulfilled, i.e. $c_i x$ is out of the tolerance interval.

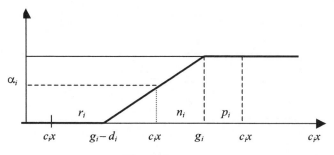

Figure 1.

In the same way, if inequalities are $\widetilde{\leq}$, from eq. (5) (see fig. 2):

$$\mu_i(x) = 1 \Leftrightarrow a_i x + n_i = b_i, \text{ where } n_i \geq 0$$
$$\mu_i(x) = \alpha_i \in (0,1] \Leftrightarrow a_i x - p_i = b_i, \text{ where } p_i = (1 - \alpha_i) t_i \qquad (8)$$
$$\mu_i(x) = 0 \Leftrightarrow p_i \geq t_i \Leftrightarrow a_i x - t_i - q_i = b_i, \text{ where } q_i \geq 0$$

where n_i, p_i are negative and positive deviation of targets. And q_i is the amount by which the constraint is strongly violated.

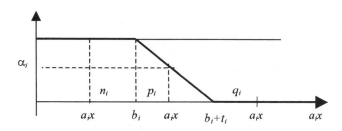

Figure 2.

Similarly for flexible equalities $\cong$ (see fig. 3):

$$\mu_i(x) = \alpha_i \in (0,1] \Leftrightarrow \begin{cases} c_i x + n_i = g_i, \text{ where } n_i = (1-\alpha_i)d_i \\ or \\ a_i x - p_i = b_i, \text{ where } p_i = (1-\alpha_i)t_i \end{cases}$$

$$\mu_i(x) = 0 \Leftrightarrow \begin{cases} n_i \geq d_i \Leftrightarrow c_i x + d_i + r_i = g_i, \text{ where } r_i \geq 0 \\ or \\ p_i \geq t_i \Leftrightarrow a_i x - t_i - q_i = b_i, \text{ where } q_i \geq 0 \end{cases}$$

(9)

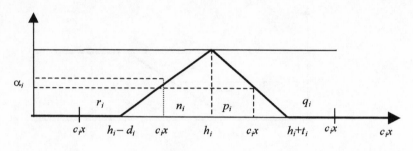

Figure 3.

According to the above considerations, we can write the model (3) as follows:

$$\text{Max } w_1\left(1-\frac{n_1}{d_1}\right)+...+w_q\left(1-\frac{n_q}{d_q}\right)+w_{q+1}\left(1-\frac{n_{q+1}}{d_{q+1}}-\frac{p_{q+1}}{t_{q+1}}\right)+...+w_k\left(1-\frac{n_k}{d_k}-\frac{p_k}{t_k}\right)+$$

$$+w_{k+1}\left(1-\frac{p_{k+1}}{t_{k+1}}\right)+...+w_m\left(1-\frac{p_m}{t_m}\right)$$

s.t.
$$\begin{array}{ll} c_i x + n_i - p_i = g_i & i = 1,...,q \\ c_i x + n_i - p_i = h_i & i = q+1,...,k \\ a_i x + n_i - p_i = b_i & i = k+1,...,m \\ n_i \leq d_i & i = 1,...,k \\ p_i \leq t_i & i = q+1,...,m \\ x \geq 0, p_i \geq 0, q_i \geq 0 \end{array}$$

(10)

Which is equivalent to the next formulation:

$$\text{Min} \quad w_1 \frac{n_1}{d_1} + \ldots + w_q \frac{n_q}{d_q} + w_{q+1}\left(\frac{n_{q+1}}{d_{q+1}} + \frac{p_{q+1}}{t_{q+1}}\right) + \ldots + w_k\left(\frac{n_k}{d_k} - \frac{p_k}{t_k}\right) +$$

$$+ w_{k+1}\frac{p_{k+1}}{t_{k+1}} + \ldots + w_m \frac{p_m}{t_m} \tag{11}$$

With the same feasible set as model (10).

Observe that we have transformed the GP problem (2), into a flexible one, whose objective function expresses the DM's satisfaction function [7,8] according to the deviation values n_i, p_i and the tolerance margins d_i, and t_i.

The feasible set of problem (10) could be the empty set. It means that DM's requirements have been excessive, i.e. DM has suggested a rigid maximum deviation of targets.

Using LINDO as a problem solver it is possible, from its unfeasibility report, to know what the relationships are on the feasible set that may have been unfulfilled. For simplicity, if we suppose that they are the first and the last ($i = 1$ and $i = m$), that have been described in the third line of eqs. (7), (8), or (9), besides maximizing the total measure of fulfillment of constraints $F(\alpha_1, \alpha_2, \ldots, \alpha_{k+m})$, we have to minimize the excess over the tolerance interval for constraints 1 and m. Then we rewrite model (11) as the following bi-objective program:

$$\text{Min} \quad w_1 \frac{n_1}{d_1} + \ldots + w_q \frac{n_q}{d_q} + w_{q+1}\left(\frac{n_{q+1}}{d_{q+1}} + \frac{p_{q+1}}{t_{q+1}}\right) + \ldots + w_k\left(\frac{n_k}{d_k} - \frac{p_k}{t_k}\right) +$$

$$+ w_{k+1}\frac{p_{k+1}}{t_{k+1}} + \ldots + w_m \frac{p_m}{t_m}$$

$$\text{Min} \quad \frac{1}{g_1} r_1 + \frac{1}{b_m} q_m$$

$$
\begin{aligned}
\text{s.t.} \quad & c_1 x + n_1 + r_1 - p_1 = g_1 \\
& c_i x + n_i - p_i = g_i & & i = 2,\ldots,q \\
& c_i x + n_i - p_i = h_i & & i = q+1,\ldots,k \\
& a_i x + n_i - p_i = b_i & & i = k+1,\ldots,m-1 \\
& a_m x + n_i - p_i - q_m = b_m \\
& n_1 = d_1 \\
& n_i \le d_i & & i = 2,\ldots,k \\
& p_i \le t_i & & i = q+1,\ldots,m-1 \\
& p_m = t_m \\
& x \ge 0, \, p_i \ge 0, q_i \ge 0
\end{aligned}
\tag{12}
$$

Where r_1 and q_m are the amounts by which constraints 1 and m are strongly unfulfilled (see eqs. (7) and (8)).
Our proposal will be illustrated by an example.

4. An illustrative example

Company C manufactures two products P_1 and P_2, using three different materials M_1, M_2 and M_3. The company knows that to produce 1 ton of product P_1 requires 2 tons of material M_1, 4 tons of M_2 and 10 tons of M_3, while to produce 1 ton of P_2 requires 5 tons of M_1, 1 tons of M_2 and 5 tons of M_3. The total amount of available materials is limited to 20 tons of M_1, 16 tons of M_2, and 45 tons of M_3. Each ton of P_1 requires 15 hours of labor and each ton of P_2 requires 5 hours of labor and the whole labor capacity of the company is 80 hours. The production capacity is 4 tons for P_1 and 5 tons for P_2. And, owing to market necessities, it must produce at least 2 tons of P_1 and 2 tons of P_2. It also knows that product P_1 yields a profit of 24 monetary units, while P_2 yields 8 monetary units. But unfortunately, it is pointed out that product P1 yields 3 units of pollution per ton and product P_2 yields 1 unit of pollution per ton. The company is trying to figure out how many units of products P_1 and P_2 should be produced to maximize the total profit and to minimize the amount of pollution.
This problem can be formulated as the following bi-objective linear programming problem:

$$\text{maximize} \quad 24x_1 + 8x_2$$
$$\text{minimize} \quad 3x_1 + x_2$$
$$\text{subject to} \quad 2x_1 + 5x_2 \leq 20$$
$$4x_1 + x_2 \leq 16$$
$$10x_1 + 5x_2 \leq 45$$
$$15x_1 + 5x_2 \leq 80 \quad\quad\quad (13)$$
$$x_1 \leq 4$$
$$x_2 \leq 5$$
$$x_1 \geq 2$$
$$x_2 \geq 2$$
$$x_1 \geq 0, x_2 \geq 0$$

To solve such conflicting linear objective functions simultaneously, we assume that the decision-maker is able to establish aspiration levels for the objective functions and that some small slack or surplus might be acceptable in the constraints:

To achieve at least 130 monetary units of total profit, with a tolerance interval of 20 m.u.

To keep the pollution level below 12 units with a tolerance interval of 2 units.

The tolerance intervals for the total availability of materials M_1, M_2 and M_3 are respectively 4, 3, and 10 tons.

The labor capacity can, at most, increase by 8 hours or decrease by 8 hours.

The production capacity for products P_1 and P_2 can grow at most by 1 ton or by 2 tons respectively.

The market necessities could decrease, at most, by 0.5 tons.

From now on we will not distinguish between objectives and constraints, and we will only speak of goals. Also we may accept that the attainment of goals is flexible. Then model (13) is written as follows (see eq. (2))

Find x

s.t.
$$24x_1 + 8x_2 \gtrsim 130 \quad \text{(total profit)}$$
$$3x_1 + x_2 \lesssim 12 \quad \text{(environmental impact)}$$
$$\left.\begin{array}{l} 2x_1 + 5x_2 \lesssim 20 \\ 4x_1 + x_2 \lesssim 16 \\ 10x_1 + 5x_2 \lesssim 45 \end{array}\right\} \quad \text{(materials)}$$
$$15x_1 + 5x_2 \cong 80 \quad \text{(employment)}$$
$$\left.\begin{array}{l} x_1 \lesssim 4 \\ x_2 \lesssim 5 \end{array}\right\} \quad \text{(production capacities)}$$
$$\left.\begin{array}{l} x_1 \gtrsim 2 \\ x_2 \gtrsim 2 \end{array}\right\} \quad \text{(market necessities)}$$
$$x_1 \geq 0, x_2 \geq 0$$

(14)

Using eq. (4), (5) and (6) we define the corresponding fuzzy sets that represent the flexible relationship and whose membership function $\alpha_i = \mu_i(x)$ represent the degree in which each goal is attained.

Now we ask the decision-maker if the goals have different importance. We suppose that he gives us the following information:
- First group of goals, production capacities: 26 %
- Second group of goals, environmental impact: 23%
- Third group of goals, total profit 20%.
- Fourth group of goals, employment: 17%.
- Fifth group of goals, materials: 9%
- Sixth group of goals, market necessities: 6%

Also we assume that the goals which are in the same group have the same weight. Then we can write model (13) as follows (see eq. (3)):

$$\text{Max} \quad F(\alpha_1, \alpha_2, \ldots, \alpha_{10}) = 0.2\alpha_1 + 0.23\alpha_2 + 0.09\left(\frac{1}{3}\alpha_3 + \frac{1}{3}\alpha_4 + \frac{1}{3}\alpha_5\right) +$$

$$+ 0.17\alpha_6 + 0.26\left(\frac{1}{2}\alpha_7 + \frac{1}{2}\alpha_8\right) + 0.06\left(\frac{1}{2}\alpha_9 + \frac{1}{2}\alpha_{10}\right) \tag{15}$$

s.t.

$$\mu_i(x) = \alpha_i$$
$$0 < \alpha_i \leq 1 \qquad i = 1, 2, \ldots, 10$$
$$x \geq 0$$

Below, according to model (11), we can reformulate the above problem as follows:

$$\text{Min} \quad 0.2\frac{n_1}{20} + 0.23\frac{p_2}{2} + 0.09\left(\frac{1}{3}\frac{p_3}{4} + \frac{1}{3}\frac{p_4}{3} + \frac{1}{3}\frac{p_5}{10}\right) + 0.17\left(\frac{n_6}{8} + \frac{p_6}{8}\right) +$$

$$+ 0.26\left(\frac{1}{2}\frac{p_7}{0.5} + \frac{1}{2}\frac{p_8}{1}\right) + 0.06\left(\frac{1}{2}\frac{n_9}{0.5} + \frac{1}{2}\frac{n_{10}}{0.5}\right)$$

s.t.

$24x1 + 8x2 + n1 - p1 = 130$

$3x1 + x2 + n2 - p2 = 12$

$2x1 + 5x2 + n3 - p3 = 20$

$4x1 + x2 + n4 - p4 = 16$

$10x1 + 5x2 + n5 - p5 = 45$

$15x1 + 5x2 + n6 - p6 = 80 \tag{16}$

$x1 + n7 - p7 = 3.5$

$x2 + n8 - p8 = 3$

$x1 + n9 - p9 = 2$

$x2 + n10 - p10 = 2$

$n1 < 20, \ p2 < 2, \ p3 < 4, \ p4 < 3, \ p5 < 10, \ n6 < 8, \ p6 < 8,$

$p7 < 0.5, \ p8 < 1, \ n9 < 0.5, \ n10 < 0.5,$

$x_1, x_2 \geq 0, \ n_i, p_i \geq 0 \quad i = 1, 2, \ldots, 10$

This problem is infeasible. If we use LINDO as solver, we find that it is sufficient to correct one of the following constraints:

3) $-p2 + 3x1 + x2 + n2 = 12$

7) $n6 - p6 + 15x1 + 5x2 = 80$

3) $p2 <= 2$

7) $n5 <= 8$

According to this result, to make the problem feasible the decision-maker should increase the tolerance margins of pollution and labor hours. Then we reformulate problem (13) as a bi-objective problem in which we assume that the tolerance margins of pollution and labor hours can be exceeded:

$$\text{Min } 0.2\frac{n_1}{20} + 0.23\frac{p_2}{2} + 0.09\left(\frac{1}{3}\frac{p_3}{4} + \frac{1}{3}\frac{p_4}{3} + \frac{1}{3}\frac{p_5}{10}\right) + 0.17\left(\frac{n_6}{8} + \frac{p_6}{8}\right) +$$

$$+ 0.26\left(\frac{1}{2}\frac{p_7}{0.5} + \frac{1}{2}\frac{p_8}{1}\right) + 0.06\left(\frac{1}{2}\frac{n_9}{0.5} + \frac{1}{2}\frac{n_{10}}{0.5}\right)$$

$$\text{Min } \frac{q_2}{12} + \frac{r_6}{80}$$

s.t.

$$24x_1 + 8x_2 + n_1 - p_1 = 130 \tag{17}$$
$$3x_1 + x_2 + n_2 - p_2 - q_2 = 12$$
$$2x_1 + 5x_2 + n_3 - p_3 = 20$$
$$4x_1 + x_2 + n_4 - p_4 = 16$$
$$10x_1 + 5x_2 + n_5 - p_5 = 45$$
$$15x_1 + 5x_2 + n_6 + r_6 - p_6 = 80$$
$$x_1 + n_7 - p_7 = 3.5$$
$$x_2 + n_8 - p_8 = 3$$
$$x_1 + n_9 - p_9 = 2$$
$$x_2 + n_{10} - p_{10} = 2$$

$n_1 < 20$, $p_2 = 2$, $p_3 < 4$, $p_4 < 3$, $p_5 < 10$, $n_6 = 8$, $p_6 < 8$, $p_7 < 0.5$, $p_8 < 1$, $n_9 < 0.5$, $n_{10} < 0.5$
$x_1, x_2 \geq 0$, $q_2, r_6 \geq 0$, $n_i, p_i \geq 0$ $i = 1,2,\ldots,10$

Where we have done $p_2 = 2$, and $n_6 = 8$, and we have included two new non-desirable deviation variables: q_2 and r_6, that represent the amount by which the tolerance margins of pollution and employment are exceeded (see eqs. (7) and (8)). By means of the second objective function we try to minimize this excess. To solve problem (17) we formulate the following mono-objective program:

$$\text{Min } 0.2\frac{n_1}{20} + 0.23\frac{p_2}{2} + 0.09\left(\frac{1}{3}\frac{p_3}{4} + \frac{1}{3}\frac{p_4}{3} + \frac{1}{3}\frac{p_5}{10}\right) + 0.17\left(\frac{n_6}{8} + \frac{p_6}{8}\right) +$$

$$+ 0.26\left(\frac{1}{2}\frac{p_7}{0.5} + \frac{1}{2}\frac{p_8}{1}\right) + 0.06\left(\frac{1}{2}\frac{n_9}{0.5} + \frac{1}{2}\frac{n_{10}}{0.5}\right) + \frac{q_2}{12} + \frac{r_6}{80} \tag{18}$$

With the same feasible set of model (17)

Table 1 shows the optimal solution for model (18). Let us compare our approach with the classic weighted goal-programming method: to solve our initial problem (13) through this method, we write it as follows:

$$\text{Min } 0.2\frac{n_1}{130} + 0.23\frac{p_2}{12} + 0.09\left(\frac{1}{3}\frac{p_3}{20} + \frac{1}{3}\frac{p_4}{16} + \frac{1}{3}\frac{p_5}{45}\right) + 0.17\left(\frac{n_6}{80} + \frac{p_6}{80}\right) +$$

$$+ 0.26\left(\frac{1}{2}\frac{p_7}{3.5} + \frac{1}{2}\frac{p_8}{3}\right) + 0.06\left(\frac{1}{2}\frac{n_9}{2} + \frac{1}{2}\frac{n_{10}}{2}\right)$$

s.t.

$$24x1+8x2+n1-p1=130 \qquad\qquad (19)$$
$$3x1+x2+n2-p2=12$$
$$2x1+5x2+n3-p3=20$$
$$4x1+x2+n4-p4=16$$
$$10x1+5x2+n5-p5=45$$
$$15x1+5x2+n6-p6=80$$
$$x1+n7-p7=3.5$$
$$x2+n8-p8=3$$
$$x1+n9-p9=2$$
$$x2+n10-p10=2$$
$$x_1, x_2 \geq 0,\ n_i, p_i \geq 0 \quad i = 1,2,\ldots,10$$

Table 1 shows the optimal solution for model (19).

Table 1

VARIABLE	TOLERANCE INTERVAL	OPTIMAL SOLUTION OF OUR MODEL	OPTIMAL SOLUTION OF CLASSICAL MODEL
x_1		3.666667	3.500000
x_2		3.000000	2.000000
n_1	20	18.000000	30.000000
$p_2(+q_2)$	2	2.000000	0.500000
p_3	4	2.333333	0.000000
p_4	3	1.666667	0.000000
p_5	10	6.666667	0.000000
$n_6(+r_6)$	8	10.000000	17.500000
p_6	8	0.000000	0.000000
p_7	0.5	0.166667	0.000000
p_8	1	0.000000	0.000000
n_9	0.5	0.000000	0.000000
n_{10}	0.5	0.000000	0.000000
p_1	∞	0.000000	0.000000
n_2	∞	0.000000	0.000000
n_3	∞	0.000000	3.000000
n_4	∞	0.000000	0.000000
n_5	∞	0.000000	0.000000
n_7	∞	0.000000	0.000000
n_8	∞	0.000000	1.000000
p_9	∞	1.666667	1.500000
p_{10}	∞	1.000000	0.000000

Let us compare the two optimal solutions above. Table 1 shows that our approach (models (17), (18)) is more balanced than the classic method (model (19)) regarding the aspiration levels of the decision-maker. We can see that in this model (19) more goals are fully achieved but the tolerance margin of profit and employment has been greatly exceeded. This could be unacceptable to the decision-maker. However with our method only the tolerance margin of employment is surpassed -by just two hours.

5. Summary and conclusions

In classic goal programming, the DM has to provide crisp goals and he/she cannot express a satisfaction degree concerning observed target deviations. In this paper we have proposed a new approach of flexible GP: by means of the fuzzy logic we have tried to lessen both the drawbacks.

We have constructed a problem formulation taking into account not only goal achievements but also minimizing the amounts by which constraints may be strongly unfulfilled. This usually expresses the DM's preferences better than the classical approach.

The flexible relationships in a GP problem are described by fuzzy sets whose membership function, $\alpha_i = \mu_i(x)$, represents the degree in which each relationship is attained. To obtain a linear program, we have used the simplest shapes of membership function i.e. linear shapes, which are valid for most practical applications.

Our solution maximizes a global measure for the degrees of achievement of goals. We have used the weighted mean, although more complex aggregation functions may also be considered.

The solution obtained through our approach is more balanced than the classic one with regard to the achievement of the aspiration levels of objective functions because, in general, it is preferable to satisfy fewer goals in total, with only minimum deviations in those which are not satisfied.

References

[1] Arenas, M.M., Bilbao, A., Rodriguez, M. V., Jiménez, M. (1996): "A Fuzzy Solution Approach to a Fuzzy Linear Goal Programming Problem", in Günter Fandel & Tomas Gal (Eds.), *Multiple Criteria Decision Making*, Lecture Notes in Economics and Mathematical Systems 448, pp.255-264, Springer, New York.

[2] Arenas, M.M., Bilbao, A., Rodriguez, M. V., Jiménez, M. (1998): "Fuzzy Parameters multiobjective linear programming problem: Solution analysis", in Theo Stewart y Rob van den Honert (Eds.), *Trends in Multicriteria Decision Making* , Lecture Notes in Economics and Mathematical Systems 465, pp. 128-137, Springer, New York.

[3] Charnes, A. and Cooper, W.W. (1997): "Goal programming and multiple objective optimisation", *European Journal of Operational Research*, 1 (1), pp. 39-54.

[4] Hannan, E. L. (1981): "Linear Programming with Multiple Fuzzy Goals", *Fuzzy Sets and Systems* 6, pp. 235-248.

[5] Jones, D.F. and Tamiz, M. (1995): "Expanding the flexibility of goal programming via preference modelling techniques", *Omega* 23 (1), pp. 41-48.

[6] Lai, Y.J. and Hwang, C.L. (1993): *Multi-Objective fuzzy Mathematical Programming: Theory and Applications*, Lecture Notes in Economics and Mathematical Systems 404, Springer, Berlín.

[7] Martel, J.-M. and Aouni, B. (1990): "Incorporating the Decision Maker's Preferences in the Goal Programming Model". *Journal of Operational Research Society* 41(12), pp. 1121-1132.

[8] Martel, J.-M. and Aouni, B. (1998): "Diverse Imprecise Goal Programming Model Formulations". *Journal of Global Optimization* 12, pp. 127-138.

[9] Narashimhan, R. (1980): "Goal programming in fuzzy environment". *Decision Sciences* 11, pp. 325-336.

[10] Ramik, J. (2000): "Fuzzy goals and fuzzy alternatives in goal programming problem". *Fuzzy Sets and Systems* 111, pp. 81-86.

[11] Sakawa, M. (1993): "Fuzzy sets and interactive multiobjective optimisation". *Applied Information Technology Series*, Plenum Press, New York.

[12] Tanaka, H.; Asai, K. (1984): "Fuzzy linear programming problems with fuzzy numbers". *Fuzzy Sets and Systems* 13, pp. 1-10.

[13] Torra I Reventós, V. (1998): "On considering constraints of different importance in fuzzy constraints satisfaction problems". *International Journal of Uncertainty, Fuzziness and Knowledge-Based Systems*. Vol. 6, N° 5, pp. 489-481.

[14] Zimmermann, H.J. (1978): "Fuzzy programming and linear programming with several objective functions", *Fuzzy sets and systems* 1 (1), pp. 45-55.

[15] Zimmermann, H.J. (1991): *Fuzzy Sets. Theory and Its Applications*. Kubler Academic Publishers, Boston.

Trade-offs - A Lost Dimension in Multiple Criteria Decision Making

Ignacy Kaliszewski *

1   Introduction

The majority of multiple criteria decision making (MCDM) algorithms are based on the following scheme:

> the outcomes (vectors of values of criteria) of alternatives are compared and on that base the decision maker (DM) selects an alternative to become her best choice.

An alternative approach is to base selection process on a measure of the potential of an alternative to become the best choice, where the potential of the alternative is represented by its trade-offs.

The concept of trade-off has been present in MCDM from the very beginning of the field. In course of time more and more stress has been put on computational tractability of multiple criteria decision making and gradually trade-off, which calculations can be computer intensive, has earned a status of an interesting theoretical construct but of little practical importance. Only recently methods to assess values of trade-offs at negligible computational cost have been proposed. This opens a way to revive the ideas of exploiting this notion in MCDM algorithms.

The presentation sumarizes research efforts in trade-off assessments and trade-off calculations, as well as in reviving the trade-off concept in MCDM.

2   Trade-offs and MCDM

When we nowadays speak about MCDM we almost exclusively refer to interactive methods. In interactive methods selection of alternatives is organised step-wise with DM interactions. The rationale behind interactive decision making is to provide means to overcome two key problems in MCDM:

---

*Systems Research Institute, Polish Academy of Sciences, ul. Newelska 6, 01-447 Warszawa, Poland, kaliszew@ibspan.waw.pl.

- the DM's value function is usually not known,

- the DM's preferences may change or evolve as interactive decision process progresses.

In interactive decision making the DM evaluates a sequence of feasible alternatives to a decision problem. The intent is that each alternative is an improvement (has a better evaluation) over the previous one. To fulfil this aim at each step the DM interacts with a model of the problem, directing herself by previous judgments and decisions as well as her current preferences.

Interactive decision making can be viewed then as a walk around the set of feasible alternatives. Along the walk the DM stops at certain outcomes to analyze and evaluate. The walk ends when the DM makes her final choice of the most preferable alternative. In the simplest case the walk can be random (with no monotonous improvements of alternative evaluations guaranteed), otherwise it can be structured according to any of existing interactive MCDM methods.

In a natural way the DM tends to confine her walk to efficient alternatives. Passing from one efficient alternative to another efficient alternative she trades on values of outcome components (criteria) since, by the principle of efficiency, any gain in one component is compensated by a loss in at least one other component. At any alternative the DM may decide to continue her walk or terminate. In the majority of interactive decision making methods the DM makes her decisions on the base of values of outcome components (criteria). She can also decide on the base of the maximal relative change of values of outcome components as she moves (or considers moving) from an alternative to an alternative. Those relative changes are called, generically, trade-offs.

If DM knows in advance which alternative she goes next (or she likes to go next), related trade-offs can be easily calculated. At the extreme, if alternatives are explicitly given by a list, all trade-offs are calculable at any time. In general, however, the DM may want to know trade-offs for each potential move prior to specifying the next alternative in her walk. In this presentation we concentrate ourselves on the problem of determining trade-offs in advance.

3 Problem Definition and Basic Notions

We shall refer in the sequel to the following MCDM underlying model:

$$"\max" f(x) \text{ s.t. } x \in X_0 \subseteq X, \tag{1}$$

where $f : X \to R^k$, $k \geq 2$, $f = (f_1, f_2, ..., f_k)$, is a vector of criteria $f_i : X \to R$, X_0 is the set of feasible alternatives (decisions, solutions), and "max" stands for the operator of determining all efficient alternatives of X_0.

In what follows we shall be interested in properties of elements $f(x)$ (*outcomes*) of the set $f(X_0)$ (*the outcome set*) and therefore we shall identify alternatives with their outcomes using the notation $y = f(x)$ and $f(X_0) = Z$. Consequently, all the discussion and result presentation will be in terms of outcomes y.

Let $\bar{y} \in Z$. The following are commonly accepted definitions of various types of efficiency.

An outcome $\bar{y} \in Z$ is:

weakly efficient if there is no y, $y \in Z$, such that $y_i > \bar{y}_i$, $i = 1, ..., k$,

efficient if $y_i \geq \bar{y}_i$, $i = 1, ..., k$, $y \in Z$, implies $y = \bar{y}$,

properly efficient if it is efficient and there exists a finite number $M > 0$ such that for each i we have

$$\frac{y_i - \bar{y}_i}{\bar{y}_j - y_j} \leq M$$

for some j such that $y_j < \bar{y}_j$, whenever $y \in Z$ and $y_i > \bar{y}_i$.

4 Trade-off Definition

Before defining trade-offs, let us observe that in MCDM the notion of trade-off is confusingly applied to two different types of objects, namely to value functions and to outcome sets. Consequently, in the first case trade-off is defined as some specific (usually local) properties of the explicit or implicit value function whereas in the second case as a limit of relative changes in criteria when moving away from a given outcome along feasible directions. In this paper we shall exploit the concept of trade-off understood in the latter sense.

Let $\bar{y} \in Z$, $Z \subseteq \mathcal{R}^k$. For $i = 1, ..., k$, we denote:

$$Z_i^<(\bar{y}) = \{y \in Z \mid y_i < \bar{y}_i,\ y_l \geq \bar{y}_l,\ l = 1, ..., k,\ l \neq i\}.$$

Definition 1 *Let* $\bar{y} \in Z$. **Trade-off** $T_{ij}^G(\bar{y})$ *involving criteria* i *and* j, $i, j = 1, ..., k$, $i \neq j$, *is defined as*

$$\sup_{y \in Z_j^<(\bar{y})} \frac{y_i - \bar{y}_i}{\bar{y}_j - y_j}.$$

We adopt the convention that if $Z_j^<(\bar{y}) = \emptyset$, then $T_{ij}^G(\bar{y}) = -\infty$, $i = 1, ..., k$, $i \neq j$.

A simpler but less general construct is so called *point-to-point trade-off* which is defined as

$$\frac{y_i - \bar{y}_i}{\bar{y}_j - y_j},$$

where $y_i - \bar{y}_i \geq 0$, $\bar{y}_j - y_j > 0$.

Point-to-point is a meaningful concept for all cases in which perspective outcomes are either explicitly given or can be easily determined.

5 A Lost Dimension

There is no direct and easy way to calculate trade-offs as defined above. Efforts have been concentrated on calculating trade-offs for specific instances of the problem (1), namely for linear problems (with polyhedral outcome sets) and convex problems (problems where the outcome set Z is R_+^k-convex, i.e. the set $Z - R_+^k$ is convex, where R_+^k denotes the nonnegative orthant; convexity of Z clearly entails its R_+^k-convexity). Results obtained, mathematically involved and therefore of little appeal to MCDM practitioners, have not made as yet their way to interactive decision making algorithms. All this together makes that trade-offs - a powerful carrier of information on mutual relations among alternatives - has been left unexploited for long.

A revival of the idea to exploit trade-offs in interactive MCDM comes from the fact that recently simple and fully operational methods to calculate *assessments* of trade-offs have been proposed. The methods are based on the following argument.

The process of deriving efficient outcomes (and therefore also efficient alternatives) can be interpreted as supporting the outcome set Z by geometric constructs: hyperplanes (the hyperplane method) or displaced cones (the cone method).

The hyperplane method

The method relies on applying weights $\lambda_i > 0$, $i = 1, ..., k$, to criteria $f_i(x)$ and summing the products to get

$$\sum_{i=1}^{k} \lambda_i f_i(x), \tag{2}$$

which in the k-dimensional (criteria) space represents a hyperplane. To derive an efficient outcome the hyperplane is moved in the direction of increasing value of (2) (cf. Figure 1). An outcome which maximizes (2) (we assume the maximum exists) is (properly) efficient. In other words, at an efficient outcome the hyperplane (2) is tangent to Z for some $\lambda_i > 0$, $i = 1, ..., k$.

As will be seen in the next section, a hyperplane tangent to Z at an efficient y provides assesments of trade-offs at y. This observation has been

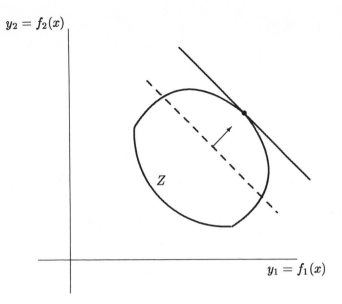

Figure 1

fully exploited in MCDM only recently. Moreover, if a tangent hyperplane is unique, it provides the exact values of trade-offs. On the other hand, if there is more than one hyperplane tangent Z at y, each tangent hyperplane provides trade-off assessments.

Supprisingly but quite logically, assesments of trade-offs are independent of y and depend only on the corresponding hyperplane: any efficient outcome derived with help of a given hyperplane has the same trade-off assesment. This opens a way for a method to derive only those outcomes for which trade-offs assesment are favourable by:

1. selecting hyperplanes which provide favourable trade-off assessments,

2. using those hyperplanes to derive efficient outcomes.

The cone method

The hyperplane approach to derive efficient outcomes is not a universal method. Its limitation comes from the following observation:

any (properly) efficient outcome is an element of a tangent hyperplane only if the outcome set Z is R_+^k-convex.

If Z is not R_+^k-convex, not all efficient outcomes can be derived by the hyperplane method. However,

1. any weakly efficient outcome y is an element of the displaced cone $\{y\} + R_+^k$,

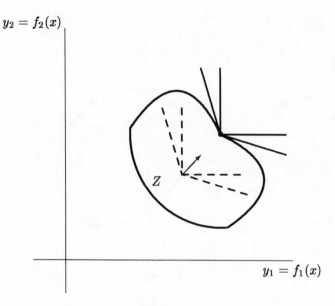

Figure 2

2. any properly efficient outcome y is an element of a displaced cone $\{y\}+C$, where $R_+^k \subseteq intC$ ($int()$ denotes *interior*) and C is a convex cone,

(cf. Figure 2).

These observations give rise to some results presented in the next section by which it is possible to derive only those outcomes for which trade-off assesments are favourable, in the same manner as when exploiting hyperplanes. The results are applicable to general MCDM underlying model (1) (R_+^k-convexity is not required).

As we shall see, with the hyperplane method and the cone method trade-off assessments come with efficient outcomes at no extra computational cost.

6   Assessing Trade-offs

In this section we present results which provide trade-off assessments **prior** to generating outcomes. In other words, by the presented results it is possible to generate outcomes which satisfy preimposed bounds on trade-offs.

Theorem 1 shows how to generate properly efficient outcomes by solving a problem which is a mathematical realization of the hyperplane method and Theorem 2 establishes trade-off assessments.

The problem (4) is equivalent to a computationally friendly formulation:

$$\min_{y \in Z} t$$
$$t \geq \lambda_i((y_i^* - y_i) + \rho e^k (y^* - y)), \ i = 1, ..., k.$$

All the problems in Theorem 3 - Theorem 10 can be reformulated in a similar manner .

Theorem 3 shows how to generate properly efficient outcomes by solving a problem which is a mathematical realization of the cone method. Theorem 4 repeats the result of Theorem 3 but provides more freedom in selecting parameters ρ. of the corresponding problem. The result of Theorem 5 establishes trade-off assessment for selected pairs of indices taken from the set I_1; trade-offs for pairs of indices with at least one index not in I_1 can take any values. Theorem 6 is a variant of Theorem 5 for $I_1 = I$.

Theorem 7 - Theorem 10 are equivalents of Theorem 3 - Theorem 6 with a different problem to be solved. The difference between problem (4) and problem (5), which both relate to so called Tchebycheff scalarization, at a glance are very similar and the practical difference between them is negligible as long as the parameters ρ. in the scalarization problems are treated merely as a technical factor. This situation changes when these parameters are interpreted as a valuable source of trade-off information. Observe that trade-off assessments for outcomes derived by solving problem (4) are independent of parameters λ., in contrast to assessments relating to problem (5).

Theorem 1 *Assume that Z is convex. An outcome $\bar{y} \in Z$ is properly efficient if and only if there exists a vector $\lambda > 0$ such that $\bar{y}$ solves the problem*

$$\max_{y \in Z} \sum_i \lambda_i y_i . \tag{3}$$

Theorem 2 *Let $\bar{y}$ solve problem (3). Then*

$$T_{ji}^G(\bar{y}) \leq \frac{\lambda_i}{\lambda_j}$$

for each $j, i = 1, ..., k$, $j \neq i$.

Let y^* be an element of $\mathcal{R}^k$ such that $Z \subset y^* - R_+^k$. Let $I = \{1, ..., k\}$ and let e^k denote k-dimensional vector whose all components are equal 1.
Let $I_1 \subseteq I$, $|I_1| \geq 2$, $I_2 = I \setminus I_1$.

Theorem 3 *An outcome $\bar{y} \in Z$ is properly efficient if and only if there exist $\lambda_i > 0$, $i \in I$, and $\rho > 0$, such that $\bar{y}$ solves*

$$\min_{y \in Z} \max_i \lambda_i((y_i^* - y_i) + \rho e^k(y^* - y)). \qquad (4)$$

Theorem 4 *An outcome $\bar{y} \in Z$ is properly efficient if and only if there exist $\lambda_i > 0$ and $\rho_i > 0$, $i \in I$, such that $\bar{y}$ solves problem (6), i.e. the problem*

$$\min_{y \in Z} \max_i \lambda_i((y_i^* - y_i) + \sum_{t \in I} \rho_t(y_t^* - y_t)). $$

Theorem 5 *An outcome $\bar{y} \in Z$ is weakly efficient and for each $i \in I_1$ and each $t \in I_1$, $i \neq t$, $T_{ti}^G(\bar{y})$ is bounded from above by a positive finite number if and only if there exist $\lambda_i > 0$, $i \in I$, and $\rho_i > 0$, $i \in I_1$, such that $\bar{y}$ solves*

$$\min_{y \in Z} \max[\max_{i \in I_1} \lambda_i((y_i^* - y_i) + \sum_{t \in I_1} \rho_t(y_t^* - y_t)), \ \max_{i \in I_2} \lambda_i(y_i^* - y_i)]. $$

Any solution to the above problem satisfies $T_{ti}^G(\bar{y}) \leq (1 + \rho_i)\rho_t^{-1}$, $i \in I_1$, $t \in I_1$, $t \neq i$.

With $I_1 = I$ Theorem 5 reduces to the following result.

Theorem 6 *Suppose $\bar{y}$ solves the following problem*

$$\min_{y \in Z} \max_i \lambda_i((y_i^* - y_i) + \sum_{t \in I} \rho_t(y_t^* - y_t)), $$

where $\lambda_i > 0$ and $\rho_i > 0$ for each i. Then,

$$T_{ti}^G(\bar{y}) \leq (1 + \rho_i)\rho_t^{-1} $$

for each $i, t \in I$, $i \neq t$.

Theorem 7 *An outcome $\bar{y} \in Z$ is properly efficient if and only if there exist $\lambda_i > 0$, $i \in I$, and $\rho > 0$, such that $\bar{y}$ solves*

$$\min_{y \in Z} \max_i \lambda_i(y_i^* - y_i) + \rho e^k(y^* - y). \qquad (5)$$

Theorem 8 *An outcome $\bar{y} \in Z$ is properly efficient if and only if there exist $\lambda_i > 0$ and $\rho_i > 0$, $i \in I$, such that $\bar{y}$ solves problem (10), i.e. the problem*

$$\min_{y \in Z} \max_i \lambda_i(y_i^* - y_i) + \sum_{t \in I} \rho_t(y_t^* - y_t).$$

Theorem 9 *An outcome $\bar{y} \in Z$ is weakly efficient and for each $i \in I_1$ and each $t \in I_1$, $i \neq t$, $T_{ti}^G(\bar{y})$ is bounded from above by a positive finite number if and only if there exist $\lambda_i > 0$, $i \in I$, and $\rho_i > 0$, $i \in I_1$, such that $\bar{y}$ solves*

$$\min_{y \in Z} \max[\max_{i \in I_1} \lambda_i(y_i^* - y_i) + \sum_{t \in I_1} \rho_t(y_t^* - y_t), \ \max_{i \in I_2} \lambda_i(y_i^* - y_i)].$$

Any solution to the above problem satisfies $T_{ti}^G(\bar{y}) \leq (\lambda_i + \rho_i)\rho_t^{-1}$, $i \in I_1$, $t \in I_1$, $t \neq i$.

With $I_1 = I$ Theorem 9 reduces to the following result.

Theorem 10 *Suppose $\bar{y}$ solves the following problem*

$$\min_{y \in Z} \max_i \lambda_i(y_i^* - y_i) + \sum_{t \in I} \rho_t(y_t^* - y_t),$$

where $\lambda_i > 0$ and $\rho_i > 0$ for each i. Then,

$$T_{ti}^G(\bar{y}) \leq (\lambda_i + \rho_i)\rho_t^{-1}$$

for each $i, t \in I$, $i \neq t$.

7   Trade-offs Revisited

With the results of Section 7 it is now technically possible to involve trade-off type of information into interactive decision making framework. At simplest, we can eliminate from the decision process all outcomes with excessive trade-offs by a versatile trade-off filtering method. We can propose even more active involvement of the trade-off concept into the decision process by giving the DM chance to express her preferences only in terms of trade-offs. The most interesting and promising approach seems to be to let the DM to express freely her preferences *both* in terms of values of outcome components (criteria) and trade-offs. Some efforts in the aforementioned directions have been already reported (c.f. the next section for references).

It must be stressed here that because of negligable computational effort required to derive trade-off assesments, involving trade-offs into decision making is a win-win strategy: it offers a new tool at virtually no cost.

8 An Annotated Bibligraphy

If an outcome set is convex, efficient outcomes can be derived by solving problem (3). This wisdom belongs to the folklore of MCDM and its origin can be perhaps attributed to the early days of mathematical programming (Kuhn,Tucker (1951). The most referenced paper on that subject is (Geoffrion (1968)).

If an outcome set is convex and smooth, trade-offs are provided by vectors normal to the outcome set (Kuhn,Tucker (1951)). If the outcome set is only convex, trade-offs are characterized by normal cones (Henig,Buchanan (1992), Halme (1991)).

In the general case, where convexity does not hold (as e.g. in the case of discrete programming), to derive efficient outcomes scalarizations based on the so called Tchebycheff norms (4) and (5) were proposed:

scalarization (4) - in Choo,Atkins (1983), Wierzbicki (1986), Kaliszewski (1987);

scalarization (5) - in Wierzbicki (1980,1990), Steuer,Choo (1983), Steuer (1986), Kaliszewski (1987,1994).

Trade-off assessment resulting from different forms of scalarizations as presented in the section 6 were proved:

Theorem 5 and Theorem 6 - in Kaliszewski, Michalowski (1995a,b),

Theorem 9, Theorem 10, Theorem 2 - in Kaliszewski (2000).

Trade-offs can be calculated directly which involves maximization of a hiperbolic function (cf. the definition of trade-off). An alternate approach is to calculate trade-offs by parametric programming methods (Kaliszewski (1993)).

The possibility to set bounds on trade-offs prior to generating the corresponding outcomes was exploited in interactive MCDM algorithms proposed in the following works: (Kaliszewski (1998, 2000)), (Kaliszewski,Michalowski (1999)).

The existence of relations between parameters ρ and weights λ, as shown by Theorem 3, has been exploited to bring a new dimension in MCDM algorithms of the Zionts-Wallenius type (Kaliszewski (1998,2000)).

An application of a decision making method based entirely on using trade-off information to portfolio selection was reported in Jog et al. (1999).

Point-to-point trade-offs are most often associated with the Zionts-Wallenius decision making algorithm (Zionts, Wallenius (1983)).

References

[1] Choo, E.U., Atkins, D.R. (1983), "Proper efficiency in nonconvex programming". *Mathematics of Operations Research*, 8, 467-470.

[2] Geoffrion, A.M. (1968), "Proper efficiency and the theory of vector maximization". *Journal of Mathematical Analysis and its Applications*, 22, 618-630.

[3] Halme, M. (1992), "Local characterizations of efficient solutions in interactive multiple objective programming". *Acta Academiae Oeconomicae Helsingiesis*, Series A: 84.

[4] Henig, M.I. Buchanan, J. (1992), "Tradeoff directions in multiobjective optimization problems". Mathematical Programming 1997, 78, 357-374.

[5] Jog, V., Kaliszewski, I., Michalowski, W. (1999), "Using attribute tradeoff information in investment". *Journal of Multi-Criteria Decision Analysis*, 8, 189-199.

[6] Kaliszewski, I.,

(1987) "A modified weighted Tchebycheff metric for multiple objective programming". *Computers and Operations Research*, 14, 315-323.

(1993) "Calculating trade-offs by two-step parametric programming". *Central European Journal of Operational Research and Economics*, 2, 291-315.

(1994) *Quantitative Pareto Analysis by Cone Separation Technique.* Kluwer, Dordrecht.

(1998) "Using tradeoff information in Zionts-Wallenius type decision making algorithms". In: *Methods and Applications of Operational Research*, (ed. T. Trzaskalik), part II, 265-278, Akademia Ekonomiczna, Katowice, 1998, (in Polish); English version: Systems Research Institute Report, Report PMMiO, 8/96, 1996.

(2000) "Using trade-off information in decision-making algortihms". *Computers & Operations Research*, 27, 161-182.

[7] Kaliszewski, I., Michalowski, W.,

(1995a) "Generation of outcomes with selectively bounded trade-offs". *Foundations of Computing and Decision Sciences*, 20, 113-122.

(1995b) "Efficient solutions and bounds on global trade-offs". *Journal of Optimization Theory and Applications*, 94, 381-394.

[8] Kuhn, H.W., Tucker, A. (1951), Nonlinear programming. *Proceedings of the Second Berkeley Symposium on Mathematics, Statistics, and Probability*, University of California Press, Berkeley.

[9] Steuer, R.E. (1986), *Multiple Criteria Optimization: Theory, Computation and Application*. John Wiley & Sons, New York.

[10] Steuer, R.E. , Choo, E.U. (1983), "An interactive weighted Tchebycheff procedure for multiple objective programming". *Mathematical Programming*, 26, 326-344.

[11] Wierzbicki, A.P.,

(1980) The use of reference objectives in multiobjective optimization. Multiple Criteria Decision Making; Theory and Applications (ed. G. Fandel, T. Gal), Lecture Notes in Economics and Mathematical Systems, 177, 468-486, Springer Verlag, Berlin.

(1986) On the completeness and constructiveness of parametric characterizations to vector optimization problems. *OR Spectrum*, 8, 73-87.

(1990) "Multiple criteria solutions in noncooperative game theory", Part III: Theoretical Foundations. Discussion Paper 288, Kyoto Institute of Economic Research, Kyoto University.

[12] Zionts, S., Wallenius, J. (1983), "An interactive multiple objective linear programming method for a class of underlying nonlinear utility functions". *Management Science*, 29, 519-529.

Multiple Objective Path Optimization
for Time Dependent Objective Functions

Michael M. Kostreva
Laura Lancaster
Clemson University

Department of Mathematical Sciences

Clemson, South Carolina 29634-0975 USA

flstgla@clemson.edu

Abstract

The study of time dependent, non-monotone increasing objective functions is interesting for several applications of multiple objective path optimization. In this paper an algorithm which finds the set of non-dominated paths is derived and shown to converge. This algorithm does not reduce to dynamic programming, even for constant cost functions.

1. Introduction

Dynamic programming (DP) is a mathematical technique used to solve optimization problems by a sequential process. It takes a complex optimization problem with many decisions and variables and reduces it into a set of simpler problems with fewer decisions and variables. The principle of optimality given by Richard Bellman[1] is a partial description of the phenomena of DP, and it implicitly assumes cost functions which are both separable and monotonic. In this paper we wish to consider multiple objectives on each arc of a network, and these functions need not be monotone increasing. This feature leads to the break down of both the above assumptions of DP, and hence to the requirement of a new type of algorithm for the solution of such a problem.

The paper presents an algorithm for finding *all* non-dominated solutions to multiple objective time-dependent network programming problems. Such an algorithm will apply to more general problems than most existing methods, because of the lack of assumptions on the cost functions. It will also not require a time grid, which was used in [16] in order to comprehend very general cost functions. We claim that these are the advantages of the new method.

2. New Algorithm

2.1. The problem

Consider a directed network with each arc having a transition cost function associated with it. This transition cost function gives the travel time from the start node of the arc to the end node of the arc. This transition cost function is dependent on time. For a given path in this network the time of arrival at the specific node of the path can be calculated using the transition cost functions. Each arc also has several other time-dependent cost functions associated with it. We will consider a shortest path problem with multiple time-dependent cost functions. The problem is to find all Pareto optimal paths from a specific start node to one or many destination nodes.

One solution method would be to enumerate all the paths from the start node to a destination node and then use VMIN to find all the nondominated paths. However costly, this is, of course, always a last resort method. One might hope that a simple application of dynamic programming or Dijkstra`s algorithm would work. However, the fact that the transition cost function and all other cost function are dependent on time causes difficulties with these methods. One difficulty lies in the fact that the arcs do not have unique costs. The cost of an arc depends on the time of arrivals at the arcs, and this is turn depends on the path taken to arrive at the start node of the arc. Thus, the costs of the arts are not independent of the paths. It is possible that arriving at a node later could actually result in a lower cost than arriving at the node early. Thus, the monotonicity assumption necessary for Bellman`s Principle of Optimality [1] is broken. Kostreva and Wiecek`s Algorithm One [16] gets around this problem by finding all the possible cost of each arc given a specific time-grid for arrival times at the arcs. This algorithm works, but has limitation in that it is restricted to the integrality of time and requires vast amounts of memory. Getachew [10] presented a recursive algorithm that is done in two phases. The first phase uses time-invariant backward dynamic programming and the second phase uses forward time-variant costing of the paths found in phase one. This algorithm has advantages over Algorithm One in that it does not require a discrete time grind and potentially uses less memory. However, it still has the limitation that it requires each cost function to have an upper and lower bound and that the lower bound be known. Kostrewa and Wiecek [16] also presented a second algorithm called Algorithm Two which uses forward dynamic programming. It overcomes the problem of monotonicity by requiring that all of the cost functions and the transition cost function be monotone increasing with respect to time. This prevents the problem stated earlier: Arriving at a path later may result in lower cost function. This is prevented because all of the costs increase with time.

The algorithm presented here is most similar to Kostrewa and Wiecek's Algorithm Two. However, it does *not* require that the cost functions be monotone increasing with respect to time. The only requirement is that the time function is nonnegative. Otherwise, any type of cost function is allowed. This algorithm overcomes the problem of monotonicity by generalizing dynamic programming to weaken the Principle of Optimality as given by Bellman [1]. The algorithm uses a forward dynamic programming type method. However, no path is thrown away that could possibly lead to an optimal solution at a later time, even thought currently the path is not optimal. The algorithm is not formally presented after some definitions.

Preliminary Definitions

Consider a connected directed network **G** with a set of nodes, $N = \{1, 2, \dots, n\}$, and a set directed arcs, $A = \{(i_0, i_1), (i_2, i_3), (i_4, i_5), \dots\} \subset N \times N$, which link the nodes.

Definition 1

a) *For the arc* (i, j), *node i is the* **start node** *and node j is the* **end node**. So, for example (2, 3) is the arc from node 2 to node 3. And (3, 2) is the arc from node 3 to node 2.

b) *Let* $\sigma(j) \in N$ *be the set of all nodes i where* $(i, j) \in A$ *for the network* **G**.

c) *A* **path**, *P, from node* i_0 *to node* i_p *is the sequence of directed arcs* $P = \{(i_0, i_1), (i_1, i_2), \dots, (i_{p-1}, i_p)\}$ *where the start node of each arc is the end node of the preceding arc in the node sequence* $i_0, i_1, \dots, i_p$.

d) *A path from node* i_0 *to node* i_p, $P = \{(i_0, i_1), (i_1, i_2), \dots, (i_{p-1}, i_p)\}$ *is* **acyclic** *if* $i_j \neq i_k$ *for any* i_j, i_k *in the sequence of nodes along the path P.*

e) *Let* Π *be the set of all acyclic paths in the Network* **G**.

The network has a transition cost function associated with each edge. This is the time to travel from the start node of the arc to the end node of the arc. Using these transition cost functions, the time of arrival at every node along a path can be calculated by an arrival function.

Definition 2

a) *For the arc (i, j) the* **transition cost function,** $a_{ji} : \mathbf{R}^+ \cup \{0\} \to \mathbf{R}^+ \cup \{0\}$, *is the time to travel from node i to node j. It is dependent on time, $t \geq 0$, where the time is the arrival time at node i.*

b) *For the path, $p \in \Pi$, where $p = \{(i_0, i_1), (i_1, i_2), ..., (i_{q-2}, i_{q-1}), (i_{q-1}, i_q)\}$, the* **arrival function** $A : (P \in \Pi) \times (N \in \mathbf{N}) \to \mathbf{R}^+ \cup \{0\}$ *is defined recursively as*

$$A(p, i_0) = 0 \tag{3.1}$$
$$A(p, i_q) = A(p, i_{q-1}) + a_{i_{q-1}, i_q}(A(p, i_{q-1})) \tag{3.2}$$

assuming that A has been defined for all nodes preceding i_q in path p.

c) *Each arc (i, j) has an associated cost vector of cost functions, $c_{ij} : \mathbf{R}^+ \cup \{0\} \to \mathbf{R}^{m+} \cup \{0\}$, which is dependent on time, $t \geq 0$.*
So, $c_{ij}(t) = (c_{ij_1}(t), c_{ij_2}(t), ..., c_{ij_m}(t))$.

d) *Let $[c_{ij}(t)]_1 = a_{ij}(t)$.*

e) *The cost to traverse the path, $p \in \Pi$ is*

$$[c(p)] = \sum_{(i,j) \in p} [c_{ij}(A(p, i))]. \tag{3.3}$$

The only assumption made about these cost vectors are that they are non-negative. It is often the case that the transition cost function is one of the objectives. Note that for convenience we will let the transition cost function be the first cost function in the cost vector.

Definition 3

a) *An acyclic path, $p \in \Pi$, from node i to node j is* **nondominated** *if there is no other acyclic path, $\bar{p} \in \Pi$, from node i to node j with $[c(\bar{p})] \leq [c(p)]$ and $[c(\bar{p})]_r < [c(p)]_r$ for some $r \in \{1, ... , m\}$.*

b) *An acyclic path that is not nondominated is* **dominated**.

c) *An acyclic path, $p \in \Pi$, from node i to node j is* **nondominated*** *if there is no other acyclic path, $\bar{p} \in \Pi$, from node i to node j with $[c(\bar{p})]_1 = [c(p)]_1$, $[c(\bar{p})]_i \leq [c(p)]_i$, $i = 2, ... , m$, and $[c(\bar{p})]_r < [c(p)]_r$ for some $r \in \{2, ... , m\}$. If $[c(p)]_1 = \infty$, then p is* **not** *nondominated* if there are any other acyclic paths, $\hat{p} \in \Pi$, from node i to j where $[c(\hat{p})]_1 \neq \infty$.*

d) *An acyclic path that is not nondominated* *is* **dominated***.

This algorithm finds the set of all nondominated paths from a specific starting node in N, the origin, to all other nodes in the network. For simplicity, assume the origin node is node 1 and that the initial time to leave the origin node is $t_0 = 0$.

Definition 4

a) *Let* $\{\mathbf{D_j}\}$ *be the set of all acyclic paths,* $p \in \Pi$, *which leave the origin node at* $t = 0$ *and lead to node j.*

b) *Let* $\{\mathbf{D_j^{(k)}}\}$ *be the set of all acyclic paths,* $p \in \Pi$, *of a most k arcs which leave the origin node at* $t = 0$ *and lead to node j.*

c) *Let* $\{\mathbf{Eff(D_j)}\}$ *be the set of all acyclic paths,* $p \in \Pi$, *which leave the origin node at* $t = 0$, *lead to node j, and are nondominated.*

d) *Let* $\{\mathbf{Eff^*(D_j)}\}$ *be the set of all acyclic paths,* $p \in \Pi$, *which leave the origin node at* $t = 0$, *lead to node j, and are nondominated**.

e) *The function* **VMIN** *computes the vector costs of all acyclic nondominated paths from the origin to node j,* $\{Eff(D_j)\}$, *from the set of all acyclic paths from the origin to node j,* $\{D_j\}$.

f) *The function* **VMIN*** *computes the vector costs of all acyclic nondominated** *paths from the origin to node j,* $\{Eff^*(D_j)\}$, *from the set of all acyclic paths from the origin to node j,* $\{D_j\}$.

g) *Let* $\{\mathbf{PreEff^*(D_j)}\}$ *be the set of all acyclic paths,* $p \in \Pi$, *which leave the origin node at* $t = 0$ *and lead to node i,* $\forall i \in \sigma(j)$, *then lead from node i to node j by one arc, and are nondominated** *from the origin to node i.*

h) *Let* $\{\mathbf{PreEff^*(D_j^{(k)})}\}$ *be the set of all acyclic paths,* $p \in \Pi$, *which are of at most k arcs, leave the origin node at* $t = 0$, *lead to node i,* $\forall i \in \sigma(j)$, *and then lead from node i to node j by one arc, and are nondominated** *from the origin to node i.*

Definition 5

a) *Let* $[\mathbf{G_j(t^u)}]$ *be the vector cost of the acyclic path* $u \in \{D_j\}$ *that leaves the origin node at* $t = 0$, *arrives at node j at time* t^u, *and is nondominated.*

b) *Let* $\{[\mathbf{G_j}]\} = [[G_j(t^u)], u=1,..., N_j\}$ *be the set of vector cost of all acyclic paths in* $\{Eff(D_j)\}$ *that are nondominated, where* N_j *is the number of nondominated paths from the origin to node j.*

c) Let $[\mathbf{G}_j^*(\mathbf{t}^u)]$ be the vector cost of the acyclic paths $u \in \{PreEff^*(D_j)\}$ that leaves the origin node at $t = 0$ and arrives at node j at time t^u.

d) Let $\{[\mathbf{G}_j^*]\} = \{[G_j^*(t^u)], u = 1,..., N_j^*\}$ be the set of vector cost of all acyclic paths in $\{PreEff^*(D_j)\}$, where N_j^* is the number of paths in $\{PreEff^*(D_j)\}$.

e) Let $[\mathbf{G}_j^*(\mathbf{t}^u)^{(k)}]$ be the vector cost of the acyclic paths $u \in \{PreEff^*(D_j)^{(k+1)}\}$ that leaves the origin node at $t = 0$ and arrives at node j at time t^u in at most $k+1$ arcs.

f) Let $\{[\mathbf{G}_j^{*(k)}]\} = [G_j^*(t^u)^{(k)}], u=1,..., N_j^{*(k)}\}$ be the set of vector cost of all acyclic paths in $\{PreEff^*(D_j)^{(k+1)}\}$ that are of at most $k + 1$ arcs, where $N_j^{*(k)}$ is the number of paths in $\{PreEff^*(D_j)^{(k+1)}\}$.

g) Let $\{[\mathbf{S}_j^{i^{(k)}}]\}$ be the set of vector costs of all acyclic nondominated paths in $\{[G_j^{*(k-1)}]\}$ which go from the origin node to node i, do not contain the node j, and are of at most k arcs.

Definition 6

a) The function $\mathbf{A}_j$ computes the vector costs of all acyclic paths that do not contain node j from any set of paths vector costs.

b) Let $\{\mathbf{P}_j^{i^{(k)}}\} = \{\mathbf{A}_j \{[G_j^{*(k-1)}]\}, i \neq j$, be the set of all acyclic paths of at most k arcs that start at the origin node and lead to node i without using node j.

c) Let $\mathbf{N}_j^{iA(k)}$ be the number of paths in $\{\mathbf{P}_j^{i^{(k)}}\}$.

These notations and definitions are used in the new algorithm which is presented next.

The Algorithm

The following is the new algorithm which finds all nondominated paths from the origin node to all other nodes in the network. Without loss of generality, assume the origin node is node 1. Thus, the algorithm finds $\{Eff(D_j)\}$ for all $j = 2,3, ...,n$. The first step in the algorithm simply finds all paths of at most one arc which emanate from the origin starting at time t = 0, $\{[G_j^{*(0)}]\}, j = 2, ..., n$. If no arc exists from node 1 to some node k, then $[c_{1k}(0)] = \infty$.

Step 2 is the most computationally intensive part of the algorithm. It iterates until the sets $[\{[G_j^{*(k)}]\}], k = 1, 2, 3, ...,$ converge. This step has three parts. The first part of Step 2 finds the vector costs of all nondominated[*] paths which leave the origin node at t = 0 and go to node i without using node j which are of at most k arcs in length. The second part of Step 2 takes the vector costs found in the first part of this step and adds on the cost of an additional arc. This gives the set $[\{[G_j^{*(k)}]\}], k = 1, 2, 3, ...$. The last part of Step 2 simply checks to see if two consecutive iterations give the same set of vector costs.

In the second part of Step 2 the set $[\{G_j^{*(k)}\}]$ for a particular node j and iteration k must be found by first calculating the set $\{[S_j^{i(k)}]\}$, the set of vector costs of all acyclic nondominated[*] paths in $\{[G_i^{*(k-1)}]\}$ which go from the origin node to node i, for all $i \in \sigma(j)$, do not contain j, and are of at most k arcs. Once this is found, the cost of traversing the arc (i, j) at the calculated arrival time at node i is added to every vector cost in $\{[S_j^{i(k)}]\}$. The reason for finding this set $\{[S_j^{i(k)}]\}$ instead of simply using $\{[G_j^{*(k-1)}]\}$ is because it is possible to have cycling. Cycling can occur because of the time-dependent nature of the cost function. It is possible that there is an arc in the network where one of the costs decreases as time increases. Thus, it might be beneficial to cycle for a while or possibly forever before traversing a certain arc. Finding $\{[S_j^{i(k)}]\}$ makes sure that all paths are acyclic, as the function A_j is performed on $\{[G_j^{*(k-1)}]\}$ to eliminate any paths that would cause cycles.

Step 3 finds the convergent set $\{[G_j^{*}]\}$, and the paths associated with those vector costs, $\{PreEff^{*}(D_j)\}$. It is important to note that these paths are not necessarily nondominated[*]. Step 4 is the last step, which finds all nondominated[*] paths from the origin node to all other nodes in the network by taking **VMIN** of all the vector costs from Step 3. The paths associated with these nondominated vector costs are found from the set $\{PreEff^{*}(D_j)\}$ found in Step 3.

Step 1: Find an initial vector $[\{[G_j^{*(0)}]\}], j = 1, 2, ..., n,$ where

$$\{[G_1^{*(0)}]\} = \{\mathbf{0}\}$$
$$\{[G_j^{*(0)}]\} = \{c_{ij}(0)], j = 2, ..., n\}$$

Step 2: Calculate the vectors $[\{[G_j^{*(k)}]\}], j = 1, 2, \dots, n$, for $k = 1,2,3, \dots$, as follows:

If $j = 1$, then

$$\{[G_1^{*(k)}]\} = \{0\}$$

else

(i) $\{[S_j^{i(k)}]\} = \mathbf{VMIN}^* \{A_j\{[G_i^*(t^n)^{(k-1)}], n = 1, \dots, N_j^{*(k)}\}\}$ for all $i \in \sigma(j)$.

(ii) $\{[G_i^*(t^l)^{(k)}], l = 1, \dots, N_j^{*(k)}\} = \{[G_i^*(t^n)^{(k-1)}] + [c_{ij}(t^n)]\}$, for all $[G_i^*(t^n)^{(k-1)}] \in \{[S_j^{i(k)}]\}, n = 1, \dots, N_j^{iA(k)}, i \in \sigma(j)$.

(iii) If $[\{[G_i^{*(k+1)}]\}] = [\{[G_j^{*(k)}]\}], j = 2, \dots, n$ go to Step 3. If not repeat Step 2.

The sequence of sets $[\{G_j^{*(k)}]\}, k = 1,2,3, \dots$, converges to the set $\{[G_j^*]\}$. The set $\{\text{PreEff}^*(D_j)\}$ can be found by keeping track of the arcs added to each paths in $\{[G_j^{*(k)}]\}$.

Step 3: To calculate the set of vector costs of all nondominated paths from the origin node to node $j, j = 2, \dots, n$, $\{[G_j]\} = \mathbf{VMIN} \{[G_j^*]\}$. The actual set of nondominated paths $\{\text{Eff}(D_j)\}$ can be found from the paths in $\{\text{PreEff}^*(D_j)\}$ associated with $\{[G_j]\}$.

In the first part of Step 2 it is important that $\mathbf{VMIN}^*$ is performed on the set $\{A_j\{[G_i^*(t)^{(k-1)}]\}\}$ instead of the set $\{A_j\{[G_i^*(t)^{(k-1)}]\} + [c_{ij}(t)]\}$, which becomes $\{[G_j^{*(k)}]\}$, since doing the latter would possibly eliminate a path that could be needed in a later iteration. This is because not all vector costs of paths in $\{[G_j^{*(k)}]\}$ can necessarily be used in the $k+1$ iteration for some specific node l due to the fact that they may cause cycling. Thus, the vector cost of the path $p_0 \in \{[G_j^{*(k)}]\}$ may dominate* the vector cost of the path $p_l \in \{[G_j^{*(k)}]\}$ but p_0 may not be able to be used in the $k + 1$ iteration due to cycling. Thus, the vector cost corresponding to the path p_l is needed. For example, suppose $\mathbf{VMIN}^*$ is performed on the set $\{\{[S_3^{2^{(3)}}]\} + [c_{23}(t)]\}$ in the second part of Step 2 instead of on $\{A_3\{[G_2^*(t)^{(2)}]\}\}$ in the first part of Step 2. Also suppose that the vector cost corresponding to the path $p_l \in \{\{[S_3^{2^{(3)}}]\} + [c_{23}(t)]\}$ is dominated* by $p_0 \in$

$\{\{[\,S_3^{\,2^{(3)}}\,]\} + [c_{23}(t)]\}$ and thus dropped from the set $\{[\,G_3^*(t)^{(3)}\,]\}$. In the fourth iteration of Step 2, suppose the arc (3, 4) is in $\mathbb{S}$, and suppose that $p_1 \notin \{A_4\{[\,G_3^*(t)^{(3)}\,]\}\}$. Then, assuming that p_0 was not dominated* by any other vector cost, the vector cost corresponding to p_0 should be included in $\{[\,S_4^{\,3^{(4)}}\,]\}$.

Complexity

In the worst case scenario, this algorithm could be run on a completely connected time-dependent network where the traversal times were such than no path eliminations were due to finding nondominated* paths. This would mean enumerating all paths in the network from the origin node to every other node in the network. This would involve finding $(n-1)! \sum_{k=0}^{n-2} \frac{1}{k!}$ paths.

Theory

Theorem 1 *A nondominated* path p that leaves the origin at time $t_0 = 0$ and arrives at node j at time t_j, has the property that for each node i lying on this path, a subpath p_1, that leaves the origin node at time $t_0 = 0$ and arrives at node i at time t_1, $t_i \leq t_j$, is nondominated*.*

Proof. Assume that p_1 is dominated*. Thus, there exists a $\overline{p}$ that leaves the origin node at $t = 0$ and arrives at node i at time $\overline{t_i} = t_i$ such that $[c(\overline{p})]_k \leq [c(p_1)]_k$, $k = 2, \ldots, m$, and $[c(\overline{p})]_r < [c(p_1)]_r$ for some $r \in \{2, \ldots, m\}$. Clearly $[c(\overline{p})]_1 = [c(p_1)]_1$.

Both paths p_1 and $\overline{p}$ leave the origin node at $i = 0$ and lead to node i at the same time. Since they both arrive at node i at the same time, the cost to go from node i to node j does not change depending on which path p_1 or $\overline{p}$ you take, call this part p_2. Thus, we have to paths from origin node to node j such that their total cost is respectively:

$$[c(p_1)] + [c(p_2)] \text{ and } c[(\overline{p})] + [c(p_2)]$$

Since $[c(p_1)]_1 = [c(\overline{p})]_1$ we know that

$$[c(\,p\,)]_1 + [c(p_2)]_1 = [c(p_1)]_1 + [c(p_2)]_1$$

and since $[c(\,p\,)]_k \le [c(p_1)]_k$, $k = 2, ..., m$, then we know that

$$[c(\,p\,)]_i + [c(p_2)]_i \le [c(p_1)]_i + [c(p_2)]_i, i = 2, ..., m$$

and since $[c(\,p\,)]_r < [c(p_1)]_r$ for some $r \in \{2, ..., m\}$, then we know that

$$[c(\,p\,)]_r + [c(p_2)]_r < [c(p_1)]_r + [c(p_2)]_r \text{ for some } r \in \{2, ..., m\}.$$

Thus (p_1, p_2) is dominated* by $(\,p\,, p_2)$. $\square$

Theorem 2 $\{[S_j^{i(k)}]\}$ *is the set of vector costs of all acyclic nondominated* paths of length at most k arcs going from the origin node to node i that do not contain node j.*

Proof. For $j = 1, ..., n$, $\{[S_j^{i(k)}]\} = \textbf{VMIN}^* \{A_j\{[G_i^{*(k-1)}]\}\}$ for all i, $i \ne j$, and $\{[G_i^{*(k-1)}]\}$ is the set of vector costs of all acyclic paths in $\{\text{PreEff}^*(D_j^{(k)})\}$. $A_j\{[G_i^{*(k-1)}]\}$ computes the vector costs of all acyclic paths in $\{\text{PreEff}^*(D_j^{(k)})\}$ that do not contain the node j. All vector costs found by $\textbf{VMIN}^* \{A_j\{[G_i^{*(k-1)}]\}\}$ must be nondominated*, by definition of $\textbf{VMIN}^*$. Also, all paths associated with these vector costs must be acyclic, since the vector costs in $\{[S_j^{i(k)}]\}$ are associated with paths that come from $\{\text{PreEff}^*(D_j^{(k)})\}$.

Suppose there exists an acyclic nondominated* path, p, on at most k arcs going from the origin node to node i that does not contain node j such that $p \notin \{[S_j^{i(k)}]\}$. Then $[c(p)] \notin \{A_j\{[G_i^{*(k-1)}]\}\}$, since by definition of $\textbf{VMIN}^*$, the nondominated* path p must be in $\{[S_j^{i(k)}]\}$. If $[c(p)] \in \{[G_i^{*(k-1)}]\}$, but not in $\{A_j\{[G_i^{*(k-1)}]\}\}$, then p must contain the node j. Thus, $[c(p)] \notin \{[G_i^{*(k-1)}]\}$ and $p \notin \{\text{PreEff}^*(D_i^{(k)})\}$.

$\{\text{PreEff}^*(D_i^{(k)})\}$ is the set of all acyclic paths of at most k arcs that leave the origin at $t_0 = 0$ and lead to node l, for all $l \in \sigma(j)$, then lead l to node i by one arc, and are nondominated* to node l. Otherwise, p would be in $\{\text{PreEff}^*(D_i^{(k)})\}$. This contradicts Theorem 1, which says that all subpaths of a nondominated[*] paths must be nondominated[*]. Thus, p can not be nondominated[*]. □

Theorem 3 *The iterative step in the algorithm computes the set of all vector costs corresponding to all acyclic paths from the origin node to node j, $j = 2, ...,$ n, where each of the subpaths from the origin to node i, $i \in \sigma(j)$, is nondominated[*].*

Proof. Assume $k = 1$. Then for all $j = 2, ..., n$

$\{[G_j^{*(1)}]\}$ = the vector costs of all nondominated[*] paths in $\{[P_j^{i(1)}]\}$, for all $i \in \sigma(j)$ plus the vector cost of the link from node i to node j if $\{D_j^{(2)}\} \neq \varnothing$.

$$\{[G_j^{*(1)}]\} = \{[\infty]\} \text{ if } \{D_j^{(2)}\} = \varnothing.$$

If $\{D_j^{(2)}\} \neq \varnothing$, then there exist at least one acyclic path from the origin node to node j consisting of one or two arcs. Thus, there is some node i such that $\{D_i^{(1)}\} \neq \varnothing$ and $(i, j) \in \mathbf{A}$. In step one, all of the vector costs of one arcs path are obtained. In the first iteration of step two $\{[S_j^{i(1)}]\} = \{[G_i^{*(0)}]\}$ for all $i \in \sigma(j)$, since each $\{[G_i^{*(0)}]\}$ is just the vector cost of paths of at most one arc from the origin to node i if $\{D_i^{(1)}\} \neq \varnothing$. Thus, the vector cost in $\{[S_j^{i(1)}]\}$ is nondominated[*]. The second part of step two adds the vector cost of each path in $\{[S_j^{i(1)}]\}$ where $\{D_i^{(1)}\} \neq \varnothing$ and the vector cost associated with traversing the arc from node i to node j where $i \in \sigma(j)$. (Note: $\{[S_j^{1(1)}]\} = \{0\}$ and is not associated with a one arc path.) Thus, the second part of step two finds the vector costs of all one and two arc paths from the origin node to node j that are in $\{\text{PreEff}^*(D_j^{(2)})\}$.

If $\{D_j^{(2)}\} = \varnothing$, then the one arc path from the origin node to node j has vector cost of $[\infty]$. For two arc paths, if $(i,j) \in \mathbf{A}$ then the arc $(1, i) \notin \mathbf{A}$. Thus, $\{[G_j^{*(0)}]\} = \{[\infty]\}$ causing $\{[S_j^{i(1)}]\} = \{[\infty]\}$. If $(i,j) \notin \mathbf{A}$ then $\{[S_j^{i(1)}]\} = \varnothing$ and $\{[G_j^{*(1)}]\}$ remains the same value as $\{[G_j^{*(0)}]\}$. Thus $\{[G_j^{*(1)}]\} = \{[\infty]\}$.

Now, assume that the iterative step is true for k, $k > 1$. We need to show that it is true for $k + 1$. For $j = 2, ..., n$,

$\{[G_j^{*(k+1)}]\}$ = the vector costs of all nondominated* paths in $\{[P_j^{i(k+1)}]\}$ for all $i \in \sigma(j)$ plus the vector cost of the link from node i to node j if $\{D_j^{(k+2)}\} \neq \varnothing$.

$\{[G_j^{*(k+1)}]\} = \{[\infty]\}$ if $\{D_j^{(k+2)}\} = \varnothing$.

If $\{D_j^{(k+2)}\} \neq \varnothing$, then there exist at least one acyclic path of at most $k + 2$ arcs leaving from the origin node at $t_0 = 0$ and arriving at node j. In the kth iteration, vector costs of all acyclic paths in $\{\text{PreEff}^*(D_i^{(k+1)})\}$ for all $i \in \sigma(j)$ are found. In the first part of step two in the $k + 1$ iteration, the vector costs of all acyclic nondominated* paths with at most $k + 1$arcs from the origin node to node i that do not contain node j are found in $\{[S_j^{i(k+1)}]\}$ for all $i \in \sigma(j)$ where $\{D_i^{(k+1)}\} \neq \varnothing$. The second part of step two adds the vector cost of traversing the arc from node i to node j. Thus, the vector costs of all paths in $\{\text{PreEff}^*(D_i^{(k+2)})\}$ are found.

If $\{D_j^{(k+2)}\} = \varnothing$, then there are no paths of at most $k + 2$ arcs that leave the origin node at $t_0 = 0$ and reach node j. Thus, either $\{[S_j^{i(k+1)}]\} = \{[\infty]\}$ or $(i,j) \notin \mathbf{A}$ meaning that $\{[S_j^{i(k+1)}]\} = \varnothing$ and $\{[G_j^{*(k+1)}]\}$ remains the same value as $\{[G_j^{*(k)}]\}$. Thus $\{[G_j^{*(k+1)}]\} = \{[\infty]\}$. $\square$

Theorem 4 $\{Eff(D_j)\} \subseteq \{PreEff^*(D_j)\}$

Proof. Suppose there exist a path $p_0 \in \{\text{Eff}(D_j)\}$, but $p_0 \notin \{\text{PreEff}^*(D_j)\}$ that consist of k arcs. The fact that $p_0 \in \{\text{Eff}(D_j)\}$ implies that p_0 is acyclic and there exists no acyclic path, p^*, going from the origin node to node j such that $[c(p^*)] \leq [c(p_0)]$ and $[c(p^*)]_r < [c(p_0)]_r$ for some $r \in \{1, \ldots, m\}$. However, since p_0 is acyclic and $p_0 \notin \{\text{PreEff}^*(D_j)\}$, this implies that the subpath of p_0, p, which goes from the origin node to node i in $k - 1$ arcs is not nondominated*. Thus, there is another path from the origin node to node $i, \hat{p}$, which dominates* p. Therefore $[c(\hat{p})]_1 = [c(p)]_1, [c(\hat{p})]_k \leq [c(p)]_k, k = 2, \ldots, m,$ and $[c(\hat{p})]_r < [c(p)]_r$ for some $r \in \{2, \ldots, m\}$. Thus $[c(\hat{p})] \leq [c(p)]$ and $[c(\hat{p})]_r < [c(p)]_r,$ for some $r \in \{2, \ldots, m\}$., Thus the path $\hat{p}$ dominates p. Since p is the subpath of path p_0 which leads to node i in $k{-}1$ arcs. The cost of path p_0 is $[c(p)]+[c_{ij}([c(p)]_1)]$.

This cost of the path p_1 which uses subpath $\hat{p}$ and the arc (i, j) is $[c(\hat{p})]+[c_{ij}([c(\hat{p})]_1)]$. However, since $[c(p)]_1 = [c(\hat{p})]_1$, then $[c_{ij}([c(p)]_1)] = [c_{ij}([c(\hat{p})]_1)]$. So, $[c(p_1)]_1 = [c(p_0)]_1$, $[c(p_1)]_k \leq [c(p_0)]_k$, $k = 2, \ldots , m$, and $[c(p_1)]_r < [c(p_0)]_r$, for some $r \in \{2, \ldots , m\}$. Thus, p_0 is dominated by p_1. But, since $p_0 \in \{\text{Eff}(D_j)\}$ then p_0 cannot be dominated. Contradiction. $\square$

Theorem 5 *Taking the vector minimum, **VMIN**, of the set of the vector costs of all paths in $\{PreEff^*(D_j)\}$, $\{[G_j^*]\}$, gives the set of vector costs of all nondominated paths from the origin node to node j, $\{[G_j]\}$.*

Proof. Since $\{[G_j^*]\}$ is the set of vector costs of all paths in $\{PreEff^*(D_j)\}$, then taking the vector minimum, **VMIN**, of $\{[G_j^*]\}$ finds the vector costs of all nondominated paths from the origin node to node j since $\{\text{Eff}(D_j)\} \subseteq \{PreEff^*(D_j)\}$. $\square$

As mentioned earlier in chapter 2, Carraway *et al.* [3] worked on a generalization of MODP using a preference function. Since their generalization of MODP did not assume monotonicity they could no longer use Bellman's famous principle of optimality. Several weakened principles of optimality can also be found in work by Lee [25].

We can apply similar logic to have a weak principle of optimality for the new algorithm. A strong principle of optimality for a MODP problem would be stated as: *A nondominated path must consist of subpaths that are nondominated.* While this principle is true for most dynamic programming problems where the monotonicity assumption is satisfied, the new algorithm is based on the following weak principle of optimality. *A nondominated path must consist of subpaths that can be part of a nondominated path.* Stated more formally:

Weak Principle of Optimality *A nondominated path p that leaves the origin at time $t_0 = 0$ and arrives at node j at time t_j, has the property that for each node i lying on this path, a subpath p_1, that leaves the origin node at time $t_0 = 0$ and arrives at node i at time t_i, $t_i \leq t_j$, is nondominated**.

Proof. From Theorem 3, the algorithm computes the set of all vector costs of all acyclic paths, $\{PreEff^*(D_j)\}$, from the origin to node j, $j = 2, \ldots, n$, where each of the subpaths from the origin to node i, $i \in \sigma(j)$, is nondominated*. From Theorem 1, every subpath $\hat{p}$ that leaves the origin node at $t_0 = 0$ and arrives at node i, $i \in \sigma(j)$ at time t_i, has the property that for every node k on the path $\hat{p}$ that leaves the origin node at $t_0 = 0$ and arrives at node k at time t_k, $t_k \leq t_i$, is also nondominated*. Thus, every path $p \in \{\text{PreEff}^*(D_j)\}$ that leaves the origin node at $t_0 = 0$ and arrives at node j at time t_j, has the property that for every node i lying on the path p, a subpath that leaves the origin node at $t_0 = 0$ and arrives at node i at time t_i, $t_i \leq t_j$, is also nondominated*. Theorem 4 showed that the set of nondominated paths from the origin node to some node j, $j = 2, ..., n$, is a subset of the set $\{\text{PreEff}^*(D_j)\}$. Thus, every nondominated path p that leaves the origin at time $t_0 = 0$ and arrives at node j at time t_j, has the property that for each node i lying on this path, a subpath p_1, that leaves the origin node at time $t_0 = 0$ and arrives at node i at time t_i, $t_i \leq t_j$, is nondominated*. $\square$

Thus, the algorithm retains all subpaths that *can* lead to a nondominated path. At the and of the algorithm all nondominated paths are found from the set $\{\text{PreEff}^*(D_j)\}$ for all j, $j = 2, ... , n$, by the **VMIN** operation.

3. Conclusions

The new algorithm presented in this paper finds all non-dominated paths from an origin node to every other node, in a network that has multiple time-dependent cost functions specified on each link. There are no restrictions on these functions, except that the time function be nonnegative. Because of the generality, the method can be used in many applications. Fire egress, process control, and multiple objective time-dependent knapsack problems have been solved with it. We note that it is best used when its generality is required, due to consideration of complexity of computations. If all objective functions are monotone increasing, then Algorithm 2 of [16] is likely to perform the calculations in a more effective manner. From experience, problems of fire egress and time dependent knapsack problems associated with capital budgeting on longer time horizons contain such general objective functions.

Bibliography

1. R. E. BELLMAN. *Dynamic Programming*, Princeton University Press, Princeton, N.J., (1957).

2. T. A. BROWN AND R. E. STRAUCH. "Dynamic Programming in Multiplicative Lattices", *Journal of Mathematical Analysis and Application* **12**, 364-370, (1965).

3. R. L. CARRAWAY, T. L. MORIN, AND H. MOSKOWITZ. "Generalized Dynamic Programming for Multicriteria Optimization", *European Journal of Operational Research* **44**, 95-104, (1990).

4. K. L. COOKE AND E. HALSEY. "The Shortest Route Through a Network with Time-Dependent Internodal Transit Times", *Journal of Mathematical Analysis and Applications* **14**, 493-498, (1966).

5. H.W. CORLEY AND I. D. MOON. "Shortest Paths in Networks with Vector Weights", *Journal of Optimization Theory and Applications* **46**, 79-86, (1980).

6. H. G. DAELLENBACH AND C. A. DEKLUYVER. "Note on Multiple Objective Ddynamic Programming", *Journal of the Operational Research Society* **31**, 591-594, (1980).

7. E. W. DIJKSTRA. "A Note on Two Problems in Connexion with Graphs", *Numerische Mathematik* **1**, 269-271, (1959).

8. S. E. DREYFUS. "An Appraisal of Some Shortest-Path Algorithms", *Operations Research* **17**, 395-412, (1969).

9. M. EMSTERMANN. *Time Dependency in Multiple Objective Dynamic Programming: The General Monotone Increasing Case*, Masters Project, Department of Mathematical Sciences, Clemson University, S.C., USA, (1993).

10. T. GETACHEW. *An Algorithm for Multiple-Objective Network Optimization with Time Variant Link-Costs*, Ph.D. dissertation, Clemson, S.C., USA, (1992).

11. J. HALPERN. "Shortest Route with Time Dependent Length of Edges and Limited Delay Possibilities in Nodes", *Zeitschrift für Operations Research* **21**, 117-124, (1977).

12. R. HARTLEY. "Vector Optimal Route by Dynamic Programming", *Mathematics of Multiobjective Optimization*, P. Serafini, Ed. , 215-224, (1984).

13. T. IBARAKI. "Enumerative Approaches to Combinatorial Optimization – Part II", *Annals of Operations Research* **11**, 343-440, (1987).

14. D. E. KAUFMAN AND R. L. SMITH. "Minimum Travel Time Paths in Dynamic Networks with Application to Intelligent Vehicle-Highway Systems", University of Michigan, Transportation Research Institute, IVHS Techniccal Report, **90-11**, (1990).

15. D. E. KAUFMAN AND R. L. SMITH. "Fastest Paths in Time-Dependent Networks for Intelligent Vehicle-Highway Systems Application", *IVHS Journal* **1(1)**, 1-11, (1993).

16. M. M. KOSTREVA AND M. M. WIECEK. "Time Dependency in Multiple Objective Dynamic Programming", *Journal of Mathematical Analysis and Applications* **173**, 289-307, (1993).

17. D. LI AND Y. Y. HAIMES. "Multiobjective Dynamic Programming: The state of the Art.", *Control Theory and Adv. Tech.* **5**, No. 4, 471-483, (1989).

18. S. P. BRADLEY, A. C. HAX, AND T. L. MAGNATI. *Applied Mathematical Programming*, Addison-Wesley Publishing Company, Reading, MA, (1977).

19. L. G. MITTEN. "Preference Order Dynamic Programming", *Management Science* **21**, No. 1, 43-46, (1974).

20. G. L. NEMHAUSER. *Introduction to Dynamic Programming*, John Wiley and Sons, Inc. New York, (1966).

21. A. ORDA AND R. ROM. "Shortest-Path and Minimum-Delay Algorithms in Networks with Time-Dependent Edge-Length", *Journal of the AMC* **37**, 607-625, (1990).

22. A. B. PHILPOTT AND A. I. MEES. "Continuous-Time Shortest Path Problems with Stopping and Starting Costs", *Applied Math. Lett.* **5**, 63-66, (1992).

23. A. B. PHILPOTT AND A. I. MEES. "A Finite-Time Algorithm for Shortest Path Problems with Time-Varying Costs", *Applied Math. Lett.* **6**, 91-94, (1993).

24. H. J. SEBASTIAN. "Dynamic Programming for Problems with Time-Dependent Parameters", *Differential Equations* **14**, 242-249, (1978).

25. E. S. LEE. "Dynamic Programming and Principles of Optimality", *Journal of Mathematical Analysis and Applications* **65**, 586-606, (1978).

26. B. VILLAREAL AND M. H. KARWAN. "Multicriteria Integer Programming: A (Hybrid) Dynamic Programming Recursive Approach", *Mathematical Programming* **21**, 204-223, (1981).

27. M. WILSON. *A Time Dependent Vector Dynamic Programming Algorithm for the Path Planning Problems*, Masters Project, Department of Mathematical Sciences, Clemson University, Clemson, USA, (1992).

28. J. WHITE. *Dynamic Programming*, Holden-Day, San Francisko, CA, (1969).

Multicriteria Decision Support in Bargaining, a Problem of Players' Manipulations

Lech Kruś

Systems Research Institute, Polish Academy of Sciences

Newelska 6, 01-447 Warsaw, Poland

e-mail krus@ibspan.waw.pl

Abstract. The paper relates to construction of computer based systems for decision support in negotiations. A special case of distributed decision making – a class of bargaining situations is considered. DSS (decision support systems) utilizing mathematical model of decision situation can serve as a tool supporting unilateral and multilateral analysis made by negotiating sides (players). A problem of players' manipulations is discussed. What does it mean fairness? How can players manipulate using DSS? Can we minimize the players' manipulations applying game theoretical solution concepts in DSS? How can interactive procedures be constructed? This sort of questions is discussed in the paper.

Keywords: modeling, negotiations, multicriteria decision making.

1   Introduction

A negotiation process is in general very sensitive to possible manipulations - cheating of the negotiating sides. Similar sensitivity can be observed in the case of interactive procedures implemented in many computer-based systems supporting negotiations.

Let us look at a simple two party - one issue bargaining. A buyer and a seller negotiate the price. Each has his own reservation price as it is shown on fig. 1. The reservation prices are based on the BATNA concept (abbreviation to "Best Alternative to Negotiated Agreement" - a concept presented by Fisher and Ury (1981). The space between these two prices is the zone of agreement. The buyer will not agree for the price higher than r_b and respectively the seller will not agree for the price lower than r_s. In this zone the bargainers can settle an agreement price but might not come to any agreement, even if the zone is not empty. The information about the reservation price is strictly protected by each of the sides. It is typical, that the sides try to manipulate proposing consecutive offers during negotiations. The buyer tries to give the impression of lower reservation price, than it really is, why the seller - vice-versa. The agreement price, if accepted highly depends on the impressions. If the first offer of the buyer is too low and if the first offer of the seller - too high, the sides may not come to any agreement.

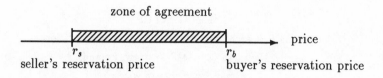

Fig. 1: A simple one issue two parties bargaining.

There are of course examples of manipulation free mechanisms for very specific problems, for example "I cut, you choose" procedure for cake allocation. There are extensions of the procedure proposed by Hugo Steinhaus (Steinhaus fair-division procedure reported by Raiffa, 1982), see also (Young, 1982). Groves and Ledyard (1977) have proposed the solution of so called Free-Rider problem in the case of allocation of funds for public goods. The mechanism is based on an punishment idea realized in the so-called "double payment". An interesting procedure has been proposed by Kulikowski at al. (1981) supporting fair allocation of founds for research projects.

However in general case the problem of constructing manipulation free interactive procedures for negotiation support is still open. This problem is discussed in the paper.

The bargaining problem in the case of two and many issues is modeled in the classical game theory in terms of utilities as it is presented in fig. 2. In the axes of the players' utilities a set S of possible agreements is presented as well as a status quo point d. Two parties (players) can reach any of the payoffs from the agreement set S, if they unanimously agree. The status quo point called the disagreement point defines payoffs of the players in the case when they do not reach such an agreement. Situations in which bargaining occurs normally contain two elements: an element of common interest and an element of conflicting interest. Without common interest there is nothing to bargain for; without conflicting interests there is nothing to bargain about. The exact nature and extent of these different interests are often determined by the preferences of the parties involved. Since preferences are personal matters, each party's information about the other's preferences is likely to be incomplete. To realize the common interests, the parties must exchange information about their preferences.

The axiomatic theory of bargaining following Nash (1950) assumes that complete information about all parameters of interests is given. A solution of the bargaining problem is considered as a method to choose a feasible point for each problem. Different solution concepts are formulated under assumptions of different properties (called axioms) the solution should fulfill. The argumentation for acceptance of the solution concept by the players is the following: if rational players agree on a selected set of axioms - principles and accept them as fair, why they should not accept the solution concept which fulfills the axioms.

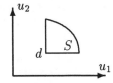

Fig. 2: A bargaining problem in the space of utilities.

The case of incomplete information, where the bargaining parties have a common interests in sharing information about their preferences but each party also needs to act strategically to maximize its individual gain falls into class of noncooperative games of incomplete information (Harsanyi 1967), (Harsanyi, Selten, 1972), and others. Chatterjee and Ulvila (1979) analyzed a single-factor model of distributive bargaining and a multiple-factor model of integrative bargaining. The analysis shows that the presence of private information generates a potential conflict between maximization of individual gain and joint gains. It explains why collectively desirable outcomes are not reached in practice. Truthful revelation, the maxmin strategy may be a good choice for a "satisficing" bargainer.

Talking about cheating and manipulation free procedures we should answer the question: what does it mean fairness? Following Raiffa (1982) we can say that it is impossible to formalize the notion of fairness for practice, despite the fact that there is a literature on the abstract form of fairness. We can say rather about feeling of fairness by particular player. If the player accepts a consensus payoff as fair - he will support the agreement. We can expect that if all the players fill that the agreement is fair, they will have no intentions to abandon it. In such a case we can expect that the agreement will be stable.

In the paper a special case of distributed decision making problem - a class of bargaining situations is considered in which there are several parties - players, each having multiple objectives and conflicting interests. It is assumed that a mathematical model is given which describes the set of admissible decisions of the players, and allows calculation of players' payoffs as dependent on assumed values of the decision variables. The payoffs are measured by multiple criteria, in general different for each player. Due to practical reasons the criteria are not aggregated to any utility functions of the players. The payoffs are analyzed in multicriteria spaces of the players. The model does not include preferential structure of the players. The model implemented in a decision support system is used for decision analysis. Using the model the consequences of different actions of the players can be derived. This model should not be mixed up with models describing entire negotiation process.

Ideas of multi-objective modeling and optimization applied in negotiation and mediation support have been discussed among others in the papers by Wierzbicki (1983), Vetschera 1990, Wierzbicki, Krus, Makowski (1994), Krus (1991, 96). In the papers by Krus, Bronisz (1993, 94), Krus(1996), Krus, Bronisz (1996) game theoretical solution concepts which can be used in interactive procedures supporting negotiations have been proposed. This paper discusses the problem of players' manipulations. It is considered among others, as far the properties of the solution concepts and construction of the interactive procedures can prevent possible cheating of the players.

2 Description of decision situation

We assume that n sides - players are involved in a negotiation process. Each player has some decision variables and some assumed criteria measuring his payoff. Each player can have in general different criteria. Each payoff depends on decision variables of all the players.

Let the vector of decision variables of the player i $(i = 1, 2, \ldots, n)$ be denoted by $x_i = (x_{i1}, x_{i2}, \ldots, x_{ik_i})$, where k_i is the number of the variables and the payoff of the player i be defined by the vector of criteria $y_i = (y_{i1}, y_{i2}, \ldots, y_{im_i})$, where m_i is the number of the criteria.

A substantive model describing the decision problem is given by:

a set of admissible decisions $X_0 \subset R^K$, $x = (x_1, x_2, \ldots, x_n) \in X_0$, $K = \sum_i k_i$, where R^K is the space of all the decisions of all the players,

a vector of players' criteria $y = (y_1, y_2, \ldots, y_n) \in R^M$, $M = \sum_i m_i$, where R^M is the space of all the criteria of all the players,

a function $f : X_0 \to R^M$.

Assuming that the function f is continuous and the set $X_0 \subset R^K$ is compact, we have the compact set of attainable outcomes. The last set is denoted by Y_0.

We assume that utility functions aggregating player's criteria are not given explicitly. However each player has in mind preferences among his own criteria. Therefore, in the multicriteria payoffs space a partial ordering is introduced with use of the following cone D.

$$D = \{ y \in R^M : \quad y_{ij} \geq 0, \ j = 1, 2, \ldots, m'^i,$$
$$y_{ij} \leq 0, \ j = m'^i + 1, \ldots, m_i, \ \text{for } i = 1, 2, \ldots, n \},$$

where respectively the objectives to be maximized are indexed by $j = 1, 2, \ldots, m'^i$, and to be minimized — by $j = m'^i + 1, \ldots, m_i$.

We say that an element $y \in R^M$ **dominates** an element $z \in R^M$, and write $y \gg z$ if $y \in z + int(D)$. An element $y \in R^M$ **weakly dominates** an element $z \in R^M$, (in writing $y > z$) if $y \in z + D \setminus \{0\}$.

With use of the cone Pareto and weakly Pareto optimal elements of an arbitrary set Q_0 are defined. Pareto optimal (nondominated) elements $\hat{q}$ of the set Q_0 can be defined as the elements which belong to the set: $\hat{Q}_0 = \{\, \hat{q} \in Q_0 : Q_0 \cap (\hat{q} + D \setminus \{0\}) = \emptyset \,\}$. Weakly Pareto optimal (weakly nondominated) elements $\hat{q}^w$, are defined as the elements which belong to the set: $\hat{Q}_0^w = \{\, \hat{q} \in Q_0 : Q_0 \cap (\hat{q} + \operatorname{int} D) = \emptyset \,\}$.

An example of a set Y_0 of attainable outcomes in the case of two criteria y_1, y_2 is given in the fig. 3. Let a status quo point d be given in the set Y_0. Players have incentives for negotiations, if there exists a nonempty set S of mutual benefits. If the set is empty there is nothing to bargain for.

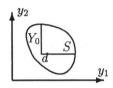

Fig. 3: A set of attainable payoffs and the agreement set S in the space of criteria.

The set of attainable payoffs is in general not given explicitly. However with use of the model implemented on a computer, one can derive some elements of the set for given decision variables. The model is assumed to be a base for decision analysis made by the players.

In the following the multicriteria bargaining problem will be considered, defined for n players by a pair (S, d), where $S \subset Y_0 \in R^M$ is so called agreement set, and d is a disagreement point, called also status quo point. The agreement set defines the payoffs of the players in case of their unanimous agreement. If the agreement is not reached the payoffs are defined by the point d. The bargaining problem describes a decision situation in which players can obtain some benefits, if they will cooperate, for example in realization of a joint project. The agreement set describes benefits of the players in case of cooperation in comparison to the status quo point describing their payoffs in the case when each player acts independently. The problem consists in finding reasonable solution - a point in the set S accepted by all the players and close to their preferences. The solution is looked for by means of negotiations.

3 Negotiation decision support systems

There exists a number of procedures and computer based systems already elaborated for negotiation support, for example MEDIATOR (Jarke et al. 1987), SCDAS (Lewandowski, Johnson, Wierzbicki 1986, Lewandowski 1989), NEGO (Kersten 1985, 88), MCBARG (Krus, Bronisz Lopuch, 1990), ICANS (Thiessen, Loucks 1992), GMCR (Fang et al. 1993), NEGOTIATION ASSISTANT (Rangaswamy, Shell 1997). See also Bui (1985), Korhonen et al. (1986), DeSanctis, Gallupe (1987). Comprehensive reviews on negotiation analysis are given by Sebenius(1992) and Young(1991). A methodological survey on group decision and negotiation support can be found in (Vetschera 1990).

In the following we consider a class of computer based systems, which utilize a mathematical model of decision problem. The fig. 4 shows on a scheme, how the model and optimization tools can be used for negotiation support. Two types of analysis are considered which can be supported by the system: unilateral analysis and multilateral analysis.

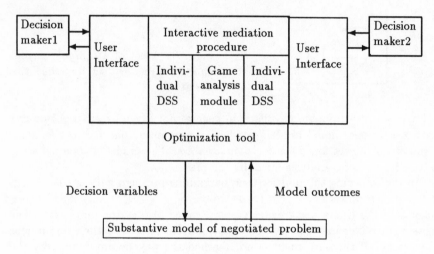

Fig. 4: General structure of DSS.

In the case of unilateral analysis each player acts with the system independently and no real interactions among the players take place. Each player can learn the problem, comparing different options of the decision variables and obtainable payoffs. He can not only better understand the nature of the problem, but can also learn, what are his preferences among criteria measuring his payoff. This kind of analysis is supported by "Individual DSS" module presented on the scheme. In the MEDIATOR system (Jarke et al. 1987) the unilateral analysis is based on evaluation of a utility function representation using PREFCALC system (Jacket-Lagreze, 1985). In MCBARG system (Krus at al. 1990) the multicriteria decision support based on Wierzbicki's reference point approach is used (Wierzbicki, 1982, 86). In this case players (decision makers) interact with the system using not directly their decision variables, but reference points defined in the spaces of players' criteria. The system derives on an output - the outcomes (payoffs), which are Pareto optimal in the set Y_0 and close to the reference points. The outcomes are calculated with use of an optimization tool according to the relations of the substantive model of the negotiated problem. When optimization calculations are made, the decision variables are also derived. Each player (decision maker) interacts with the system by "User interface" - a module providing menus for system operation, readable graphical presentation of results etc.

Multilateral analysis is made under joint actions of players. Each player can learn what he can really obtain when real - human counter players look for reasonable solution according to their own preferences.

In the case of MEDIATOR system a joint problem representation is constructed, and interactive analysis in the space of utilities is made in which players look for Pareto optimal consensus.

In MCBARG system an interactive procedure based on generalized solution concepts to multicriteria bargaining problem has been proposed and applied. The procedure serves as a mediation tool, which can aid the players to find the consensus on the Pareto frontier of the Y_0 set. The analysis is supported by the modules called "Interactive mediation procedure" and "Game analysis module" presented on the scheme. The "Game analysis module" calculates payoffs of the players according to assumed game theoretical solution concepts. The payoffs are calculated under introduced by the players reference points representing their preferences.

The procedure relates to two level distributed decision making problem.

The lower level deals with unilateral analysis. Each player independently assumes reference level for the criteria (reference point in the space of criteria) he would like to reach. The computer based DSS, using the model relations, calculates the attainable, Pareto optimal payoff being close to the reference point. The process can be repeated. Each player can generate (using the system) a number of attainable payoffs, assuming different reference points. In this way each player can analyze – scan the set of attainable Pareto optimal payoffs and can select the payoff which is the most preferred one. In the analysis each player has to assume the reference points of counterplayers. The selected payoff is sent to the upper level.

The upper level relates to coordination problem. The most preferred payoffs of all the players are collected. On the base, the cooperative outcome is calculated with use of assumed solution concept of the bargaining problem. The obtained outcome and payoffs of particular players are sent to the lower level for further analysis. On the lower level the players again independently analyze the problem in the way presented above. The coordination problem is solved in an iterative process. At each iteration the players independently analyze the problem on the lower level and improved cooperative outcome is calculated on the upper level.

4 Analysis of players' manipulations

The multicriteria bargaining problem formulated in section 2 is a generalization of the classical unicriteria bargaining problem. In the case of classical problem preferences of any player are expressed by given utility functions. A number of solution concepts have been proposed and axiomatized for the classical problem (see Nash, 1950, Raiffa, 1953, Kalai and Smorodinsky, 1975, Roth, 1979, Thomson, 1980, Imai, 1983).

There are questions to be discussed:

How the solution concepts to bargaining problem can be generalized on multicriteria problem and utilized in the multilateral analysis and in mediation support? Can application of the solution concepts prevent possible players' manipulation?

There are two ways of players' manipulations. A player can manipulate in problem definition, redefining for example criteria (changing scales of the criteria) or adding additional insignificant criteria. A player can report false values of parameters required in the interactive mediation procedure (expressing for example false preferences). In both the cases the player tries to increase his payoff.

A generalization of Raiffa-Kalai-Smorodinsky solution concept on the case of multicriteria bargaining problem has been given by Krus, Bronisz (1993) in the following theorem. The result is based on a new concept of so called relative utopia point (RA utopia) defined in R^M space. In the following we assume that all criteria are maximized. We assume also that each player makes unilateral analysis of the problem using reference point approach of multicriteria optimization. He assumes reference points in his multicriteria space of payoffs, and the decision support system calculates nondominated outcomes being in the set S. Let the player i select his preferred nondominated point $\hat{y}_i$.

A point $u \in R^M$ is an **utopia point relative to the players' aspirations (RA utopia point)** if for each player $i \in N$, there is an individually nondominated point $\hat{y} \in S$ such that $u_i = \hat{y}_i$.

The RA utopia point is a composition of preferred nondominated points selected by all the players. The RA utopia point significantly differs from the concept of ideal point (called also utopia). Let us see that the classical **ideal (utopia) point** $I(S, d) = (I_1(S, d), I_2(S, d), \ldots, I_M(S, d))$ is defined by $I_k(S, d) = \max\{y_k : y \in S, \ y \geq d\}$ for $k \in [1, \ldots, M]$.

Theorem 1 *Krus, Bronisz, 1993. Let the multicriteria bargaining problem (S, d) satisfy the following conditions:*

(i) S is compact and there is $y \in S$ such that $y > d$,
(ii) S is comprehensive, i.e. for $y' \in S$ if $d \leq y \leq y'$ then $y \in S$.
(iii) For any $y' \in S$, let $Q(S, y') = \{\, i : y \geq y', \ y_i > y'_i \ \text{for some } y \in S \,\}$. Then for any $y' \in S$, there exists $y \in S$ such that $y \geq y'$, $y_i > y'_i$ for each $i \in Q(S, y')$.

Then there exists a unique function $G(S, d, u) = \max_{\geq} \{y \in S : \ y = d + h(u - d)$ for some $h \in R\}$ which fulfils the following set of axioms:

A1. Weak Pareto optimality.
*   A point $G(S, d, u)$ is weak Pareto optimal in S.*

A2. Invariance under positive affine transformations of criteria.

Let $T : R^M \longrightarrow R^M$ be an arbitrary affine transformation such that $T_k y = (a_k y_k + b_k)$, $a_k > 0$ for $k \in M$. Then $G(TS, Td, Tu) = TG(S, d, u)$.

A3. Anonymity.

For any permutation on $[1, \dots, M]$, π, let π^* denote the permutation on R^M. Then $\pi^* G(S, d, u) = G(\pi^* S, \pi^* d, \pi^* u)$.

A4. Restricted monotonicity.

Let we consider two multicriteria bargaining problems (S, d) and (S', d). Let $U(S, d)$ denote the set of all relative utopia points of the problem (S, d).

If $u \in U(S, d) \cap U(S', d)$ and $S \subseteq S'$ then $G(S, d, u) \leq G(S', d, u)$. ■

Discussion

The theorem generalizes Raiffa-Kalai-Smorodinsky solution concept on the Multicriteria bargaining problem. The first three axioms are usually imposed on solutions of axiomatic bargaining problem. Axiom $A1$ says that the players behave in a rational way trying optimize their payoffs. Axiom $A2$ demands that a solution does not depend on selected affine measure of any criterion. Axiom $A3$ says that a solution does not depend on the order of the players, nor on the order of the criteria. The last axiom $A4$ assures that all the players benefit (or at least not lose) from any enlargement of the agreement set, if the RA utopia point does not change.

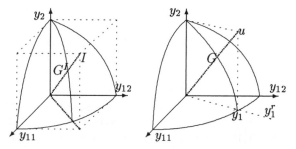

Fig. 5: Solution concepts to multicriteria bargaining problem.

An illustration of the generalized solution concept based on the RA utopia is presented in fig. 5 (on the right hand side) and compared to a straight-forward generalization based on the Ideal point (left hand side). The figure illustrates bargaining problem of two players. The player 1 has two criteria: y_{11}, y_{12}. The player 2 has one criterion y_2. In the three coordinates an agreement set S is presented. The status quo point d is at the origin. Let y_1^r be the reference point of the player 1, and $\hat{y}_1$ his preferred nondominated payoff. The nondominated payoff of the player 2 is $\hat{y}_2$. The RA utopia u is the composition of the last two points. Let us take the line linking the origin and the RA utopia point. The solution G proposed in the theorem 1 is formulated as the intersection of the line with the Pareto frontier of the set S.

The left-hand side of the figure illustrates a natural straightforward generalization of the Raiffa-Kalai-Smorodinski solution concept G^I based on the Ideal point I. Let us see that in this case the payoffs of the players generated by the solution concept do not depend on the players' preferences. Therefore this particular concept hardly can be used in the decision support.

The proposed solution concept based on RA utopia has an interesting property presented in the following theorem.

Let

u_i denote projection of the RA-utopia point on the multicriteria space of the player i,

H denote n-dimensional hyperplane generated by the points $d, u_1, u_2, \ldots, u_n$,

T denote mapping from H to R^n defined by:

$$T(d + (a_1(u_1 - d_1), a_2(u_2 - d_2), \ldots, a_n(u_n - d_n))) = (a_1, a_2, \ldots, a_n),$$

G denote generalized Raiffa-Kalai-Smorodinsky solution concept to the bargaining problem (S, d), and G^n denote Raiffa-Kalai-Smorodinsky concept to the classical problem $(T(S \cap H), T(d))$.

Theorem 2 *If*

(i) S is compact and there is $y \in S$ such that $y > d$,

(ii) S is comprehensive, i.e. for $y' \in S$ if $d \leq y \leq y'$ then $y \in S$.

then $T(G(S, d, u)) = G^n(T(S \cap H), T(d))$. ∎

Proof. The classical bargaining problem $(T(S \cap H), T(d))$ is normalized, i.e. the disagreement point $T(d)$ is equal to $\mathbf{0}$ and the ideal point $I(T(S \cap H), T(d)) = T(u) = \mathbf{1}$. We have $G^n(T(S \cap H), T(d)) = \max_{\geq} \{a \in T(S \cap H) : a = T(d) + h(I(T(S \cap H), T(d)) - T(d))$ for some $h \in R\} = \max_{\geq} \{T(x) \in T(S \cap H) : x = d + h(u - d)$ for some $h \in R\} = T(G(S, d, u))$. □

The result is illustrated in fig. 6 in the case of two players. Let $\hat{y}_1'^r$ be nondominated point selected by the player 1 and $\hat{y}_2$ selected by the player 2. The hyperplane H' is defined by the two points and the origin (i.e. status quo point d). The dimensionality of the hyperplane is equal to the number of players. The RA-utopia point U' and the solution to the multicriteria bargaining problem G' lye on the hyperplane. Applying the transformation T we can consider the solution in two dimensional space (of two players). The theorem shows that the classical n–person Raiffa-Kalai-Smorodinsky solution concept can be applied directly to the multicriteria bargaining problem if we confine consideration to the outcomes in $S \cap H'$, i.e. to intersection of the agreement set S with the hyperplane H'.

On the base of the theorem other classical solution concepts can be considered and applied in multicriteria bargaining problem. Examples of Egalitarian solution concept (denoted by E) and Nash solution (N) are marked on the figure. The Nash solution concept (Nash, 1950) maximizes product of the players' payoffs. It satisfies the axioms of Pareto optimality, symmetry, scale invariance and of independence of irrelevant alternatives. The Egalitarian solution concept maximizes gain of equal coordinates. It satisfies axioms of weak Pareto optimality, symmetry and of strong monotonicity.

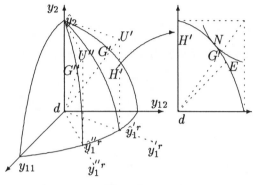

Fig. 6:

Let us discuss how the solution depends on player's references. What will happen if a player reports false preferences? Preferences of a player are defined by selected reference point and preferred nondominated outcome. In the figure two nondominated points $\hat{y}_1'^r$ and $\hat{y}_1''^r$ are denoted. Each of the points generates another hyperplane, H' and H'' respectively. If the player 1 changes his preferences and moves from the point $\hat{y}_1'^r$ to the point $\hat{y}_1''^r$, then we deal with a pivot of the hyperplane from H' to H'', and the solution will move from G' to G''. The selected by the player nondominated outcome defines a direction starting from the status quo payoff. The direction reflects preferences of the player. According to the direction the multicriteria cooperative payoff is generated due to the solution concept.

Let the player report his preferences incorrectly. That means, the player does not report the point reflecting his real preferences (for example $\hat{y}_1'^r$), but reports false point $\hat{y}_1''^r$. The cooperative payoff, according to the solution concept, will move from G' to G''. Interests of counterplayers are protected by the solution concept formula. The player who tries to cheat can lose himself, because his payoff will not be close to his real preferences but to the false ones.

In the following definition and theorem a continuity of solution concepts is discussed.

Definition 1 *We say that a solution to multicriteria bargaining problem is continuous with respect to players' aspirations, if for any sequence of reference points $\{y_i^{rt}\}_{t=1}^{\infty}$ for $i = 1, 2, \ldots n$ such that in the limit as t goes to infinity, y_i^{rt}*

converges to y_i^r for all $i = 1, 2, \ldots, n$, we have that $G(S, d, u(y^{rt}))$ converges to $G(S, d, u(y^{rt}))$, where $y^{rt} = (y_1^r, y_2^r, \ldots, y_2^r)$.

Theorem 3 *If the agreement set S is compact, convex, comprehensive and there exists a point $x \in S$ dominating status quo point d, then*

- *generalized multicriteria solution based on Raiffa, Kalai, Smorodinsky concept,*

- *multicriteria solution based on Egalitarian solution concept,*

are continuous with respect to players aspirations in multicriteria bargaining problem. ∎

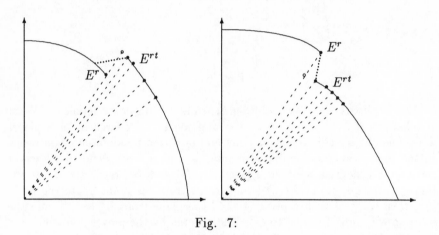

Fig. 7:

Proof. Let us consider first the egalitarian solution concept, and a sequence of reference points, y_i^{rt} converging to y_i^r, defined for all $i = 1, 2, \ldots, n$. For each t, on the points y_i^{rt}, $i = 1, 2, \ldots, n$, and on the status quo point d, a hyperplane H^{rt} can be constructed in the way presented at the theorem 2. In each of the hyperplanes the egalitarian solution E^{rt} is defined as the intersection of the line of equal gains with the pareto frontier of the set S. Let the sequence $\{E^{rt}\}_t$ does not converge to E^r, where E^r is the egalitarian solution in the case of the reference points y_i^r, $i = 1, 2, \ldots, n$. That means, the sequence converges to a point lying on the line linking the origin point d with the point E^r, but with the lower or higher distance from the origin, than the E^r point (see the construction on the following figure). If the sequence converges to a lower point, then we construct the line segments linking the E^r point with the E^{rt} points. The segments include points that not belong to the set S. The contradiction to the convexity of S. We deal with the similar contradiction, if the sequence $\{E^r t\}_t$ converges to a higher point than E^r.

Line segments can be constructed in the way shown on the right hand side of the figure. That means, the sequence $\{E^{rt}\}_t$ converges to the point E^r.

Let in the case of generalized Raiffa-Kalai-Smorodinsky (R-K-S) solution, $\hat{y}_i^{rt}$, and $\hat{y}_i^r$ denote the nondominated points corresponding to the reference points y_i^{rt}, and y_i^r respectively, where i is the number of player. In the criteria space of the player i we construct the line linking the origin and the reference point y_i^{rt}. The nondominated point of any player i is calculated as the intersection of the line with the pareto frontier of the projection of the set S on the criteria space of the player i. Because the projection of the convex set is convex, we show, in the similar way as in the case of egalitarian solution, that the sequence $\{\hat{y}_i^{rt}\}_t$ converges to $\hat{y}_i^r$. Therefore the sequence of relative utopia points $\{U^{rt}\}_t$ converges to U^r point. Let us construct lines linking the origin and the points U^{rt}, and denote the respective generalized R-K-S solutions by G^{rt}. The generalized R-K-S solution is formulated as the intersection of the line and pareto frontier of the set S. Using the way presented in the case of egalitarian solution we prove that the sequence $\{G^{rt}\}_t$ converges to the point G^r. □

An interactive procedure supporting multilateral analysis has been presented in details in (Krus, Bronisz, Lopuch 1990) and utilized in MCBARG computer based system. It is assumed that negotiation process consists of some number of rounds. Let t denote number of the round. Then according to the procedure a sequence of mediation proposals d^t is generated in rounds $t = 1, 2, \ldots, T$ defined by:

$$(*) \qquad \begin{aligned} d^0 &= d, \\ d^t &= d^{t-1} + \alpha^t * \left[G^t - d^{t-1} \right] \qquad \text{for} \quad t = 1, 2, \ldots, T \end{aligned}$$

where

α^t is so called confidence coefficient assumed by players in the round t, $0 < \epsilon < \alpha^t < 1$, ϵ is any small, positive number,

T is a minimal number t for which $d^t = d^{t-1}$ or $T = \infty$.

In each round players make independently unilateral analysis. Each player assumes a number of reference points and learns possible payoffs calculated by the system. Each player finishing the unilateral analysis is asked to select his preferred payoff or preferred reference point indicating the payoff. He is also asked to define the confidence coefficient - a positive number less than 1. The system calculates cooperative solution G on the base of preferred reference points selected by the players. The payoffs d^t presented to the players should be considered as mediation proposals. The proposal is calculated as the cooperative solution decreased by multiplication with the value of confidence coefficient according to the above formula. In the next round the players deal with a "smaller" bargaining problem, as it is illustrated in fig. 8. The mediation proposal d^1 calculated in the round 1 becomes status quo point in the round 2. In the second round the players deal with the fragment of the agreement set S dominating the point d^1. The set is unilaterally analyzed by the players and they again select theirs preferred payoffs and reference points. The next mediation proposal can be calculated.

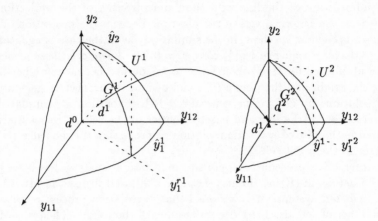

Fig. 8: Mediation proposals d^1, d^2 generated by the system.

Let us see that using the confidence coefficient a player can protect himself against unpredictable payoffs. A lower confidence coefficient results in lower increase of payoff in the round. (Each player defines his own coefficient, and α^t takes minimum value of the coefficients). If lower confidence coefficients are assumed in particular rounds then the more rounds are required to reach final multilateral cooperative payoff on the pareto frontier of the set S. The players have in such a case more possibilities to analyze the decision problem in details.

5   Final remarks

The paper discusses problem of players' manipulations in interactive procedures supporting negotiations. A class of decision support systems utilizing mathematical model of decision situation is considered. The paper continues the line of previous research linking multicriteria optimization methods and new solution concepts to multicriteria bargaining problem.

New results include among others an analysis of relations between generalized solutions of multicriteria bargaining problem and respective solutions of classical (unicriteria) problem (Theorem 2), an analysis of continuity of the multicriteria solution concept with respect to reference points reported by players (Theorem 3), discussion of the properties of the solutions and of the interactive mediation procedure in the context of possible players' manipulations.

On the base of the Theorem 2 different classical solution concepts can be generalized on multicriteria case and applied in the interactive procedure. Each of the solutions fulfills a different set of properties (axioms). The axioms according to the game theory express some fairness rules imposed on the payoffs that is derived according to an assumed solution concept. For example the Anonymity axiom assures that all the players and all criteria are treated in the same way (no one is privileged, nor wronged). The axiom of Invariance under affine positive transformation (called also the Scale invariance axiom) says that any player can not benefit changing scale of any criterion. It seems reasonable, that if a player accepts a selected set of axioms, he should agree on payoffs satisfying the axioms.

It has been illustrated that the solution concept protects counterplayers payoffs against possible player's manipulations. The player reporting false preferences can lose himself.

Coefficients of "limited confidence" assumed by players in particular round of the interactive procedure can protect the players against unpredictable payoffs calculated by the system as the agreement solution. Each player can decrease improvement of all the players' payoffs in particular round and can increase the number of rounds in which analysis is made.

Further research on the players' manipulation problem is required. It should include among others, problems of information structure in interactive procedures, generalization of other solution concepts on the multicriteria case, analysis of the concepts in interactive procedures, experiments with human players.

References

Bui, T.X.(1985). N. A. I.: A Consensus Seeking Algorithm for Group Decision Support Systems. *Proc. of the IEEE Conference on Cybernetics and Society*, IEEE, N.Y., pp. 380-384.

Chatterje K., J. Ulvila (1983), Bargaining with shared information, *Decision Science*, Vol. 13, pp.380-404.

DeSanctis, G., B. Gallupe (1987). A Foundation for the Study of Group Decision Support System, *Management Science*, Vol.33, pp. 589-609.

Fang L., K.W.Hipel, D.M. Kilgore (1993) Interactive Decision Making, John Wiley&Sons, New York.

Fisher R., Ury W.(1981) Getting to Yes. Hougton Mifflin, Boston.

Groves T., Ledyard J. (1977). Optimal Allocation of Public Goods: A Solution to the Free-Rider Problem, Econometrica 45, 783-809.

Harsanyi, J. (1967-68), Games of Incomplete Information Played by "Bayesian" Players. *Management Science*. Vol. 14, pp. 149-182, 320-334, 486-502.

Harsanyi, J.C., R. Selten (1972). A Generalized Nash Solution for Two–Person Bargaining Games with Incomplete Information. Management

Sciences, Vol. 18, pp. 80–106.

Imai, H. (1983). Individual Monotonicity and Lexicographical Maxmin Solution. *Econometrica*, Vol. 51, pp. 389–401.

Jacquet-Lagreze, E. (1985). PREFCALC, Version 2.0, EURO=DECISION, BP 57, 78530 Buc, France.

Jarke, M., M.T. Jelassi, M.F. Shakun (1987). Mediator: Towards a negotiation support system. *European Journal of Operational Research* 31, pp. 314–334, North-Holland.

Kalai, E., M. Smorodinsky (1975). Other Solutions to Nash's Bargaining Problem. *Econometrica*, Vol. 43, pp. 513–518.

Kersten, G.E. (1985). NEGO - Group Decision Support System, *Information and Management*, Vol. 8, pp. 237-385

Kersten, G.E. (1988). A Procedure for Negotiating Efficient and Non–Efficient Compromises. *Decision Support Systems* 4, pp. 167–177, North-Holland.

Korhonen, P., H. Moskowitz, J. Wallenius, S. Zionts (1986). An Interactive Approach to Multiple Criteria Optimization with Multiple Decision–Makers. *Naval Research Logistics Quarterly*, Vol. 33, pp. 589–602, John Wiley & Sons.

Kruś, L. (1991). Some Models and Procedures for Decision Support in Bargaining. In P. Korhonen, A. Lewandowski, J. Wallenius (Eds), Multiple Criteria Decision Support. *Lectures Notes in Economics and Mathematical Systems*, Springer Verlag, Berlin.

Krus, L. (1996). Multicriteria Decision Support in Negotiations. *Control and Cybernetics* Vol (1996) No. 6, pp. 1245-1260.

Krus L., P. Bronisz, (1993), "Some New Results in Interactive Approach to Multicriteria Bargaining". In Wessels J., A.P. Wierzbicki (Eds), " User - Oriented Methodology and Techniques of Decision Analysis and Support", *Lecture Notes in Economic and Math. Systems*, Springer Verlag, Berlin.

Krus L. P. Bronisz (1994) "On n-person Noncooperative Multicriteria Games Described in Strategic Form". *Annals of Operation Research*, Vol. 51, J. C. Balzer AG, Sci. Publ, USA, pp. 83-97.

Krus L. P. Bronisz (1996) "Solution Concepts in Multicriteria Cooperative Games without Side Payments". In J. Dolezal (Ed.): System Modelling and Optimization, Chapman and Hall Publ.

Krus, L., P. Bronisz, B. Lopuch (1990). "MCBARG - Enhanced. A System Supporting Multicriteria Bargaining". CP–90–006, IIASA, Laxenburg, Austria.

Lewandowski, A., Johnson S., Wierzbicki A. P. (1986). A prototype Selection Committee Decision Analysis and Support System SCDAS: Theoretical Background and Computer Implementation. WP-8627, IIASA, Laxenburg Austria.

Lewandowski, A. (1989). SCDAS - Decision Support System for Group Decision Making: Theoretic Framework. *Decision Support Systems*, 5, 403-423.

Nash, J.F. (1950). The Bargaining Problem. *Econometrica*, Vol. 18, pp. 155–162.

Raiffa, H. (1953). Arbitration Schemes for Generalized Two-Person Games. *Annals of Mathematics Studies*, No. 28, pp. 361–387, Princeton.

Raiffa, H. (1982). The Art and Science of Negotiations. Harvard Univ. Press, Cambridge.

Rangaswamy, A., G.R. Shell (1997) Using Computers to Realize Joint Gains in Negotiations: Toward an "Electronic Bargaining Table", Management Science, Vol. 43, No. 8, pp.1147-1163.

Roth, A.E. (1979). Axiomatic Models of Bargaining. *Lecture Notes in Economics and Mathematical Systems*, Vol. 170, Springer-Verlag, Berlin.

Sebenius, J.K. (1992) Negotiation Analysis: A Characterization and Review. Management Sci. Vol. 38, pp. 18-38.

Thiessen, E.M., D.P. Loucks (1992) Computer Assisted Negotiation of Multi-objective Water Resources Conflicts, Working Paper, School of Civil and Envir. Eng., Cornell University, Ithaca, NY.

Thomson, W. (1980). Two Characterization of the Raiffa Solution. *Economic Letters*, Vol. 6, pp. 225–231.

Vetschera, R. (1990). Group Decision and Negotiation Support - a Methodological Survey. *OR Spectrum*, 17, pp. 67-77.

Wierzbicki, A.P. (1982). A Mathematical Basis for Satisficing Decision Making. *Mathematical Modeling*, Vol. 3, pp. 391–405.

Wierzbicki, A.P. (1983). Negotiation and Mediation in Conflicts I: The Role of Mathematical Approaches and Methods. In H. Chestnat et al. (Eds): Supplemental Ways to Increase International Stability. Pergamon Press, Oxford.

Wierzbicki, A.P. (1986). On the Completeness and Constructiveness of Parametric Characterization to Vector Optimization Problems. *OR-Spectrum*, Vol. 8, pp. 73-87.

Wierzbicki, A. P., L. Krus, M. Makowski (1993), "The Role of Multi-Objective Optimization in Negotiation and Mediation Support". *Theory and Decision*, special issue on "International Negotiation Support Systems: Theory, Methods, and Practice" Vol. 34, No. 2.

Young, H.P. (1991); Negotiation Analysis, in H.P. Young(Ed.) Negotiation Analysis, Univ. of Michigan Press, Ann Arbor, MI.

Young H.P. (1982), Cost Allocation. Prentice Hall. New York.

Some Concepts of Solution for a Game under Uncertainty

Moussa Larbani[1] and Fatiha Kacher

Department of Mathematics, Faculty of Sciences, University of Tizi-Ouzou, 15000 Tizi-Ouzou, Algeria.

[1] e-mail: larbani@usa.net

Abstract. We present some concepts of solution for a decision making problem involving several decision makers in a conflict and unknown parameters in the case of complete ignorance of their behaviour. In our model we assume that the decision makers (players) have formed a coalition structure.

Keywords. Game, equilibrium, uncertainty, multi-objective problem.

1 Introduction

Usually, real decision making problems involve unknown parameters, which are generally due to lack of information. Studies on decision making problems involving several decision makers in a conflict with unknown parameters in the case of complete ignorance of their behaviour are at their beginning. The first important result in this field of research has been obtained by Zhukovskii [10]. He has introduced the NS- equilibrium concept for a non co-operative game under uncertainty. This concept results from the combination of the concept of Nash equilibrium for a non co-operative game [6] and a weak Pareto (Slater) optimal solution for a multi-objective problem [8]. An approach for the determination of the NS-equilibrium is proposed in [3].

The solutions we propose in this paper are the result of the combination of a concept of solution from game theory and some notions of solution from multiple criteria decision making (MCDM) theory. These solutions take into account both the aspect of conflict and the aspect of decision making under uncertainty [4]. Furthermore, we give sufficient conditions for the existence of such solutions and study the problem of their determination. The results of this work are a generalisation of the concept of NS-equilibrium presented in [10] in the sense that we consider the case where the players can form coalitions and we use other concepts of solution from MCDM theory.

The paper is organized as follows. The section 2 is devoted to the problem statement and the definition of its solutions; in section 3 we prove existence theorems of the introduced solutions; in section 4 we discuss the problem of determination of such solutions and, finally, we give a conclusion.

2 The statement of the problem and the definition of solutions

Let us consider the following n-person game under uncertainty
$$< I, X, Y, f(x,y) > \tag{1}$$
where $I=\{1,...,n\}$ is the set of players; $X=\prod_{i\in I} X_i$ is the set of issues of the game

(1); $X_i \subset R^{n_i}$, $n_i \geq 1$, X_i the set of strategies of the *ith* player, $X \subset R^s$,
$s=\sum_{i\in I} n_i$; $x=(x_1,..,x_n) \in X$ is an issue of the game where $x_i \in X_i$ is the strategy of

the *ith* player; Y is the set of unknown parameters, $Y \subset R^p$, $p \geq 1$, $y \in Y$ is the vector of unknown parameters ; $f=(f_1,..,f_n)$, where $f_i : X \times Y \to R$ is the objective function of the *ith* player.

Definition 1. [9] A coalition structure of the game (1) is a partition of the set of the players.

Assumptions. In the game (1), we suppose that :
1- players are rational;
2- each player knows the objective function and the set of strategies of each of the remaining players;
3- all players only know the domain Y where the vector of unknown parameters can take its values.
4- players have formed a coalition structure;
5- side payments are not permitted;
6- there is not enforceable agreements between coalitions of the formed coalition structure.

The game takes place as follows: when all players have chosen their respective strategies x_i, $i \in I$, we obtain the issue $x=(x_1,..,x_i,..,x_n)$ and if the unknown parameters take the value y then each player $i \in I$ receives the payoff $f_i(x,y)$. The aim of each player in this game, by choosing his strategy, is to maximize his objective function taking into account the formed coalition structure and the possible realizations of the unknown parameters.

Notations. Let S denote the set of all coalition structure and let $P \in S$ be the coalition structure formed by players, for any coalition $k \in P$, the set $X_k = \prod_{i \in k} X_i$ denotes the set of strategies of k; we denote by x_k any element of X_k; $\forall x \in X$ and $\forall x^0 \in X$, $(x_k, x_{I-k}^0) = (x^0 // x_k)$ is an issue of the game (1) where the strategies of the players of the coalition k, in the issue x^0, are substituted for the corresponding ones in the issue x, particularly, $x = (x_k, x_{I-k}) = (x // x_k)$; for any coalition $k \subset I$ the function defined by

$$\varphi_k(x,y) = \sum_{i \in k} f_i(x,y), \quad \forall (x,y) \in X \times Y$$

represents the objective function of the coalition k.

Note that from assumptions 5 and 6 we deduce that the strategic possibilities of any coalition k of the coalition structure formed is limited to the set $X_k = \prod_{i \in k} X_i$.

Remark 1. Let P be the coalition structure formed by players $(P \in S)$. The assumptions 1-6, enable us to classify the game (1) as a cooperative game under uncertainty in the complete ignorance case, in normal form without side payments, with a coalitions structure. The game (1) has the following properties.

1. If $x = x^0$ (x^0 fixed in X), in (1), we obtain the multi-objective problem [8]:
$$<Y, f(x^0, y)>.$$

2. If we fix a realization of the unknown parameters $y = y^0$ in (1), we obtain the n-person game $< I, X, f(x, y^0) >$.

From assumptions 1-6 (cited above), we deduce that a solution for the game (1) has to satisfy at least the following conditions:

1. take into account the non cooperative behaviour of the coalitions of the formed coalition structure P;

2. express the collective interest of the players against all possible realizations of the unknown parameters.

Throughout this paper we assume that the coalition structure P is formed and that the following conditions are met:

a) $Y, X_i, i = \overline{1,n}$ are non empty, convex and compact sets;

b) $f_i: X \times Y \rightarrow R, \overline{1,n}$ are continuous on $X \times Y$.

The following definitions reflect the cited above conditions that a solution has to satisfy.

Definition 2. A pair $(x^0, y^0) \in X \times Y$ is called N-S-G equilibrium (generalized Nash-Slater equilibrium) if :

1. $\forall k \in P, \forall x_k \in X_k$, the system of inequalities
$$f_i(x^0, y^0) \leq f_i(x^0 // x_k, y^0), \quad i \in k,$$
where at least one of them is stringent, is impossible.

2. $\forall k \in P$, $\displaystyle \max_{x_k \in X_k} \min_{x_{I-k} \in X_{I-k}} \sum_{i \in k} f_i(x_k, x_{I-k}, y^0) \leq \sum_{i \in k} f_i(x^0, y^0)$.

3. $\forall y \in Y$ the system of inequalities

$$f_i(x^0, y) < f_i(x^0, y^0), \quad i \in I,$$

is impossible.

Definition 3. A pair $(x^0, y^0) \in X \times Y$ is called N-P-G equilibrium (Generalized Nash Pareto equilibrium) if in addition to conditions 1 and 2 of definition 2 the following condition holds:

3. $\forall y \in Y$ the system of inequalities

$$f_i(x^0, y) \leq f_i(x^0, y^0), \quad i \in I,$$

where at least one of them is stringent, is impossible.

Definition 4. A pair $(x^0, y^0) \in X \times Y$ is called N-G-G equilibrium (Generalized Nash Geoffrion equilibrium) if in addition to conditions 1-3 of definition 3 the following condition holds:

4. there exists a number $\theta > 0$ such that

$$\forall y \in Y, \ \forall i \in I \text{ such that } f_i(x^0, y) < f_i(x^0, y^0)$$

there exists $j \in I$ such that

$$f_j(x^0, y^0) < f_j(x^0, y) \text{ and } [(f_i(x^0, y^0) - f_i(x^0, y)) / (f_j(x^0, y) - f_j(x^0, y^0))] \leq \theta.$$

Remark 2.

1. The first condition of definitions 2-4 means that

    i) any deviation of a coalition $k \in P$ from its strategy x_k^0, cannot increase the payoff of all its members, this property shows that the introduced concepts are stable,

    ii) $\forall k \in P$, x_k^0 is a weak Pareto (Slater) optimal solution for the multi-objective problem $< X_k, \{f_i(x^0//x_k, y^0)\}_{i \in k} >$.

2. The second condition shows that the issue x^0 is individually rational for each coalition of P, when the unknown parameters take the value y^0.

3. The third condition in definitions 2-4 expresses the collective interests of the players against all possible realizations of the parameter y and

    i) in definition 2, y^0 is a weak Pareto (Slater) optimal solution for the multi-objective problem $< Y, f(x^0, y) >$,

    ii) in definition 3, y^0 is a Pareto optimal solution for the multi-objective problem $< Y, f(x^0, y) >$.

4. In definition 4 the conditions 3 and 4 imply that y^0 is a Geoffrion optimal (or proper efficient) solution [8] for the problem $< Y, f(x^0, y) >$.

5. We have the following relation between the three concepts:

$$\text{N-G-G} \Rightarrow \text{N-P-G} \Rightarrow \text{N-S-G}$$

this fact is a consequence of the fact that in a mutltiobjective problem a Geoffrion optimal solution is a Pareto optimal solution and a Pareto optimal solution is a weak Pareto optimal solution [8]. Thus a sufficient condition for the existence of an N-G-G equilibrium is also sufficient for the existence of N-P-G and N-S-G equilibrium.

Using the functions $\varphi_k(x,y) = \sum_{i \in k} f_i(x,y))$, $k \subset I$, we can eliminate the condition

2 of definitions 2-4. Precisely, we have the following lemmas.

Lemma 1. If a pair $(x^0, y^0) \in X \times Y$ verifies the following conditions :

1. $\forall k \in P$, $\forall x_k \in X_k$, $\varphi_k(x^0//x_k, y^0) \leq \varphi_k(x^0, y^0)$;
2. $\forall y \in Y$ the system of inequalities
$$f_i(x^0, y) < f_i(x^0, y^0), \quad i \in I,$$
   is impossible.

Then (x^0, y^0) is an N-S-G equilibrium of the game (1).

Proof. We can easily prove that the condition 1 of this lemma implies the conditions 1 and 2 of definition 2. □

Lemma 2. If a pair $(x^0, y^0) \in X \times Y$ verifies the following conditions :

1. $\forall k \in P$, $\forall x_k \in X_k$, $\varphi_k(x^0//x_k, y^0) \leq \varphi_k(x^0, y^0)$;
2. $\forall y \in Y$, $\sum_{i \in I} f_i(x^0, y^0) \leq \sum_{i \in I} f_i(x^0, y)$.

Then (x^0, y^0) is an N-G-G, N-P-G and N-S-G equilibrium of game (1).

Proof. It suffices to verify the third and forth conditions of definition 4. We have

$$\forall y \in Y, \quad \sum_{i \in I} f_i(x^0, y^0) \leq \sum_{i \in I} f_i(x^0, y) \Rightarrow$$

$$\min_{y \in Y} \sum_{i \in I} f_i(x^0, y) = \sum_{i \in I} f_i(x^0, y^0),$$

then, y^0 is a Geoffrion optimal solution of the multi-objective problem $<Y, f(x^0, y)>$ [7]. We deduce that (x^0, y^0) is a N-G-G equilibrium of the game (1). □

3 The problem of existence

In the previous section we introduced some concepts of equilibrium for the game (1). Now we will study the problem of the existence of such solutions. Generally, the existence of solutions in game theory are proved by fixed points theorems [1]. However, using this approach it is very difficult to derive constructive algorithms for the determination of these solutions. In this paper we use the approach presented in [3] from which, in the next section, we derive an algorithm for the determination of the introduced solutions. We are going to prove the existence theorems of N-S-G and N-G-G equilibrium, the existence of the N-P-G equilibrium is a consequence of the point 5) of remark 2.

3.1 The existence of N-S-G equilibrium

In this subsection we consider the function $\phi_{k_0}(.,.) : Z \times T \rightarrow R$,

$(z,t) \rightarrow \phi_{k_0}(z, t)$ defined by

$$\phi_{k_0}(z,t) = \varphi_{k_0}(x,y) - \varphi_{k_0}(x,y') + \sum_{k \in P} [\varphi_k(x//x'_{k_1},y) - \varphi_k(x,y)] \qquad (2)$$

where $z \in Z = X \times Y$, $t \in T = X \times Y$, $z = (x,y)$, $t = (x',y')$, $k_0 \subset I$.

The following lemma shows the relation between the N-S-G equilibrium and the function $\phi_{k_0}(.,.)$.

Lemma 3. If there exists $\bar{z} = (\bar{x}, \bar{y}) \in Z$ such that

$$\phi_{k_0}(\bar{z},t) \leq 0, \qquad \forall t \in T \qquad (3)$$

then $\bar{z}$ is an N-S-G equilibrium of the game (1).

Proof.

1) Let $k \in P$ setting $t = (\bar{x}//x_k, \bar{y})$ in (2), according to (3) and (2), we obtain

$$\phi_{k_0}(\bar{z},t) \leq 0 \Rightarrow \varphi_k(\bar{x}//x_k,y) - \varphi_k(\bar{x},\bar{y}) \leq 0$$

then

$$\forall k \in P, \forall x_k \in X_k, \varphi_k(\bar{x}//x_k,y) \leq \varphi_k(\bar{x},\bar{y}).$$

Thus the first condition of lemma 1 is satisfied.

2) Setting $t = (\bar{x},y)$ in (2), we obtain

$$\phi_{k_0}(\bar{z},t) \leq 0 \Rightarrow \varphi_{k_0}(\bar{x},\bar{y}) \leq \varphi_{k_0}(\bar{x},y), \forall y \in Y$$

hence

$$\min_{y \in Y} \varphi_{k_0}(\bar{x},y) = \varphi_{k_0}(\bar{x},\bar{y})$$

then $\bar{y}$ is a weak Pareto optimal (Slater) solution for the multi-objective problem $<Y, f(\bar{x},y)>$ [7], we deduce that $\bar{z} = (\bar{x}, \bar{y})$ verifies the condition 2 of lemma 1. Thus, by this lemma, we conclude that $\bar{z} = (\bar{x}, \bar{y})$ is an N-S-G equilibrium of the game (1). □

Using lemma 3, let us prove a theorem of existence of N-S-G equilibrium of the game (1).

Theorem 1. If in the game (1) the following conditions are met:

1. the function $t_k \rightarrow \varphi_k(x//t_k,y)$ is concave, $\forall (x,y) \in X \times Y$, $\forall k \in P$;

2. there exists $k_0 \subset I$ such that $y \rightarrow \varphi_{k_0}(x,y)$ is convex over Y, $\forall x \in X$.

Then the game (1) has at least one N-S-G equilibrium.

Proof. Using lemma 3, one has only to prove that there exists $\bar{z} = (\bar{x}, \bar{y}) \in Z$ such that the inequality (3) holds. By conditions **a)**, **b)** and conditions of theorem 1, we deduce that the function $\phi_{k_0}(.,.)$ verifies the following properties :

- the function $z \rightarrow \phi_{k_0}(z,t)$ is continuous, $\forall t \in T$;

- the function $t \rightarrow \phi_{k_0}(z,t)$ is concave, $\forall z \in Z$.

Thus the conditions of the Ky Fan inequality [1] are met. Hence there exists $\bar{z}=(\bar{x}, \bar{y}) \in Z$ such that $\phi_{k_0}(\bar{z},t) \leq \max_{z \in T} \phi_{k_0}(z,z)$, $\forall t \in T$, but by construction we have $\phi_{k_0}(t,t)=0$, $\forall t \in T$ hence $\phi_{k_0}(\bar{z},t) \leq 0$, $\forall t \in T$ according to lemma 3, we deduce that $\bar{z}=(\bar{x}, \bar{y})$ is an N-S-G equilibrium of the game (1). □

3.2 The existence of N-G-G equilibrium

In this subsection we establish some sufficient conditions for the existence of the N-G-G equilibrium using a certain real valued function. Since an N-G-G equilibrium is also an N-P-G equilibrium then these conditions are also sufficient for the existence of an N-P-G equilibrium.

Let us consider the function $\phi(.,.):Z \times T \rightarrow R$, $(z,t) \rightarrow \phi(z,t)$ defined by

$$\phi(z,t)=\sum_{k \in P} [(\varphi_k (x// x'_k,y) - \varphi_k (x, y'))] \tag{4}$$

where $z \in Z=X \times Y$, $t \in T= X \times Y$, $z=(x,y)$, $t=(x', y')$.

The following lemma shows the relation between the N-G-G equilibrium of the game (1) and the function (4).

Lemma 4. If there exists $\bar{z}=(\bar{x}, \bar{y}) \in Z$ such that $\phi(\bar{z},t) \leq 0$, $\forall t \in T$ then $\bar{z}$ is an N-G-G equilibrium of the game (1).

Proof.

1) Let $k \in P$ setting $t=(\bar{x}// x_k, \bar{y})$ in (4), according to the condition of lemma and (4), we obtain

$$\phi(\bar{z},t) \leq 0 \Rightarrow \varphi_k (\bar{x}// x_k, \bar{y}) - \varphi_k (\bar{x}, \bar{y}) \leq 0$$

then

$$\forall k \in P, \forall x_k \in X_k, \varphi_k (\bar{x}// x_k, \bar{y}) \leq \varphi_k (\bar{x}, \bar{y}).$$

Thus the first condition of lemma 2 is satisfied.

2) setting $t=(\bar{x},y)$ in (4), we obtain

$$\phi(\bar{z},t) \leq 0 \Rightarrow \sum_{k \in P} \varphi_k (\bar{x}, \bar{y}) \leq \sum_{k \in P} \varphi_k (\bar{x},y), \forall y \in Y.$$

We have $\sum_{k \in P} \varphi_k (x,y) = \sum_{i \in I} f_i(x,y)$, $\forall (x,y) \in X \times Y$

hence

$$\sum_{i \in I} f_i(\bar{x}, \bar{y}) \leq \sum_{i \in I} f_i(\bar{x},y), \forall y \in Y \Rightarrow \min_{y \in Y} \sum_{i \in I} f_i(\bar{x},y) = \sum_{i \in I} f_i(\bar{x}, \bar{y})$$

then $\bar{y}$ is a Geoffrion optimal solution for the multi-objective problem

$<Y, f(\overline{x},y)>$ [7], we conclude that $\overline{z}=(\overline{x}, \overline{y})$ verifies the condition 2 of lemma 2, which completes the proof of lemma 4. $\square$

Using lemma 4, let us prove the theorem of existence of N-G-G equilibrium of the game (1).

Theorem 2. If in the game (1) the following conditions are met :

1. the function $t_k \rightarrow \varphi_k (x//t_k, y)$ is concave, $\forall (x,y) \in X \times Y$, $\forall k \in P$;

2. the function $y \rightarrow \sum_{i \in I} f_i(x,y)$ is convex on Y, $\forall x \in X$.

Then the game (1) has at least one N-G-G equilibrium.

Proof. One has only to prove that there exists $\overline{z}=(\overline{x}, \overline{y}) \in Z$ such that the condition of lemma 4 holds. By conditions **a)**, **b)** and conditions of theorem 2, we deduce that the function $\phi(.,.)$ verifies the Ky Fan inequality's conditions [1]. Hence there exists $\overline{z}=(\overline{x}, \overline{y}) \in Z$ such that

$$\phi(\overline{z},t) \leq \max_{z \in T} \phi(z,z), \quad \forall t \in T$$

but by construction we have $\phi(t,t)=0$, $\forall t \in T$, hence

$$\phi(\overline{z},t) \leq 0, \quad \forall t \in T$$

according to lemma 4, we deduce that $\overline{z}=(\overline{x}, \overline{y})$ is an N-G-G equilibrium of the game (1). $\square$

Remark 3. The theorem 2 implies also the existence of the N-P-G equilibrium.

4 Algorithm for the determination of N-S-G and N-G-G equilibrium

We now present an algorithm for the determination of an N-S-G equilibrium. In addition to conditions **a)** and **b)** we suppose that conditions of theorem 1 are verified. Let us consider the functions $\phi_{k_0}(z,t)$ defined in (2) and $z \rightarrow g(z)$ defined by

$$g(z)= \max_{t \in T} \phi_{k_0}(z,t), \quad z \in Z,$$

we have the following algorithm.

Algorithm

Let $z^0 \in Z$ be the initial issue, suppose that we have calculated z^l in the step l then

i) solve the optimization problem $\max_{t \in T} \phi_{k_0}(z^l,t)$, we obtain $\widetilde{t}$

if $\phi_{k_0}(z^l,\widetilde{t}) \leq 0$, stop: z^l is an N-S-G equilibrium; else go to ii);

ii) set, $z^{l+1}= z^l-\lambda_l d_l$ where $d_l=\widetilde{t} - z^l$ and λ_l is a solution of the optimization problem $\min_{\lambda \in [0.1]} g(z^l + \lambda d_l)= g(z^l + \lambda_l d_l)$ then return to i).

It is easy to prove that the sequence $(z^l)_{l\geq0}$, generated by this algorithm, verifies the following property.

Property 1. If the sequence $(z^l)_{l\geq0}$ converges to a point z^* then z^* is an N-S-G equilibrium of the game (1).

Using the Zangwill's theorem we study the convergence of this algorithm. Let us consider the following multi-valued maps:

$$D(z^l)=\{d_l=\tilde{t}-z^l,\ \varphi_{k_0}(z^l,\tilde{t})=\max_{t\in T}\varphi_{k_0}(z^l,t)\},$$

$$M(z^l,d_l)=\{\ \bar{z}=z^l+\lambda_t d_l,\ d_l\in D(z^l),\ \min_{\lambda\in[0,1]}g(z^l+\lambda d_l)=g(z^l+\lambda_t d_l)\ \},$$

$$G(z)=\{\ \tilde{t}\in Z\ /\ g(z)=\varphi_{k_0}(z,\tilde{t})\}\ \text{and the set}\ \Omega=\{\ \bar{z}\in Z\ /\ g(\bar{z})\leq 0\}.$$

Remark 4. According to lemma 3, if $\bar{z}\in\Omega$ then $\bar{z}$ is an N-S-G equilibrium of the game (1).

The following propositions guarantee the convergence of this algorithm.

Proposition 1.[2] If $z\to\varphi_{k_0}(z,t)$ is a convex and differentiable function $\forall t\in T$; the set $G(z)$ is reduced to a single point $t(z)$, $\forall z\in Z$ and the function $z\to t(z)$ is continuous on Z, then $z\to g(z)$ is a descent function for the algorithm.

Proposition 2. [2] Under the assumptions of proposition 1, $M(.,.)$ is a closed map in $\Omega^c=Z-\Omega$.

According to Zangwill's theorem (Global convergence theorem) [5], the following proposition establishes the convergence of the algorithm.

Proposition 3. Under the assumptions of proposition 1, either the algorithm converges in a finite number of steps to an N-S-G equilibrium or each convergent subsequence of the sequence $(z^l)_{l\in N}$ converges to a point in Ω which, by remark 4, is an N-S-G equilibrium of the game (1).

Remark 5. If we consider the function defined in (4), we can construct an analogous algorithm for the determination of N-G-G equilibrium and justify its convergence by the same way.

Let us illustrate this algorithm by an example.

Example. Suppose that in the game (1):

$I=\{1,2,3\}$, $n=3$, $n_i=1$, $X_i=[-1,1]$, $i=1,2,3$; $Y=[-1,1]\times[-1,1]$; $f=(f_1,f_2,f_3)$,

$x=(x_1,x_2,x_3)$, $y=(y_1,y_2)$, $f_1(x,y)=x_1^2-2x_2^2+x_1y_1+x_2y_2-y_1^2$,

$f_2(x,y)=-2x_1^2-x_3^2+x_2y_2-y_1^2+y_2^2$, $f_3(x,y)=x_1^2-x_2^2-x_3^2+y_1^2+y_2^2$.

We suppose that $P=\{\{1,2\},\{3\}\}$, i.e. $k_1=\{1,2\}$, $k_2=\{3\}$; P is the coalition structure formed by the three players, then we have

$\varphi_{k_1}(x,y)=f_1(x,y)+f_2(x,y)=-x_1^2-2x_2^2-x_3^2+x_1y_1+2x_2y_2-2y_1^2+y_2^2$,

$\varphi_{k_2}(x,y)=f_3(x,y)=x_1^2-x_2^2-x_3^2+y_1^2+y_2^2$.

We can easily verify that the conditions of theorem 1 are satisfied hence this game has an N-S-G equilibrium. Let $\phi_{k_0}(z,t)$, $z=(x,y)\in X\times Y$, $t=(x',y')\in X\times Y$ be the function to maximize in the algorithm with $k_0=k_2$ then according to (2) we have

$$\phi_{k_0}(z,t) = \phi_{k_2}(z,t) = \varphi_{k_2}(x,y) - \varphi_{k_2}(x,y') + [(\varphi_{k_1}(x//x'_{k_1},y) - \varphi_{k_1}(x,y)) +$$

$$(\varphi_{k_2}(x//x'_2,y) - \varphi_{k_2}(x,y))] = -(x_1'^2 - x_1^2) - 2(x_2'^2 - x_2^2) - (x_3'^2 - x_3^2) + y_1(x_1' - x_1) +$$

$$2y_2(x_2' - x_2) - (y_1'^2 - y_1^2) - (y_2'^2 - y_2^2). \text{ Hence}$$

$$\phi_{k_0}(z,t) = t^t M t + t^t N z + z^t D z$$

with $t = (x_1', x_2', x_3', y_1', y_2')$, $z = (x_1, x_2, x_3, y_1, y_2)$ and

$$M = \begin{pmatrix} -1 & 0 & 0 & 0 & 0 \\ 0 & -2 & 0 & 0 & 0 \\ 0 & 0 & -1 & 0 & 0 \\ 0 & 0 & 0 & -1 & 0 \\ 0 & 0 & 0 & 0 & -1 \end{pmatrix}, \quad N = \begin{pmatrix} 0 & 0 & 0 & 1 & 0 \\ 0 & 0 & 0 & 0 & 2 \\ 0 & 0 & 0 & 0 & 0 \\ 0 & 0 & 0 & 0 & 0 \\ 0 & 0 & 0 & 0 & 0 \end{pmatrix}, \quad D = \begin{pmatrix} 1 & 0 & 0 & -1/2 & 0 \\ 0 & 2 & 0 & 0 & -1 \\ 0 & 0 & 1 & 0 & 0 \\ -1/2 & 0 & 0 & 1 & 0 \\ 0 & -1 & 0 & 0 & 1 \end{pmatrix}.$$

Let us consider the function $g(z) = \max_{t \in T} \phi_{k_0}(z,t)$ and the set Ω defined above.

The functions $z \to \phi_{k_0}(z,t)$ and $t \to \phi_{k_0}(z,t)$ are differentiable, the first one is strictly convex in R^5, $\forall t \in T$, the second one is strictly concave in R^5, $\forall z \in Z$. Hence $\forall z \in Z$, there exists $t(z) \in T$, such that $\max_{t \in T} \phi_{k_0}(z,t) = \phi_{k_0}(z,t(z))$ and

$\forall z \in Z$ the set $G(z)$ is reduced to a single element i.e.

$G(z) = \{t(z)\}$, $\forall z \in Z$. Since $-1/2 M^{-1} N z = (1/2y_1, 1/2y_2, 0, 0, 0)^t \in T$, $\forall z \in Z$, we obtain

$$t(z) = -1/2 M^{-1} N z, \quad \forall z \in Z. \tag{5}$$

Let $B = -1/2 M^{-1} N$ then (5) becomes $t(z) = B z$. On the other hand, we have

$$g(z) = \phi_{k_0}(z,t(z)) = z^t B^t M B z + z^t B^t N z + z^t D z = z^t [B^t M B + B^t N + D] z = z^t \Lambda z,$$

with $\Lambda = B^t M B + B^t N + D = \begin{pmatrix} 1 & 0 & 0 & -1/2 & 0 \\ 0 & 2 & 0 & 0 & -1 \\ 0 & 0 & 1 & 0 & 0 \\ -1/2 & 0 & 0 & 5/4 & 0 \\ 0 & -1 & 0 & 0 & 3/2 \end{pmatrix}$

then $g(z + \lambda d) = \lambda^2 d^t \Lambda d + 2\lambda d^t \Lambda z + z^t \Lambda z = \lambda^2 d^t \Lambda d + 2\lambda d^t \Lambda z + g(z).$

Resolution

Iteration 1.

Set $z^0 = ((1,1,-1),(1,1))^t$. We have $t(z^0) = -1/2 M^{-1} N z^0 = ((1/2, 1/2, 0), (0,0))^t$

$g(z^0) = \phi_{k_0}(z^0, t(z^0)) = 15/4 > 0$ and $d_0 = t(z^0) - z^0$, $g(z^0 + \lambda d_0) = 3\lambda^2 - 6\lambda - g(z^0)$

$\min_{\lambda \in [0,1]} g(z^0 + \lambda d_0) = g(z^0 + 1 d_0) = g(t(z^0)) = 3/4 < g(z^0)$ then setting $z^1 = t(z^0)$ we obtain

$g(z^1) > 0.$

Iteration 2.

$z^1 = t(z^0) = ((1/2, 1/2, 0), (0,0))^t$, $t(z^1) = B z^1 = ((0,0,0),(0,0))^t$

$g(z^1 + \lambda d_1) = 3/4 \lambda^2 - 3/2 \lambda + g(z^1)$ with $d_1 = t(z^1) - z^1$

$\min_{\lambda \in [0,1]} g(z^1 - \lambda d_1) = g(z^1 + 1 d_1) = g(t(z^1))$, then setting $z^2 = t(z^1)$ we obtain $g(z^2) = 0.$

Thus according to remark 4, we conclude that $z^2=((0,0,0),(0,0))$ ^{t} is an N-S-G equilibrium of this game.

Conclusion

In this paper we have introduced some concepts of solution for the game (1) generalizing the N-S equilibrium proposed by Zhukovskii [10], by taking into account the coalition structure formed by players and other notions of solution of a multi-objective problem. Furthermore, we have established sufficient conditions for the existence of these solutions and studied the problem of their determination. We think that the study of the case where the behaviour of the unknown parameters has a stochastic or fuzzy character is a worthy direction of research. It would be interesting to implement these results in real decision making problems.

References

[1] Aubin. J. P, Ekland I. (1984): Applied Nonlinear Analysis. John Willey and Sons, New York.

[2] Kacher F. (1999): A Concept of Equilibrium for a Cooperative Game with a Coalition Structure in the Normal Form under Uncertainty. Magister Thesis, University of Tizi-Ouzou, Tizi-Ouzou.

[3] Larbani M. (1997), About the Existence of the N-S equilibrium for a Non cooperative Game under Uncertainty. In: Caballero R and Steuer R. (eds) Advances in Multiojective Programming and Goal Programming,. Springer Verlag, Berlin.

[4] Luce R.D and Raifa H. (1951): Games and decisions. Wiley, New york.

[5] Minoux M. (1983): Programmation mathématiques théorèmes et algorithmes. Bordas et C.N.E.T-E.N.S.T, Paris.

[6] Nash J.F. (1951): Non cooperative Games. Annals. Math., 54, 286-295.

[7] Podinovsky V.V., Nogin V.D.(1982): Pareto Optimal Solutions in Multiple Criteria Problems. Nauka, Moskow (in Russian).

[8] Steuer R. (1986): Multiple Criteria Optimization: Computation and Application. Wiley, New York.

[9] Owen G. (1968): Game Theory. W.B. Sanders company, Philadelphia, London, Toronto .

[10] Zhukovskii V.I, Tchirkry A.A. (1994): Linear-quadratic Differential Games. Naukova Dumka, Kiev (in Russian).

Towards the Development of an Integrated Multi-Objective Solution and Analysis System

S.K. Mirrazavi, D.F. Jones[1], M. Tamiz[2]

University of Portsmouth, Mercantile House,
Hampshire Terrace, Portsmouth, UK.

Abstract

This paper details some of the issues investigated and experiments conducted by the authors in the course of their design of a integrated multi-objective solution and analysis system. The role to which the concept of multiple objectives can be incorporated into the genetic algorithm framework is examined. The composition of a multi-objective fitness function is discussed, as well as its implications for the genetic operators such as selection, crossover and mutation. Current work on such issues as representation of the efficient set by genetic algorithms are reviewed. A non-aggregating randomised selection algorithm is given and illustrated by means of an example. The use of genetic algorithms for the solution of difficult goal programming models is investigated. A representative non-linear goal programming model is solved under various genetic algorithm parameter options in order to demonstrate the type of parameter sensitivity that can occur when using genetic algorithms as a solution tool.

Keywords : Multi-objective Programming, Genetic Algorithms

1 Introduction

The field of multiple objective programming is comprised of a number of techniques with different underlying philosophies but the same general aim. That is, to provide effective solutions to a decision maker faced with a situation in which there exists multiple objectives to be satisfied. It is highly probable that in such a situation the objectives are conflicting - i.e. they cannot reach their optimal values simultaneously. Multiple objective programming models occur in a wide variety of application areas - it could be argued that any non-trivial decision to be taken has to involve multi-objectives to a certain extent.

---

[1] E-mail dylan.jones@port.ac.uk
[2] E-mail mehrdad.tamiz@port.ac.uk

Some commonly used techniques for the resolution and analysis of multiple objective programming models [11] include goal programming, compromise programming, Pareto set generation methods, and interactive methods.

The common algorithmic way of solving the techniques mentioned above has been by the use of adapted versions of conventional optimisation techniques. Such techniques include the simplex method for linear models, branch and bound techniques for integer models, and various calculus based methods for non-linear models. These techniques are effective when dealing with well-defined, well-behaved models but struggle with some ill-defined or complex models.

Consequently, there has been a recent growth in heuristic search based techniques for the solution of the more difficult models in the field of optimisation. Amongst the most popular of these is the technique of genetic algorithms [4], which is described in Section 2. Genetic algorithms have been successfully used to solve many 'difficult' models from the field of optimisation [4]. The majority of this effort has been aimed at models which are single objective in their nature. However, there exist rich possibilities for the use of genetic algorithms as a solution and analysis tool for multiple objective models. This paper assesses the extent to which genetic algorithms can be, and have been, used in multiple objective programming and provides new suggestions for the incorporation and use of multiple objectives within the genetic algorithm. Also, a demonstration is given as to the sensitivity of the genetic process to the parameters required to control the genetic algorithm. This demonstration takes the form of a controlled partial factorial experiment on a non-linear goal programme that is difficult to solve using conventional methods.

The remainder of this paper is divided into five sections. Section two gives a brief overview of the relevant topics in genetic algorithms. Section three reviews the literature regarding the use of multiple objectives in genetic algorithms and examines the theoretical issues involved in multiple objective fitness function construction. Section four presents a new randomised selection algorithm and illustrates the method by means of an example. Section five gives a demonstration of how a solution can be sensitive with regard to the genetic parameters. Finally, section six draws conclusions.

2 An Overview of Genetic Algorithms

Genetic algorithms are a type of heuristic search technique. They emulate natural genetic processes in order to efficiently search large, artificial regions. The standard genetic algorithm, as considered in this paper, encodes each point in the solution space as a binary string, i.e. a series of zeros and ones. The genetic algorithm is primarily based around discrete measures, although by setting the interval between points sufficiently small, a good approximation to continuous variables can be given. When tackling a problem with decision variables, each decision variable is assigned a number of positions, or genes, on the string. This number should be sufficient to allow binary representation of all the possible values of that decision variable. Thus, each string represents a complete solution to the model. The information required of each decision variable is its lower bound, upper bound, and discrete distance between points.

A measure of fitness of the solution should exist that is calculable or able to be given a value at each solution point. This measure will act as a guiding force for the GA. The principle behind GA is one of randomised, yet intelligent search. The intelligence is given by the direction of the fitness function. The randomness is introduced by the way in which solutions combine and are changed to form new solutions.

The GA is initialised by the random selection of the first generation of points from the solution space. These solutions are then bred with each other to form successive generations of 'fitter' solutions. The mechanism of how generation $n + 1$ is formed from generation n is divided into three basic genetic operations: crossover, mutation, and selection. A fuller, tutorial-style explanation of GA is available from Goldberg [4] or from the first few chapters of Michalewicz [5].

3 Genetic Algorithms in Multi-Objective Programming

This section examines ways in which genetic algorithms have been applied to various multi-objective programming methods. Firstly, it must be recognised that a variety of solution types exist within multi-objective programming. These depend on the type of method employed. In goal programming formulations a single solution is provided that satisfices [7] the goals of the decision maker. In compromise programming [15] a compromise set is found which minimizes the distance from an ideal solution over a number of different distance methods. For generating methods [11] a set of points which are representative of the efficient set are found. Interactive methods [3] seek to provide the decision maker with a series of points which become closer to the solution most in line with their preferences.

Therefore developing about a single multiple-objective genetic algorithm is difficult, as different techniques require different solution types. There are, however certain features which multi-objective techniques have in common, which can be exploited by genetic algorithms, as well as various specialised genetic algorithm refinements that can be used to improve specific multi-objective techniques. The generalised algebraic form of a multi-objective programming model is given in section 4.

As detailed in Section 2, the genetic algorithm is composed of three basic operators, crossover, mutation, and selection. Of these three operations, crossover and mutation require little alteration in moving from a single to a multiple objective programming framework. The majority of the changes to the genetic algorithm must take place in the selection operation and in the representation of the fitness function in particular. We now detail some of the concepts and the changes necessary in this process

3.1 Multiple Objective Fitness Functions

An important characteristic of the genetic algorithm when considering multiple objectives is the fitness function. As detailed in section 2, the means of directing the genetic search is by the single-criterion measure of fitness, the fitness function. In order to successfully apply genetic algorithms to multiobjective models, means must be found of turning this into a multi-objective measure of fitness. The first attempts at this are by Schaffer [9] with his V.E.G.A. (vector evaluated genetic algorithm) directed towards the generation of a genetic population to represent the efficient set. This technique was successful to the extent that the population lay entirely along the appropriate set, but the population showed a bias towards extreme individuals (good in a single objective but poor in others), at the expense of other more balanced individuals. These problems show a certain similarity to the problem encountered when using a solely 'Manhattan weighting scheme' approach with conventional simplex-based optimisation. Solutions that emulated a Chebyshev or equilibrated distance-metric are harder to find. One solution is to form a Pareto ranking of the individuals within a generation. Those that dominate other solutions receive a higher ranking whilst the dominated solutions receive a lower ranking. The fitness function then consists of the Pareto rank. This concept is used by Srinivas and Deb [10] in their non-dominated sorting algorithm(N.D.S.A.)and by Fonseca and Fleming [1] in combination with niching techniques in their MOGA algorithm. Both of these algorithms are aimed at effective representation of the efficient set. Vicini and Quagliarella [14] apply the concept of genetic algorithm Pareto set estimation to an airfoil design model.

When solving certain types of multi-objective model, such as lexicographic goal programmes, a vector valued fitness function must be used. The fact that the fitness function is vector valued causes difficulties for the conventional 'roulette-wheel' selection which is based around a single fitness measure. For this reason it is more appropriate to use the concept of tournament selection for this type of model. In tournament selection, k individuals are selected (normally k=2) as possible candidates for the next generation and the one with the higher fitness is chosen. This type of selection can be easily extended to vectors where a lexicographic comparison between the two vectors takes place in order to determine the fitter individual. This is useful for techniques which assume a natural ordering or semi-ordering of the objectives such as lexicographic goal programming. Lexicographic goal programmes with complicating factors such as non-linearities that make them hard to solve by conventional methods can be solved using this form of tournament selection based genetic algorithm.

For techniques which allow direct normalised summation of the objectives, such as weighted goal programming and compromise programming, the normalised sum of the values of the objectives can be used as the fitness function. Murata, Ishibuchi and Tanaka [6] present such a method for the solution of a flowshop scheduling model. Gen, Ida, Lee, and Kim [2] present a genetic algorithm method for fuzzy non-linear goal programming and Sakawa, Kato, Sunada, and Shibano [8] present a genetic algorithm method for 0-1 multiobjective programming. In cases where direct comparisons and trade-offs between the methods are not allowed or desired, but neither does there exist a natural lexicographic ordering of preferences then a different way of measuring fitness must be devised. This is especially important for techniques which seek to find a single solution rather than a set of points.

One possibility is to build on the fact that the genetic algorithm is a non-deterministic search technique. So when considering multiple objectives it is permissable to allow for a degree of randomness in the choice of objectives and their contribution towards their overall fitness. Surry and Radcliffe [12] give a basic form of random choice between two objectives in the COMOGA method for single-objective GA. They recognize that constrained GA poses constraint handling problems and hence model the single objective GA as a bi-objective model where :

- Objective 1 : The conventional objective (fitness) function

- Objective 2 : Minimize the sum of infeasibilities.

An objective is chosen at random and the fitness function is calculated solely on that objective.

This idea can be extended into a multi-objective model with k objectives. The non-aggregating selection routine developed in the next section can then be used.

4   A Randomised Selection Algorithm

Given a general multi-objective model:

$$max \ \ z_1 = g_1(\mathbf{x})$$

$$\cdot$$

$$\cdot$$

$$max \ \ z_k = g_k(\mathbf{x})$$

Subject to,

$$\mathbf{x} \in \mathbf{C_s}$$

Where $\mathbf{x}$ is the set of n decision variables. g_i is the $i'th$ objective, which we assume, without loss of generality, is to be maximised. C_s is the set of hard constraints to be satisfied. A further function $\mathbf{f}(\mathbf{x})$ is defined, which represents the sum of infeasibilities (i.e. the total breakage of the constraints. Then $-f(\mathbf{x})$ is to be maximised to its ideal value of zero. Note that the new objective Max $-f(\mathbf{x})$ differs to the other k objectives in that anything other than its complete satisfaction at its ideal value of zero renders the solution infeasible and hence unimplementable.

If preferential weights for the objectives are to be permitted then the additional information $w_1, w_2, \ldots w_k$ is extracted from the decision maker, representing the relative importance of the corresponding objective. If the setting of such weights is not practical or not permitted due to the sensitivity of the objective measures then these weights are initially set equal to each other. i.e. $w_1 = w_2 = \ldots = w_k$. An initial population is then selected at random and the genetic algorithm is started as in the standard case. Crossover and mutation are performed as normal, but the selection step is altered. Each of the objectives is assigned a probability of selection P_i, where :

$$P_i = \frac{w_i}{\sum_{i=1}^{k} w_i}$$

Thus we have Monte-Carlo type probabilities for the objectives, where $\sum_{i=1}^{k} P_i = 1$. Each of the objectives is thus assigned a portion in a 'roulette wheel' according to its probability. A random number is generated between zero and one from the uniform distribution to select the objective that will be used for the fitness function.

4.1 An Example

This section uses a small multi-objective example to illustrate the concept of randomised selection. In this example it is assumed that additive summation of the objectives is not permissable. the relative importance of the objectives is, however, known *a-priori*. The example is non-linear with three objectives and three decision variables. It has the following algebraic form:

$$Max \ z_1 = -x_1^2 - 2x_2^2 - x_3^2$$

$$Max \ z_2 = x_1 x_2 x_3$$

$$Max \ z_3 = x_1 + x_2 - x_3$$

Subject to,

$$x_1 + x_2 + x_3 \leq 4$$

$$x_1, x_2, x_3 \geq 0$$

The *a-priori* weights for the objectives are given by

$$w_1 = \frac{1}{6} \quad w_2 = \frac{1}{3} \quad w_3 = \frac{1}{2}$$

The sum of infeasibilities $f(x)$ is therefore given by

$$f(x) = Max(x_1 + x_2 + x_3 - 4, 0)$$

In order to solve this model using genetic algorithms, a genetic encoding must be devised. The range of each of the three variables is determined as being between 0 and 4 by the feasible region. As the variables are continuous, a degree of accuracy must be given. It is therefore assumed that 2^5 points lie between 0 and 4, giving an accuracy of around 10^{-4}. The number of points is deliberately chosen as a power of two in order to ensure efficient execution of the genetic algorithm. Thus a 45 bit encoding is given for the three decision variables.

The genetic algorithm code used to solve the model is a modified version of a single-objective public-domain FORTRAN based code from the University of Illinois. All experimentation took place on a 133Mhz Pentium PC. The GA code is used with the following parameters.

- Population Size = 50

- Crossover Probability (p_c) = 0.6

- Mutation Probability (p_m) = 0.01

- Number of Generations = 201

Where 201 is a sufficient number of generations to allow the genetic algorithm to converge. The constraint set was handled using a penalty function approach. The penalty is scaled to be equal in magnitude to the objective function selected. Thus the three fitness functions become $z_1 + 8f(x)$, $z_2 + 8f(x)$, $z_3 + f(x)$. An alternative to a penalty function method would be to include the sum of infeasibilities $(-f(x))$ as an objective and allow it to be selected at random along with the other objectives. However, this was not found to be as good as the penalty function method in practice, as it was difficult to produce feasible solutions and to provide any convergence or meaningful movement in the objective values over the generations.

The results show a convergence around the average values.

$$x_1 = 2.067, x_2 = 1.787, x_3 = 0.183$$

This point lies on the constraint $x_1 + x_2 + x_3 \leq 4$, which is as expected as both objectives z_2 and z_3 conflict with this constraint at their ideal values. The average initial (randomly selected) values for the three objectives and the percentage of the population that is feasible are given in Table 1. This table also displays the final average values of the objectives. These are taken as an average over the final four generations to prevent any bias towards the objective chosen to be the fitness function when constructing the final generation.

Objective	z_1	z_2	z_3	Percentage Feasible
Initial	-20.988	7.805	2.149	18%
Final	-10.671	0.716	3.559	88%

Table 1 : Initial and Final Population Statistics

From Table 1 it can be seen that the population has been successfully guided from being largely infeasible to being largely feasible by the penalty function. The value of the first objective has been improved. The value of the second objective has been lowered in order to reach feasibility. The value of the third objective has been improved, despite the fact that the ideal value for this function is infeasible. This reflects the fact that the third objective has the highest weight and is hence chosen as the fitness function more frequently.

The final point reached here represents a generally satisfactory solution to the non-linear multi-objective programming example in terms of decision variable and objective values. The exact suitability of the solution depends, of course, on its relevance and implications to the particular real-world situation being modelled. In the case of a non-satisfactory solution or a case where the weights were not able to be specified *a-priori*, there exists scope for an interactive weight-setting scheme to produce suitable solutions. Also the nature of the multiple solutions available in a genetic algorithm could be exploited in order to provide alternative solutions from within the population. Niching and sharing methods could be used to maintain population diversity in this case.

5 Sensitivity of Parameters

From the preceding discussions it is clear that GA's theoretically have a good potential for producing solutions to multi-objective programming models. A problem encountered by the authors in their design of a multi-objective genetic algorithm system is the sensitivity of the solution towards the parameters. This section demonstrates this concept by means of a representative example. One problem that is encountered is the fact that genetic algorithm has more control parameters than a classical simplex-based solution method. These parameters arise out of the nature of the genetic algorithm as detailed in Section 2. The main parameters include:

- The use of elitism (Values : on,off). Elitism is a mechanism which ensures that the best individual in a generation is carried forward to the next generation [4].

- The crossover probability p_c (Values : 0.5, 0.55, 0.6)

- The mutation probability p_m (Values : 0.01, 0.02, 0.04)

- The population size (Values 31, 51, 101)

The values given for the parameters represent the range of values as recommended by the established genetic algorithm texts [4, 5]. A factorial experiment is designed around these values. The object of this experiment is to demonstrate how the change in these values affects the performance of the genetic algorithm. This is an important practical aspect to be taken into account as those wishing to solve their multi-objective models with genetic algorithms need to know the solution they obtain is robust, stable and optimal. That is, the parameter set they choose is capable of finding a good solution that will not be dominated or vary widely from solutions chosen by other parameter sets. In short, sensitivity towards parameters is not desired.

The experimentations leading to the results detailed in this paper are carried on a non-linear goal programming model. This model has 27 objectives, 12 of which are non-linear, and 33 integer decision variables. The algebraic formulation of the non-linear objectives can be found in Appendix A. The model produced a genetic string size of 99 bits. It has conflicting objectives. It is therefore designed to be a typical medium size multi-objective programming model that is moderately difficult to solve using conventional methods. Experimentations were also carried out on a range of multi-objective programming models with between 3 and 201 variables that produced genetic strings of the range 30-804. These models included complicating factors such as lexicographic priority orders, non-standard preferences [13], integer and logical restrictions, and non-linearities.

The goal programming model under experimentation has a number of local optima. For the genetic algorithm to perform well it needs to avoid converging at a local optimum but rather to find the global optimum. An important piece of data is the weight attached to the seventeenth objective w_{17}. Initial analysis shows that as w_{17} is increased two things happen. Firstly the global optimal solution changes. This occurs around the point $w_{17} = 10.5$. At this point there are two distinct global optima. At weights close to this point there exists a local optimum and a global optimum that are distinct from each other yet of similar but not identical magnitude. This is the area where any deception of the genetic algorithm (i.e. converging at the local optimum) might intuitively be expected to occur. The second thing that happens as w_{17} increases is that the model goes from being more multi-objective in nature towards being more single objective in nature as the seventeenth objective starts to dominate other objectives that conflict with it.

The goal programme was therefore run with different weights for w_{17} within the range $1 \leq w_{17} \leq 30$. Each combination of the parameter set was executed twenty times using different sets of random data in the genetic algorithm at each different weighting point. This produces a total of 3300 genetic algorithm executions in the course of the experimentation.

The two criteria used to measure the performance of the genetic algorithm for this model were:

- Percentage Deception : This measures the average level that the best solution found by a single GA execution was above the best overall solution found in all the executions for the goal programme with the same weight used for w_{17}. This figure will give the value of how far above (i.e. worse than) the optimal value a user applying a single GA execution with the relevant parameter set values is likely to be. This is an important statistic as users of GA would obviously like to find values close to the optimal value without performing large numbers of GA executions.

- Probability of Finding Optimum : This statistic measures the percentage change of the parameter set combination actually producing the best solution for that value of the w_{17} weight on a single GA execution.

A value of zero here indicates that the combination never found the optimal value. This is an important statistic for users who wish to be assured of finding the optimal value to their model.

5.1 Results and Analysis

Figures 1.1 - 1.4 show the variation of percentage deception for each of the factors over the range of w_{17} values. Figures 2.1 - 2.4 show the same information regarding the probability of finding the global optimum.

In both measures of performance the results agree with the hypotheses outlined above. That is, there is turbulence in the measures at the point where the optima are close together - that is around $10 \leq w_{17} \leq 12$. Additionally, there is a general increase in the probability of finding the optima and decrease in deception as the weight is increased and the model moves from single to multi-objective in nature.

Regarding the sensitivity of the measures to the individual factors. The use of elitism in this case proved beneficial. There was less deception with the use of elitism (figure 1.1) and figure 2.1 shows that at several weights the optimum can only be found when elitism is used. Another highly significant parameter is that of the mutation probability p_m. Figures 1.3 and 2.3 show that the higher mutation probabilities (0.02 and 0.04) led to significant increase in deception and a very low probability of finding the optimum (zero in all but one weight for $p_m = 0.02$ and zero at all weights for $p_m = 0.04$). The case of this parameter clearly shows that the genetic algorithm is sensitive to at least one parameter and therefore care must be taken when solving multi-objective models using a genetic approach to ensure that good results are obtained. A possible cause of the bad results for high mutation rates is that an unnecessarily large degree of randomness is introduced that interferes with the implicit improvement mechanisms of the genetic algorithm and therefore does not allow for the best solutions to be built.

The other two parameters proved to be less sensitive to change. Figures 1.2 and 2.2 show that there is little significant change in either performance measure across the range of values used for the crossover probability $0.5 \leq p_c \leq 0.6$. Figures 1.4 and 2.4 lead to the same conclusion regarding the population size - although there is a slight lowering in the level of deception as the population size is increased. This has to be traded off against the extra computational time involved in processing the larger number of individuals in each generation.

6 Conclusion

This paper has detailed some of the issues involved in the use of genetic algorithms as a tool for the solution and analysis of multiple objective programming models. It has shown that multiple objectives can be effectively incorporated into the genetic algorithm framework. Various attributes of the genetic algorithm can be exploited for this purpose. The reviewed work on

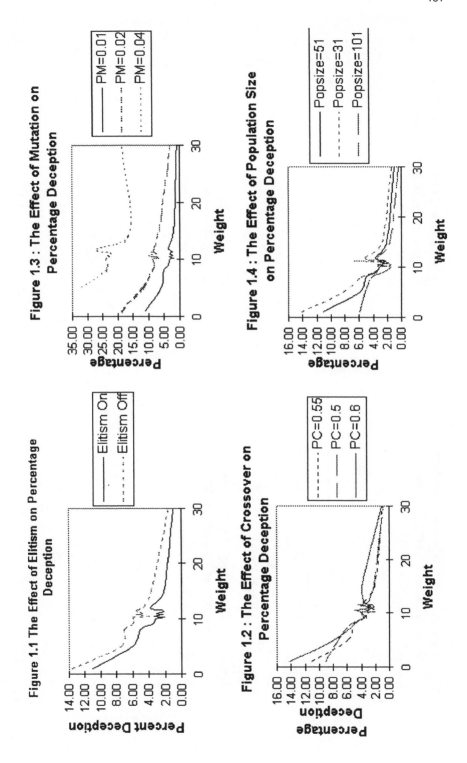

Figure 1.1 The Effect of Elitism on Percentage Deception

Figure 1.2 : The Effect of Crossover on Percentage Deception

Figure 1.3 : The Effect of Mutation on Percentage Deception

Figure 1.4 : The Effect of Population Size on Percentage Deception

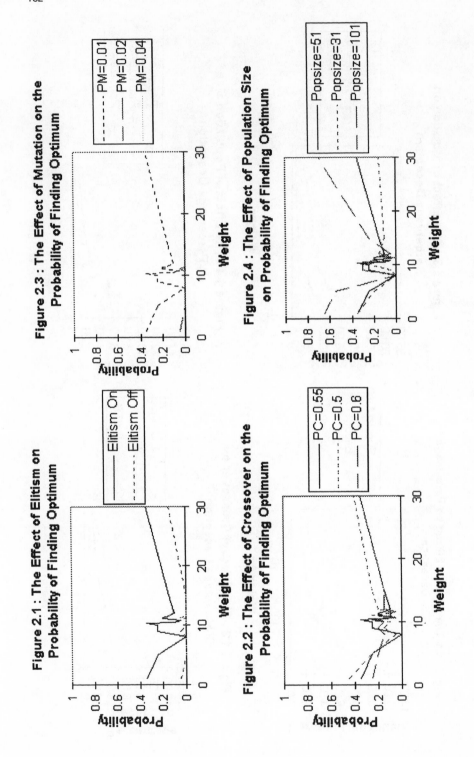

Figure 2.1 : The Effect of Elitism on Probability of Finding Optimum

Figure 2.2 : The Effect of Crossover on the Probability of Finding Optimum

Figure 2.3 : The Effect of Mutation on the Probability of Finding Optimum

Figure 2.4 : The Effect of Population Size on Probability of Finding Optimum

the representation of the Pareto efficient frontier uses the fact that the genetic algorithm produces multiple solutions at each iteration along with the advanced technique of niching. This allows effective Pareto set representation within one generation. The randomised selection algorithm uses the random search aspect of the genetic algorithm in order to ensure that an appropriate solution can be found without aggregating or summing any of the objectives. The use of tournament selection allows the solution of models with a lexicographic order of preferences to be obtained. Thus it is shown that all types of multi-objective model can be effectively handled by genetic algorithms.

Another strength of genetic algorithms is their robustness in dealing with 'difficult' objective functions. Genetic algorithms managed to produce solutions to the representative example in section 4. In fact, the only condition that is required is that each objective is defined at each point in the objective space. This flexibility means that multiple objective programming models that were hitherto not able to be analysed by conventional methods (e.g. simplex or calculus based methods) can now be solved and analysed with the help of genetic algorithms. This will also provide advances into areas such as ill-defined and stochastic multiple objective programming. The demonstration of sensitivity in Section 5 shows that whilst genetic algorithms prove a highly effective - and in some cases maybe the only - tool for solving such models, there do exist models where care must be taken over the way in which such algorithms are used. The goal programme examined showed particular sensitivity towards the use of mutation rates that are too high.

There exist possibilities for future research regarding the use of hybrid genetic methods and the concept of annealing for further refinement of the solutions produced. The multiplicity of solutions produced in each generation of a genetic algorithm should also lead to advances in the area of interactive multiple objective programming.

Acknowledgements : The authors would like to thank to the British Engineering and Physical Sciences Research Council for their sponsorship of this research (Grant no GR/M27593).

References

[1] FONESCA, C.M. and FLEMING, P.J.(1993) Genetic algorithms for multiobjective optimization : Formulation, Discussion, and Generalization, *Proceedings of the Fifth Annual Conference on Genetic Algorithms*, 416-423.

[2] GEN, M., IDA, K., LEE, J. and KIM, J.(1997) Fuzzy Nonlinear Goal programming Using Genetic Algorithm, *Computers and Industrial Engineering*, **33**, 39-42.

[3] GARDINER, L.R. and STEUER, R.(1994) Unified interactive multiple objective programming, *European Journal of Operational Research*, **74**, 391-406.

[4] GOLDBERG, D.E.(1989) *Genetic Algorithms in Search, Optimization and Machine Learning*, Addison-Wesley.

[5] MICHALEWICZ, Z.(1996) *Genetic Algorithms + Data Structures = Evolution Programs*, 3rd Edition, Springer-Verlag.

[6] MURATA, T., ISHIBUCHI, H., and TANAKA, H.(1996) Multi-objective genetic algorithm and its application to flowshop scheduling, *Computers and Industrial Engineering*, **30**, 957-968.

[7] ROMERO, C.(1991) *Handbook of Critical Issues in Goal Programming*, Pergamon Press, Oxford.

[8] SAKAWA, M., KATO, K., SUNADA, H., and SHIBANO, T.(1997) Fuzzy programming for multiobjective 0-1 programming problems through revised genetic algorithms.

[9] SCHAFFER, J.D.(1985) Multiple objective optimization with vector evaluated genetic algorithms, *Proceedings of an International Conference on Genetic Algorithms and Their Applications*, 93-100.

[10] SRINIVAS, N. and DEB, K. Multiobjective optimization using nondominated sorting in genetic algorithms, *Evolutionary Computation*, **2**, 221-248.

[11] STEUER, R.E.(1986) *Multiple Criteria Optimization : Theory, Computation, and Application*, John Wiley and Sons.

[12] SURRY, P.D. and RADCLIFFE, N.J.(1997) The COMOGA method : constrained optimisation by multiple objective genetic algorithms, *Control and Cybernetics*, **26**, 391-412. Lawrence Erlbaum.

[13] TAMIZ, M. and JONES, D.F.(1995)'Expanding the flexibility of goal programming via preference modelling techniques', *Omega*, **23**, 41-48.

[14] VICINI, A. and QUAGLIARELLA, D.(1997) Inverse and direct airfoil design using a multiobjective genetic algorithm, *AIAA Journal*, **35**, 1499-1505.

[15] ZELENY, M.(1982) *Multi-Criteria Decision Making*, McGraw Hill.

Appendix A : Non-Linear Objectives from Model in Section 5

$$x_1^2 + x_5^2 + x_8^2 + x_{10}^2 + n_{16} - p_{16} = 250$$

$$x_2^3 + x_4^3 + x_9^3 + x_{11}^3 + n_{17} - p_{17} = 1250$$

$$x_3^4 + x_7^4 + x_{12}^4 + n_{18} - p_{18} = \frac{6250}{3}$$

$$\frac{\sum_{i=1}^{16} x_i}{1 + \sum_{i=17}^{33} x_i} + n_{19} - p_{19} = 1$$

$$\frac{\sum_{i\ even} x_i}{1 + \sum_{i\ odd} x_i} + n_{20} - p_{20} = 0$$

$$x_{20}x_{21} + n_{21} - p_{21} = 1$$

$$\frac{x_4^2 + x_5^2 + x_6^2}{1 + (5 - x_1)^6 + (4 - x_{27})^6} + n_{22} - p_{22} = 1$$

$$x_{12}^2 + x_{16}^2 + x_{20}^2 + x_{24}^2 + n_{23} - p_{23} = 250$$

$$x_{13}^3 + x_{17}^3 + x_{21}^3 + x_{25}^3 + n_{24} - p_{24} = 1250$$

$$x_{14}^4 + x_{18}^4 + x_{22}^4 + x_{26}^4 + n_{25} - p_{25} = \frac{6250}{3}$$

$$x_{27}^2 x_{28}^2 x_{30}^2 + n_{26} - p_{26} = 1000$$

$$x_{31}^2 x_{32}^2 x_{33}^2 + n_{27} - p_{27} = 1000$$

Dynamic Discrete Programming with Partially Ordered Criteria Set

Tadeusz Trzaskalik

Department of Operation Research, the University of Economics,
ul. Bogucicka 14, 40-226 Katowice, Poland, ttrzaska@figaro.ae.katowice.pl

Sebastian Sitarz

Institute of Mathematics, the Silesian University, ul. Bankowa 14,
40-007 Katowice, Poland, ssitarz@ux2.math.us.edu.pl

Abstract. This paper presents a model of dynamic, discrete, decision-making problem with partially ordered set (exactly the set with transitive and antisymmetric relation). We also show Bellman's Principle of this kind of a problem by means of properties of maximal elements. Numerical procedures are formulated and an example is given for illustrative purposes. In this example we apply fuzzy parameters of the model.

Keywords. Dynamic programming, principle of optimality, partially ordered set, fuzzy numbers.

1. Introduction

Most of decision-making problems of human activity consist of sequential decision problems and have multiply objectives. These objectives can be described by means of elements from partially ordered set.

Initially, Brown and Strauch [1] present the applicability of the principle of optimality to a class of multi-criteria dynamic programming (MCDP) with a lattical order. Since then, the vector principle of optimality has been described in many papers. Mitten [5] shows a method for solving multistage decision in which the real valued objective function is replaced by preference relation. Wu [9] studies the dynamic property of the efficient solutions of dynamic systems and shows that they posses a chain property necessary for establishing the fundamental equation. Henig [2] defines a dynamic model where returns are in a partially ordered set, and shows that Bellman's principle is valid with respect to maximal returns. Assumptions of separability and monotonicity of MCDP are needed to guarantee that each nondominated solution can be computed. Classical definitions are discussed in Yu and Seiford [10], Li and Haimes [4] and Trzaskalik [7].

In this paper we will consider separable and monotone backward processes with finite number of periods, states and decision variables. Each period decision is described by use of elements from partially ordered set (here: the relation that partially orders the set is transitive and antisymmetric). Applying these models we will classify many of discrete MCDP. Optimality equations are formulated by means of properties of maximal elements. For illustration, we present a numerical example with fuzzy parameters.

2. Process Realizations

The formulation of the process realizations and dynamic process P defined below comes from Trzaskalik [8]. We consider a discrete dynamic process, which consist of T periods. Let for $t=1,\ldots,T$

• Y_t is the set of all feasible state variables at the beginning of period t.

• Y_{T+1} is the set of all states at the end of the process.

• $X_t(y_t)$ is the set of all feasible decision variables for period t and state $y_t \in Y_t$.

We assume that all these sets are finite.

• $D_t \cong \{d_t = (y_t, x_t): y_t \in Y_t, x_t \in X_t(y_t)\}$ is the set of all period realizations in period t.

• $\Omega_t: D_t \rightarrow Y_{t+1}$ are given transformations.

• $D \equiv \{d = (d_1, \dots, d_T): \forall_{t \in \{1, \dots, T\}}\ y_{t+1} = \Omega_t(y_t, x_t)$ and $x_T \in X_T(y_T)\ \}$ is the set of all process realizations d.

• $D_t(y_t) \equiv \{(y_t, x_t): x_t \in X_t(y_t)\}$ is the set of all realizations in period t which begin at state y_t.

• $d(y_t) \equiv (y_t, x_t, \dots, y_T, x_T)$ is the partial realization for given realization d, which begin at y_t.

• $D(y_t) \equiv \{d(y_t): d \in D\}$ is the set of all partial realizations, which begin at y_t.

• $D(Y_t) \equiv \{D(y_t): y_t \in Y_t\}$ is the set of all partial realizations, which begin at period t.

• $P \equiv \{(Y_t, Y_{T+1}), X_t(y_t), \Omega_t: t=1, \dots, T\}$ denotes discrete dynamic process, where sets $Y_1, \dots, Y_{T+1}, X_1(y_1), \dots X_T(y_T)$, functions $\Omega_1, \dots, \Omega_T$ are identified.

3. Concepts of Efficiency

We consider the following structure, functions and operators to describe multi-period criteria function of process realization.

• $(W, <)$ is a structure, where W is the set and $<$ denotes transitive $[\forall_{x,y,z \in W}$ $(x<y$ and $y<z) \Rightarrow x<z]$ and antisymmetric $[\forall_{x,y \in W}\ (x<y$ and $y<x) \Rightarrow x=y]$ relation in $W \times W$. In this paper we call the set with such relation the partially ordered set.

• $f_t: D_t \to W$, for $t=1, \dots, T$, are period criteria functions with returns in partially ordered set W.

We assume that for each period the following operators exist:

• $\square_t: W \times W \to W$ are monotone operators $(t=1, \dots T-1)$.

$$\forall_{a,b,c \in W} \quad a < b \Rightarrow c \square a < c \square b \text{ - monotonicity of } \square$$

• $F_t: D(Y_t) \to W$ are the functions defined in the following way

$$F_t \cong f_t\ \square_t\ (f_{t-1}\ \square_{t+1}\ (\dots(f_{T-1}\ \square_{T-1}\ f_T))), \quad t=T, \dots 1.$$

• $F \cong F_1$ -is called multi-period criteria function.

In further consideration we postulate maximalization of function F.

•(P, F) denotes discrete dynamic decision process. It is given, if there are defined discrete dynamic process P and multi-period criteria function F.

•Realization $d^* \in D$ is said to be efficient, if

$$\sim\exists_{d \in D} \quad (\ F(d^*) < F(d) \ \text{and} \ F(d) \neq F(d^*) \ ).$$

4. Operation Max

For each finite subset $A \subset W$ we define

$$\max(A) \cong \{a^* \in A: \sim\exists_{a \in A} \ a^* < a \ \text{and} \ a^* \neq a\}.$$

We will be using equivalent notation i.e. $\max A \cong \max(A)$.

One can easily check that, d^* is efficient, iff $F(d^*) \in \max F(D)$, where $F(D) \cong \{F(d): d \in D\}$.

Properties of mapping max

Let A, B denote finite subsets of W, then

P1. If $A \neq \varnothing$ then $\max A \neq \varnothing$.

P2. If $[A \subseteq B \ \text{and} \ \max B \subseteq A]$ then $\max B = \max A$.

Proof

P1. (indicative proof). Let n (number of elements of the set A) be an inductive argument. For n=1, it is clear that $\max A = A$.

Let n>1, then we can describe set A as follows $A = A' \cup \{a_n\} = \{a_1, \ldots, a_{n-1}\} \cup \{a_n\}$, and $\max A' \neq \varnothing$, let $a_i \in \max A'$. Observe that in two possible cases we have

1. $\sim(a_i < a_n)$ then $a_i \in \max A$.

2. $(a_i < a_n)$ then $a_n \in \max A$, we prove this fact in the following way:

since relation $<$ is antisymmetric, we get $\sim(a_n<a_i)$. Suppose that there exists such $a' \in A' \backslash a_i$ that $a_n<a'$. From transitivity of $<$ we have $a_i<a'$, what is in contradiction with the fact that $a_i \in \max A'$. $\square$

P2. We shall check that $1.\max B \subseteq \max A$ and $2.\max B \supseteq \max A$.

1. Let $x \in \max B$ then $x \in A$ and $(\sim\exists_{b \in B}: (x<b$ and $x \neq b))$. Since that $A \subseteq B$ we have $(\sim\exists_{b \in A}: (x<b$ and $x \neq b)$, which implies that $x \in \max A$.

2. Suppose that $x \in \max A$ and $x \notin \max B$. From the latter and from P1 we get existence of such $b \in \max B$ that $x<b$. Thus $b \notin A$ (in other case $x \notin \max A$), which is in contradiction with $(A \subseteq B)$. $\square$

Theorem 1

Let I be a finite index set, and for $i \in I$: $x_i \in W$, $A_i \subseteq W$, A_i are finite sets, operator $\square$ is monotone, then

$$\max\{x_i \,\square\, A_i: i \in I\} = \max\{x_i \square \max A_i: i \in I\}.$$

Proof

We use property P2, putting $A \cong (x_i \square \max A_i: i \in I)$, $B \cong \{x_i \,\square\, A_i: i \in I\}$.

We shall check that $1.A \subseteq B$ and $2.\ \max(B) \subseteq A$.

1.It's a consequence of the fact that $\max A_i \subseteq A_i$ for all $i \in I$.

2.Let $w \in \max B$. Then there exists such $k \in I$ and $a \in A_k$ that $w = x_k \square a$ and $(\sim\exists_j \sim\exists_{b \in Aj}: w<x_j \square b$ and $w \neq x_j \square b)$. Suppose that $a \notin \max A_k$. Then there exists such $b \in A_k$ that $a<b$. Since the operator $\square$ is monotone it follows that $x_k \square a < x_k \square b$, which is in contradiction with the fact that $w \in \max B$. Thus $a \in \max A_k$, and $w = x_k \square a \in x_k \square \max A_k$, it means that $w \in A$. $\square$

Corollary 1

Let I be a finite index set, and for $i \in I$: $A_i \subseteq W$, A_i are finite, then

$$\max\{A_i: i \in I\} = \max\{\max A_i: i \in I\}.$$

Proof

Let operator $\square$ -used in theorem 1- be defined as follows $x \square y \cong y$ ($\square$ is monotone), and for $i \in I$ x_i be any elements from W, then the assertion follows from above theorem. $\square$

5. Principle of Optimality

In the discrete dynamic decision process (P, F) efficient solutions exist, which is guarantied by property P1.

Theorem 2

Let (P, F) be decision dynamic process. For all $t = T-1, \ldots 1$ and all $y_t \in Y_t$ holds

$$\max \{F_t(D(y_t))\} = \max \{ f_t(d_t) \square_t \max(F_{t+1}(d(\Omega_t(d_t)))): d_t \in D_t(y_t)\}.$$

Proof

Observe that $F_t(D(y_t)) = \{f_t(d_t) \circ_t (F_{t+1}(d(\Omega_t(d_t)))): d_t \in D_t(y_t)\}$.

If we put $x_i \cong f_t(d_t)$, $A_i \cong F_{t+1}(d(\Omega_t(d_t))$, the assertion follows from Theorem 1. $\square$

Theorem 3

Let (P, F) be discrete dynamic process. Then

$$\text{Max}\{F(D)\} = \max \{\max F_1(d(y_1)): y_1 \in Y_1\}.$$

Proof

Observe that $F(D)=\{F_1(d(y_1)):y_1\in Y_1\}$, and the assertion follows from corollary 1. $\square$

6. Numerical Procedure

We present an algorithm for determination of the set of all maximal returns of the process, which is based on theorems 2-3. This procedure is stated as follows:

1. Compute max $F_T(D(y_T))$ for all states $y_T\in Y_T$.

2. For $t=T-1,\ldots,1$ compute max $F_t(D(y_t))$ for all states $y_t\in Y_t$ by using theorem 2.

3. Compute max$\{F(D)\}$ by using theorem 3.

4. Since $F(d^*)\in$ max $F(D)$, obtain the set of efficient realizations d^* generating max $F(D)$.

7. Illustrative Example

To illustrate an application of the model we use discrete dynamic program with fuzzy parameters. The process (P,F) is defined as follows:

We consider a process, which consists of 3 periods $[T=3]$, in which:

$$Y_t=\{0,1\}, \quad \text{for } t=1,2,3,4;$$

$$X_t(0) = X_t(1) =\{0, 1\}, \quad \Omega_t(y_t,0)=0 \text{ and } \Omega_t(y_t,1)=1, \quad \text{for } t=1,2,3 \text{ and } y_t\in Y_t.$$

The terms connected with the criteria function are defined as follows. Let $W=W_1\times W_2$, where

$$W_1=\{a\in\mathbf{R}: a\in(0, 1]\} \text{ is the set of real numbers } a\in(0,1],$$

$$W_2=\{(m,\alpha,\beta): m\in\mathbf{R} \text{ and } \alpha\geq0, \beta\geq0\} \text{ is the set of triangular fuzzy numbers}$$

[m is the centre, and α,β are deviation parameters].

In other words

$$W=\{\ [a,\ (m,\alpha,\beta)]\ :\ a\in(0,1],\ m\in\mathbf{R}\ \text{and}\ \alpha\geq0,\ \beta\geq0\ \}.$$

Elements of W_1 can be interpreted as degrees of feasibility of period decision and elements of W_2 can be interpreted as imprecise parameters connected with period criteria function. Relation $<$ is defined as follows:

$$[\ a_1,\ (m_1,\alpha_1,\beta_1)\ ]\ <\ [\ a_2,\ (m_2,\alpha_2,\beta_2)\ ]\ \text{iff}$$

$$a_1\leq a_2\ \text{and}\ (m_1\leq m_2\ \text{and}\ m_1-\alpha_1\leq m_2-\alpha_2\ \text{and}\ m_1+\beta_1\leq m_2+\beta_2).$$

[$\leq$ denotes traditional relation between real numbers].

Operators $\square_t$ for $t=1,2,3$ are defined as follows

$$(a_1,\ (m_1,\alpha_1,\beta_1)\ )\square_t\ (a_2,\ (m_2,\alpha_2,\beta_2)\ )\cong(\ \min\{a_1,\ a_2\},\ (m_1+m_2,\ \alpha_1+\alpha_2,\ \beta_1+\beta_2)\ ).$$

One can easily check that relation $<$ is transitive and antisymmetric and operators $\square$ are monotone. Period criteria functions are defined as follows (Fig. 1).

(y_t,x_t)	$f_1(y_t,x_t)$	$f_2(y_t,x_t)$	$f_3(y_t,x_t)$
(0,0)	0.8, (4,3,1)	0.9, (5,1,3)	0.8, (5,2,3)
(0,1)	0.8, (6,2,2)	0.9, (4,2,1)	0.8, (4,1,3)
(1,0)	0.9, (3,2,1)	0.8, (6,3,2)	0.9, (4,2,2)
(1,1)	1, (2,2,2)	0.7, (5,3,4)	0.7, (6,3,2)

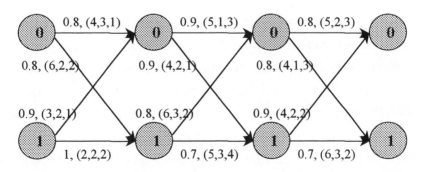

Fig. 1. The graph of the process

Applying the procedure described earlier we obtain:

t	max$\{F_t(d(0)\}$	max$\{F_t(d(1)\}$
3	[0.8, (5,2,3)]	[0.9, (4,2,2)], [0.7, (6,3,2)]
2	[0.8, (10,3,6)], [0.9, (8,4,3)]	[0.7, (11,6,6)], [0.8, (11,5,5)]
1	[0.8, (17,7,7)], [0.7, (17,8,8)]	[0.9, (11,6,4)], [0.8, (13,5,7)], [0.7, (13,8,8)]

max$\{F(D)\}$ = { [0.8, (17,7,7)], [0.7, (17,8,8)], [0.9, (11,6,4)] }

Efficient realizations are: (0,1, 1,0, 0,0), (0,1, 1,1, 1,1), (1,0, 0,1, 1,0).

8. Summary and Conclusions

The paper classifies many of discrete dynamic programming problems, in particular the ones with real-valued vector criteria function. On the basis of the introduced notions and presented theorems, it is possible to approach the model more generally; e.g. one can apply more general class of fuzzy numbers than the one presented in the example, one can use any product of partially ordered sets, or put in other approaches.

References

[1] Brown, T.A., Strauch R.E.: Dynamic programming in multiplicative lattices. J. Math. Analysis and Applications, 12, 2, (1965), 364-370.

[2] Henig, M.I.: The principle of optimality in dynamic programming with returns in partially ordered sets. Math. Of Oper. Res., 10, 3, (1985), 462-470.

[3] Li, D., Haimes Y.Y.: Multiobjective dynamic programming: the state of the art. Control Theory and Advanced Technology, 5, 4, (1989), 471-483.

[4] Li, D., Haimes Y.Y.: Extension of dynamic programming to non-separable dynamic optimization problems. Comp. & Math. Appl.,21,11/12, (1991), 51-56.

[5] Mitten, L.G.: Preference order dynamic programming. Management Science 21,1, (1974), 43-46.

[6] Trzaskalik, T.: Multicriteria discrete dynamic programming. Theory and economic applications. The University of Economics, Katowice (1990), (in Polish).

[7] Trzaskalik, T.: Multiple criteria discrete dynamic programming. Mathematics Today, XII-A, (1994), 173-199.

[8] Trzaskalik, T.: Multiobjective analysis in dynamic environment. The University of Economics, Katowice (1998).

[9] Wu, C.P.: Multi-criteria dynamic. Scientia Sinica, 23, 7, (1980), 816-822.

[10] Yu, P.L., Seiford L.: Multistage decision problems with multiple criteria. In Multiple Criteria Analysis, P. Nijkamp and J. Spronk (Eds), Gower Press, London, (1981), 235-244.

[11] Zimmermann H. J.: Fuzzy set theory and its application. Kluwer Academic Publishers, Boston/Dordrecht/London, (1991).

Dual Approach to Generalized Data Envelopment Analysis based on Production Possibility

Yeboon Yun[1], Hirotaka Nakayama[2], and Tetsuzo Tanino[3]

[1] Department of Reliability-based Information System Engineering, Faculty of Engineering, Kagawa University, Kagawa 761-0396, Japan
[2] Department of Applied Mathematics, Konan University, Kobe 658-8501, Japan
[3] Department of Electronics and Information Systems, Graduate School of Engineering, Osaka University, Osaka 565-0871, Japan

Abstract. So far, in order to evaluate the efficiency of DMUs, there have been developed several kinds of DEA models, for example, CCR model, BCC model, FDH model, and so on. These models are characterized by how to determine the production possibility set; a convex cone, a convex hull and a free disposable hull of observed data set. In this paper, we the $GDEA_D$ model based on production possibility as a dual approach to GDEA [13] and the concept of α_D-efficiency in the $GDEA_D$ model. In addition, we establish the relations between the $GDEA_D$ model and existing DEA models, and interpret the meaning of an optimal value to the problem ($GDEA_D$). Therefore, we show that it is possible to evaluate the efficiency for each decision making unit by considering surplus of inputs/slack of outputs as well as the technical efficiency. Finally, through an illustrative example, it is shown that $GDEA_D$ can reveal domination relations among all decision making units.

1 Introduction

Data Envelopment Analysis (DEA) which was originally suggested by Charnes, Cooper and Rhodes [4,5] is a method to measure the relative efficiency of decision making units (DMUs) performing similar tasks in a production system that consumes multiple inputs to produce multiple outputs. Later, Banker, Charnes and Cooper (BCC) suggested a model for estimating technical efficiency and scale inefficiency in DEA. In addition, Tulkens [10] introduced a relative efficiency to non-convex free disposable hull (FDH) [6] of an observed data and formulated as a mixed integer programming to calculate a relative efficiency for each DMU. On the other hand, relationships between DEA and multiple criteria decision analysis (MCDA) have been studied from several viewpoints by many authors. Belton [1], and Belton and Vickers [2] measured an efficiency as a weighted sum of inputs and outputs. Stewart [9] showed the equivalence between the CCR model and some linear value function model for multiple outputs and multiple inputs. Joro et al. [8] proved structural correspondence between DEA models and Multiple Objective Linear Programming

(MOLP) using an achievement scalarizing function [11]. Especially, Hamel *et al.* [7] evaluated the efficiency of DMU in terms of pseudo-concave value function by considering a tangent cone of feasible set at the most preferred solution of decision maker. Yun, Nakayama and Tanino [12,13] proposed a new model called a generalized DEA (GDEA) which can treat basic DEA models, specifically, the CCR model, the BCC model and the FDH model in a unified way. They showed the theoretical properties on relationships among the GDEA model and those DEA models and so, GDEA model made it possible to calculate the efficiency of DMUs incorporating various preference structures of decision makers. In this paper, we the GDEA_D model based on production possibility as a dual approach to GDEA and the concept of α_D-efficiency in the GDEA_D model. In addition, we establish the relations between the GDEA_D model and existing DEA dual models, and interpret the meaning of an optimal value to the problem (GDEA_D). Therefore, we show that it is possible to evaluate the efficiency for each decision making unit by considering surplus of inputs/slack of outputs as well as the technical efficiency. Finally, through an illustrative example, it is shown that GDEA_D can reveal domination relations among all decision making units.

2 Basic DEA Models

In the following discussion, we assume that there exist n DMUs to be evaluated. Each DMU consumes varying amounts of m different inputs to produce p different outputs. Specifically, DMUj consumes amounts $\boldsymbol{x}_j := (x_{ij})$ of inputs $(i = 1, \cdots, m)$ and produces amounts $\boldsymbol{y}_j := (y_{kj})$ of outputs $(k = 1, \cdots, p)$. For these constants, which generally take the form of observed data, we assume $x_{ij} > 0$ for each $i = 1, \cdots, m$ and $y_{kj} > 0$ for each $k = 1, \cdots, p$. Further, we assume that there are no duplicated units in the observed data. The $p \times n$ output matrix for the n DMUs is denoted by $\boldsymbol{Y}$, and the $m \times n$ input matrix for the n DMUs is denoted by $\boldsymbol{X}$. $\boldsymbol{x}_o := (x_{1o}, \cdots, x_{mo})$ and $\boldsymbol{y}_o := (y_{1o}, \cdots, y_{po})$ are amounts of inputs and outputs of DMUo, which is evaluated. In addition, ε is a small positive number ("non-Archimedean") and $\boldsymbol{1} = (1, \cdots, 1)$ is a unit vector. For convenience, the following notations for vectors in $\mathbb{R}^{p+m}$ will be used:

$$\boldsymbol{z}_o > \boldsymbol{z}_j \iff z_{io} > z_{ij}, \quad i = 1, \cdots, p+m,$$

$$\boldsymbol{z}_o \geqq \boldsymbol{z}_j \iff z_{io} \geqq z_{ij}, \quad i = 1, \cdots, p+m,$$

$$\boldsymbol{z}_o \geq \boldsymbol{z}_j \iff z_{io} \geqq z_{ij}, \quad i = 1, \cdots, p+m \text{ but } \boldsymbol{z}_o \neq \boldsymbol{z}_j.$$

The CCR model [5], BCC model [3] and FDH model [10] with an input oriented model were formulated as the following:

$$\begin{aligned}
\underset{\theta,\,\lambda,\,s_x,\,s_y}{\text{minimize}} \quad & \theta - \varepsilon(\mathbf{1}^T s_x + \mathbf{1}^T s_y) && \text{(CCR)}\\
\text{subject to} \quad & X\lambda - \theta x_o + s_x = \mathbf{0},\\
& Y\lambda - y_o - s_y = \mathbf{0},\\
& \lambda \geq \mathbf{0},\ s_x \geq \mathbf{0},\ s_y \geq \mathbf{0},\\
& \theta \in \mathbb{R},\ \lambda \in \mathbb{R}^n,\ s_x \in \mathbb{R}^m, s_y \in \mathbb{R}^p.
\end{aligned}$$

$$\begin{aligned}
\underset{\theta,\,\lambda,\,s_x,\,s_y}{\text{minimize}} \quad & \theta - \varepsilon(\mathbf{1}^T s_x + \mathbf{1}^T s_y) && \text{(BCC)}\\
\text{subject to} \quad & X\lambda - \theta x_o + s_x = \mathbf{0},\\
& Y\lambda - y_o - s_y = \mathbf{0},\\
& \mathbf{1}^T\lambda = 1,\\
& \lambda \geq \mathbf{0},\ s_x \geq \mathbf{0},\ s_y \geq \mathbf{0},\\
& \theta \in \mathbb{R},\ \lambda \in \mathbb{R}^n,\ s_x \in \mathbb{R}^m, s_y \in \mathbb{R}^p.
\end{aligned}$$

$$\begin{aligned}
\underset{\theta,\,\lambda,\,s_x,\,s_y}{\text{minimize}} \quad & \theta - \varepsilon(\mathbf{1}^T s_x + \mathbf{1}^T s_y) && \text{(FDH)}\\
\text{subject to} \quad & X\lambda - \theta x_o + s_x = \mathbf{0},\\
& Y\lambda - y_o - s_y = \mathbf{0},\\
& \mathbf{1}^T\lambda = 1;\ \lambda_j \in \{0,\ 1\}\ \text{for each}\ j = 1,\cdots,n,\\
& \lambda \geq \mathbf{0},\ s_x \geq \mathbf{0},\ s_y \geq \mathbf{0},\\
& \theta \in \mathbb{R},\ \lambda \in \mathbb{R}^n,\ s_x \in \mathbb{R}^m, s_y \in \mathbb{R}^p.
\end{aligned}$$

Therefore, the production possibility set P_1, P_2 and P_3 (See Figure 1-3.) in the above models, respectively, can be given by

$$\begin{aligned}
P_1 &= \{\,(y, x)\,|\,Y\lambda \geq y,\ X\lambda \leq x,\ \lambda \geq \mathbf{0}\,\},\\
P_2 &= \{\,(y, x)\,|\,Y\lambda \geq y,\ X\lambda \leq x,\ \mathbf{1}^T\lambda = 1,\ \lambda \geq \mathbf{0}\,\},\\
P_3 &= \{\,(y, x)\,|\,Y\lambda \geq y,\ X\lambda \leq x,\ \mathbf{1}^T\lambda = 1,\ \lambda_j \in \{0,1\},\ j = 1,\cdots,n\,\}.
\end{aligned}$$

Here, an output-input vector z_j of a DMUj, $j = 1,\cdots,n$ and output-input matrix Z of all DMUs respectively, denoted by $z_j := \begin{pmatrix} y_j \\ -x_j \end{pmatrix}$, $j = 1,\cdots,n$ and $Z := \begin{pmatrix} Y \\ -X \end{pmatrix}$. We denote a $(p+m) \times n$ matrix Z_o by $Z_o := (z_o,\cdots,z_o)$, where o is the index of DMU to be evaluated. Thus, P_1', P_2' and P_3' are defined by

$$\begin{aligned}
P_1' &= \{z\,|\,Z\lambda \geq z,\ \lambda \geq \mathbf{0}\,\},\\
P_2' &= \{z\,|\,Z\lambda \geq z,\ \mathbf{1}^T\lambda = 1,\ \lambda \geq \mathbf{0}\,\},\\
P_3' &= \{z\,|\,Z\lambda \geq z,\ \mathbf{1}^T\lambda = 1,\ \lambda_j \in \{0,1\},\ j = 1,\cdots,n\,\},
\end{aligned}$$

and the 'efficiency' in basic models can be transformed into the following:

Definition 1 *DMUo is said to be Pareto efficient in P'_l $(l = 1, 2, 3)$, if and only if there does not exist $(\boldsymbol{y}, -\boldsymbol{x}) \in P'_l$ such that $(\boldsymbol{y}, -\boldsymbol{x}) \geq (\boldsymbol{y}_o, -\boldsymbol{x}_o)$. Note that the Pareto efficiency for $l = 1, 2, 3$ is equivalent to the CCR efficiency, BCC efficiency and FDH efficiency, respectively.*

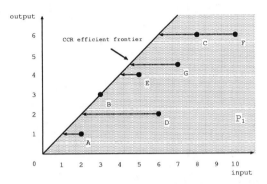

Fig. 1. CCR efficient frontier and production possibility set generated by the CCR model from the observed data.

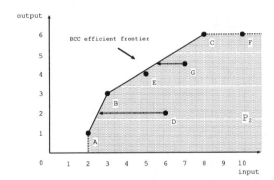

Fig. 2. BCC efficient frontier and production possibility set generated by the BCC model from the observed data.

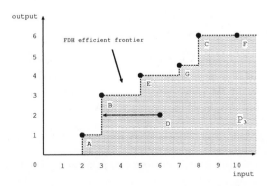

Fig. 3. FDH efficient frontier and production possibility set generated by the FDH model from the observed data.

3 GDEA Based on Production Possibility

In this section, we formulate a GDEA$_D$ model based on the production possibility and define 'α_D-efficiency' in the GDEA$_D$ model. Next, we establish relationships between the GDEA$_D$ model and basic DEA models introduced in section 1.

The GDEA model, which can evaluate the efficiency in several basic models as special cases, is as follows [13]:

$$\begin{array}{ll}\underset{\Delta,\,\mu_k,\,\nu_i}{\text{maximize}} & \Delta \hspace{6cm} \text{(GDEA)}\end{array}$$

$$\text{subject to} \quad \Delta \leqq \tilde{d}_j + \alpha\Big(\sum_{k=1}^{p}\mu_k(y_{ko}-y_{kj}) + \sum_{i=1}^{m}\nu_i(-x_{io}+x_{ij})\Big), \ j=1,\cdots,n,$$

$$\sum_{k=1}^{p}\mu_k y_{ko} - \sum_{i=1}^{m}\nu_i x_{io} = 0,$$

$$\sum_{k=1}^{p}\mu_k + \sum_{i=1}^{m}\nu_i = 1,$$

$$\mu_k, \ \nu_i \geqq \varepsilon, \ k=1,\cdots,p; i=1,\cdots,m,$$

where $\tilde{d}_j = \max\limits_{\substack{k=1,\cdots,p \\ i=1,\cdots,m}} \{\mu_k(y_{ko}-y_{kj}), \ \nu_i(-x_{io}+x_{ij})\}$ and α is a positive number.

The dual problem (GDEA$_D$) to the problem (GDEA) can be formulated as follows:

$$\begin{array}{ll}\underset{\omega,\,\kappa,\,\boldsymbol{\lambda},\,\boldsymbol{s_z}}{\text{minimize}} & \omega - \varepsilon\mathbf{1}^T\boldsymbol{s_z} \hspace{4cm} \text{(GDEA}_D)\end{array}$$

$$\begin{array}{ll}\text{subject to} & \{\alpha(Z_o - Z) + D_z\}\boldsymbol{\lambda} - \boldsymbol{\omega} + \boldsymbol{s_z} + \kappa z_o = \mathbf{0} \\[4pt] & \mathbf{1}^T\boldsymbol{\lambda} = 1, \\[4pt] & \boldsymbol{\lambda} \geqq \mathbf{0}, \ \boldsymbol{s_z} \geqq \mathbf{0},\end{array}$$

where $\boldsymbol{\omega} = (\omega,\cdots,\omega)$ and α is a given positive number. A $(p+m) \times n$ matrix $D_z := (\boldsymbol{d_1},\cdots,\boldsymbol{d_n})$ is a matrix $(Z - Z_o)$ is replaced by 0, except for the maximal component (if there exist non-unique maximal components, only one is chosen from among them) in each row.

We define an 'efficiency' for a DMUo in the GDEA$_D$ model.

Definition 2 (α_D-efficiency) For a given positive α, DMUo is said to be α_D-efficient if and only if the optimal solution $(\omega^*, \kappa^*, \boldsymbol{\lambda}^*, \boldsymbol{s_z^*})$ to the problem (GDEA$_D$) satisfies the following two conditions:

(i) ω^* *is equal to zero;*
(ii) *the slack variable* s_z^* *is zero.*

Otherwise, DMUo is said to be α_D*-inefficient.*

We, particularly, note that for an optimal solution $(\omega^*, \kappa^*, \boldsymbol{\lambda}^*, s_z^*)$ to the problem GDEA$_D$, ω^* is not greater than zero because of the strong duality of (GDEA) and (GDEA$_D$) (in linear programming problem), and the 'non-Archimedean' property of ε.

In here, we establish theoretical properties on relationships among efficiencies in basic DEA models and the GDEA$_D$ model.

Theorem 1 *Let* κ *be fixed at 0 in the problem (GDEA$_D$). DMUo is Pareto efficient in* P_3' *if and only if DMUo is* α_D*-efficient for some sufficiently small positive number* α.

Theorem 2 *Let* κ *be fixed at 0 in the problem (GDEA$_D$). DMUo is Pareto efficient in* P_2' *if and only if DMUo is* α_D*-efficient for some sufficiently large positive number* α.

Theorem 3 *DMUo is Pareto efficient in* P_1' *if and only if DMUo is* α_D*-efficient for some sufficiently large positive number* α.

4 Optimal Solutions to (GDEA$_D$)

In this section, we explain the meaning of optimal solutions ω^*, $\boldsymbol{\lambda}^*$, s_z^* to the problem (GDEA$_D$). ω^* gives a measurement of relative efficiency for DMUo. In other words, it represents the degree how inefficient DMUo is, that is, how far DMUo is from the efficient frontier generated with the given α. $\boldsymbol{\lambda}^* := (\lambda_1^*, \cdots, \lambda_n^*)$ represents a domination relation between DMUo and another DMUs. That is, it means that the DMUo is dominated by DMUj if

Table 1. An Example of 1-input and 1-output and Optimal value in the problems (CCR), (BCC) and (FDH).

DMU	input	output	CCR model	BCC model	FDH model
A	2	1	0.5	1	1
B	3	3	1	1	1
C	8	6	0.75	1	1
D	6	2	0.333	0.417	0.5
E	5	4	0.8	0.933	1
F	10	6	0.6	0.999	0.8
G	7	4	0.571	0.667	0.714

Table 2. Optimal solution to (GDEA_D) with $\alpha = 10^{-6}$ and fixed $\kappa = 0$.

DMU	ω^*	λ^*	$s_z^* = (s_x^*, \ s_y^*)$
A	0	$\lambda_A^* = 1$	$(0, 0)$
B	0	$\lambda_B^* = 1$	$(0, 0)$
C	0	$\lambda_C^* = 1$	$(0, 0)$
D	-0.5	$\lambda_B^* = \lambda_E^* = 0.5$	$(0, 0)$
E	0	$\lambda_E^* = 1$	$(0, 0)$
F	0	$\lambda_C^* = 1$	$(2, 0)$
G	0	$\lambda_E^* = 1$	$(2, 0)$

Table 3. Optimal solution to (GDEA_D) with $\alpha = 10$ and fixed $\kappa = 0$.

DMU	ω^*	λ^*	$s_z^* = (s_x^*, \ s_y^*)$
A	0	$\lambda_A^* = 1$	$(0, 0)$
B	0	$\lambda_B^* = 1$	$(0, 0)$
C	0	$\lambda_C^* = 1$	$(0, 0)$
D	-7.803	$\lambda_B^* = 0.765, \ \lambda_C^* = 0.235$	$(0, 0)$
E	-0.441	$\lambda_B^* = 0.631, \ \lambda_C^* = 0.369$	$(0, 0)$
F	0	$\lambda_C^* = 1$	$(20, 0)$
G	-8.281	$\lambda_B^* = 0.378, \lambda_C^* = 0.622$	$(0, 0)$

Table 4. Optimal solution to (GDEA_D) with $\alpha = 10$ and non-fixed κ.

DMU	ω^*	λ^*	$s_z^* = (s_x^*, \ s_y^*)$	κ^*
A	-11.333	$\lambda_C^* = 1$	$(0, 0)$	38.667
B	0	$\lambda_B^* = 1$	$(0, 0)$	0
C	-2.571	$\lambda_B^* = 1$	$(0, 0)$	-5.929
D	-24.500	$\lambda_C^* = 1$	$(0, 0)$	7.750
E	-2.778	$\lambda_B^* = 1$	$(0, 0)$	-3.444
F	-7.500	$\lambda_C^* = 1$	$(0, 0)$	-1.250
G	-8.727	$\lambda_C^* = 1$	$(0, 0)$	2.818

λ_j for some $j \neq 0$ is positive. s_x^* represents the slack of inputs and s_y^* does the surplus of outputs for performance of the DMUo.

Consider an illustrative example as shown in Table 1. Table shows the results of the CCR-efficiency, BCC-efficiency and FDH-efficiency, respectively,

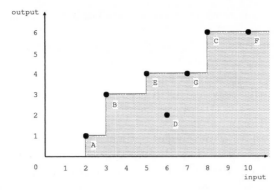

Fig. 4. Efficient frontier generated by GDEA$_D$ model with $\alpha = 10^{-6}$ and fixed $\kappa = 0$.

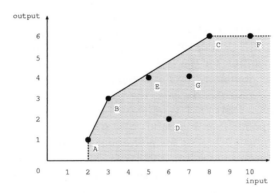

Fig. 5. Efficient frontier generated by GDEA$_D$ model with $\alpha = 10$ and fixed $\kappa = 0$.

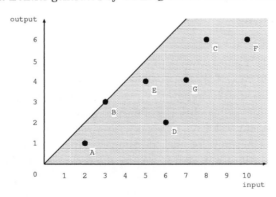

Fig. 6. Efficient frontier generated by GDEA$_D$ model with $\alpha = 10$ and non-fixed κ.

in the example. Table 2 shows the optimal solution $(\omega^*, \kappa^*, \boldsymbol{\lambda}^*, \boldsymbol{s}_z^*)$ to the problem (GDEA$_D$) $(\varepsilon = 10^{-6})$ when α is given as 10^{-6} and κ is fixed at 0. Table 3 shows the optimal solution $(\omega^*, \kappa^*, \boldsymbol{\lambda}^*, \boldsymbol{s}_z^*)$ to the problem (GDEA$_D$)

($\varepsilon = 10^{-6}$) when α is given by 10 and κ is fixed at 0. Finally, Table 4 shows the optimal solution $(\omega^*, \kappa^*, \boldsymbol{\lambda}^*, \boldsymbol{s}_z^*)$ to the problem (GDEA$_D$) ($\varepsilon = 10^{-6}$) when α is given as 10. Here, we can see that the FDH-efficiency, BCC-efficiency and CCR-efficiency are equivalent to the α-efficiency, respectively, from the result of Tables 2-Tables 4 and Figure 4-Figure 6. In other words, the FDH-efficiency, BCC-efficiency and CCR-efficiency can be obtained by changing the parameter α in the GDEA$_D$ model.

Now, we interpret a meaning of optimal solutions $(\omega^*, \kappa^*, \boldsymbol{\lambda}^*, \boldsymbol{s}_z^*)$ to the problem (GDEA$_D$). Note that ω^* gives a measurement of relative efficiency for DMUo. In other words, it represents the degree how inefficient DMUo is, that is, how far DMUo is from the efficient frontier generated with the given α. $\boldsymbol{\lambda}^* := (\lambda_1^*, \cdots, \lambda_n^*)$ represents a domination relation between DMUo and another DMUs. That is, it means that the DMUo is dominated by DMUj if λ_j for some $j \neq o$ is positive. For example, as seen in Table 2, the optimal solution for the DMU D is $\lambda_B^* = 0.5$ and $\lambda_E^* = 0.5$, and hence DMU D is dominated by DMU B and DMU E. (See Figure 4.) In addition, in Table 3, the optimal solution for the DMU E is $\lambda_B^* = 0.631$ and $\lambda_C^* = 0.369$, and hence DMU E is dominated by linear combination of DMU B and DMU C. (See Figure 5.) As seen in Table 4, the optimal solution for the DMU C is $\lambda_B^* = 1$, and hence DMU D is dominated by a point on line through DMU B and original point. (See Figure 6.) $\boldsymbol{s}_x^*$ represents the slack of inputs and $\boldsymbol{s}_y^*$ does the surplus of outputs for performance of the DMUo. For instance, DMU G has the optimal solution $\omega^* = 0$, $\lambda_E^* = 1$ and $\boldsymbol{s}_x^* = 0$, and it is α-inefficient because $\boldsymbol{s}_x^*$ is not equal to zero although $\omega^* = 0$. It implies that DMU G has the surplus amount of input than DMU E with the same output.

5 Conclusions

In this paper, the GDEA$_D$ model based on production possibility as a dual approach to GDEA and the concept of α_D-efficiency in the GDEA$_D$ model have been proposed. The relations between the GDEA$_D$ model and existing DEA dual models have been established, and the meaning of an optimal value to the problem (GDEA$_D$) has been interpreted. Therefore, it is possible to evaluate the efficiency for each decision making unit by considering surplus of inputs/slack of outputs as well as the technical efficiency. Moreover, through an illustrative example, it has been shown that GDEA$_D$ can reveal domination relations among all decision making units. Finally, through the study on GDEA in the paper, it will be expected that GDEA makes it helpful to evaluate an efficiency of complex management systems such as banks, chain stores, communications enterprise, hospitals, etc. Moreover, GDEA is promising to be very useful method to construct decision support systems such as administrative reforms of (local) governments, engineering design, schools, courts, and so on.

References

1. Belton, V. (1992) An Integrating Data Envelopment Analysis with Multiple Criteria Decision Analysis. Proceedings of the Ninth International Conference on Multiple Criteria Decision Making:Theory and Applications in Business, Industry and Commerce, eds. A. Goicoechea, L. Duckstein and S. Zoints (Springer-Verlag, Berlin), 71–79.
2. Belton, V., Vickers, S.P. (1993) Demystifying DEA-A Visual Interactive Approach Based on Multiple Criteria Analysis. Journal of Operational Research Society **44**, 883–896.
3. Banker, R.D. , Charnes, A., Cooper, W.W. (1984) Some Models for Estimating Technical and Scale Inefficiencies in Data Envelopment Analysis, Management Science **30**, 1078–1092.
4. Charnes, A., Cooper, W.W., Rhodes, E. (1978) Measuring the Efficiency of Decision Making Units, European Journal of Operational Research **2**, 429–444.
5. Charnes, A., Cooper, W.W., Rhodes, E. (1970) Measuring the Efficiency of Decision Making Units, European Journal of Operational Research **3**, 339.
6. Deprins, D., Simar, L., Tulkens, H. (1984) Measuring Labor-Efficiency in Post Offices, The Performance of Public Enterprises:Concepts and Measurements, eds. M. Marchand, P. Pestieu and H. Tulkens (North Holland, Amsterdam), 247–263.
7. Halme, M., Joro, T., Korhonen, P., Salo, A, Wallenius, J. (1999) A Value Efficiency Approach to Incorporating Preference Information in Data Envelopment Analysis, Management Science **45**, 103–115.
8. Joro, T., Korhonen, P., Wallenius, J. (1998) Structural Comparison of Data Envelopment Analysis and Multiple Objective Linear Programming, Management Science **44**, 962–970.
9. Stewart, T.J. (1996) Relationships Between Data Envelopment Analysis and Multiple Criteria Decision Analysis, Journal of Operational Research Society **47**, 654–665.
10. Tulkens, H. (1993) On FDH efficiency: Some Methodological Issues and Applications to Retail Banking, Courts, and Urban Transit, Journal of Productivity Analysis **4**, 183–210.
11. Wierzbicki, H. (1980) The use of Reference Objectives in Multiobjective Optimization, Multiple Objective Decision Making, Theory and Application, eds. G. Fandel and T. Gal, Springer-Verlag, New York.
12. Yun, Y.B. , Nakayama, H., Tanino, T. (2000) On efficiency of Data Envelopment Analysis, Forthcoming in Proceedings of the 14th International Conference on Multiple Criteria Decision Making, Charlottesville, Virginia, USA.
13. Yun, Y.B. , Nakayama, H., Tanino, T. (1999) A Generalization of DEA Model, Journal of the Society of Instrument and Control Engineers (SICE) **35**, 1813–1818.

II

APPLICATIONS

Using Interactive Multiple Objective Methods to Determine the Budget Assignment to the Hospitals of a Sanitary System

Rafael Caballero[1], Trinidad Gómez[1], M. Puerto López del Amo[2], Mariano Luque[1], José Martín[2], Julián Molina[1] and Francisco Ruiz[1]

1. Departamento de Economía Aplicada (Matemáticas). Campus El Ejido s/n. University of Málaga. Spain.
2. Escuela Andaluza de Salud Pública. Granada. Spain.

Abstract. One of the main problems that the decision centers of public sanitary systems must face is the budget distribution among the different hospitals of the system. Sanitary, economical, and political criteria must be combined to take the final decision. In this paper, a combined procedure, which uses several interactive multiple objective methods, is applied to the specific problem of the Andalusian Public Health Service. The performance of the system is studied, and the final results are commented by the decision-makers.

Keywords. Multiobjective Programming. Interactive Methods. Health Economy. Budget Assignment.

1
Introduction

The Spanish National Health Service (SNS) shares, with the rest of the European Health Services, the necessity to find compatibility between the ethic principles of universality and equality of access to the sanitary services, and the requirements given by the European Union. The regulating agency (as is the case of the Catalonian Health Service, or the private insurers) or the corporate center of a public hierarchy (as, for example, the National Service, INSALUD, or the Andalusian Service, SAS), must solve the problem of the budget assignment among a given set of hospitals. This problem constitutes the central element of their strategy when elaborating and concretizing the so-called Contract-Program. Depending on the analysis of the objectives formulated in the Contract-Program and on the application of certain preference revelation systems to the decision center, its attributes and priorities are characterized as budgets, activity vectors and risk transference to the providers.

The buyers, or corporate centers of the regional Health Services (as, for example, the SAS), which are placed within a specific institutional environment and have a 'limited rationality', usually wish to search for a solution which simultaneously satisfies several objectives, rather than optimizing a single one. For this reason, multiobjective programming techniques seem to be very appropriate for the modeling and resolution of the corresponding problem. And within these techniques and in this context, interactive techniques can be very helpful tools in order to find the optimal parameters of the contracts and to identify the potential contradictions existing among the objective of the decision center. Therefore, the main aim is to drive the regulating agency, through the use of interactive multiobjective techniques, towards the values that yield an equilibrium among all the objectives.

A great part of the literature related to Health Economy problems assumes that the regulating center has got a single objective to optimize (production efficiency of the hospitals, gross social benefit, etc.), which can be insufficient in this decisional context. The number of papers where multicriteria techniques are applied to the sanitary field are still scarce, and most of them are centered in activity planning and budget assignment at a intern level within a hospital. In these papers, Goal Programming is the most widely used approach. For example, let us point out the work by Lee (1973), that evaluates the compatibility and priority structure of the goals formulated for the annual resource assignment planning. The objective considered are: assuring the necessary human resources to provide an adequate service to the patients; replacing or acquiring new equipment; increasing the salaries in an adequate way; adjusting the ratios staff/patients; adequate distribution of the different professional categories at the hospital; adequate nursing staff; and costs. Panitz (1988) describes a situation where a Mental Health center must select the services that should be offered and determine the optimal staff, so that the number of hours devoted to the patients is maximized, as well as the staff's occupation. Kwak and Lee (1997) presented a model for the strategic planning and the limited resources assignment in a sanitary organization. A sensitivity analysis was carried out in order to improve the applicability of the model. Arenas et al. (1998) analyze the intern coherence of the objectives, and the possibility to improve the functioning of a surgical unit at a general hospital, taking into account the occupation, staff availability and economical constraints. Rodríguez et al. (1998) formulate a planning model for two surgical units of a general hospital in order to reduce the waiting lists (both the number of patients and the length of stay in the lists), while the minimization of costs is also considered as a objective.

In this work, the advantages of the interactive techniques in this field are studied. Besides, the model is not centered in a single hospital, but comprises a whole regional sanitary system. Namely, the aim of this paper is to apply a decision system, which incorporates several interactive techniques, so that the decision-makers can analyze different possible solutions and 'build', in some sense, the strategy that best fits their requirements. At the same time, the opinions of the decision-makers about the process and the final solution are given, in order to validate the decision system, designed by Luque (2000), for real applications. It must be pointed out that the model developed was previously described and studied by Martín et al. (2000), but using non-interactive techniques.

2
Description of the Model

The final aim of the model is to determine the number of units for each activity line in each hospital and, thus, the budget assignment, so that the desires of the decision center (a regulating agency or the corporate center of a public hierarchy) are satisfied. Therefore, the decision variables are denoted by x_{ij}, which represents the level corresponding to activity i ($i = 1,...,r$) at hospital j ($j = 1,...,n$). Consequently, there are $r \cdot n$ variables, where r is the number of activity lines, and n is the number of hospitals.

The model will be applied to the particular case of the budget assignment among the 16 regional hospitals ($n = 16$) of the Andalusian Health Service (SAS), and considering 12 activity lines ($r = 12$). The objectives of the decision center will be organized in a hierarchy tree, so that the decision-maker can assess weights or other parameters to a certain set of objectives at the same time. This structure will be commented later on.

The model is formed by 5 blocks of technical constraints which give lower and upper limits for the activity level depending on several factors, and a set of objectives which can be classified in two groups: increasing the efficiency level of the system and decreasing the total expense. These objectives, of course, cause a great degree of conflict, which is the main feature of the problems where multiobjective techniques are applied.

2.1
Technical Constraints

The admissible set of activity levels is determined by the following constraints:
- The global activity level for each line i must lie between two prefixed values, denoted by L_{x_i} and U_{x_i}, that is,

$$L_{x_i} \le \sum_{j=1}^{n} x_{ij} \le U_{x_i} \qquad i = 1, ..., r$$

- Each activity level in each hospital must be, at least a 80%, and not more than a 130% of the activity level achieved in the previous year, h_{ij}, that is:

$$0.8 h_{ij} \le x_{ij} \le 1.3 h_{ij} \qquad i = 1, ..., r \quad j = 1,...,n$$

These constraints assure that no exaggerated increases or drastic decreases are experimented by any activity line at any hospital.
- In each hospital, the total number of available hours of the surgical rooms (HQj) cannot be surpassed. If the mean number of surgical hours required for the activity line i is denoted by HQ_{x_i}, then these constraints can be formulated as follows:

$$\sum_{i=1}^{r} x_{ij} \cdot HQ_{x_i} \le HQ_j \qquad j = 1,...,n$$

- Besides, in each hospital the total number of available days of stay (hospitalizations), Ej, cannot be surpassed. Therefore,

$$\sum_{i=1}^{r} x_{ij} \cdot E_{x_i} \le E_j \qquad j = 1,...,n$$

where E_{x_i} denotes the mean days of stay for activity i.

- Finally, the total number of available off patient consulting hours, HCj, cannot be surpassed either in any hospital. If the mean number of hours for each off patient visit is denoted by HC, and the variable corresponding to the off patient activity in hospital j is denoted by x_{1j}, then these constraints can be written in the following way:

$$x_{ij} \cdot HC \le HC_j \qquad j = 1,...,n$$

In total, the model has $r + 3\,n$ technical constraints, and $2 \cdot r \cdot n$ simple bounds on the variables.

2.2
Objectives

Let us now describe the objectives set by the decision centers:

- First, the decision center wishes to maximize the global activity levels of those lines whose waiting lists are longer, while they prefer to keep the rest of the lines at the same levels. Anyway, at this first stage it will be assumed that all the activity lines are to be maximized, given that the ulterior interactive process will allow the decision-makers to give levels for certain activity lines.

$$\text{Max } f_i = \sum_{j=1}^{n} x_{ij} \qquad i = 1, 2,...,r$$

With respect to these objectives, it must be noted that, as it was previously commented, the global level of each activity line has got upper and lower bound, as well as the activity levels per hospitals, so that traumatic changes do not take place in the system. Such changes would make the solution too expensive in economical and/or political terms to be assumed.

- On the other hand, the decision center wishes to minimize the budget assignment to each hospital. For this assignment, it is considered that the 80% of the activity that was carried out the previous year is financed with the 80% of its historical cost (c_j), while the rest of the activity ($x_{ij} - 0.8 \cdot h_{ij}$) is valued at its efficient cost π_i. These efficient costs are given in Martin et al. (2000). Therefore, we have the following objective functions:

$$\text{Min } f_{j+r} = \sum_{i=1}^{r} \left((x_{ij} - 0.8 h_{ij}) \cdot \pi_i + 0.8 \cdot c_j \right) \qquad j = 1,...,n$$

- The last objective of the decision center is to carry out the budget assignment so that the global budget is minimized, taking into account the same considerations of the previous group of objectives:

$$\text{Min } f_{r+n+1} = \sum_{j=1}^{n} \sum_{i=1}^{r} \left(\left(x_{ij} - 0.8h_{ij} \right) \cdot \pi_i + 0.8 \cdot c_j \right)$$

Thus, the aim of the model is to find the activity levels that maximize the global activity in each line, and minimize both the budget assignments to each hospital, and the global expense. It is evident that the greater the activity levels are, the greater the costs will be. This high degree of conflict among the objectives motivates the use of the interactive techniques in order to search the final solution.

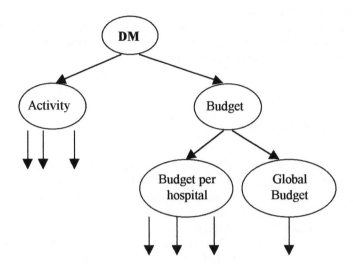

Fig 1. Hierarchical structure of the objectives

Taking into account the technical constraints and the objectives of the model, the multiobjective problem to be considered is the following:

$$\text{Max } f_i = \sum_{j=1}^{n} x_{ij} \qquad i = 1, 2, \dots, r$$

$$\text{Min } f_{j+r} = \sum_{i=1}^{r} \left(x_{ij} - 0.8h_{ij} \right) \cdot \pi_i + 0.8 \cdot c_j \qquad j = 1, \dots, n$$

$$\text{Min } f_{r+n+1} = \sum_{j=1}^{n} \sum_{i=1}^{r} \left(x_{ij} - 0.8h_{ij} \right) \cdot \pi_i + 0.8 \cdot c_j$$

subject to:

$$L_{x_i} \le \sum_{j=1}^{n} x_{ij} \le U_{x_i} \qquad i = 1, \dots, r$$

$$0.8h_{ij} \le x_{ij} \le 1.3h_{ij} \qquad i = 1, \dots, r; \quad j = 1, \dots, n$$

$$\sum_{i=1}^{r} x_{ij} \cdot HQ_{x_i} \leq HQ_j \qquad j = 1,2,...,n$$

$$\sum_{i=1}^{r} x_{ij} \cdot E_{x_i} \leq E_j \qquad j = 1,2,...,n$$

$$x_{ij} \cdot HC \leq HC_j \qquad j = 1,...,n$$

$$x_{ij} \geq 0 \qquad i = 1,...,r \; ; \quad j = 1,...,n$$

At a previous stage, the objectives were structured in order to help the regulating agency to provide the information required. This structuring, which was adapted in a natural way to the description of the $r + n + 1$ objectives, is given by the hierarchical structure shown in figure 1.

3
Solution and Results

The data for the application of the previously described model belong to the Andalusian Health Service (SAS), that plays the role of the decision center within the public net of regional hospitals of Andalucía. As it has been commented above, 16 hospitals have been considered, and the decision makers have grouped the different activities in 12 main lines.

The resolution has been carried out using a decision system developed by Luque (2000), named PROMOIN. The system comprises several classic interactive methods, which the user can choose along the process, so that it is possible to switch from one method to another, and to transfer information among the algorithms.

The program gives the user the possibility to carry out a normalization of the objectives other than the standard ones, using certain values as divisors which may have some meaning for the decision maker. In this particular case, the decision center decided to use the following normalizations: On the one hand, the activity levels were normalized dividing them by the corresponding maximum level, that is, its upper bound U_{x_i}. On the other hand, the budget assignments to each hospital were normalized dividing them by the amount of the funds required by each hospital:

$$g_1, g_2,...., g_n$$

Finally, for the global budget objective, the value G has been used, which is a global budget requirement established by the decision center as the result of a negotiation with the fiscal authorities.

As a result of these normalizations, the values of the objective functions shown to the user along the process are the following:

$$\text{Max} \ \frac{1}{U_{x_i}} f_i = \frac{1}{U_{x_i}} \sum_{j=1}^{n} x_{ij} \qquad i \in \{1,2,\dots,r\}$$

$$\text{Min} \ \frac{1}{g_j} f_{j+r} = \sum_{i=1}^{r} \left(x_{ij} - 0.8 h_{ij}\right) \cdot \frac{\pi_i}{g_j} + 0.8 \cdot \frac{c_j}{g_j} \qquad j = 1,\dots,n$$

$$\text{Min} \ \frac{1}{G} f_{r+n+1} = \sum_{j=1}^{n} \sum_{i=1}^{r} \left(x_{ij} - 0.8 h_{ij}\right) \cdot \frac{\pi_i}{G} + 0.8 \cdot \frac{c_j}{G}$$

Let us observe that the values of the objective functions corresponding to the normalized activity levels will always be less or equal to 1, and they reach the value 1 only when the activity level is at its upper bound. Therefore, the values of the normalized objectives can be interpreted as the percentage of the upper bound. On the other hand, the normalized values of the hospital budget objectives can be interpreted as the percentage of the required amount that each hospital would be assigned, and the normalized global budget objective is the percentage of the total budget assignment.

Besides, from the technical point of view, all the objectives corresponding to budget requirements can be simplified:

$$\text{Min} \ \frac{1}{g_j} f_{j+r} = \sum_{i=1}^{r} \left(x_{ij} - 0.8 h_{ij}\right) \cdot \frac{\pi_i}{g_j} + 0.8 \cdot \frac{c_j}{g_j} \ \equiv$$

$$\equiv \ \text{Min} \ \sum_{i=1}^{r} x_{ij} \cdot \frac{\pi_i}{g_j} - \sum_{i=1}^{r} 0.8 h_{ij} \cdot \frac{\pi_i}{g_j} + 0.8 \cdot \frac{c_j}{g_j} \ \equiv \ \text{Min} \ \sum_{i=1}^{r} x_{ij} \cdot \frac{\pi_i}{g_j}$$

and,

$$\text{Min} \ \frac{1}{G} f_{r+n+1} = \sum_{j=1}^{n} \sum_{i=1}^{r} \left(x_{ij} - 0.8 h_{ij}\right) \cdot \frac{\pi_i}{G} + 0.8 \cdot \frac{c_j}{G} \ \equiv$$

$$\equiv \ \text{Min} \ \sum_{j=1}^{n} \sum_{i=1}^{r} x_{ij} \cdot \frac{\pi_i}{G} - \sum_{j=1}^{n} \sum_{i=1}^{r} 0.8 h_{ij} \cdot \frac{\pi_i}{G} + 0.8 \cdot \frac{c_j}{G} \ \equiv \ \text{Min} \ \sum_{j=1}^{n} \sum_{i=1}^{r} x_{ij} \cdot \frac{\pi_i}{G}$$

Once the multiobjective model has been stated and processed, let us show the corresponding resolution process. The particular data have been taken from Martín et al. (2000).

At a first stage, the decision makers wished to give a greater importance to the objectives regarding the activity levels. The analysts chose the G-D-F method (see Geoffrion, Dyer and Feinberg, 1972) which, although it can possibly generate non-efficient solutions, it can give good approximations at the first iterations. The first iteration was made using the following weights:

Weights for the set of activity levels objectives = 3
Weights for the budget objectives = 1

The G-D-F method gives at each iteration a set of solutions among which the decision maker is asked to chose one. In this case, the solution chosen can be seen in table 1.

As all the activity levels, except one (number 9), were at their upper bounds, the decision makers said they wished to relax the activity levels, in order to improve some of the budget assignment values, provided that there are cases where the budget assignment to a hospital is a 20% greater than the corresponding fund requirement. Besides, it would be much more comfortable for the decision makers to give aspiration levels for the budget assignment objectives. For this reason a reference based algorithm (namely, the interactive method described in Wierzbicki, 1980) is chosen to continue the process. Given that the objective functions have been previously normalized, equal weights are given to all the objectives in the scalarized achievement function.

Table 1. Solution at iteration #1.

Activity Levels											
1	2	3	4	5	6	7	8	9	10	11	12
1,000	1,000	1,000	1,000	1,000	1,000	1,000	1,000	0,943	1,000	1,000	1,000
Budget assignment to the hospitals															
1	2	3	4	5	6	7	8	9	10	11	12	13	14	15	16
1,22	1,05	1,27	1,01	0,80	0,93	1,05	0,84	0,76	0,80	0,67	0,90	0,81	1,24	0,80	0,96
Global budget assignment															
1,1071															

Namely, the decision makers set the reference levels for all the hospitals equal to 1 (that is, at their required levels) , except hospitals 13 and 14, where the required values are considered to be too high with respect to the expenses of the previous year. The reference value for the global budget objective is set to the value obtained in the previous iteration. Thus, the reference point is the following:

$$\overline{\mathbf{q}}^2 = \left(\overline{q}_1^2,...,\overline{q}_{12}^2,\overline{q}_{13}^2,...,\overline{q}_{28}^2,\overline{q}_{29}^2\right)$$

where:

$$\overline{q}_i^2 = 1 \quad i = 1,...,12 \text{ with } i \neq 9$$

$$\overline{q}_9^2 = 0.9429$$

$$\overline{q}_i^2 = 1 \quad i = 13,...,28 \text{ with } i \neq 25 \wedge i \neq 26$$

$$\overline{q}_{25}^2 = 0.95 \quad \overline{q}_{26}^2 = 0.95$$

$$\overline{q}_{29}^3 = 1.10$$

Using this reference point, the interactive method gives several solutions, among which the decision maker has to choose one. The solution chosen is the following:

Table 2. Solution at iteration #2

Activity Levels											
1	2	3	4	5	6	7	8	9	10	11	12
1,000	1,000	1,000	1,000	1,000	1,000	1,000	1,000	0,943	1,000	1,000	1,000
Budget assignment to the hospitals															
1	2	3	4	5	6	7	8	9	10	11	12	13	14	15	16
1,00	1,00	1,00	1,00	1,00	1,00	1,00	1,00	0,76	1,00	0,91	1,00	0,95	0,95	0,80	1,00
Global budget assignment															
1,1071															

With this new solution, the activity levels have been kept at their previous values, while the hospital budgets, which were somewhat unbalanced before, have been readjusted, and the global expense has been kept at its previous value. This new solution implies a re-assignation of the different activities to the hospitals, so that the global activity level is kept. The regulating agency considered that the solution was good, but still they proposed to generate another one changing some reference levels. Namely, they set to 1 the reference level for activity line number 9, while the reference levels for hospitals 13 and 14 are lowered, and a increase of a 3/100 is allowed in the global expense. Therefore, we have the following reference point:

$$\overline{\mathbf{q}}^3 = \left(\overline{q}_1^3, \dots, \overline{q}_{12}^3, \overline{q}_{13}^3, \dots, \overline{q}_{28}^3, \overline{q}_{29}^3\right)$$

where:

$\overline{q}_i^3 = 1 \quad i = 1, \dots, 12$

$\overline{q}_i^3 = 1 \quad i = 13, \dots, 28 \text{ with } i \neq 25 \wedge i \neq 26$

$\overline{q}_{25}^3 = 0.9 \quad \overline{q}_{26}^3 = 0.9$

$\overline{q}_{29}^3 = 1.13$

Given these reference levels, the solution chosen by the decision-makers is:

Table 3. Solution at iteration #3.

Activity Levels											
1	2	3	4	5	6	7	8	9	10	11	12
0,993	0,993	0,993	1,000	0,993	0,993	0,993	0,993	0,993	0,993	0,993	1,000

Budget assignment to the hospitals															
1	2	3	4	5	6	7	8	9	10	11	12	13	14	15	16
1,01	1,01	1,01	1,01	1,01	1,01	1,01	1,01	1,01	1,01	1,01	1,01	0,91	0,91	1,01	1,01

Global budget assignment
1,1356

The solution obtained in this iteration was highly appreciated by the regulating agency, given that their expectations had been achieved. Nevertheless, they still wanted to iterate again, with the aim of obtaining slightly better values for the budgetary objectives through the modification of certain activity levels. In order to carry out this new iteration, it was decided to switch to the STEM method (see Benayoun et al., 1971), so that the decision makers could state exactly which objectives they wanted to improve, which ones did they wish to relax, and how far could this relaxation go. The values given by the decision-makers can be found in table 4. Given these values, the solution obtained is shown in table 5

The decision-makers were finally satisfied with this solution, and they decided to end the process. As it can be observed, the normalized activity levels are all very close to 1 (between 0,97 and 1), and that means that all the activity lines have been significantly increased. At the same time, the normalized budget objectives are all around 1. Some of them have been kept under this value, following the desires of the decision-makers.

Table 4. Requirements for iteration # 4. The symbol '=' means that the DM wishes to keep the objective at its present value. '↓' means that the DM admits a decrease of the objective up to the value given below. '↑' means that the DM wishes to improve the value of the objective.

Activity Levels											
1	2	3	4	5	6	7	8	9	10	11	12
=	↓	↓	↓	↑	↓	=	↓	↓	↓	↓	=
	0,97	0,97	0,98		0,98		0,98	0,97	0,98	0,98	
Budget assignment to the hospitals											
1	2	3	4	5	6	7	8	9	10	11	12	13	14	15	16
↑	↑	↑	↑	↑	↑	↑	↑	↑	↑	↑	↑	=	=	↑	↑
Global budget assignment											
=											

Table 5. Solution at iteration #4.

Activity Levels											
1	2	3	4	5	6	7	8	9	10	11	12
0,993	0,973	0,973	0,98	0,993	0,983	0,993	0,983	0,973	0,983	0,983	1,000
Budget assignment to the hospitals											
1	2	3	4	5	6	7	8	9	10	11	12	13	14	15	16
0,95	0,97	0,98	0,98	1,01	0,99	0,99	1,01	1,01	1,01	1,01	1,01	0,91	0,91	1,01	1,01
Global budget assignment											
1,119											

4
Conclusions

To conclude, the following considerations about the interactive process can be pointed out:

- From the point of view of the analysts, the valuation of the interactive decision system is positive, given that the implementation allowed us to adapt the process to the decision-makers' requirements in a flexible and dynamic way. In this sense, it is important to point out how easily the process reacts to changes in the way the decision-makers provide the information. Besides, this application lets us confirm the original motivation to develop the system. Real decision-makers, rather than limiting themselves to the requirements of the particular algorithm, tend to observe the solution at each iteration and to express their opinion in a rather primary way, reacting to the aspects they consider being more relevant in the current solution. Therefore, this implementation has created a framework within which the analyst is capable to adapt the process to these reactions of the decision-makers, with, relatively, not much effort.
- As for the decision-makers, the satisfaction degree with the process and the final solution was high. As a matter of fact, the decision makers commented when the process was over that this type of iteration gave them a high degree of freedom when expressing their opinions and preferences.

At the same time, they were satisfied with the way the method adapted itself to the new requirements. It is important to point out that the decision-makers had previous experience with the use of other Multiobjective Programming techniques, and, therefore, they had more elements to judge the behavior of both the methods and the implementation.

- Finally, it must be pointed out that this experience confirms once more that, despite the greater or lower friendliness of the computer environment, the analyst is still completely necessary in the process of resolution of a real problem. If a given user does not know in depth the basic lines of behavior of the interactive methods, he or she will not be able to react in the same way when choosing the most suitable technique to each situation. Therefore, this implementation can be considered as a valuable help tool for the analysts.

References

Arenas M.M., Lafuente E., Rodríguez M.V. (1998): Goal Programming Model for Evaluating an Hospital Service Performance. In Caballero, R., Ruiz F., and Steuer, R.E. (Eds.): Advances in Multiple Objective and Goal Programming. Lectures Notes in Econommics and Mathematical Systems 455:, Springer, Berlin. pp. 57-65.

Benayoun, R., Montgolfier, J., Tergny, J. and Laritchev, O. (1971): Linear Programming with Multiple Objective Functions: Step Method (STEM). Mathematical Programming, 1, 366-375.

Geoffrion, A.M., Dyer, J.S. and Feinberg, A. (1972): An Interactive Approach for Multi-Criterion Optimization, with an Application to the Operation of an Academic Department. Management Science, 19 (4), 357-368.

Kwak, N.K. and Lee C.H. (1997): A Linear Goal Programming Model for Human Resource Allocations in a Health-Care Organization. Journal of Medical Systems, 21(3). 129-140.

Lee, S.M. (1973): An Aggregative Resource Allocation Model for Hospital Administration. Socio-Economic Planning Sciences, 7(4), 381-395.

Luque, M. (2000): Multiple Criteria Decision Making in Integer and Continuos Variables. Compuational Implementation and Applications to Economy (In Spanish). PhD Thesis. University of Málaga, Spain.

Martín, J.J., López del Amo, P., Caballero, R., Gómez, T., Molina, J. and Ruiz, F. (2000): A Goal Programming Scheme to Determine the Budget Assignment Among the Hospitals of a Sanitary System. In Zanakis, S.H., Doukidis, G. and Zopounidis, C. (Eds.):Recent Developments and Applications in Decision Making. Kluwer Academic Publishers (In print).

Panitz, E. (1988): The Services Mix Decision in Not-for-Profit Organizations: A Math Programming Approach to Community Mental Health Service Mix Selection. PhD Thesis, University of Kentucky.

Rodríguez, M.V., Arenas, M., Bilbao, A. and Cerdá E. (1998): Management of Surgical Waiting Lists in Public Hospitals. Working Paper of the Instituto Complutense de Análisis Económico (ICAE), 9817. Universidad Complutense. Madrid.

Wierzbicki, A.P. (1980): The Use of Reference Objectives in Multiobjective Optimization. In Fandel, G. and Gal, T. (Eds.):Multiple Criteria Decision Making Theory and Application, Lecture Notes in Economics and Mathematical Systems 177, Springer-Verlag, Heidelberg, pp. 468-486.

Fuzzy Multi-objective Approach to the Supply Chain Model

Yuh-Wen Chen[1] and Gwo-Hshiung Tzeng[2.]

[1] Department of Industrial Engineering, Da Yeh University, 112 Shan-Jeau Rd., Da-Tsuen, Chang-Hwa 51505, Taiwan

E-mail: profchen@mail.dyu.edu.tw, Tel: +886(4)8528469 ext 4120, Fax: +886(4)8520781

[2] Energy and Environmental Research Group, Institute of Traffic and Transportation, and Institute of Technology Management, College of Management, National Chiao Tung University, 1001, Ta-Hsueh Rd., Hsinchu 300, Taiwan.

Abstract – Modern businesses face a more severe and challenging environment than before. For example, if an enterprise is requested to provide adequate commodities to its customers in different areas, it should be able to determine its own supply chain (SC) at the lowest-cost level immediately. If the enterprise's response is not in time, the customers will feel unsatisfied and reduce their loyalty. The SC problem is formulated as a multi-level decision making problem in this study. Study results show that the fuzzy multi-objective approach can easily provide a satisfied solution at an acceptable achievement level of desired goals. Therefore, our study is valuable when designing a large-scale SC for practical use.

Keywords: supply chain (SC), fuzzy, multi-objective, enterprise.

1. Introduction

The concept of supply chain (SC) is popularly used and discussed in recent years [15][16][26]. However, a simple way to formulate the SC problem and find an appropriate SC solution are still be explored [23][26]. The basic SC problem can be described as follows: if an enterprise is requested to provide adequate commodities to its customers on time, it should be able to determine its own appropriate purchase/production/transportation network at the lowest-cost level as soon as possible. Thus, the SC problem is defined as how to design the appropriate purchase/production/transportation network. The SC problem includes at least four major works in a sequential decision process. First, the enterprise should decide the demand quantity of original materials from each original material supplier. Second, it should appropriately assign these original materials to the manufacturing partners for production use. Third, the enterprise should also plan the production quantity of each manufacturing partner; and fourth, it should choose the appropriate logistics partners so as to transport these produced merchandises to its customers. Since each partner involved in the SC has its own objective and constraints, these partners are playing a Stackelberg game [17] in a SC problem. In this study, the appropriate SC design is regarded as a multi-level decision making problem, which is difficult to be resolved [21]. Since the SC dominates the operation efficiency of an enterprise [16][23], the network of aforementioned four major works in a SC should be appropriately designed so as to make customers satisfied and keep their loyalty.

Thus, this study mainly focuses on: (a) how to translate conceptual SC framework to an operational model; (b) how can we reduce the computational complexity when solving this SC problem; and (c) validate our SC formulation and resolution method. The numerical example is illustrated by two different original material suppliers, three different manufacturing partners, two different logistics partners and three different customers. Furthermore, this SC design is considered across three different time periods. We also assume each partner involved in our SC (not including customers) has its own objective and constraints. Study results show that our model formulation is simple and our resolution approach is easy to be operated. Therefore, our SC model is a valuable beginning when designing a large-scale SC for practical use.

This paper is organized as follows: in Section 2, our problem's characteristics: the SC framework, the multi-level programming problems (MLPP) and the fuzzy multi-objective programming (FMOP) are illustrated. In Section 3, the SC model is formulated. Furthermore, a fuzzy resolution approach is illustrated and applied to find the SC solution. In Section 4, an assumed example is used to validate our model and resolution process. Finally, the conclusions and recommendations are available in Section 5.

2. Conceptual Framework of SC, Multi-level Programming Problems and Fuzzy Multi-objective Programming

In this section, we will introduce the basic concepts and framework of SC in Section 2.1. The multi-level programming problems (MLPP) are illustrated in Section 2.2, and the fuzzy multi-objective programming (FMOP) is shown in Section 2.3.

2.1 Conceptual Framework of SC

The SC concept, which includes the appropriate decision of purchasing materials, producing merchandises and transporting commodities so as to maximize each partner's satisfaction degree in a SC. The concept of an appropriate SC is popularly discussed in recent years. For example, we find issues of model construction and methods for supply chain design [16][22][26], exploring the timely demand to reduce inventories [4], fuzzy modeling of a supply chain [15], an interactive approach for the future European supply chain [14], designing the green supply chain [20], and multi-level decision making problems [21][27], etc.

However, a simple and general approach to the SC solution is also necessarily explored [16][23][26] – this is why we present this paper. In practice, implementing a supply chain by integrating demand/supply management is a fairly complex but necessary process, which should be combined with the multi-level and multi-objective consideration [20][27]. This multi-level and multi-objective process comprises three key components: demand planning, supply planning and inventory deployment [4]. If the *just in time* (JIT) strategy is successful used in an enterprise, then the demand and supply functions within or outside the enterprise are the dominant cost buckets in the SC. In a practical SC, a consumer product may be handled as many as 12 different organizations [23]. We only present a simple model in Figure1 to introduce the operation process in a SC.

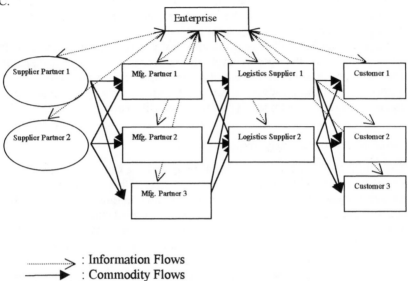

............> : Information Flows
———▶ : Commodity Flows

Figure 1 Supply Chain Model

The enterprise's operation process can be described as follows. First, customers ask the enterprise to provide adequate commodities. Second, the enterprise seeks its appropriate partners of supplier, manufacturing and logistics. The enterprise also decides the appropriate commodity flow between any two partners of different functions at the same time. Of course, the appropriate commodity flow should satisfy each partner with the level of lowest-cost and highest-profit, e.g., maximizing the net profit. Finally, the commodity flow is running from the up-stream suppliers, through the manufactures and logistics partners, then to the down-stream customers – the commodity flow should be established to meet each different partner's objective and constraints. Thus, the SC problem is obviously a typical multi-level programming problem [21][27]. The information flows in Fig.1 indicate the necessary information exchanging during the purchase/production/transportation periods, e.g., ordering information. Furthermore, the information flows may be operated on-line by Internet services as the electronic business (e-business) increasingly develops.

Since the SC model in Figure1 includes at least four kinds of partners, an important question arises from our mind: how to design the appropriate purchase/production/transportation network (SC) to satisfy each partner's goal?

That is why we implement a simple model to guide the enterprises *how to* design and manage their own SC. Furthermore, our model can be expanded by database interfaces, e.g., *Excel, Access* and optimization modules, e.g., *Visual Basic, Lindo* to make faster decisions.

This problem of designing the appropriate SC is also explained in Figure 1 – this problem can be defined to find the appropriate purchase/production/transportation network among all partners involved. This SC problem includes four major decisions, which we had discussed in Section 1. Therefore, the appropriate design of SC can be regarded as a three-level (the level of supplier, manufacturing and logistics) programming problem. In the first level, the enterprise purchases the necessary quantity of original materials from the supplier partners. In the second level, the enterprise asks the manufacturing partners to produce adequate merchandises for customers. In the third level, the enterprise seeks qualified logistics partners to efficiently ship merchandises of customers. This aforementioned SC formulation will clearly presented in Section 3.

2.2 Multi-level Programming Problems (MLPP)

The MLPP is defined as mathematical programming that solves decentralized planning problems with multiple decision makers (DMs) in a multi-level or hierarchical organization [1]. The MLPP often has the following features [27]: (a) interactive decision makers (DMs) exist within a predominantly hierarchical structure; (b) execution of decision is sequential, form the upper to a lower-level; (c) each DM independently maximizes his own net profits, but is affected by the actions of other DMs through externalities; and (d) the external effect on a decision maker's (DM's) problem can be can be reflected in both the objective function and the set of decision space. The basic resolution concept of MLPP is that an upper-level DM sets his goal or decisions and asks each subordinate level of the organization for their optimum which are calculated separately; the lower-level DM's decisions are then returned to the upper-level to maximize the DM's objective value. This process will be iterated until all the DMs feel almost satisfied.

Taking the two-level programming problem as an example, the general form of a two-level programming problem can be illustrated as follows [25]:

$$\underset{x}{Min}\ f_u(x,y) \qquad\qquad (1)\ \text{where } y \text{ solves}$$

$$\underset{y}{Min}\ f_l(x,y)$$

$$st\ x,y \in XY = \{x,y \in R^n \mid g_j(x,y) \le 0, j = 1,2,...,m\}$$

where

$f_u(x,y)$: the objective function of the upper level (leader), $i = 1,2,...,k$;

$f_l(x,y)$: the objective function of the lower level (follower);

x, y: the decision variable;

XY: the feasible solution set;

$g_j(x, y)$: the inequality constraint, $j = 1, 2, ..., m$.

Namely, let $\hat{x}$ denotes the decision made by the leader, and then the follower solves the following problem:

$$\underset{y}{Min} \; f_l(\hat{x}, y) \tag{2}$$

$$st \; \; \hat{x}, y \in XY = \{x, y \in R^n \mid g_j(\hat{x}, y) \le 0, j = 1, 2, ..., m\}$$

If the follower chooses an optimal solution $y(\hat{x})$ to the Equation (1) with a rational response, and. assuming that the follower chooses the rational response, the leader also makes the decision so as to minimize the objective function $f_u(\hat{x}, y(\hat{x}))$. Then a solution derived from the aforementioned procedure is defined as a Stackelberg solution [17]. We can easily prove the following results by the definitions of MLPP and FMOP: it is clear that if the XY: (feasible solution set) can be clearly defined and determined, the aforementioned Stackelberg solution process is identical to finding the solution space in XY by maximizing each DM's achievement level of goals. In this case, the aforementioned bi-level programming problems (BLPP) are translated to the fuzzy bi-objective programming problems. Using the aforementioned results, the MLPP with more than two levels and a clear solution space can be deduced to equal the fuzzy multi-objective programming problems. In this study, we only use a linear model; thus, our solution space of the SC problem is convex and able to be clearly defined.

2.3 Fuzzy Linear Multi-objective Programming

The general concept of fuzzy linear multi-objective programming was first introduced by Tanaka et al. [18] in the fuzzy decision framework by Bellman and Zadeh [2]. Following the fuzzy decision or the minimum operator by Bellman and Zadeh [2] together with any type of membership function respectively, they proved that there exist equivalent linear programming problems. The fuzzy multi-objective programming has been rapidly developed and applied by Tanaka's contribution. For example, we found the fuzzy multi-criteria facility location problem [3], the fuzzy multiobjective linear programming [10], fuzzy approaches to multicriteria programs [11], fuzzy vs. minmax weighted multiobjective linear programming [12], fuzzy multiobjective combinatorial optimization problems [19]. We introduce Zimmermann's fuzzy linear programming with i linear objective functions as follows [7][18]:

$$Min \; f(x) = (f_1(x), f_2(x), ..., f_i(x))^T \tag{3}$$

$$st \; Ax \le b, \; x \ge 0$$

where

$f_i(x)$: the objective function, $f_i(x)=c_i x$, $i=1,2,...,p$;

x: the decision variable, $x=(x_1,x_2,...,x_n)^T$;

b: the right hand side (RHS) value, $b=(b_1,b_2,...,b_m)^T$;

A: the coefficient matrix, $A=[a_{ij}]_{m\times n}$.

For each of the objective function $f_i(x)=c_i x$, $i=1,2,...,p$; of this problem, assuming that the decision maker has a fuzzy goal – the objective $f_i(x)$ should be substantially less than or equal to some value p_i. Thus, the corresponding linear membership function $\mu_i^L(f_i(x))$ is defined as:

$$\mu_i^L(f_i(x))=\begin{cases} 0 & ; f_i(x)\le f_i^- \\ \dfrac{f_i(x)-f_i^-}{f_i^+-f_i^-} & ; f_i^- \le f_i(x)\le f_i^+ \\ 1; f_i(x)\ge f_i^+ \end{cases} \quad (4)$$

where f_i^- denotes the objective value of pessimistic expectation by a decision maker, and f_i^+ denotes the objective value of optimistic expectation by a decision maker. This is shown in Figure 2 [9].

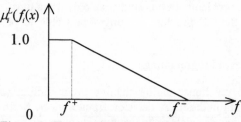

Figure 2. The Achievement Level for Fuzzy Objectives

Using such linear membership function $\mu_i^L(f_i(x))$, $i=1,2,...,k$; and apply the operator of Bellman and Zadeh (1970), the original problem can be changed as:

$$\underset{i}{Min} \quad \mu_i^L(f_i(x)) \quad (5)$$

$st \quad Ax\le b$

$\quad x\ge 0$

Interpreting the auxiliary variable λ, Eq. (5) is rewritten as follows:

$$Max \; \lambda \quad (6)$$

$st \; \lambda \le \mu_i^L(f_i(x))$, $i=1,2,...,p$;

$$Ax \leq b$$
$$x \geq 0$$

Eq. (4) will be our fuzzy transformation in the next section.

3. Model Construction and Resolution

We have realized that the appropriate design of SC is a very important issue but is difficult to be resolved from Section 2. To formulate our three-level SC model, we should consider the conflicting objectives among different partners at the same time. Before we propose the following mathematical formulation, our assumption should be stated first: the practical SC behavior is assumed to be a three-level decision problem, which is discussed in Section 2.1 and Fig. 1. Second, the routing problem [5] between any two levels is not considered in our simple SC model. Third, the assumed parameters in our SC model are fixed during different periods (not including the customer' demand).

Therefore, we formulate this SC model from each level by the following objectives and constraints:

(a) The supplier partner's objective and constraints

The supplier partner's objective is assumed to maximize its own net profit in each demand period t. This objective function is shown in Equation (7).

$$Max \ f_{s,t} = \sum_m \sum_e p_s^e x_{sm,t}^e - \sum_m \sum_e c_s^e x_{sm,t}^e, \qquad \forall s \in S, \forall t \quad (7)$$

where

$x_{sm,t}^e$: the decision variable, the shipped quantity of original material e from supplier s to Mfg. partner m in period t.

S denotes the set of all supplier partners;

p_s^e : the sale price of original material e for supplier s ;

c_s^e : the average total cost of original material e for supplier s ;

Furthermore, the first constraint of the supplier partner is the storage space constraint:

$$\sum_m \sum_e x_{sm,t}^e \leq space_s, \qquad \forall s \in S, \forall t \quad (8)$$

The $space_s$ shows the available storage space in supplier s. And Equation (9) is the capacity constraint:

$$\sum_m \sum_e wt_s^e x_{sm,t}^e \leq awt_s, \qquad \forall s \in S, \forall t \quad (9)$$

The wt_s^e represents the unit working time for original material e; the awt_s denotes the total available working time of supplier s.

(b) The Mfg. partner's objective and constraints

The Mfg. partner's objective is similar to that of a suppler partner. This objective function is shown in Equation (10), which also achieves to maximize each Mfg. partner's net profit:

$$Max\ f_{m,t} = \sum_l p_m x_{ml,t} - \sum_l c_m x_{ml,t}, \qquad \forall m \in M, \forall t \qquad (10)$$

where

$x_{ml,t}$: the decision variable, the shipped quantity of merchandises from Mfg. partner m to logistics partner l in period t.

M denotes the set of all Mfg. partners;

p_m: the sale price of merchandise for Mfg. partner m ;

c_m: the average total cost of merchandise for Mfg. partner m;

Similarly, Equation (11) is the storage space constraint; Equation (12) is the capacity constraint:

$$\sum_l x_{ml,t} \le space_m, \qquad \forall m \in M, \forall t \qquad (11)$$

$$\sum_m wt_m x_{ml,t} \le awt_m, \qquad \forall m \in M, \forall t \qquad (12)$$

The $space_m$ shows the available storage space of Mfg. partner m; the wt_m represents the unit working time for merchandise of Mfg. partner m; the awt_m denotes the total available working time of Mfg. partner m. Furthermore, we consider the different Mfg. partner possess the different production ability, e.g., if there are two Mfg. partners A and B to produce the same Z, and two different available original materials X and Y; perhaps A consumes 2 unit Y and one unit X to produce one unit Z, while B consumes 2 unit X and one unit Y to produce one unit Z – this constraint is shown as follows:

$$x_{ml,t} = \sum_e \sum_{s \in S} pa_m^e x_{sm,t}^e, \forall m \in M, \forall t \qquad (13)$$

The pa_m^e indicates when one unit x_{ml} is produced, the original material e of pa_m^e unit will be consumed by Mfg. partner m.

(c) The logistics. partner's objective and constraints

The logistics. partner's objective is also achieving to maximize each logistics partner's net profit, this is shown in Equation (14) .

$$Max\ f_{l,t} = \sum_c p_{lc} x_{lc,t} - \sum_c c_{lc} x_{lc,t}, \qquad \forall l \in L, \forall t \qquad (14)$$

where

$x_{lc,t}$: the decision variable, the shipped quantity of merchandises from logistics partner l to customer c in time period t.

L denotes the set of all logistics partners;

p_{lc}: the transportation price from logistics partner l to customer c;

c_{lc}: the average total cost for transporting merchandise from logistics partner l to customer c.

We assume each logistics partner has its own capacity (cap_l); thus, this constraint is shown in Equation (15):

$$\sum_l x_{lc,t} \le cap_l, \quad \forall t \qquad (15)$$

We also assume the logistics partners are able to meet the needs of all customers; thus, $\sum_c x_{lc,t}$ should equal to the total demand of customer c:

$$\sum_c x_{lc,t} = d_{c,t}, \forall t \qquad (16)$$

$d_{c,t}$: the given value, it denotes the total demand of customer c in time period t.

In addition to the Equations (7)-(16), the network flows from the upper-level (suppliers) to the lower-level (customers) should be the same between any two levels. This constraint is shown as in Equation (16)-(17).

$$\sum_m \sum_l x_{ml,t} = \sum_l \sum_c x_{lc,t} = \sum_c d_{c,t}, \forall t \qquad (17)$$

$$\sum_m x_{ml,t} = \sum_l x_{lc,t}, \quad \forall l, \forall c, \forall t \qquad (18)$$

Equations (7)-(18) are our SC model structure. From Equations (7) to (18), we can design the appropriate purchase/production/transportation network (supply chain). This solution will help an enterprise to decide its own advantage chain, which includes the purchase strategy, production strategy and transportation strategy. Our SC problem is considered across three time periods and with two different original material suppliers, three different Mfg. partners, two different logistics partners and three different customers. Assuming each partner has its own net profit objective (not including customers), by the λ transformation illustrated in Equation (1)-(3), Equations (7)-(18) can be rewritten as a fuzzy combinatorial optimization problem in Equation (19).

$$Max \ \lambda$$

$$st$$

$$\lambda \le \mu_s(f_{s,t}), \quad \forall s \in S, \forall t \qquad (19)$$

$$\lambda \le \mu_m(f_{m,t}), \quad \forall m \in M, \forall t$$

$$\lambda \le \mu_l(f_{l,t}), \quad \forall l \in L, \forall t$$

and Equations (8)-(9); (11)-(13); (15)-(18).

To resolve the linear problem in Equation (19), we can find the maximal λ by the branch and bound procedure [6]. However, the corresponding solution to the same λ is not necessarily unique [24][25]. Thus, the appropriate SC solution we find is a non-inferior solution set in FMOP [18] instead of only one single optimal solution.

4. Numerical Example

In Section 4, we use a numerical example to validate our model of Equation (19) by FMOP. The model structure is also illustrated in Fig. 1– which contains two different types of original materials: X and Y; two different original material suppliers, three different manufacturing partners, two different logistics partners, three different customers and three demand periods. Each partner involved in the SC model has its own objective and constraints – these objectives and constraints are shown in *Appendix*.

We assume the merchandise demand in different periods is as follows: (a) customer 1 needs 200 units, customer 2 also needs 200 units and customer 3 needs 100 units in the first period; (b) customer 1 needs 100 units, customer 2 needs 200 units and customer 3 needs 100 units in the second period; and (c) customer 1 needs 200 units, customer 2 also needs 100 units and customer 3 needs 200 units in the third period. By the fuzzy multi-objective approach, we can easily find the results in Table 1.

Thus, the designed commodity flow for three demand periods is easily obtained (see Table 1). A decision maker can efficiently derive the initial results within a few seconds just by *LINDO* software – this obviously can promote the reaction speed to an uncertain circumstances. More sensitivity analysis should be made as the model parameter changes. However, this paper mainly focuses on the SC model formulation and validation by the fuzzy multi-objective approach. We can conclude that our formulation and approach are both workable and valuable. We do provide an operational and workable approach to the SC solution, a decision maker can easily apply the results in Table 1 to command his own appropriate SC. Compared with the other related issues of SC, this study successfully translates the conceptual framework to a manageable SC model by a more simple and clear way. The SC techniques are now also moderated with the computer interface by our efforts, we try to integrate the database system and the optimizing module so as to help an enterprise moving faster and gaining much more.

5. Conclusions and Recommendations

First, this study successfully translates the conceptual framework of SC to a MLPP; second, since the MLPP is degenerated to a FMOP problem if the solution space can be clearly defined in a MLPP, we apply the fuzzy multi-objective approach to reduce the computational complexity of such a SC problem. The computation results are more easily obtained than before and satisfied. Third, Our model is easy to be understood and handled by the techniques of FMOP. The SC techniques proposed in this paper should be considered for more computer applications and help the decision maker "*do the right thing faster*".

Table 1 Computational Results of the SC Model in Each Period

Variable	Global Achievement Level λ =0.12		
	Produced or Shipped Quantity		
	$t=1$	$t=2$	$t=3$
Original material X Produced in Supplier Partner 1	354	226	0
Original material Y Produced in Supplier Partner 1	232	337	324
Original material X Produced in Supplier Partner 2	0	0	378
Original material Y Produced in Supplier Partner 2	12	97	81
Material Flow X from Supply Partner 1 to Mfg. Partner 1	70	100	0
Material Flow X from Supply Partner 1 to Mfg. Partner 2	185	79	0
Material Flow X from Supply Partner 1 to Mfg. Partner 3	99	47	0
Material Flow X from Supply Partner 2 to Mfg. Partner 1	0	0	42
Material Flow X from Supply Partner 2 to Mfg. Partner 2	0	0	175
Material Flow X from Supply Partner 2 to Mfg. Partner 3	0	0	161
Material Flow Y from Supply Partner 1 to Mfg. Partner 1	140	200	2
Material Flow Y from Supply Partner 1 to Mfg. Partner 2	92	40	161
Material Flow Y from Supply Partner 1 to Mfg. Partner 3	0	0	0
Material Flow Y from Supply Partner 2 to Mfg. Partner 1	0	0	81
Material Flow Y from Supply Partner 2 to Mfg. Partner 2	5	0	0
Material Flow Y from Supply Partner 2 to Mfg. Partner 3	7	97	0
Commodity Produced in Mfg. Partner 1	140	200	83
Commodity Produced in Mfg. Partner 2	185	79	173
Commodity Produced in Mfg. Partner 3	99	47	161
Commodity Flow from Mfg. Partner 1 to Logistics Partner 1	108	137	83
Commodity Flow from Mfg. Partner 1 to Logistics Partner 2	32	63	0
Commodity Flow from Mfg. Partner 2 to Logistics Partner 1	40	20	173
Commodity Flow from Mfg. Partner 2 to Logistics Partner 2	145	59	0
Commodity Flow from Mfg. Partner 3 to Logistics Partner 1	98	47	0
Commodity Flow from Mfg. Partner 3 to Logistics Partner 2	1	0	161
Commodity Flow from Logistics Partner 1 to Customer 1	0	0	0
Commodity Flow from Logistics Partner 1 to Customer 2	146	104	56
Commodity Flow from Logistics Partner 1 to Customer 3	100	100	200
Commodity Flow from Logistics Partner 2 to Customer 1	200	100	200
Commodity Flow from Logistics Partner 2 to Customer 2	54	96	44
Commodity Flow from Logistics Partner 2 to Customer 3	0	0	0

Moreover, our SC model can be regarded as a basis for simulating the partner behavior of a SC in the near future. Many advanced topics should be continuously explored. For example, How to arrange the product flows between different Mfg. partners? How to manage the original materials so as to minimize the material inventory cost and maximize the variety of customer's need? How to appropriately design the production schedule in a SC? How to tackle the uncertain parameters of a SC model [2][21]? How to combine the SC techniques with the Internet to make a real-time control? How to apply the vehicle routing problem [5] between any two partners in a SC? How to evolve the appropriate alliance strategy in a SC by genetic algorithms or other algorithms [8][13]? ...,etc. These problems are worthy explored from this beginning.

References

[1] Bard, J. F. and Falk, J. E., "An explicit solution to the multi-level programming problem," Computers and Operations Research, Vol. 9, No. 1, pp. 77-100, 1982.

[2] Bellman, R. E. and Zadeh, L. A., "Decision making in fuzzy environment," Management Science, Vol. 17B, No. 3, pp. 141-164, 1970.

[3] Bhattacharya U., Rao, J. R. and Tiwari, R. N., "Fuzzy Multi-criteria Facility Location Problem," Fuzzy Sets and Systems, Vol. 51, No. 3, pp. 277-287, 1992.

[4] Bourland, K. E., Powell, S. G. and Pyke, D. F., "Exploiting timely demand information to reduce inventories," European Journal of Operational Research, Vol. 92, No. 2, pp. 239-253, 1996.

[5] Current, J. R., ReVelle, C. S. and Cohon, M. B., "The maximum covering/shortest path problem: A multiobjective network design and routing formulation," European Journal of Operational Research, Vol. 21, No. 1, pp. 189-199, 1985.

[6] Demeulemeester, E. and Herroelen, W., "A branch-and bound procedure for the multiple resource-constrained project scheduling problem," Management Science, Vol. 38, No. 12, pp. 1803-1818, 1992.

[7] Fedrizzi, M., Kacprzyk, J., and Roubens, M., Interactive Fuzzy Optimization, Spring-Verlag, New York, 1991.

[8] Goldberg, D. E., Genetic Algorithms in Search, Optimization and Machine Learning, Addison Wesley Publishing Co., Massachusetts, 1989.

[9] Hannan E. L., "Linear Programming with Multiple Fuzzy Goals," Fuzzy Sets and Systems, Vol. 6, No. 1, pp. 235-248, 1981.

[10] Ida, K. and Gen, M., "Improvement of Two-phase Approach for Solving Fuzzy Multiobjective Linear Programming," Journal of Japan Society for Fuzzy Theory and Systems, Vol. 9, No. 1, pp. 115-121, 1997.

[11] Lee, E. S. and Li, R. J., "Fuzzy multiple objective programming and compromise with Pareto optimum, " Fuzzy Sets and Systems, Vol. 53, No. 3, pp. 275-288, 1993.

[12] Martison, F. K., "Fuzzy vs. Minmax Weighted Multiobjective Linear Programming: Illustrative Comparison," Decision Sciences, Vol. 24, No. 4, pp. 809-824, 1993.

[13] Michalewicz, Z., Genetic algorithms + Data Structures = Evolution Programs, Springer-Verlag Press, Berlin, 1996.

[14] Oxe, G., "Reducing overcapacity in chemical plants by linear programming," Decision Sciences, Vol. 24, No. 4, pp. 809-824, 1993.

[15] Petrovic, D., Roy, R. and Petrovic, R., "Modeling and simulation of a supply chain in an uncertain environment," European Journal of Operational Research, Vol. 109, No. 2, pp. 299-309, 1998.

[16] Pyke, D. F. and Cohen, M. A., "Performance characteristics of stochastic

integrated production-distribution systems," European Journal of Operational Research, Vol. 68, No. 1, pp. 23-48, 1993.

[17] Rasmusen, E., *GAMES AND INFORMATION: AN INRRODUCTION TO GAME THEORY*, Blackwell Publishers, Oxford, 1989.

[18] Sakawa M., *Fuzzy Sets and Interactive Multiobjective Optimization*, Plenum Press, New York, 1989.

[19] Sakawa, M., Kato, K., Sunada, H. and Shibano, T., "Fuzzy Programming for Multiobjective 0-1 Programming Problems through Revised Genetic Algorithms," European Journal of Operational Research, Vol. 97, No. 2, pp. 149-158, 1997.

[20] Sarkis, J., "Evaluating environmentally conscious business practices," European Journal of Operational Research, Vol. 107, No. 1, pp. 159-174, 1998.

[21] Shih, H-S, Lai, Y-J and Lee, E. S., "Fuzzy approach for multi-level programming problems," Computers Operations Research, Vol. 23, No. 1, pp. 73-91, 1996.

[22] Thomas, D. J. and Griffin, P. M., "Coordinated supply chain management," European Journal of Operational Research, Vol. 94, No. 1, pp. 1-15, 1996.

[23] Tyndall, G., Gopal, C., Partsch, W. and Kmuauff, J., *Supercharging Supply Chains: New ways to increase value through global operational excellence*, John Wiley & Sons, Inc., 1998.

[24] Tzeng, G. H. and Tsaur, S. H., "Application of Multiple Criteria Decision Making for Network Improvement Plan Model," Journal of Advanced Transportation, Vol. 31, No. 1, pp. 49-74, 1997.

[25] Tzeng, G. H. and Chen, Y. W., "Implementing an Effective Schedule for Reconstructing Post-earthquake Road-network Based on Asymmetric Traffic Assignment– An Application of Genetic Algorithm," International Journal of Operations and Quantitative Management (IJOQM), Vol. 4, No. 3, pp. 229-246, 1998.

[26] Vidal, C. J. and Goetschalckx, M., "Strategic production-distribution models: a critical review with emphasis on global supply chain models," European Journal of Operational Research, Vol. 98, No. 1, pp. 1-18, 1997.

[27] Yu, P. L. and Seiford, L., *Multilevel Decision Problems with Multiple Criteria Analysis – Operation Method*, edited by Nijkamp, P., Gover Publishers, 1981.

Appendix

1. The objective and constraints of supplier partner 1:

Max $3X+4Y-X-Y$

st $X+Y \leq 400$

$2X+Y \leq 600$

2. The objective and constraints of supplier partner 2:

Max $4X+3Y-2X-Y$

st $X+Y \leq 600$

$X+2Y \leq 500$

3. The objective and constraints of Mfg. partner 1:

Max $2Z-Z$

st $Z = 2X+Y$

$\quad Z \leq 200$

$\quad 5Z \leq 1000$

4. The objective and constraints of Mfg. partner 2:

Max $4Z-2Z$

st $Z = X+2Y$

$\quad Z \leq 600$

$\quad 2Z \leq 600$

5. The objective and constraints of Mfg. partner 3:

Max $3Z-2Z$

st $Z = X+Y$

$\quad Z \leq 300$

$\quad 3Z \leq 900$

6. The objective and constraints of logistics partner 1:

Max $6Z_1+7Z_2+9Z_3-Z_1-Z_2-2Z_3$

st $Z_1+Z_2+Z_3 \leq 500$

where

Z_1: the shipped quantity from logistics partner 1 to customer 1

Z_2: the shipped quantity from logistics partner 1 to customer 2

Z_3: the shipped quantity from logistics partner 1 to customer 3

7. The objective and constraints of logistics partner 2:

Max $7Z_a+6Z_b+7Z_c-3Z_a-Z_b-Z_c$

st $Z_a+Z_b+Z_c \leq 1000$

where

Z_a: the shipped quantity from logistics partner 2 to customer 1

Z_b: the shipped quantity from logistics partner 2 to customer 2

Z_c: the shipped quantity from logistics partner 2 to customer 3

8. The customer demand in each period:

when $t=1$, Customer 1 needs 200 units, Customer needs 200 units, Customer 3 needs 100 units;

when $t=2$, Customer 1 needs 100 units, Customer needs 200 units, Customer 3 needs 100 units;

when $t=3$, Customer 1 needs 200 units, Customer needs 100 units, Customer 3 needs 200 units;

Goal Programming Model for Airport Ground Support Equipment Parking

Sydney C. K. Chu

Department of Mathematics, University of Hong Kong, Hong Kong

schu@hku.hk

We propose a model for daily parking decisions of airside ground support equipment (GSE) at the Hong Kong International Airport. It is envisaged as a planning model of GSE parking problem arising from the need to handle complex transport requirements dictated by flight schedules in an efficient way. The goal programming formulation to actually compute parking decisions will be presented with illustrative numerical results.

Key words: airport ground support equipment, planning model, goal programming

INTRODUCTION

We propose a model for daily parking decisions of airside ground support equipment (GSE) at the Hong Kong International Airport. GSE refers to the pre-specified set of vehicular equipments (such as one low-deck loader, two passenger ladder-steps, six tractors, etc) required to service an arrival or a departure of a particular type of aircraft (such as a Boeing 747). GSE are punctually needed at the aircraft side and promptly returned (or parked) as airside equipments to various designated areas after use.

Airline operation has traditionally been one of the hottest subject area of real Operations Research (OR) applications [1]. GSE parking naturally falls within the logistic sub-area of such operations management. It is interesting to note that, even though there exists a tremendous amount of both theoretical studies and practical solutions on airline operational logistics as a whole, very little result seems to be available on the specific aspect of *GSE parking optimization*. We believe that there are mainly two (among possibly other) reasons: Firstly, GSE parking is regarded as a rather routine operation, best left to the "front-line" operating staff's practical experience. Secondly, the complex and dynamic nature of hundreds or thousands of such detailed GSE movements appears so tedious to be well "managed", let alone actually "optimized" (or being regarded as a futile effort).

While there is certain trade wisdom in the above two assertions, we believe that a properly streamlined and simplified modeling is possible *and* useful. By trimming minor minute operating details, its simplified mathematical modeling "with a fresh view" can produce *planning decisions*. These can restore the exceedingly complicated real-time states of the system in operation back to a *target, or "optimized" state* of orderly positioning of GSE before or after use. We can actually obtain simple operating instructions for GSE staff to follow, minimizing unnecessary movements and dis-organized retrieving and returning of all GSE under their consideration. We believe our approach is a completely new and different attempt on GSE parking decisions, which we have seen little reporting in the open literature. (This paper contains therefore few cited available references on related work, as a rather big contrast to most OR work on airline logistics.)

Our result here can be envisaged as a planning model of GSE parking problem arising from the need to handle complex transport requirements dictated by flight schedules in an efficient way. Rather uncharacteristic of a planning model, it actually computes simple rules for prescribing GSE parking operations. The goal programming (GP) formulation will be presented with illustrative numerical results, based on simplified actual flights and requirements data [2].

BASE GSE MOVEMENT MODEL

The base GSE movement model considers five types of equipments: Passenger Ladder-Step, Medium-Deck Loader, Low-Deck Loader, Conveyor, and Low-Deck Loader for Boeing 767. They will be referred to by their respective abbreviations of: Pax step, MDL, LDL, Conv, and LDL-767 for convenience. The model is in fact just a GP variance of a generalized transportation problem (TP) based on the following crucial observation that leads to such a simplification. The GSE parking areas are modeled as the (generalized) source nodes and the aircraft parking bays as the (again, generalized) sink nodes. Retrieving a piece of GSE of a certain type represents a movement from source to sink — a usual TP shipment. After its use, this specific piece of GSE is promptly returned to its designated (as calculated from the model) parking area. Since the return is in exactly the opposite direction (from sink to source), all GSE movements (pairs of retrievals and returns) can be modeled as (doubled) TP shipments. We give below the model indices, the definitions of its variables and parameters, followed by the model formulation itself.

Model Indices, Variables and Parameters

- $i =$ GSE parking area index, $i = 1, \cdots, I(= 4)$
- $j =$ Flight bay (group) index, $j = 1, \cdots, J(= 11)$
- $k =$ GSE type index, $k = 1, \cdots, K(= 5)$

- A_i = Area (in m^2) of parking area i
- F_j = Number of flights docked (daily) at bay j ($N \equiv \sum_j F_j$)
- S_k = Unit space requirement (in m^2) of GSE type k
- C_k = (Physical) Number of GSE units under consideration

- C_{ik} = Parking limit in area i for GSE type k ($\leq A_i/S_k$)
- D_{jk} = Daily demand at bay j on GSE type k (= $\sum_{f_j} r_{jk}(f_j)$, where r_{jk} = required GSE type k of flight f_j)

- T_{ijk} = Travel time from area i to bay j of GSE type k ($T \equiv \sum_{i,j,k} T_{ijk}$)
- L_{ijk}, U_{ijk} = Lower, Upper bounds on daily transport movements

- x_{ijk} = Decision variable representing the daily number of area i to bay j movements of GSE type k
- m_{ik}, p_{ik} = Deviation variables of (GSE movement) supply constraints
- n_{jk}, q_{jk} = Deviation variables of (GSE movement) demand constraints

The Base GSE Model (a generalized TP)

(0) $\quad$ Min $\quad T * \left(\dfrac{1}{J} \sum_{i,k} p_{ik} + \dfrac{1}{I} \sum_{j,k} n_{jk} \right) + \sum_{i,j,k} T_{ijk}\, x_{ijk}$

$\qquad$ Subject to
(Space Constraints)

(1) $\qquad\qquad \sum_{j,k} S_k\, x_{ijk} \leq A_i * g(i) \qquad\qquad (\forall i)$

(2) $\qquad\qquad \sum_{i,j,k} S_k\, x_{ijk} \leq \dfrac{N}{I} \sum_i A_i$

(Supply Constraints)

(3) $\quad \sum_j x_{ijk} + m_{ik} - p_{ik} = C_{ik} * g(i) \qquad\qquad (\forall i, k)$

(Demand Constraints)

(4) $\qquad\quad \sum_i x_{ijk} + n_{jk} - q_{jk} = D_{jk} \qquad\qquad (\forall j, k)$

$$(5) \qquad \sum_{i,j} x_{ijk} \leq \sum_{j} D_{jk} \qquad (\forall k)$$

(Bounds, or Scenario Setting Constraints)

$$(6) \qquad L_{ijk} \leq x_{ijk} \leq U_{ijk} \qquad (\forall i,j,k)$$

An important key feature of this model is provided by the function $g(i)$ – the estimated number of times area i is used, as appeared on the RHS of (1) and (3) above. Its explicit form is as derived below.

For each area i, the percentage of supply-demand matching movement (of all equipment types) to a certain bay j is equal to

$$\frac{\sum_{k} x_{ijk}}{\sum_{k} D_{jk}}$$

Hence, the number of times of such movements from i to j is given by

$$F_j \frac{\sum_{k} x_{ijk}}{\sum_{k} D_{jk}}$$

And the total number from i (to all bays) is thus

$$\sum_{j} F_j \frac{\sum_{k} x_{ijk}}{\sum_{k} D_{jk}} \qquad (\forall i)$$

Consequently, $g(i)$ is defined to be the above (after re-arranging sums):

$$(7) \qquad g(i) \equiv \sum_{j,k} \left[\frac{F_j}{\sum_{\ell} D_{j\ell}} \right] x_{ijk} \qquad (\forall i)$$

Finally, substituting (7) into (1) and (3), we get their alternative explicit forms (1') and (3') below.

$$(1') \qquad \sum_{j,k} S_k\, x_{ijk} \leq A_i * \sum_{j,k} \left[\frac{F_j}{\sum_{\ell} D_{j\ell}} \right] x_{ijk} \qquad (\forall i)$$

$$(3') \qquad \sum_{j} x_{ijk} + m_{ik} - p_{ik} = C_{ik} * \sum_{j,k} \left[\frac{F_j}{\sum_{\ell} D_{j\ell}} \right] x_{ijk} \quad (\forall i,k)$$

Note that the real time nature of individual flights' requirements is not explicitly modeled. Instead, demands are daily figures, which have vastly simplified the structure of an otherwise dynamic model. This is achieved through the use of our function $g(i)$, for every parking area i as explained above.

MODEL DATA AND RESULTS

The whole input data is quite voluminous, as it includes the actual daily flight schedules and actual arrival/departure time-and-location records for a (representative) month (of the winter schedule). For our purpose here, this data is used solely for the calculation of the averaged daily demand in terms of the number of flights to serve at every aircraft parking bay and hence its requirement of GSE of specific types there. We therefore show these consolidated demand data respectively in Tables 1 and 2, as an illustration. For completeness, constant problem parameters, for items such as the sizes (in m^2) of parking areas, are given in Table 3.

Data Tables

Flight bay	Pax(Gen)	Pax(Bulk)	Pax(767)	Comb	Total(F_j)
$j = 1$	14	0	0	0	14
$j = 2$	4	0	0	0	4
$j = 3$	18	1	0	1	20
$j = 4$	10	0	1	0	11
$j = 5$	20	0	0	0	20
$j = 6$	8	2	0	0	10
$j = 7$	11	7	1	0	19
$j = 8$	1	2	0	0	3
$j = 9$	0	1	0	0	1
$j = 10$	14	0	1	0	15
$j = 11$	0	1	0	0	1

Table 1. Data table (F_j).

As a side remark, we note that the 11 flight bays in Tables 1 and 2 actually refer to "grouped" flight bays. There are a total of some ninety individual docking sites, including both inner bays and outer bays.

j	$k=1$(Pax step)	$k=2$(MDL)	$k=3$(LDL)	$k=4$(Conv)	$k=5$(LDL767)
1	28	0	28	28	0
2	8	0	8	8	0
3	39	1	37	39	0
4	22	0	21	21	1
5	40	0	40	40	0
6	18	0	16	20	0
7	31	0	23	37	1
8	4	0	2	6	0
9	1	0	0	2	0
10	30	0	29	29	1
11	1	0	0	2	0

Table 2. Data table (D_{jk}).

A_1	A_2	A_3	A_4
$4,874$	$2,915$	$1,366$	$4,133$

S_1	S_2	S_3	S_4	S_5
37.58	107.6	54.55	25.71	54.44

C_1(Pax step)	C_2(MDL)	C_3(LDL)	C_4(Conveyor)	C_5(LDL-767)
24	2	50	33	7

	$k=1$	$k=2$	$k=3$	$k=4$	$k=5$	
$i=1$	0	0	0	0	0	
$i=2$	78	27	54	113	54	(C_{ik})
$i=3$	36	13	25	53	25	
$i=4$	110	38	76	161	76	

Table 3. Data table (A_i, S_k, C_{ik}).

Results

The numerical results computed by the model (coded in LINGO [3]) are given in Tables 4 to 8, for the respective types of GSE of: Pax step, MDL, LDL, Conveyor, and LDL-767. The entries in each table (above the double horizontal dividing lines) are the computed model outputs, showing the numbers $\{x_{ijk}\}$ of optimized daily (double) movements between pairs of flight bays and parking areas. For each parking area, a total is tallied from which *and the actual item count* of pieces of that specific type of GSE (for example, 24 for $k = 1$: Pax step, in Table 3) we give the pro rata figure of pieces allocated to park there. A rounding integer number of equipment allocation is obtained (for the same example, 10 for $i = 2$: area V, in Table 4) for each parking area. These final target numbers of parking decisions are summarized together in Table 9. The short LINGO code is given in the Appendix.

$(x_{i,j,k=1})$	$i = 2(V)$	$i = 3(M)$	$i = 4(Q)$
$j = 1$			28
$j = 2$			8
$j = 3$	39		
$j = 4$		22	
$j = 5$			40
$j = 6$	18		
$j = 7$	31		
$j = 8$	4		
$j = 9$	1		
$j = 10$		30	
$j = 11$		1	
Total $(\sum_j x_{i,j,k=1})$	93	53	76
Prop allocation (of 24)	10.05	5.73	8.22
Equipment allocation	10	6	8

Table 4. Results: Equipment Allocation ($k = 1$: Pax step).

$(x_{i,j,k=2})$	$i = 2(V)$	$i = 3(M)$	$i = 4(Q)$
$j = 1$			
$j = 2$			
$j = 3$	1		
$j = 4$			
$j = 5$			
$j = 6$			
$j = 7$			
$j = 8$			
$j = 9$			
$j = 10$			
$j = 11$			
Total $(\sum_j x_{i,j,k=2})$	1	0	0
Prop allocation (of 2)	2.00	0.00	0.00
Equipment allocation	2	0	0

Table 5. Results: Equipment Allocation ($k = 2$: MDL).

$(x_{i,j,k=3})$	$i = 2(V)$	$i = 3(M)$	$i = 4(Q)$
$j = 1$			28
$j = 2$			8
$j = 3$	37		
$j = 4$		21	
$j = 5$			40
$j = 6$	16		
$j = 7$	23		
$j = 8$	20		
$j = 9$			
$j = 10$		29	
$j = 11$			
Total $(\sum_j x_{i,j,k=3})$	96	50	76
Prop allocation (of 50)	21.62	11.26	17.12
Equipment allocation	22	11	17

Table 6. Results: Equipment Allocation ($k = 3$: LDL).

$(x_{i,j,k=4})$	$i=2(V)$	$i=3(M)$	$i=4(Q)$
$j=1$			28
$j=2$			8
$j=3$	39		
$j=4$		21	
$j=5$			40
$j=6$	20		
$j=7$		37	
$j=8$	6		
$j=9$	2		
$j=10$		29	
$j=11$		2	
Total ($\sum_j x_{i,j,k=4}$)	67	89	76
Prop allocation (of 33)	9.53	12.66	10.81
Equipment allocation	9	13	11

Table 7. Results: Equipment Allocation ($k=4$: Conveyor).

$(x_{i,j,k=5})$	$i=2(V)$	$i=3(M)$	$i=4(Q)$
$j=1$			
$j=2$			
$j=3$			
$j=4$		1	
$j=5$			
$j=6$			
$j=7$	1		
$j=8$			
$j=9$			
$j=10$		1	
$j=11$			
Total ($\sum_j x_{i,j,k=5}$)	1	2	0
Prop allocation (of 7)	2.33	4.67	0.00
Equipment allocation	2	5	0

Table 8. Results: Equipment Allocation ($k=5$: LDL-767).

	Pax step	MDL	LDL	Conveyor	LDL(767)
V	10	2	22	9	2
M	6	0	11	13	5
Q	8	0	17	11	0

Table 9. GSE Model Results: Equipment Allocation Summary

While Table 9 is a summary of all the *target* parking decisions, Tables 4-8 are also very useful in providing the individual GSE movement recommendations. As an example, Table 4 (for GSE type $k = 1$) recommends respectively, 10, 6, and 8 Pax steps at parking areas V, M, and Q. It further recommends that flights docked at bays ($j =$) 3,6,7,8,9 are served from area V; bays 4,10,11 from area M; and bays 1,2,5 from area Q. The expected numbers of (double) movements are given by the individual values of x_{ijk} in the table. Entirely similar information can be read off from Tables 5-8 for the other four GSE types.

CONCLUDING REMARKS

We remark here that there is a further important major type of GSE, the tractors, that is not under our consideration here. This is because there is precisely one large designated common area ($i = 1$: area R) to park all tractors (from all airport ground service operators). Therefore, no locational parking decisions are relevant for tractors at this HK airport. (From Table 3, $C_{i=1,k} = 0$ $\forall k$ has the effect of reserving area R.)

A second remark necessary here is the omission of the GSE used for cargo flights (in addition to the passenger flights considered in this work here). Since there are separate locations and (overall independent) operations of three cargo terminals, there are designated GSE (uses and parking areas) separated from those of passenger flights. However, it is a straightforward extension if one is to apply our GSE parking model to cargo flights as well. Even its manual management and decision making will in fact be easier, as the parking areas of cargo flights are usually right in front of the cargo terminals, hence in close proximity of one another.

Our final words on concluding this study on GSE parking problem are that, with a novel view of modeling, a simple GP formulation can go a long way towards producing usefully rationalized decision rules, yet concise enough to be of importance and valuable to the operational management and staff alike.

APPENDIX

Lingo Code for the Base GSE Movement Model.

```
MODEL:
!  A Ground Service Equipment (GSE) Parking Problem;
!  Linear Goal Programming formulation;
SETS:
   II / 1..@FILE( "GSE.ldt") / :  A, G;
   JJ / 1..@FILE( "GSE.ldt") / :  F;
   KK / 1..@FILE( "GSE.ldt") / :  S, E;
   IJ( II, JJ);
   IK( II, KK) : C, M, P, XIK;
   JK( JJ, KK) : D, N, Q;
   IJK( II, JJ, KK) : T, L, U, X;
ENDSETS
DATA:
   A = @FILE( "GSE.ldt");
   F = @FILE( "GSE.ldt");
   S = @FILE( "GSE.ldt");
   E = @FILE( "GSE.ldt");
   C = @FILE( "GSE.ldt");
   D = @FILE( "GSE.ldt");
   T = @FILE( "GSE.ldt");
   L = @FILE( "GSE.ldt");
   U = @FILE( "GSE.ldt");
ENDDATA

!  Minimize Deviations and Overall Transport Time;
   MIN = @SUM( IJK: T) * ( @SUM( IK: P)/@SIZE( JJ)
       + @SUM( JK: N)/@SIZE( II))
       + @SUM( IJK: T * X) ;
   Total_N = @SUM( JK : N) ; ! Output variable;
   Total_P = @SUM( IK : P) ; ! Output variable;
@FOR( II(i):
   @SUM( JJ(j)| F(j) #GT# 0:
   F(j)*@SUM( KK(k):  X(i,j,k)) / @SUM( KK(k):D(j,k))) = G(i));
@FOR( II(i):
   @SUM( JK(j,k):  S(k) * X(i,j,k)) <= A(i) * G(i));
   @SUM( IJK(i,j,k):  S(k) * X(i,j,k))
       <= @SUM( JJ: F) * @SUM( II: A) / @SIZE(II);
@FOR( IK(i,k):
   @SUM( JJ(j):  X(i,j,k)) + M(i,k) - P(i,k) = G(i) * C(i,k));
@FOR( JK(j,k):
   @SUM( II(i):  X(i,j,k)) + N(j,k) - Q(j,k) = D(j,k));
```

```
@FOR( KK(k):  @SUM( IJ(i,j):  X(i,j,k)) <= @SUM(JJ(j):D(j,k)));
@FOR( KK(k):  @SUM( IJ(i,j):  X(i,j,k)) <= @SUM( JJ : F)*E(k));
@FOR( IK(i,k):  @SUM( JJ(j):  X(i,j,k)) = XIK(i,k)) ; !Output;
@FOR( IJK: @BND( L, X, U));
END
```

REFERENCES

[1] Cook, T.M. Ed. (1989) Airline operations research. *Interfaces*, **39**,(4) 1-68.

[2] Hongkong Airport Services, Limited (1998) *Flights records, equipments and transport data*.

[3] Schrage, L. (1999) *Optimization Modeling with LINGO*, 3/e, Lindo Systems inc.

Multicriteria Decision Aid in Inventory Management

Cezary Dominiak

University of Economics Katowice, ul. Bogucicka 14, Katowice, Poland
dominiak@ae.katowice.pl

Abstract

This paper is concerned with multicriteria decision aiding in the inventory management problem. We examine a re-order cycle policy when the constraint of value of single order is taken into consideration. The proposed multicriteria decision aiding procedure for making an order is presented. This procedure uses Interactive Multicriteria Goal Programming algorithm. In the last part of the paper a simple numerical example is presented.

1. Introduction

An appropriate inventory management has a fundamental meaning for success achievement, especially for trading companies because it has great influence on total costs, service level and determines the base for carrying on marketing strategy.

The fundamentals of inventory management was developed by Harris [7], which proposed the Economic Lot Size (ELS) model for deterministic demand case. The solution for varying demand was proposed by Wagner and Within [20]. The modification of ELS for the infinite horizon may be found in [18] and such models are called power-of-two-policies. In reality we have to consider jointly a number of items and warehouse capacity. The earliest references to this problem appears in [4], [9]. But authors considered the case where every item is replenished with any coordination with other items.

Models for situations where all items share the same interval are called Rotation Cycle policies and were proposed by Hall [8]. Advanced models for varying demand and for multi-item case may be found in [1], [2], [6], [12], [15], [19]. The stochastic approach for inventory management was proposed by Scarf [14] and recent solutions we can find in e.g. [13], [21].

In this paper we propose a multicriteria model for decision aiding in the process of order preparation, which will help to determine the number of goods ordered. We consider the trading company that operates in re-order cycle policy - it means that the time between orders is given and it is constant for each supplier.

In the first paragraph of this paper we discuss the general issues which bring us about formulation of the above problem as a multicriteria decision making problem. Next, the proposed mathematical model is presented. During the decision support process we propose the use of an Interactive Multicriteria Goal Programming [16], which is shortly described in the fourth paragraph. Finally, the simple numerical example and conclusions are presented.

2. General considerations

In the case of a trading company running a re-order cycle policy a staff responsible for making an order (decision maker-DM) has the following information (for each item): the current stock level, the quantity of items that have already been ordered but have not been delivered yet, the lead time (time between placing an order and the receipt of the goods), the demand forecast for the lead time and forecast for period between the goods reception on the basis of current order and the goods reception on the base of next order. Further, this period of time we will call the period to cover.

Most of the above discussed values are not exactly deterministic. But, in spite of that we will not consider these values as random variables for the following reasons: first, in case when we have a large number of items the computing process comes to be very complex and may take too much time and effort than it would be acceptable by DM. Moreover, when we consider new products (without history) we have no basis to compute the necessary statistical parameters. The similar situation takes place when we run on rapidly growing market. In that case we have the necessary data but there is a serious risk that such data used for statistical predictions may give us the noncredible results. Finally, we assume that decision support procedure should be simple and as much as possible and thanks to that should be easy to understand for DM (who very often has not advanced statistical background).

We propose to use for those uncertain values two parameters: lower and upper limits which may be arbitrary (intuitively) settled by DM, but of course they may be estimated on the ground of statistical methods and they may represent the upper and lower limits of confidence levels of forecasts. It should be pointed out that such approach enables to reflect directly the risk inclination of DM [2].

Typically in the inventory management models, which are prepared for the re-order cycle policy, we examine the time period divided into subperiods and we want to minimise the total operating cost which includes the setup costs, the holding costs and the cost of sales loss (see : . [3] pp. 150-200).

In our model we consider the single period only (i.e. period to cover) for which we have to prepare an order. We are interested in such order preparation which enables us to gain the maximum value of sales profit ratio, ensures us to fulfil the sales plans, enables to take into consideration the constraint settled on the maximum value of an order and finally, helps to reduce the holding costs of items that will be stored beyond the period to cover. Such understanding of holding costs comes from the assumption: if the reception of goods is at the beginning of the period to cover we don't have to consider the holding costs within period to cover because, in any way, we have to pay this costs. Thus we propose to reduce the holding costs that are created by surplus at the end of period to cover only.

In our decision aiding model we propose to consider the following criteria functions: the value of sales profit ratio, the holding cost, the cost of sales loss and the value of an order. These criteria may have a different meaning for DM. For example: the cost of the sales loss is typically hypothetical cost, but on the other hand the holding cost is the real cost we have to pay. Thus the importance of these criteria may be different for various DM, because they may depend on the market strategy, risk aversion etc. So, we suggest taking into account these criteria separately and as a result we propose to use the multicriteria approach.

3. The proposed model

We assume that DM has to prepare an order for N items denoted as $W_1,...,W_N$. For each item we have given or computed the following parameters:

- purchase price (p),
- sales profit ratio (r),
- single unit stock capacity (c),
- the holding cost (ic),
- lower (il) and upper (iu) forecast of stock volume for the beginning of period to cover,
- lower (dl) and upper (du) demand forecast for period to cover,
- volume of sales plan (dg) for period to cover.

We assume that lower and upper limits of all values are described in such way that the probability of their exceed is close to zero. The holding costs include also the capital costs and the real holding costs. The holding costs are estimated on the ground of lower limits of demand forecast for periods following the period to cover and in that way describes the holding cost if the single unit will be in stock at the end of period to cover. The basic decision variables describe suggested quantities of items to be ordered: $X_1, ..., X_N$. In our model we consider four criteria functions:

The sales profit ratio (max)

$$F^1 = \sum_{i=1}^{N} p_i r_i X_i \rightarrow \max$$

(1)

The holding cost (min)

$$F^2 = \sum_{i=1}^{N} ic_i N_i^+ \rightarrow \min$$

(2)

where

$$\underset{i=1,...,N}{\forall} X_i + N_i^- - N_i^+ = dl_i - iu_i$$

(3)

thus the total holding cost is computed on the basis of surplus of items at the end of period to cover when we assume that at the beginning of period to cover occurs the upper level of stock and then lower demand occurs in the period to cover.

The cost of sales loss (min)

$$F^3 = \sum_{i=1}^{N} p_i r_i Z_i^- \rightarrow \min$$

(4)

where

$$\underset{i=1,\dots,N}{\forall} X_i + Z_i^- - Z_i^+ = du_i - il_i$$

(5)

thus the cost of lost sales is computed on the basis of shortage of items at the end of period to cover when we assume that at the beginning of period to cover occurs the lower stock and then upper demand occurs in the period to cover.

The value of ordered items (min)

$$F^4 = \sum_{i=1}^{N} p_i X_i \rightarrow \min$$

(6)

We consider the following set of constraints. The first group of constraints ensures us to keep the stock buffer at the end of period to cover to protect us against delay of next delivery:

$$\underset{i=1,\dots,N}{\forall} dg_i - iu_i + b_i \geq 0$$

(7)

Where b_i is the buffer size computed on the basis of future demand (in next period after period to cover) and on the ground of standard deviations of lead time. Next we take into consideration the our requirements concerned with demand in the period to cover:

$$N_i^- \leq \alpha_i (dl_i - iu_i)$$

(8)

$$Z_i^+ \leq \beta_i (du_i - il_i)$$

(9)

where α_i, and β_i are arbitrary settled by DM and describe maximum deviations from stages implicated by our desire that stock at the beginning of period to cover (after reception of items) does not exceed the upper limits of demand and from the other hand the stock should not be lower than lower limit of demand in period to cover. The next constraint ensures not to exceed the total stock capacity:

$$\sum_{i=1}^{N} c_i (X_i + iu_i) \leq C$$

(10)

where C maximum stock capacity. Moreover, we take into account constraints which may be settled by suppliers on maximum quantities of items to be ordered:

$$\sum_{i=1}^{N} X_i \le M_i$$

(11)

and finally decision variables should be nonnegative:

$$\underset{i=1,...,N}{\forall}\ X_i, N_i^+, N_i^-, Z_i^+, Z_i^- \ge 0$$

(12)

4. An Interactive Multicriteria Goal Programming algorithm

In the decision support session we apply the IMGP method. Some important advantages are connected with the IMGP. First of all the DM does not have to give his preference information on a priori basis but has to consider all kinds of choices and trade-off questions which may be relevant ([17] p.104). Another important advantage of IMGP is its relatively simple and easy to understand idea. Finally the DM during an interactive procedure has to answer the simple questions:

1 Is the given solution acceptable or not?
2. Which goal value needs to be improved?
3. How much should this goal value be improved at least?
4. Do you accept the consequences of the proposed improvement of the value of the indicated goal variable? (see.: [17] p.250)

The general scheme of the applied IMGP is presented on Figure 1.

Thus in the presented multicriteria model we consider the following single criterion problems:

Problem 1: Maximise F^1,	subject to (3), (5), (7),...,(12)
Problem 2: Minimise F^2,	subject to (3), (5), (7),...,(12)
Problem 3: Minimise F^3,	subject to (3), (5), (7),...,(12)
Problem 4: Minimise F^4,	subject to (3), (5), (7),...,(12)

From the second iteration according to DM's choices an appropriate constraint is added in each iteration to above problems.

Figure 1. The flow chart of the IMGP procedure

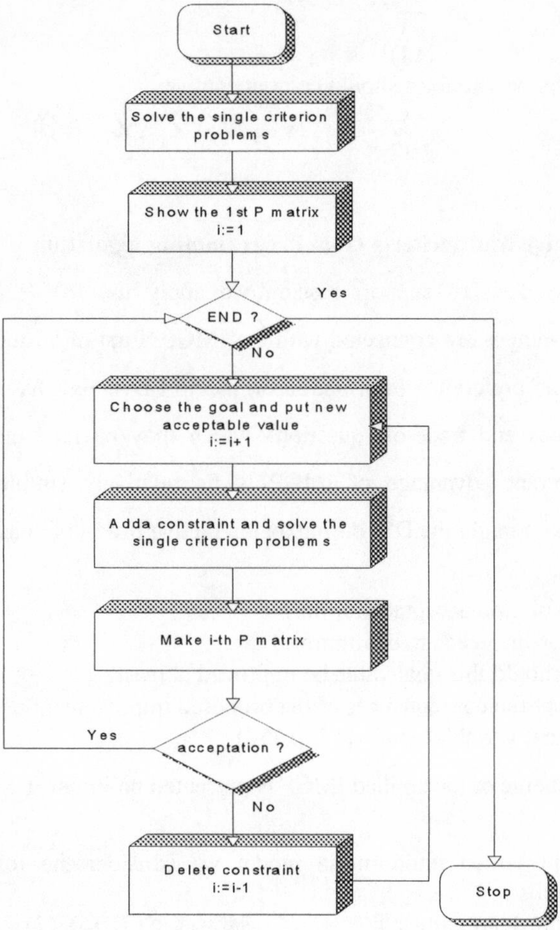

5. An illustrative example

In this paragraph we present a numerical example of decision support session using the above described model and method. Let us assume that we are faced to problem preparing of an order for 10 items. The data are presented in the table 1. In the first iteration we obtain the optimal solutions of single criterion problems that are presented in the table 2. The first potency matrix contains values shown in the table 3.

Table 1 The input data

	W1	W2	W3	W4	W5	W6	W7	W8	W9	W10
p.	10	12	15	17	20	35	15	25	8	12
R	25%	18%	12%	30%	14%	10%	15%	18%	54%	23%
Ic	0,75	0,8	0,92	0,6	1,5	1,2	0,32	0,85	0,4	0,8
C	1,2	1,5	0,95	0,9	1,2	0,6	9	2,5	0,45	0,78
Il	1000	500	200	500	1200	200	1300	1400	1500	320
Iu	1200	600	250	650	1400	300	1380	1600	1700	400
Dl	1950	1000	450	1950	2350	400	2800	2000	4900	2450
Du	2500	1450	800	2650	3000	800	3800	2600	5900	3200
Dg	2350	1200	600	2200	2750	700	3500	2200	5200	2700
B	220	115	120	300	300	170	350	220	400	270

Table 2 The optimal solutions of single criterion problems (Iteration 1)

	F^1	F^2	F^3	F^4
Problem 1	69 266	7 228	0	292 831
Problem 2	55 054	4 298	7 915	233 320
Problem 3	62 969	5 925	0	266 210
Problem 4	55 054	4 298	7 915	233 320

Table 3 The first obtained potency matrix and DM's decision

	F^1	F^2	F^3	F^4
OPT	69 266	4 298	0	233 320
PES	55 054	7 228	7 915	292 831
Decision				<250 000

The DM chooses the goal whose value should be improved and inputs a new acceptable value. Let us assume that DM wanted to reduce the value of an order at maximum 250 000. Then the second iteration is carried out (see Table 4). Let us assume that the DM accepts the new optimistic values of objectives and decides to reduce the acceptable holding cost to 4 500 and next decides to improve the sales profit ratio to 57 231. The optimistic and pessimistic values obtained in all iterations and DM's decisions are presented in the table 4 and 5.

Table 4 The next iterations and DM's decisions

	F^1	F^2	F^3	F^4
OPT	61 798	4 298	2 583	233 320
PES	55 054	5 168	7 915	250 000
		<4500		

Table 5 The next iterations and DM's decisions

	F^1	F^2	F^3	F^4
OPT	57 231	4 298	5 741	233 320
PES	55 054	4 500	7 915	237 365
	>57231			
OPT	57 231	4 500	5 753	237 351
PES	57 231	4 500	5 752	237 351

When the optimistic and acceptable values of the criteria of considered goals are equal (with desired tolerance limit) then the procedures stops. The obtained values of decision variables are presented in the table 6.

Table 6 Final solution - decision variables

	W1	W2	W3	W4	W5	W6	W7	W8	W9	W10
X	1370	715	470	1850	1650	570	2470	820	4404	2570
N(+)	620	315	270	550	700	470	1050	420	1204	520
Z(-)	130	235	130	300	150	30	30	380	0	310

6. Conclusions

In this paper we proposed the multicriteria approach to inventory management. This is a new approach which enables to take into consideration individual goals and preferences in the order preparation process.

The separation of basic components of total costs enables DM to flexible adjust quantities ordered according to current financial and market conditions. Finally in the proposed model the uncertainty of future demand may be easy incorporated without any additional computational problems.

The model presented in this paper may be easy applied in a real life situation in trading companies running in re-order cycle policy. Even for quite large problems the computations may be done using MS Excel and add-ins like e.g. What's Best!. It enables easy data transfer from other applications and preparation of final documents. For the cases with large number of decision variables it is possible to use popular optimising software like Lindo, LINGO or SAS.

References

[1] Aggarwal A., Park J.K (1990): Improved Algorithms for Economic Lot Size Problems. Working Paper, Laboratory for Computer Science, MIT, Cambridge.

[2] Atkins D.R., Iyogun P. (1988): A Heuristic with Lower Bond Performance Guarantee for the Multi-Product Dynamic Lot Size Problem. IIE Transactions 20, pp.369-373.

[3] Bramel J., Simchi-Levi D. (1997): The Logic of Logistics. Springer Verlag, New York.

[4] Churchman C.W., Ackoff R.L. and Arnoff E.L. (1957): Introduction to Operations Research. John Wiley & Sons Ltd., New York.

[5] Dobson G. (1987): The Economic Lot Scheduling Problem: A Resolution of Feasibility Using Time Varying Lot Sizes. Oper. Res. 35, pp. 764-771.

[6] Florian M., Lenstra J.K., Rinnooy Kan A.H.G. (1980): Deterministic Production Planning: Algorithms and Complexity. Management Sci. 26, pp. 669-679.

[7] Harris F., (1915): Operations and Costs. Factory Management Series. A.W.Shaw Co. Chicago, pp.48-52.

[8] Hall N.G., (1988): A Multi Item EOQ Model with Inventory Cycle Balancing. Noval Research Logistics 35, pp. 319-325.

[9] Holt C.C., (1958): Decision Rules for Allocating Inventory to Lots and Costs Foundations for Making Aggregate Inventory Decisions. J. Ind. Eng. 9, pp. 14-22.

[10] Inglehart D. (1963): Optimality of (s,S) Policies in the Infinite Horizon Dynamic Inventory Problem. Management Sci. 9, pp. 259-267.

[11] Inglehart D. (1963): Dynamic Programming and Stationary Analysis In Inventory Problems. In: Multi-Stage Inventory Models and Tehniques. Scarf H., Guilford D., Shelly M., (eds) Stanford University Press, Stanford, pp. 1-31.

[12] Joneja D. (1990): The Joint Replenishment Problem. New Heuristics and Worst-Case Performance Bounds. Oper. Res. 38, pp. 711-723.

[13] Porteus E.L. (1990): Stochastic Inventory Theory. In: Handbooks of Operations Research and Management Science, the volume on Stochastic Models, Heyman D.P., Sobel M.J. (eds), Amsterdam, pp.605-652.

[14] Scarf H.E. (1960): The Optimalities of (s,S) Policies in the Dynamic Inventory Problem. In: Mathematical Methods in the Social Sciences, Arrow K., Karlin S., Suppes P. (eds), Stanford University Press, pp.196-202.

[15] Silver E.A., Meal H.C. (1973): A Heuristic for Selecting Lot Size Quantities for the Case of a Deterministic Time-Varying Dimand Rate and Discrete Opportinities for Replenishment. Production Inventory Management 14, pp.64-74.

[16] Spronk J. (1980): Interactive Multiple Goal Programming for Capital Budgeting and Financial Planning, Boston.

[17] Nijkamp P., Spronk J. (1980): Interactive Multiplie Goal Programming: an Evaluation and Some Results. In: Multiple Decision Making Theory and Application, Ed. G. Fandel, T. Gal, Springer, Berlin, s. 278-293

[18] Roundy R., (1985): 98%-Effective Integer Ratio for One Warehouse Multi-Retailer Systems. Management Sci. 31, pp.1416-1430.

[19] Wagelmans A., Van Hoesel S., Kolen A. (1992): Economic Lot Sizing: An O(n logn) Algorithm that Runs in Linear Time in the Wagner-Whitin Case. Oper. Res. 40, Suppl.No.1, pp. S145-S156.

[20] Wagner, H.M., Whitin T.M. (1958): Dynamic Version of the Economic Lot Size Model. Management Sci. 5, pp. 89-96.

[21] Zipkin K. (1997): Foundations of Inventory Management. Irwin Burr Ridge, IL.

Solution Concepts in Multiple Criteria Linear Production Games*

F.R. Fernández[1], M.A. Hinojosa[2], A. Marmol[3], J. Puerto[1]

[1] Departamento de Estadística e Investigación Operativa.
Universidad de Sevilla.
C/ Tarfia s/n 41013-Sevilla. Spain. e-mail: fernande@cica.es

[2] Departamento de Economía y Empresa. Universidad Pablo de Olavide.
Ctra. de Utrera Km. 1 41012-Sevilla. Spain. e-mail: mahinram@dee.upo.es

[3] Departamento de Economía Aplicada III. Universidad de Sevilla.
Avda. Ramón y Cajal nº 1, 41018-Sevilla, Spain. e-mail: amarmol@cica.es

Abstract

The goal of this paper is to explore the solutions concepts of the multi-objective linear production game. Several stability conditions can be defined since one can have various interpretations of an improvement within the multicriteria framework. We present different solution concepts and explore the relationships among them for TU games whose characteristic function assigns a set of vectors to each coalition of players. These concepts generalize the classic ideas of solution for scalar games and can be considered under different preference structures. The special features of the linear production problem make possible to obtain allocations of the rewards among the players that are solutions of the linear production game associated.

Key Word: Multi-commodity linear production problem, TU multi-objective game, non-dominated solutions.

*The research of the authors is partially supported by the Spanish Ministerio de Educación y Cultura grant n. PB97-07-07

1. Introduction

Game theory is a mathematical theory for modelling and analyzing conflict situations involving a number of players with possibly divergent interests. Moreover, in cooperative game theory the players are allowed to make binding agreements. Thus, each subgroup (coalition) of the players can form a coalition. This implies that each coalition can guarantee itself a certain vector payoff without involving the other players. If each coalition's payoff consists of a set of vectors, we are left with the class of transferable utility games that we will analyze. If such a game is played and all the players decide to cooperate, then an interesting question which arises is how the total revenue vectors should be allocated among the various players. The natural extension of the idea of allocation used in scalar games to multiple criteria games consists of using a payoff matrix whose rows are allocations of the criteria.

Among all the allocations of a game, we are interested in those which cannot be beaten by the worth given to the coalitions. In scalar games, to beat an allocation with respect to a coalition means to find another allocation which gives more worth to the members of that coalition (equivalently, which gives not less worth). Nevertheless, in vector-valued games to get more worth is not equivalent to not to get less worth. Thus there are two ways of analyzing the situation which correspond to two different solution concepts for these games. In the first one, we do not admit less worth than what we already can achieve by ourselves. This would lead us to get more. In the second one, we accept compromise payoffs which get worse in some of the criteria provided that we increase in some others. Our previous discussion has shown that at least two different orderings are possible in the set of allocations in vector-valued games. These two orderings lead to two different concepts of improvement. Depending on the concept of improvement that has been established, it is possible to consider allocations such that each coalition gets a payoff which is not worse that what it can guarantee by itself, or allocations in which each coalition reaches better payoff than those it can guarantee by itself. In this context, multiple criteria games can be used to model economic situations in which the agents by cooperation can obtain bundles of a fixed set of goods. In particular we concentrate on linear production problems that can be modelled as multi-commodity games.

By using the cooperative game theory, 13 considered linear production programming problems in which several decision makers pool resources to produce some goods. He gave an allocation scheme of the total revenue by adopting a point in the core of the cooperative game arising from the production programming problem. Subsequently extensions of the production model and relationships between other optimization problems and the cooperative games have been studied in relation to Owen's work. See, for example, 1, 11, 14, 5, 6, 3, 7, 12, 15 and 8.

The goal of the paper is to analyze the linear production programming problem with several decision makers in multi-objective environments. We consider a joint project with several decision makers who produce some goods and the revenue yielding by cooperation among them should be maximized and allocated among them fairly. In section 2, some concepts in multi-commodity games are briefly reviewed. We formulate a production programming problem as a multi-objective linear programming problem and show that a multi-commodity game arises from the problem. In section 3, imputation concepts are introduced according with the two different orderings that are possible in the set of allocations in multi-commodity games. In section 4 different solution concepts that involve the collective rationality principle are introduced and existence conditions are provided. We also illustrate the concepts and results with several examples.

2. Basic Concepts

A multi-commodity cooperative game is a pair (N, V), where N is the set of players, $N = \{1, 2, \ldots, n\}$, and V is a map, the characteristic function of the game, that associates to each coalition $S \subseteq N$ a nonempty, comprehensive and compact subset $V_S \subseteq \mathbb{R}^m_{\geqq}$, $V_\emptyset = \{0\}$. Let G^V denote the class of multi-commodity games. Here $\mathbb{R}^m_{\geqq} = \{x \in \mathbb{R}^m \mid x_j \geq 0 \quad \forall j = 1, 2, \ldots, m\}$ and a set $A \subset \mathbb{R}^m_{\geqq}$ is called comprehensive if $b \in A$ and $0 \leqq a \leqq b$ imply $a \in A$. The class G^v of the vector-valued cooperative games may be considered a subclass of G^V.

Each coalition will be interested in the nondominated vectors in the associated characteristic set: $E(V_S) = \{z \in V_S \mid \nexists w \in V_S, z \leq w\}$.

Resources	Players			The grand coalition
R_i	1	2	3	N
R_1	139	181	110	$b_1^N = 430$
R_2	140	87	183	$b_2^N = 410$
R_3	130	225	215	$b_3^N = 570$

Figure 1: Resources.

We now concentrate on multi-commodity games arising from linear production situations. A multi-objective linear production programming problem is described as follows. Each of the n decision-makers (players) is in possesion of a resource vector, $b^i = \left(b_1^i, b_2^i, \ldots, b_q^i\right)$ $i = 1, 2, \ldots, n$, and p kinds of goods are produced by cooperation of the decision makers. A coalition $S \subset N$ will have a total of $b_l^S = \sum_{i \in S} b_l^i$ $l = 1, 2, \ldots, q$ units of the lth resource. A unit of the kth good $(k = 1, 2, \ldots, p)$, requires a_{lk} units of the lth resource $(l = 1, 2, \ldots, q)$. We formulate the production model as an m objective linear programming problem. For a coalition $S \subset N$, the m-objective linear programming problem is represented as:

$$
\begin{aligned}
max \quad & z(\mathbf{x}) = C\mathbf{x} \\
s.a: \quad & A\mathbf{x} \leqq B^S \\
& \mathbf{x} \in I\!R_{\geqq}^p
\end{aligned}
$$

where "max" means vector maximization, $C \in \mathcal{M}_{m \times p}$ is the price matrix, $A \in \mathcal{M}_{q \times p}$ is the technological matrix and $B^S = \left(b_1^S, b_2^S, \ldots, b_q^S\right)^t$ is the resource vector for coalition S.

The feasible decision set for S is $F_S = \left\{\mathbf{x} \in I\!R^p \,/\, A\mathbf{x} \leqq B^S, \mathbf{x} \in I\!R_{\geqq}^p\right\}$, and the characteristic set in the corresponding multi-commodity game $(N, V) \in G^V$ for coalition S is $V_S = \left\{\mathbf{z} \in I\!R^m \,/\, \mathbf{z} \leqq C\mathbf{x} \quad \forall \mathbf{x} \in F_S\right\}$.

Example 1.1 8 *Consider the following bi-criteria linear production programming problem with three decision makers (players). Each of the players initially possesses three kinds of resources as shown in Figure 1.*

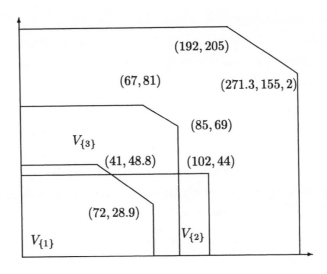

Figure 2: Characteristic sets.

For coalition N the problem is formulated as:

$$\begin{aligned}
max \quad & z_1(x) = 2.5x_1 + 5x_2 \\
max \quad & z_2(x) = 3x_1 + 2x_2 \\
s.a: \quad & 2x_1 + 9x_2 \le 430 \\
& 6x_1 + 4x_2 \le 410 \\
& 8x_1 + 9x_2 \le 570 \\
& x_1, x_2 \ge 0
\end{aligned}$$

The characteristic sets for the coalition N and for all the players are represented in Figure 2. ◁

In the multi-commodity game $(N, V) \in G^V$, if all the players cooperate, the problem than arises is how to allocate the total revenue among the players. We are interested in the nondominated vectors of the characteristic set V_N.

An allocation of $\mathbf{z} \in E(V_N)$ is a $m \times n$ matrix, $Y(\mathbf{z})$. The columns of $Y(\mathbf{z})$ represent a player's payoff. Thus $Y^i(\mathbf{z}) = \left(y_1^i, y_2^i, \ldots, y_m^i\right)^t$ are the payoffs of player i with respect to each of the m criteria. The total payoff for a coalition $S \subset N$ is $Y^S = \sum_{i \in S} Y^i$. The rows, $Y_j(\mathbf{z}) = \left(y_j^1, y_j^2, \ldots, y_j^n\right)$, represent the payoffs of each player on criterion j.

A first approach to find solutions of the game $(N, V) \in G^V$ consists of reducing the problem to the case of a vector-valued characteristic function. This is done by considering vectors that improve all the vectors of the characteristic sets.

For the game $(N, V) \in G^V$, the maximal of the set $E(V_S)$, $S \subset N$, is the m-dimensional vector whose components are the maxima componentwise among all the vectors in $E(V_S)$. We will denote it by V_S^M. The minimal in $E(V_S)$ is the vector that is improved componentwise by all the points of $E(V_S)$, that is, its components are the minima among the components of all the vectors of $E(V_S)$. We will denote it by V_S^m.

These vectors make possible to construct, what we will call the game of the maximals.

Definition 1.1 *For each* $z \in E(V_N)$ *we define the game of the maximals,* (N, V_z), *as follows:* $V_z(N) = z + I\!R_{\geq}^m$ *and* $V_z(S) = V_S^M + I\!R_{\geq}^m$ $\forall S \subset N$.

The solutions of these games will help to find solutions of the original game $(N, V) \in G^V$.

Definition 1.2 *For each* $z \in E(V_N)$, *an allocation with respect to* z *is a* $m \times n$ *matrix* Y *such that* $Y_j^N(z) = z_j$ $\forall j = 1, 2, \ldots m$, *i.e.,* $Y^N(z) = z$.

We will denote by $I^*(N, V; z)$ the set of allocations with respect to z for the game $(N, V) \in G^V$. The set of all the allocations of the game is $I^*(N, V) = \bigcup_{z \in E(V_N)} I^*(N, V; z)$. Notice that $I^*(N, V; z) = I^*(N, V_z)$ for each $z \in E(V_N)$.

Then $I^*(N, V) = \bigcup_{z \in E(V_N)} I^*(N, V_z)$.

3. Imputations

In what follows, we are interested on those allocations that have certain properties of equilibrium and stability.

Initially, we consider two different concepts of improvement. By the first one, a vector is preferred to another vector if it is better componentwise. This idea leads to what we will call preference imputations. To establish the concept of preference imputation, one can think that a certain allocation of the vector $z \in E(V_N)$ is acceptable for a player if what he achieves is better than at least one of the nondominated payoffs that he can guarantee by himself. But a more demanding player may not accept the solution if what he gets does not improve all the nondominated payoffs that he can achieve by himself.

By the second ordering, a vector is preferred to another one if it is not worse componentwise. This notion leads to what we will call nondominated or generalized imputation.

Therefore we can define three different concepts of imputation.

Definition 1.3 *Let $Y \in I^*(N,V)$ be an allocation of the game $(N,V) \in G^V$. Let Y^i denote the i-th column of matrix Y.*

Y is a strict preference imputation if $Y^i \in V_{\{i\}}^M + \mathbb{R}_{\geqq}^m \quad \forall i \in N$.

Y is a preference imputation if $Y^i \in V_{\{i\}} + \mathbb{R}_{\geqq}^m \quad \forall i \in N$.

Y is a generalized imputation if $Y^i \notin V_{\{i\}} \setminus E(V_{\{i\}}) \quad \forall i \in N$.

The situation for a two criteria game can be represented as:

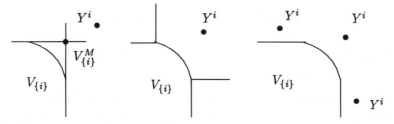

We will denote by $I(N,V;\cap,\mathbf{z})$ the set of all the strict preference imputations associated to $\mathbf{z} \in E(V_N)$ and by $I(N,V;\cap)$ the set of all the strict preference imputations of the game. Therefore $I(N,V;\cap) = \bigcup_{\mathbf{z} \in E(V_N)} I(N,V;\cap,\mathbf{z})$. Notice that a strict preference imputation is an ideal allocation of an efficient payoff vector of V_N from an individual point of view. Nevertheless it is not always possible in the linear production game to find such allocations. In fact, it happens that the set $I(N,V;\cap)$ is not empty if and only if, the maximal of the set $\sum_{i=1}^n V_{\{i\}}$ is included in the characteristic set of the grand coalition, V_N. We will denote by $E(V_N, PE)$ the vectors of V_N that have a strict preference imputation, thus $E(V_N, PE) = \left(\sum_{i=1}^n V_{\{i\}}^M + \mathbb{R}_{\geqq}^m\right) \cap E(V_N)$ (see 9). In Example 1.1 it is not possible to find an efficient vector of the set V_N that can be allocated by a strict preference imputation. Indeed the sum of the maximals of the characteristic sets of each player is $(259, 173.8) \in \left(E(V_N) + I\!R_{\geq}^m \right) \setminus E(V_N)$. This is not general. If each player lacks of one different resource, none of the players can produce individually, and therefore cooperation is necessary. The maximal of the set $\sum_{i=1}^n V_{\{i\}}$ is the null vector and all the efficient vectors of V_N can be allocated by a strict preference imputation. That is, $E(V_N, PE) = E(V_N)$.

If the individual rationality principle is established with an order based in componentwise preference, but an allocation is considered acceptable when it improves some of the efficient payoffs that the player can guarantee, the solution concept of the game is extended to preference imputations. The set of preference imputations associated to $z \in E(V_N)$ will be denoted by $I(N, V; \cup, z)$ and the set of all preference imputations of the game will be denoted by $I(N, V; \cup)$: $I(N, V; \cup) = \bigcup_{z \in E(V_N)} I(N, V; \cup, z)$. In general, for the linear production multicriteria game, it is not possible to find preference imputations for every payoff vector that the coalition can achieve. In Example 1.1 it is not possible to allocate vector $(192, 205) \in E(V_N)$ by a preference imputation because it is not possible to allocate the total amount of the first resource, 192, among the three players by a preference imputation because Player 1 will not accept less than 41, Player 2 will not accept less than 102, and Player 3 will not accept less than 67 (see Figure 2). The sum of these amounts is 210, which exceeds the total available. Nevertheless in the production game it is always possible to find preference imputations due to the balancedness property (the game (N, V) is said to be balanced if, for any balanced collection β, with balancing coefficients $(\alpha_S)_{S \in \beta}$, $\sum_{S \in \beta} \alpha_S V_S \subseteq V_N - I\!R_{\geq}^m$; the game is said to be strictly balanced if, $\sum_{S \in \beta} \alpha_S V_S \subseteq V_N^m - I\!R_{\geq}^m$). Notice that a strictly balanced game is a balanced game. The production game is balanced 8, but it is not strictly balanced (see Example 1.1).

By the balancedness property the relation $\sum_{i=1}^n V_{\{i\}} \subseteq E(V_N) - I\!R_{\geq}^m$ holds for multiple criteria linear production games since $V_N - I\!R_{\geq}^m = E(V_N) - I\!R_{\geq}^m$. Therefore, it is possible to allocate some vectors $z \in E(V_N)$ by preference imputations.

Theorem 1.1 *The vectors in the set $E(V_N, P) = \left(\sum_{i=1}^{n} V_{\{i\}}\right) + I\!R_{\geqq}^{m} \cap E(V_N)$ can be allocated by a preference imputation.*

Proof: Consider $z_1 \in E(V_N, P)$, $z_2 \in z_1 - I\!R_{\geqq}^{m} \cap E\left(\sum_{i=1}^{n} V_{\{i\}}\right)$ and $b = z_1 - z_2 \geq 0$. Since $z_2 = \sum_{i=1}^{n} z^i$, with $z^i \in E(V_{\{i\}})$, let Y be a $m x n$ matrix whose columns are $Y^i = z^i + \frac{b}{n}$. The matrix Y is an allocation of z_1 because $Y^N = z_2 + b = z_1$ and constitutes a preference imputation. $\square$

The set of generalized imputations associated to $z \in E(V_N)$ will be denoted by $I(N, V; z)$ and the set of all generalized imputations of the game will be denoted by $I(N, V)$. It is clear that $I(N, V) = \bigcup_{z \in E(V_N)} I(N, V; z)$.

Notice that the inclusion relationships among the imputation sets considered above are $I(N, V; \cap) \subseteq I(N, V; \cup) \subseteq I(N, V)$.

4. Solutions Conceps

Apart from the "individual rationality principle" used to define the imputation concepts, we consider now the "collective rationality principle" in the different imputation sets. Therefore a collective improvement concept is needed. This collective improvement concept may be based on the same order than the individual improvement concept used in the imputation set or on a different order. In the first case, we are left with the core concepts: the traditional concept of core if the improvement concept is "not be worse" an the preference core and strict preference core if the improvement concept is "be better componentwise". In the second case we will consider that the players individually will not accept an allocation if there is not improvement componentwise but collectively they will accept an imputation that assigns a joint payment not worse than what they can obtain by themselves. This leads us to a new concept of solution: imputations nondominated by allocations (INDA).

4.1. Strict preference imputations nondominated by allocations. Strict preference core

Definition 1.4 *A strict preference imputation of a vector in $E(V_N, PE)$ is said to be a strict preference imputation nondominated by allocations (strict preference INDA) if no coalition has any objection to the allocation.*

$$INDA(N, V; \cap) = \left\{ Y \in I(N, V; \cap) \,/\, Y^S \notin V_S \setminus E(V_S) \quad \forall S \subset N, \, |S| > 1 \right\}.$$

In our Example 1.1, if player 1 lacks of resource 1, player 2 lacks of resource 2 and player 3 lacks of resource 3, none of the players can produce. Therefore, as $V_{\{i\}} = \{0\}$, every allocation of a vector in $E(V_N)$ is a strict preference imputation. Moreover the allocation $Y = \begin{pmatrix} 50 & 50 & 92 \\ 60 & 60 & 85 \end{pmatrix} \in \mathcal{M}_{2\times 3}$, of vector $(192, 205) \in E(V_N)$ is an INDA. The question that arises is whether every vector in $E(V_N, PE)$ may be allocated by a strict preference INDA. It can be established that, due to its special structure, in the linear production game it is always possible to construct strict preference imputations nondominated by allocations if F_N has an efficient face, G, such that $CG \cap E(V_N, PE) \neq \emptyset$.

A strict preference imputation is an ideal allocation from an individual point of view, as each player obtains more that what he could guarantee by himself in every criterion. If we think the same way when applying the collective rationality principle, we obtain a more restrictive concept of solution: the strict preference core. Such solutions are ideal allocations from both the individual and the collective perspective because each player and each coalition get better payoff vectors in every criterion than all the efficient payoffs of the characteristic set.

Definition 1.5 *The strict preference core, $C(N, V; \cap)$, is defined as the set:*
$$C(N, V; \cap) = \left\{ Y \in I^*(N, V) / Y^S \in V_S^M + I\!R_{\geqq}^m \quad \forall S \subset N \right\}.$$

In general, it happens that $C(N, V; \cap) \subseteq INDA(N, V; \cap)$ and the inclusion relation can be strict.

It is wellknown that balancedness is a necessary and sufficient condition for the existence of core solution in scalar games (see 2). It is easy to prove that this condition may be extended to vector-valued games if we consider the cartesian product core (see 9). If $z \in E(V_N)$, the elements of the core of the game $(N, V) \in G^V$ associated to z coincide with the set of vectors in the core of the game of the maximals $(N, V_z) \in G^v$. Therefore a necessary and sufficient condition for the existence of strict preference allocations associated to $z \in E(V_N)$ is that the game $(N, V_z) \in G^v$ is balanced. Then we can obtain the strict preference core from the cores of the games of the maximals,

$C(N,V;\cap) = \bigcup_{\mathbf{z}\in E(V_N)} C(N,V_{\mathbf{z}})$. The following result establishes that strict balancedness is a necessary and sufficient condition for nonemptiness of the strict preference core.

Theorem 1.2 *There exist allocations of the strict preference core for every* $\mathbf{z} \in E(V_N)$ *if and only if the game is strictly balanced.*

<u>Proof</u>: First consider $\mathbf{z} \in E(V_N)$ and $Y \in C(N,V;\cap)$ associated to $\mathbf{z}$. Then $Y^N = \mathbf{z} \in E(V_N)$ and $Y^S \geq V_S^M \quad \forall S \subset N$. For each $S \subset N$, $\mathbf{w}_S \in V_S$, let us consider the vector-valued game whose characteristic function is defined as $v(S) = \mathbf{w}_S \in V_S$, $v(N) = \mathbf{z} = Y^N$. This game is balanced because Y is a solution of the cartesian product core of the vector-valued game. Therefore, for every balanced collection β, with balancing vector $\{\alpha_S\}_{S\in\beta}$ we have $\sum_{S\in\beta} \alpha_S \mathbf{w}_S \leq \mathbf{z}$. Since $\mathbf{w}_S \in V_S$ is arbitrary the condition $\sum_{S\in\beta} \alpha_S V_S \subseteq \mathbf{z} - I\!\!R_{\geq}^m$ holds. Moreover, $\mathbf{z} \in E(V_N)$ is arbitrary too, hence, $\sum_{S\in\beta} \alpha_S V_S \subseteq V_N^m - I\!\!R_{\geq}^m$ and (V,N) is strictly balanced.

Reciprocally, if (V,N) is strictly balanced for every balanced collection β, with balancing vector $\{\alpha_S\}_{S\in\beta}$ we have $\sum_{S\in\beta} \alpha_S V_S \subseteq V_N^m - I\!\!R_{\geq}^m$. Then $\sum_{S\in\beta} \alpha_S V_S^M \subseteq V_N^m - I\!\!R_{\geq}^m$ and for every $\mathbf{z} \in E(V_N)$, the game defined as $v(S) = V_S^M \in V_S$, $v(N) = \mathbf{z} = Y^N$ is balanced. Hence there is an allocation of $\mathbf{z}$ in the cartesian product core of this vector-valued game and, therefore, in the strict preference core of (N,V). $\qquad\square$

The multicriteria linear production game is always balanced but not strictly balanced. The game in Example 1.1 is not strictly balanced.

4.2. Preference imputations nondominated by allocations.
Preference core

In the set of preference imputations of a game, the collective rationality principia can also be adopted considering nondominance rather than preference. That is, even if a player do not accept an allocation if it does not improve in every criterion at least one of the payoffs that he could get by himself, the coalition, as a group, would accept a total payoff if it is not worse than any of the payoffs that it can guarantee collectively.

Definition 1.6 *A preference imputation that allocates a vector in* $E(V_N, P)$ *is said to be a preference imputation nondominated by allocations (preference*

268

INDA) if no coalition has any objection to the allocation: $INDA(N, V; \cup) =$

$$= \{Y \in I(N, V; \cup) / Y^S \notin V_S \setminus E(V_S) \quad \forall S \subset N, \, |S| > 1\}.$$

In Example 1.1, allocation $Y = \begin{pmatrix} 72 & 120 & 70 \\ 29.03 & 53.14 & 78.86 \end{pmatrix}$ of vector $(262, 161.03) \in E(V_N)$ that is an INDA because the characteristic sets for the different coalitions are:

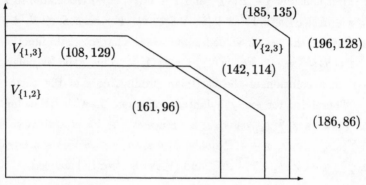

It is not difficult to prove that if there exists an efficient face $G \subseteq F_N$ such that $CG \cap E(V_N, P) \neq \emptyset$, we can allocate some vectors of the set $CG \cap E(V_N, P)$ by a preference INDA.

It follows from the definition, that $INDA(N, V; \cap) \subseteq INDA(N, V; \cup)$ because $I(N, V; \cap) \subseteq I(N, V; \cup)$. Moreover $INDA(N, V; \cup) \cap I(N, V; \cap) = INDA(N, V; \cap)$.

Componentwise preference that is required individually in the preference imputations, can be also extended to the coalitions. In this sense, a coalition will accept an allocation of an efficient payoff vector of V_N if and only if the payoffs that is assigned to the coalition improve in all the criteria some of the payoffs that the coalition can achieve by itself, that is, the payoffs improve some efficient vector of V_S.

Definition 1.7 *An allocation, Y, of vector $z \in E(V_N)$ is in the preference core of $(N, V) \in G^V$ if $Y^N = z$ and $Y^S \in E(V_S) + \mathbb{R}^m_{\geqq} \quad \forall S \subset N$. We denote $Y \in C(N, V; \cup, z)$. The preference core is the set: $C(N, V; \cup) = \bigcup_{z \in E(V_N)} C(N, V; \cup, z)$*

It follows from the above definition that $C(N,V;\cup) \subseteq INDA(N,V;\cup)$ and the inclusion relation may be strict.

4.3 Nondominated Core

If we consider the improvement concept based on the weak order, both individually and collectively, the solution concept that emerges is the nondominance core.

Definition 1.8 *The nondominated or generalized core of the game, $C(N,V)$, is the set: $C(N,V) = \{Y \in I^*(N,V) / Y^S \notin V_S \setminus E(V_S) \quad \forall S \subset N\}$.*

Due to the balancedness property, the core of the linear production multicriteria game is not empty 2. Moreover it is possible to find an allocation in the core for every vector $\mathbf{z} \in E(V_N)$. Nevertheless, it is important to find allocations of the nondominance core of the multiobjective linear production game in a systematic way. Such allocations can be obtained from the dual problem of the production problem. Let us consider the production problem for coalition $S \in \mathcal{N}$, with equality constraints (adding q slack variables):

$$\begin{aligned} max \quad & z(\mathbf{x}) = C\mathbf{x} \\ s.a: \quad & \mathbf{x} \in F_S, \end{aligned} \tag{1}$$

where $F_S = \left\{\mathbf{x} \in \mathbb{R}^{p+q} / A\mathbf{x} = B^S, \mathbf{x} \in \mathbb{R}^{p+q}_{\geq}\right\}$. The last q columns of $C \in \mathbb{R}^{m \times (p+q)}$ are null and matrix $A \in \mathbb{R}^{q \times (p+q)}$ has a $q \times q$ submatrix that is the identity.

The dual problem, see 10, is:

$$\begin{aligned} min \quad & g_S(U) = UB^S \\ s.a: \quad & U \in T \end{aligned} \tag{2}$$

where $T = \left\{U \in \mathbb{R}^{p+q} / UAw \leq Cw \quad \text{for no} \quad w \in \mathbb{R}^p_{\geq}\}\right\}$

It is possible to prove that from the efficient solutions of (2), solutions of the core can be obtained.

Theorem 1.3 *Let $\mathbf{x}^* \in F_N$ be an efficient solution of the linear production problem (1) for the grand coalition. There exists a solution of the dual problem (2), $U^* \in T$, such that $z(\mathbf{x}^*) = g_N(U^*)$. In addition, matrix $Z \in$*

$\mathbb{R}^{m \times n}$, *whose columns are obtained as* $Z^i = U^* B^i$, *is an allocation of the* *nondominance core.*

Proof: The existence of a solution of the dual problem 2, $U^* \in T$, such that $z(\mathbf{x}^*) = g_N(U^*)$, follows from the result established in 10 (Theorem 6). We are going to prove that matrix Z, with $Z^i = U^* B^i$, is an allocation of the nondominance core. First thing, we see that Z is an allocation of an efficient point of V_N because $Z^N = U^* B^N = g_N(U^*) = z(\mathbf{x}^*) \in E(V_N)$. Moreover, U^* is a feasible solution for the production problem of any other coalition $S \subset N$.

If U^* is an efficient solution of the dual problem for coalition S, it follows from Theorem 6 in 10, that there exists an efficient solution $\mathbf{x}^0$ of the primal problem, (1), such that $U^* B^S = C \mathbf{x}^0$, and hence $U^* B^S \in E(V_S)$.

If U^* is not an efficient solution of the dual problem (2), then $U^* B^S \notin E(V_S) - \mathbb{R}^m_{\geq}$ because the inequality $z(\mathbf{x}) \geq g(U)$ never holds when $\mathbf{x}$ and U are primal and dual feasible respectively (10, lema 3). $\qquad \square$

Remark that, by this procedure, it is possible to find an allocation of the nondominance core associated to each efficient vector of the characteristic set V_N, that is, all the feasible payoffs that the grand coalition can achieve admit a stable allocation among the players, because no coalition can improve its payoffs if it does not cooperate with the other players.

5. References

1. BIRD G.C.(1981) *Cores of Nonatomic Linear Production Games.* Mathematics of Operations Research, 6, pp. 420-423.

2. BONDAREVA O.N.(1963) *Some Applications of the Methods of Linear Programming to the Theory of Cooperative Games.* Problemy Kubernetiki, Vol. 10, pp. 119-139.

3. DERKD J.J.M., TIJS S.H. (1986) *Stable Outcome for Multi-Commodity Flow Games.* Methods of Operations Research, 55, pp. 493-504.

4. DERKD J.J.M., TIJS S.H. (1986) *Totally Balanced Games and Flow Games.* Methods of Operations Research, 54, pp. 335-347.

5. DUBEY P., SHAPLEY L.S. (1984) *Totally Balanced Games arising from Controled Programming Problems.* Mathematical Programming, 29, pp. 245-267.

6. ENGELBRECHT-WIGGANS, GRANOT D. (1985) *On Market Prices in Linear Production Games.* Mathematical Programming, 32, pp. 366-370.

7. GRANOT A. (1980) *A Generalized Linear Production Model. A Unifying Model.* Mathematical Programming, 34, pp. 212-222.

8. HAIMES Y., STEUER R. (EDS) (2000) *Research and Practice in Multiple Criteria Decision Making. Lecture Notes in Economics and Mathematical Systems, 487, pp. 125-136*

9. HINOJOSA M.A. (2000) *Juegos Cooperativos Vectoriales con Información Adicional.* Tesis Doctoral. Universidad de Sevilla.

10. ISERMANN H. (1976) *On Some Relations between a Dual Pair of Multiple Objective.* Operations Research, Vol. 22, pp. 33-41.

11. KALAI E. ZEMEL E. (1982) *Generalized Network Problems yielding Totally Balanced Games.* Operations Research, 30, pp. 998-1008.

12. NOUWELAND A. VAN DEN, AARTS H., BORM P. (1990) *Multi-Commodity Games.* Methods of Operations Research, Vol 63, pp. 329-338.

13. OWEN G. (1975) *On the Core of Linear Production Games.* Mathematical Programming, 9, 358-370.

14. ROSENMLLER J. (1994) *L.P.-games with Sufficiently Many Players.* International Journal of Game Theory.

15. TANINO T., MURANAKA Y., TANAKA M (1990) *On Multiple Criteria Characteristic Mapping Games.* Procceding of MCDM'92, Taipei, 1992, pp. 63-72.

Identifying Important Attributes for the Siberian Forests Management Using Rough Sets Analysis[*]

Matti Flinkman[1], Wojtek Michalowski[2], Sten Nilsson[3], Roman Slowinski[4], Robert Susmaga[4], and Szymon Wilk[4]

Abstract

This presentation discusses identification of attributes that are considered essential for a development of sustainable forest management practices in the Siberian forests. This goal is accomplished through an analysis of net primary production of phytomass (NPP), which is used to classify the Siberian ecoregions into compact and cohesive NPP performance classes. Rough Sets (RS) analysis is used as a data mining methodology for the evaluation of the Siberian forest database. In order to interpret relationships between various forest characteristics, so called *interesting rules* are generated on a basis of a reduced problem description.

Keywords: Rough sets, knowledge discovery, sustainable development, forest management

1. Introduction

Two key issues in the development of sustainable forest management practices in the boreal forest zone are:

---

[*] This is the abridged version of the paper to be published in *INFOR*.

[1] Department of Forest Industry Market Studies, Swedish University of Agricultural Sciences, Uppsala, Sweden.

[2] School of Business, Carleton University, Ottawa, Canada.

[3] Sustainable Boreal Forest Resources Project, International Institute for Applied Systems Analysis, Laxenburg, Austria.

[4] Institute of Computing Science, Poznan University of Technology, Poznan, Poland.

a) Identification and evaluation of the current and desired state of forest ecosystems that are essential for the proper functioning of the ecosystem; and

b) The study of the impact of alternative forest management regimes on the functioning of the ecosystem.

This paper deals primarily with the analysis of the current ecosystem functions of the Siberian forests by using a comprehensive database maintained at the International Institute for Applied Systems Analysis (IIASA). Knowledge established through such an analysis might, in turn, form a basis for further work on the development of sustainable management practices.

The analysis presented here draws on the framework established by the Statement of Principles on Sustainable Forest Management at the 1992 UN Conference on Environment and Development (UNCED, 1992). Despite the comprehensive nature of this framework, its principal shortcoming is that its components and performance indicators associated with them are treated in isolation rather than in a comprehensive manner (Nilsson, 1997a). In order to address this shortcoming, this paper relies on the *ecosystem functioning* as a core concept, implying that the appropriate and desirable functioning of all aspects of forest management is necessary to support ecosystem services.[1]

In this study, the considered forest ecosystem attributes are chosen from abiotic, biotic, and human induced factors, and thus describe the interactions between land-uses, vegetation types, forest density, site-class, age, and different aspects of human activities. The identification of the attributes that contribute the most to the explanation of the ecosystem functioning is a first step towards developing sustainable forest management practices. It is this step that is described in this paper in greater detail.

The data component of this study is described in Section 2. The data set contains information on a number of attributes recorded at ecoregion level. The decision as to which attributes should be selected is complex because there are a significant number of possible attributes. In keeping with the idea of a comprehensive approach, it is necessary to consider cross-classifications reflecting the different roles of attributes in describing different conditions. This task will be accomplished through the combination of a Rough Set (RS) analysis with a heuristic evaluation of the possible sets of attributes providing similar

---

[1] Delivery of ecosystem services involves: (1) Capture of solar energy and conversion into biomass that is used for food, building materials and fuels; (2) Breakdown of organic wastes and storage of heavy metals; (3) Maintenance of gas balance in the atmosphere that supports human life: absorption and storage of carbon dioxide and release of oxygen for breathable air; (4) Regeneration of nutrients in form essential to plant growth, e.g. nitrogen fixation and movement of those nutrients.

descriptive accuracy. The principles for RS analysis are introduced in Section 3. Use of the RS methodology on a data set derived from the Siberian forest database is also described in Section 3. Section 4 presents a discussion of the results.

2. Siberian Forest Database

The Siberian forest database contains information relevant to the cornerstone areas of the Sustainable Boreal Forest Resources Project at IIASA (Nilsson, 1997b). Nearly 5000 attributes describing abiotic, biotic, and human induced conditions are included in the database. The spatial coverage of the collected information is aggregated at different levels. The highest level covers the whole of Siberia. There are sub-levels for 65 administrative regions, 65 ecological regions (ecoregions), 360 landscapes, and 2500 forestry enterprises. All database items can be related to some spatial aggregation level that allows spatial descriptions of abiotic, biotic, and anthropogenic conditions.

For purposes of this study, data aggregated at the ecoregion level was extracted from the Siberian forest database (see Appendix 1). This data set contains a sample of the original abiotic and biotic attributes and attributes for human induced conditions. In addition, a number of modified attributes known as CODE-descriptors and SHDI-descriptors, describing the structure of certain distributions have been developed for each ecoregion. In creating the CODE-descriptor, the original distribution data (for example, the age distribution of a forested area) has been categorized into few (4-7) share classes. This allows the creation of a number of distribution "profiles". The SHDI-descriptors were created based on Shannon diversity index formula (Shannon and Weaver, 1962). The SHDI-descriptor represents the degree of diversity of the attribute under consideration. For example, an attribute with only a few dominating classes results in a low diversity value for the SHDI-descriptor, while an evenly distributed share results in a high value.

3. Problem Analysis

The study is based on the hypothesis that the classification of Siberian ecoregions into different classes based on the net primary production of phytomass (NPP) will reflect different types of land-use and biogeophysical conditions (Shvidenko, *et al.* 1997). The net primary production of phytomass is an estimated measure of an ecoregion's total production potential of phytomass in t/ha/year, calculated according to Bazilevich (1993). The NPP measure includes all land uses, including agricultural land, within an ecoregion. Therefore, such a classification will capture a number of the factors assumed to be associated with the level of ecosystem functioning. It is not a straightforward exercise to create a cohesive description of each ecoregion in terms of its ecosystem functioning, because there are a significant number of attributes that might be considered as the candidates for such a description. Therefore, RS analysis (Pawlak, 1991; Slowinski, 1992) was used to develop such a description. Methodological considerations associated with this issue are presented in Section 3.1, whereas the application of RS analysis to the NPP classification problem is described in Section 3.2.

An important aspect of any policy analysis is the explanation of the relationships between problem components. One of the best methods for conveying such information is provided by decision rules that are logical statements of the type *if... then...* We use them in our study to generate interesting rules for the reduced problem representation. The interesting rules provide a helpful explanation of the role of attributes and the significance of their specific values.

3.1. Methodological Considerations

The methodology used to analyze the relationships among the attributes describing the ecosystem functioning of the Siberian forests is based on RS theory. This theory was first proposed by Pawlak (1991) to study classification problems in a computer science. In order to obtain the most useful results from a basic RS analysis, it is considered best to use symbolic (qualitative) data rather than continuous-valued (quantitative) information. If quantitative information is used, the domains of continuous-valued attributes should be discretized (categorized) prior to the analysis. The data set under consideration consists of *objects* (also known as *examples* or *cases*) representing Siberian ecoregions. The characteristics of these ecoregions are described by discrete values of the attributes. The set of attributes is usually divided into two disjoint subsets, called *condition* and *decision* attributes. Condition attributes express some descriptive information about the ecoregions, whereas the decision attributes describe a classification assigned to the ecoregion. The set of ecoregions described by attributes and represented in a table format is called *a decision table*. This table is then further analyzed to reduce the number of condition attributes (such a reduced set is called *reduct*) while maintaining a good approximation of the original set. Detailed description of the RS theory and its applications can be found in Pawlak (1991) and Slowinski (1992) among others.

3.2. The NPP Classification Problem

The set of condition attributes used in the classification problem consists of[1]: MOUNTAIN, PERMAFROST, AV_AIR_TEM, AV_SOIL_TE, AV_MAX_SOI, AV_MIN_SOI, TOT_PRECIP, WIND, SUM_T10, SUM_T5, SUM_PREC10, SUM_PREC5, DURATION_1, DURATION_5, SNOW_COVER, Vext-SHDI, FA/Area, FF-CODE, FF-SHDI, BON-CODE, BON-SHDI, DENS-CODE, DENS-

---

[1] See Appendix 1 for a full list of the attribute and for an explanation of their abbreviations.

SHDI, AgAr-CODE, AgAr-SHDI, AgVo-CODE, AgVo-SHDI, POP/sqkm, Autow/sqkm, Railw/sqkm and Riverw/sqkm. The results of the analysis based on the above set of the attributes are described in the following section.

3.2.1 The Reduct

Each ecoregion was assigned into one of three NPP classes (L, M and H, denoting the *low*, *medium* and *high* class of the NPP, respectively), according to ecoregion's potential phytomass production capacity calculated according to Bazilevich (1993). Through the RS analysis, the original set of 31 attributes was then reduced and the following good *reduct* was identified: *relief conditions* (MOUNTAIN); *snow cover conditions* (SNOW_COVER); *share of forested area of total ecoregion area* (FA/Area); *forest fund profile consisting of forest land, non-forest land and lease* (FF-CODE); *age profile of growing stock consisting of 5 age class categories* (AgVo-CODE); and *density of railway network* (Railw/sqkm)

The *age profile of growing stock, share of forested area of total ecoregion area* and *forest fund profile consisting of forest land, non-forest land and lease* are all forest-related attributes. The *relief conditions* and *snow cover conditions* describe biogeophysical conditions, and the *density of railway network* can be considered as an indicator of ecoregion development. The reduction of the original set of 31 attributes to the 6 most relevant attributes constitutes a significant improvement over other studies due to the formal reduction of the original dataset without loss of information.

3.2.2 Generation of Interesting Rules

General knowledge statements were built using the interesting rules[1] (shown in Table 1) generated for the good *reduct*. Each row in Table 1 represents one decision rule. The conditional part of the rule is a conjunction of elementary conditions on those attributes for which values are specified (the elementary condition has the syntax *attribute = value*) and the decision part reflects assignment of an ecoregion to the specified NPP class. For example, rule 7 should be read as:

if AgVo-CODE equals to ABDBC and MOUNTAIN equals to 1, **then** NPP class is M.

An interpretation of this rule is as follows: **if** the distribution of growing stock into age classes is such that 0-5% of the growing stock is in the age class

---

[1] The principles of generating interesting rules are described in Mienko *et al.* (1996).

"youngest forest", 5-20% is "young forest", 40-60% is "middle aged forest", 5-20% is "immature forest", 20-40% is "mature and overmature forest", and relief conditions are mountainous, **then** the NPP class is medium.

The forest fund [1] profile (FF-CODE) appears to be the most frequent attribute present in conditional part of the interesting rules. This is particularly true for the high NPP class, where it appears in the conditional part of all decision rules. For the two other NPP classes, it appears in combination with a number of other attributes in most of the rules.

The column "relative rule strength" gives the percentage of all the ecoregions "covered" by a given rule (i.e., those that are classified into appropriate class by this rule). While generating the interesting rules, we use a threshold of 10%. That is, only those rules that "cover" at least 10% of the cases (ecoregions) are considered interesting rules.

4. Concluding Remarks

We evaluated the classification of the Siberian forests from the point of view of net primary production of phytomass. This required the incorporation of several descriptive aspects considered as essential for evaluating ecosystem functioning. Analysis of complex situations, characterized by many decision attributes of different character and different levels of detail, calls for a methodology that allows simplification of the descriptive requirements of the problem. In the case of the Siberian forest database, the RS methodology, enhanced with the procedure for identification of good reduct, enabled the development of a reduced (i.e., having fewer attributes) and compact description for the classification problem. The creation of such a compact description has advantages from a data mining perspective, as it requires less information to be collected and accessed, and it also facilitates analysis of data dependencies. Generation of the interesting rules demonstrates that it is possible to identify certain common features for ecoregions belonging to the same class.

There are some limitations to the data used in the analysis. As pointed out earlier, the net primary production of phytomass is an estimated measure of an ecoregion's total production potential of phytomass. Therefore, this measure does not give the actual phytomass and is not measured in situ. However, this was the only information available at the time of the study, and this data has been used in many international studies (e.g. Kolchugina and Vinson; 1993; Dixon et al., 1994; Krankina et al., 1996). On the other hand, it can be pointed out that aggregated Russian forest inventory and forest ecological data have been

---

[1] The "Forest Fund" consists of all forests and all land allocated for forest purposes

evaluated to be of the same quality as the inventories and data for other countries in the boreal zone (Raile, 1994).

Table 1. Interesting rules for the NPP classification problem[1]

Rule no.	NPP class	Elementary conditions						Relative rule strength
		AgVo-CODE	FA/Area	FF-CODE	MOUNTAIN	Railw/ sqkm	SNOW COVER	
1	L	AABAF						12%
4	L		0				LONG	56%
5	L			ECA	1		LONG	12%
6	L			ECA			LONG	12%
7	M	ABDBC			1			10%
8	M	AABBE			2			16%
9	M	ABDBC	1					10%
10	M		1	ECA		1		13%
11	M		1	GAA		0		13%
12	M	AACBD	1			1		10%
13	M		1	FBA	2		SHORT	10%
14	M		1		2	0	SHORT	16%
15	M			FBA	2	0	SHORT	10%
16	H		0	FBA	2			19%
17	H			FBA	2	1		19%
18	H		0	FBA		1		25%

[1] Values for the AgVo-CODE attribute represent different distributions of growing stock into age classes (youngest forest, young forest, middle aged forest, immature forest, and mature and overmature forest). Values of the FF-CODE attribute represent different distributions of land within forest fund into land use classes (forest land, non-forested lands, and 'long-term lease lands. The letter gives the share percentage ranging from <5% (A) to >95% (G)). Values of the MOUNTAIN attribute reflect different relief conditions, with 1 denoting mountain relief and 2 denoting plain relief condition. Values of the SNOW COVER attribute reflect different duration of a snow cover, with value LONG denoting long winter and SHORT denoting short winter. Values 0 and 1 for the attributes FA/Area and Railw/sqkm indicate either first or second interval generated by *Recursive Minimal Entropy Partitioning* discretization method (Fayyad and Irani, 1993) applied for these two attributes. All other attributes were discretized according to the value intervals provided by an expert.

In future research, some recent extensions of the RS methodology can be used for a more detailed study of Siberian forest database. In particular, extensions of RS methodology that concern attributes with preference ordered domains, and the approximation of classes by what are known as *dominance relations* instead of the classical indiscernibility relation (see Greco *et al.*, 1999), should prove useful for this kind of analysis.

Acknowledgements

The authors would like to thank Michael Gluck for comments on the first draft of the paper and Keith Compton for his editorial assistance.

R. Slowinski, R. Susmaga and S. Wilk wish to acknowledge financial support from the Polish Committee for Scientific Research (KBN). The Decision Analysis and Support Project at IIASA and Natural Sciences and Engineering Research Council of Canada (NSERC) supported research conducted by W. Michalowski while he was a senior research scholar at that institute.

References

Bazilevich, N.I. (1993). *Biological Productivity of Ecosystems of Northern Eurasia* (in Russian), Nauka, Moscow.

Dixon, R.K., Brown, S., Houghton, R.A., Solomon A.M., Trexler, M.C. and Wisniewski, J. (1994). Carbon Pools and Flux of Global Forest Ecosystems. *Science* Vol. 263, pp. 185-190.

Fayyad, U.M. and Irani, K.B. (1993). Multi-interval Discretization of Continuous-valued Attributes for Classification Learning. In: *Proceedings of the 13th International Conference on Artificial Intelligence*, Morgan Kaufmann Publishers, New York, pp. 1022-1027.

Greco, S., Matarazzo, B. and Slowinski, R. (1999). The Use of Rough Sets and Fuzzy Sets in MCDM. In: Gal, T., Hanne, T. and Stewart, T. (eds.), *Advances in Multiple-Criteria Decision Making*, Kluwer Academic Publishers, Boston, pp. 14.1-14.59.

Kolchugina, T.P. and Vinson, T.S. (1993). Comparison of Two Methods to Assess the Carbon Budget of Forest Biomes in the Former Soviet Union. *Water Air and Soil Pollution* Vol. 70, pp. 207-221.

Krankina, O.N., Harmon, M.E. and Winjum, J.K. (1996). Carbon Storage and Sequestration in the Russian Forest Sector. *Ambio* Vol. 25, pp. 396-404.

Mienko, R., Stefanowski, J., Tuomi, K. and Vanderpooten, D. (1996). Discovery-oriented Induction of Decision Rules. *Cahier du LAMSADE*, No. 141.

Nilsson, S. (1997a). Challenges for the Boreal Forest Zone and IBFRA. A Keynote address presented at the 7th International Boreal Forest Research Association Conference, Duluth, Minnesota, USA. pp. 16-20.

Nilsson, S. (ed.) (1997b). Dialogue on Sustainable Development of the Russian Forest Sector - Volume II. IIASA Interim Report (IR-97-010), International Institute for Applied Systems Analysis, Laxenburg.

Pawlak Z. (1991). *Rough Sets. Theoretical Aspects of Reasoning About Data.* Kluwer Academic Publishers, Dordrecht.

Raile, G. (1994). Evaluation of Russian Forest Inventory Data. International Institute for Applied Systems Analysis, Laxenburg. Unpublished manuscript.

Shannon, C.E and Weaver, W. (1962). *The Mathematical Theory of Communication.* University of Illinois Press, Urbana.

Shvidenko, A., Nilsson, S. and Roshov, V. (1997). Possibilities for Increased Carbon Sequestration through the Implementation of Rational Forest Management in Russia. *Water, Air and Soil Pollution* No. 94, pp. 137-162.

Slowinski, R. (ed.) (1992). *Intelligent Decision Support. Handbook of Applications and Advances of the Rough Set Theory.* Kluwer Academic Publishers, Dordrecht.

UNCED, (1992). The Global Partnership for Environment and Development. United Nations, Geneva.

Appendix 1

List of attributes used in the study

Attribute Name	Description
PhyProClass	Net Primary Production classes of Phytomass
MOUNTAIN	Relief conditions: mountain, plain or far east mountain
PERMAFROST	Permafrost: year round, seasonally or no frozen ground
AV_AIR_TEM	Average air temperature
AV_SOIL_TE	Average soil surface temperature
AV_MAX_SOI	Average max soil surface temperature
AV_MIN_SOI	Average min soil surface temperature
TOT_PRECIP	Average total precipitation
WIND	Average wind speed

Attribute Name	Description
SUM_T10	Total number of days during the growing season with average temperature above 10°C
SUM_T5	Total number of days during the growing season with average temperature above 5°C
SUM_PREC10	Total precipitation during the growing season for days with average temperature above 10°C
SUM_PREC5	Total precipitation during the growing season for days with average temperature above 5°C
DURATION_1	Duration of vegetation period where average temperature is above 10°C
DURATION_5	Duration of vegetation period where average temperature is above 5°C
SNOW_COVER	Duration of snow cover
Vext-SHDI	Shannon diversity index for vegetation types
FA/Area	Forested area of total ecoregion area in %
FF-CODE	Forest fund profile distributed by forest land, non-forest land, and lease
FF-SHDI	Shannon diversity index for forest fund profile
BON-CODE	Site class profile for all age classes
BON-SHDI	Shannon diversity index for site class profile of all age classes
DENS-CODE	Density class profile for all age classes
DENS-SHDI	Shannon diversity index for density class profile of all age classes
AgAr-CODE	Age class profile of total forested area
AgAr-SHDI	Shannon diversity index for age class profile of total forested area
AgVo-CODE	Age class profile of growing stock within total forested area
AgVo-SHDI	Shannon diversity index for age class profile of growing stock within total forested area
POP/sqkm	Population density per square kilometer
Autow/sqkm	Road density per square kilometer
Railw/sqkm	Railways density per square kilometer
Riverw/sqkm	Waterway density per square kilometer

On Optimization Model Formulation Using Neural Networks

Paweł Gąsiorowski

Division of Decision Analysis and Support,
 Warsaw School of Economics,
 Al. Niepodległości 162,
 02-554 Warsaw Poland;
 E-mail: pgasio@sgh.waw.pl

Abstract

Mathematical programming is a widely used tool in Operational Research. The first - and usually the most difficult - step of problem solving requires formulation of the model: finding the mathematical description of the relationships between decisions and their outcomes. The researcher is faced with the problem of finding the proper functions and their parameters. This kind of problems is dealt with using approximation theory.

The paper presents theorems and assumptions for using neural networks as approximators of functions in formulation of the optimization models. Thanks to neural networks' approximation capabilities the difficulties connected with finding the functional forms of relationships and their parameters can be avoided.

The method of identification of parameters is illustrated with an exemplary application in the area of bank credit portfolio optimization.

1.   Introduction

Management of organizations requires continuous decision making. Some of those decisions can be taken without many problems because either the best choice of the course of action is obvious or the decision is not important enough. In such cases, the decision making process is rather informal and intuitive (Bierman et. al., 1986). When the economic environment becomes more complicated, the decision making is more difficult as all courses of actions and their outcomes should be evaluated in systematic and objective way. The objective evaluation can be achieved by the analysis of the numerical data. Decision making based on analysis of numerical values uses the idea of the mathematical model, i.e. mathematical representation of the decision situation that enables the evaluation of possible decision alternatives (Knowles, 1989). Optimization models deal with the choice of the decision out of the set of feasible decisions.

Formulation (or identification) of the mathematical optimization problem requires two steps: defining what is the decision and evaluation of the relations between the decisions and their results, what can be further subdivided into *specification* of the relationships between variables and *estimation* of those relationships. The specification is understood as the determination of the functional form of relationships between the variables. After having this assumption one can use historical data to find the parameters of relationships (estimation). Specification and estimation of the function can be called approximation of the function.

One of the fundamental assumptions of mathematical optimization is the assumption that the parameters of the model are known (Schroeder, 1999). In practice, the parameters of objective function and parameters of constraints are rarely known with certainty (Krajewski and Ritzman, 1996). Therefore, in management optimization problem, the identification of criteria functions and constraints functions is based on the historical data that shows decisions and their outcomes. Specification of the functional form of the relationship on the basis of historical data can be performed with classical statistical methods, such as regression analysis or analysis of averages (Grabowski, 1980). However, the researcher must know the economic theory that explains certain results, i.e. the functional form of relationship between variables, before starting the search of parameters. In practice (Charemza and Deadman, 1997), when the theory is not known, the researcher is doing tests on many possible forms of relationships and chooses the best one. The choice is based on statistical methods enabling the verification of method's assumptions. Therefore, the researcher that looks for the functional relationships usually spends a lot of time on tedious and expensive searches. After having the functional form of relationship, the researcher has to spend at least the same amount of time on estimating function parameters.

In the ill-structured problems there are relationships which are difficult to be found with traditional methods due to the high preparation costs of the data that is not used in the normal course of management or due to the computational problems. In such cases the researcher must choose the functional form either on the basis of the intuition or on the basis of statistical test. There is also a risk that the data obtained in this way can be biased due to the bad understanding of relationships between economic processes or biased measurements. What is more, if the functional form is misidentified, the conclusions drawn out of the model can be non-relevant. The problem of bad decisions made with the usage of decision models is discussed in the literature (Bierman et al., 1986) showing that the main reasons of bad decisions were omission of important variables in the model and errors in finding relationships between variables.

The difficulties connected with the necessity of functional form search can be eliminated with the neural network methodology approach. The method presented in the paper should solve following problems connected with the formulation of the optimization problem: inclusion of relevant variables, user-friendly identification of relationships and the possibility of solving ill-structured problems.

2. Multiple criteria decision problem

In the mathematical optimization model there are a) *decision variables*, b) one or many *objective functions* that are defined on decision variables and for which we are looking for maximum or minimum and c) several *constraints* on the decision variables. The precise description of the mathematical optimization model is as follows.

Definition 1 (Galas et al., 1987): The set $D=\{x \in \mathbf{R}^n: g(x) \le b\}$, $D \subset \mathbf{R}^n$, where mapping $g:D \to \mathbf{R}^m$ is given by a family of m functions g_i, is said to be *feasible set*.

Definition 2 The problem of finding all $x_0 \in D$ that fulfil the condition: $\neg \exists x \in D \ \mathbf{f}(x) \ge \mathbf{f}(x^0)$, where mapping $\mathbf{f}:D_f \to \mathbf{R}^q$, $q>1$, $\mathbf{f}=[f_1,...,f_q]$, has components $f_k : D_f \to R, k \in \overline{1,q}, D \subset D_f \subset R^n$ is said to be the *mathematical maximization* problem with objective functions $f_k \ k \in \overline{1,q}$ over D. The vector x represents the decision.

Let us observe that the formulation of the problem of mathematical optimization requires identification the functions g_i and f_k.

3. Neural Networks approximation capabilities

Neural network is a concept that describes an algorithm of numerical data processing based on the analogy to the structure of neurons in human brain. The algorithm is defined with data processing units called neurons. Each neuron is an input-output unit, the example of which is shown on Figure 1.

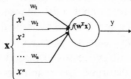

Figure 1. Graph called neurone is an algorithm made with function fl.. It is an input-output unit described by n inputs xi, n weights wi and activation function f. The output is called y. Source: [McCoulohh and Pitt, 1943].

Definition 3 (Żurada, 1996): A mapping $f_i: \mathbf{R}^n \times \mathbf{R}^n \to \mathbf{R}$, $f_i(\mathbf{x},\mathbf{w}) = f(\mathbf{w}^T\mathbf{x}) = y$, where $f: \mathbf{R} \to \mathbf{R}$ and $\mathbf{x}$, $\mathbf{w} \in \mathbf{R}^n$ is said to be *neural mapping*.

The function f is called neuron *activation function*, the vector $\mathbf{x}$ is called *neuron stimulation input vector*. Vector $\mathbf{w}$ is called *weights vector*. Value $\mathbf{w}^T\mathbf{x}$ is interpreted as *joint neuron stimulation*, and the value of activation function for the neuron joint stimulation is interpreted as the output i.e. *neuron reaction for the stimulation x*.

As an analogy to the human neural system, we can say that the reaction (output) of one neuron can be one of the stimulations (inputs) of the other neuron or neurons. Therefore it is possible to create such connection of neurons in which all inputs of the certain neuron are the reaction of the other neurons to the certain initial stimulation. It means that it is possible to create the neural network by connecting neuron outputs with inputs of next neurons. Such a network can have many inputs and many outputs and each neuron can have individual activation function and weights. An example of 9 neurons network is shown on the Figure 2.

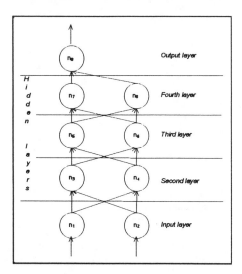

Figure 2. Example of the three hidden layer neural network.

Neural network shown on Figure 2 consists of 9 neurons expressed as circles. The weights are symbolized by connections between layers. This network has following layers: first, also called an input layer (neurons n_1, and n_2), second (neurons n_3 and n_4), third (neurons n_5, n_6), fourth (neurons n_7 and n_8), fifth, the output layer (n_9). The second, third and fourth layers create so called *hidden layers*.

When the initial vector $\mathbf{x}$ is given to the network it means that the input vector is directed to the first layer of neurons. In case of the network shown on Figure 2 this is the vector $\mathbf{x} \in \mathbf{R}^2$ such as $\mathbf{x} = [x_1, x_2]$. The first co-ordinate of vector $\mathbf{x}$ is directed to neuron n_1, the second coordinate is directed to neuron n_2. It is assumed that those neurons do not process the input information and carry it to the first hidden layer. The processed signal from the first hidden layer is directed to the next hidden or output layer. The output layer gives one or several *theoretical values* received after all mappings taking place in the network. The network shown on Figure 2 calculates one theoretical value on the output of neuron n_9. In further divagations we will call the m layer network such a network that has one input layer, m hidden layers and the output layer.

Let us begin with the analysis of one layer neural network with n units in the hidden layer that can process r element vector. Figure 3 shows such an example of network on which, for simplicity reasons, connections between neurons numbered from 3 to $r-1$ in the input layer and neurons numbered from 5 to $n-1$ in the hidden layer were omitted. The connections between neurons numbered from 5 to $n-1$ in the hidden layer and the output neuron were also omitted.

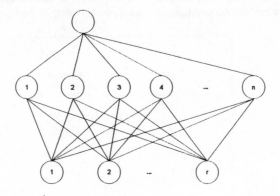

Figure 3. One layer neural network with one element in output layer, n elements in the hidden layer and r elements in input layer.

To describe the mathematical transformations taking place in one layer neural network with one output unit, n elements in the hidden layer and r elements in the input layer we will use notion of one layer functional (Modha and Hecht-Nielsen, 1993).

Definition 4: The mapping $F:\mathbf{X}\rightarrow\mathbf{R}$ such as $F(\mathbf{u})=\sum_{i=1}^{n}\beta_i\psi(A_i(\mathbf{u}))$, where $u\in X,\ \beta_i\in R,\ \ n\in N;\ \psi:R\rightarrow R$ and $A_i(\mathbf{u})$ is defined as: $A_i(\mathbf{u})=b_i+\sum_{k=1}^{r}w_{ki}u_k,\ for\ i=1,...,n$ is said to be the *one layer neural functional*. Set of all possible mappings F with given ψ, n, and the metric space X will be marked as $MF^n_\psi(X\rightarrow\mathbf{R})$ and will be interpreted as the set of one layer functionals with n units in the hidden layer.

Set $MF_\psi(X,\mathbf{R})$ of all one layer functionals with any number of hidden units is marked as: $MF_\psi(X,R)=\bigcup_{k=1}^{\infty}MF_\psi^k(X,R)$

Such mapping F is realized by one layer network with n units (neurons) in the hidden unit. The neural mapping has natural graphical interpretation that enables for interpretation as neural networks. Such mapping with two neurons in the hidden layer and three neurons in the input layer is shown on Figure 4.

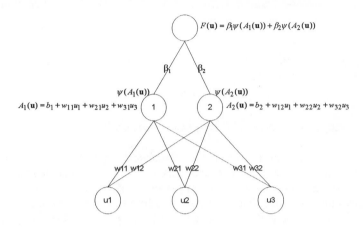

Figure 4. Mapping F realised by one layer neural network with two units in the hidden layer and three units in the input layer.

4.   Approximation with layer functionals

In this part of the paper we will present basic approximation definitions. Those definitions will be used for definition of approximation with the neural networks.

Definition 5: Let $\mathbf{w} \in \mathbf{R}^n$; vector $\mathbf{x} \in Z \subset \mathbf{R}^n$; function $H(\mathbf{w}, \mathbf{x}) = H(\mathbf{w}^{\circ} \mathbf{x}) : \mathbf{R} \to \mathbf{R}$ and function $G : \mathbf{R}^n \to \mathbf{R}$. *Approximation problem* of function G with function $H(\mathbf{w}, \mathbf{x})$ is a problem of finding such values of $\mathbf{w}$ that $\sup\limits_{\mathbf{x} \in Z} \left\| G(\mathbf{x}) - H(\mathbf{w}, \mathbf{x}) \right\|_Z$ reaches its minimum.

Definition 6: Let's consider any compact set $Z \subset \mathbf{R}^n$, continuous function $G : Z \to \mathbf{R}^s$ and set Θ of continuous functions in form of $H(\mathbf{w}, \mathbf{x})$. If for every $\varepsilon > 0$ there is such a function $H \in \Theta$, that the solution of approximation problem with function $H(\mathbf{w}, \mathbf{x})$ fulfils condition: $\sup\limits_{\mathbf{x} \in Z} \left\| G(\mathbf{x}) - H(\mathbf{w}, \mathbf{x}) \right\|_Z < \varepsilon$ then set Θ is an *uniform approximator* of function G.

Notice: We know, that the function G exists, but we do not know that function, therefore we look for the approximation of this function among the elements of set Θ.

Definition 7: Let set Δ be the set of continuous functions G. If for each function $G \subset \Delta$ set Θ is an approximator of uniform functions G, then set Θ is an *universal approximator* of Δ.

We assume that the values of function h(**x**) and its arguments are known for a finite number of points *i*. We assume that any continuous function that is a solution of approximation problem of function h(x) over set Z is also the solution of approximation problem of function h over the set spanned by the set Z.

Let X is a normed linear space over **R**. Let C(X,**R**) is set of all continuous real valued functionals with norm induced by $\|.\|_K$ where $\||\,F\,\||_K = \sup_{u \in K} |\,F(u)\,|$ and K is the compact subset of X.

The following part will cover approximation theorems with one layer and multilayer neural networks.

4.1 Approximation with one layer functional

One layer functional is a class of mathematical algorithms. The parameters of one layer functional for given activation function are number of neurons in the hidden layer and weights values for the neurons of this layer. Stone Weierstrass theorem allows to prove that it is possible to find such set of those parameters for a specific class of activation functions, that the mapping performed by one or set of one layer functionals is an universal function approximator. The process of finding weights is called *learning of neural network*. The process is aimed at the solution of approximation problem.

Definition 8 (Żurada, 1996): Let there would be a norm ρ, $r \in R^+$, **w** $\in K(\mathbf{w}^*, r)$ $\subset \mathbf{R}^n$, $\mathbf{x} \in \mathbf{R}^n$, function H(**w**,**x**):$\mathbf{R} \rightarrow \mathbf{R}^k$, and h(**x**):$\mathbf{R} \rightarrow \mathbf{R}^k$. *Learning of the neural network* is the process of solving of the approximation problem through the search of vector **w*** that gives (in sense of norm ρ) approximation of function h(x) with the chosen function H(**w**, **x**) for the series of *i* learning experiments.

For the chosen norm ρ the optimal values of parameter **w*** are found such as (Poggio and Girosi, 1990): $\exists r\, \forall \mathbf{w} : \rho[H(\mathbf{w}^*, \mathbf{x}), h(\mathbf{x})] \leq \rho[H(\mathbf{w}, \mathbf{x}), h(\mathbf{x})]$. Norm $\rho[H(\mathbf{w}, \mathbf{x}), h(\mathbf{x})]$ is the measurement of fit of H(**w**, **x**) to h(**x**). It is common to use as this norm a sum of squared differences between the theoretical values computed by the mapping H(**w**, **x**) and empirical values of h(**x**). Vector **w*** is the local extremum of function $\rho[H(\mathbf{w}, \mathbf{x}), h(\mathbf{x})]$ with respect to $\mathbf{w} \in \mathbf{R}^m$. The problem of finding the global extremum is not solved yet, therefore in this paper we will concentrate on local extremum. Number *k* corresponds to the number of outputs from the neural network.

Definition 9 (Modha and Hecht-Nielsen, 1993): If function $\psi: \mathbf{R} \rightarrow [0,1]$ is a non-descending function and $\lim_{x \to -\infty} \psi(x) = 0$, *and* $\lim_{x \to \infty} \psi(x) = 1$, then the function ψ is called *squashing function*.

The neural network literature calls squashing function ψ the neural activation function. The literature shows several types of activation function that belong to the class of squashing functions (Żurada, 1996; Tadeusiewicz, 1993; Masters, 1996).

Theorem 1 (Modha and Hecht-Nielsen, 1993): For any normed linear space X and squashing function ψ, one layer functionals $MF_\psi(X,\mathbf{R})$ are dense in $C(X,\mathbf{R})$.

The proof of this theorem is presented in (Modha and Hecht-Nielsen, 1993). The conclusion that can be drawn from Theorem 1 says that the one layer functionals are uniform approximators of continuous functionals. This conclusion leads to the statement that it is possible to approximate any real valued functional with one layer neural network.

4.2   *Approximation with multi layer functional*

The above divagations can be generalized for the complex neural network that has one output element and s hidden layers. Let us consider the network in which the elements of hidden layer are one layer neural networks. An example of such a net is shown on Figure 5.

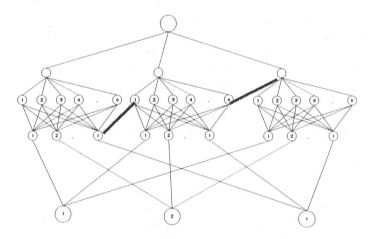

Figure 5. Multilayer network built out of three one layer networks with r - elements in the input layer, one element in output layer. Plain lines connecting elements of the net represent real valued weights. No lines mean weights equal to zero.

Weights marked as plain lines on Figure 5 can take any real values. There is an assumption that weights between some elements of the network are equal zero. Such weights can be illustrated by thick gray lines connecting: a) one of the elements in the hidden layer of single network with the output element of the neighboring network or b) one of the elements in the input layer of the single network with the element from the hidden layer of neighboring network. Other weights equal to zero were not drawn. Let us remind that in the single network weights between the input layer and hidden layer are equal one. Hence, with the assumption of weights equal to zero between chosen elements of network, the network presented on Figure 5 can simplified to the one presented on Figure 6.

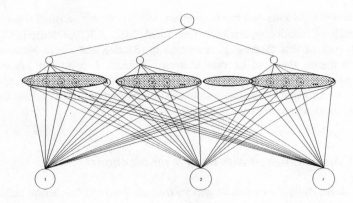

Figure 6. Multi layer network built out of k one-layer networks with r elements in the input layer and one element in the output layer. The internal networks are presented inside grey shadowed ellipses.

The clarity requires presenting a definition of the internal network.

Definition 10: Internal network is such a multi element network that possesses at least one hidden layer and output layer. The hidden layer of such a network processes values taken from the outputs of other internal networks or values taken from outputs from input elements of the multi layer network.

Let us consider the general case of network that consists of k one layer internal networks that lay in one layer (see Figure 6). Let us assume that on the output of such a network we want to approximate continuous function $F(u)$ defined on any compact set.

Theorem 2: Any real value function $F(\mathbf{u})$ defined on compact set can be approximated with accuracy of ε with n layer neural network.

The proof of Theorem 2 is presented in (Gąsiorowski and Kamiński, 1999). The proof uses functional analysis and uses the assumption that the derivative of function ψ takes absolute value not larger than M>0. The proof of Theorem 2 leads to conclusion that requirement to get accuracy of ε on the output of the whole compound network makes it necessary to get higher and higher accuracy on the outputs from the internal networks. This requirement is illustrated on Figure 7, that presents specific multi layer network with one hidden element in layers 3, 4, 5, 6.

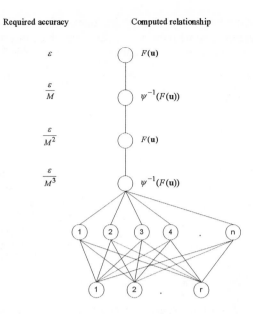

Required accuracy Computed relationship

Figure 7. Multi layer network. Overall accuracy of output approximation ε requires that output from each layer is more and more accurate.

Figure 7 can lead to such conclusion that it is possible to have situation in which addition of new layers to the neural network does not improve the quality of approximation as accuracy on outputs from single layers is required to be more and more precise. The consideration for one output neuron networks can be extended for the n-layer network with d outputs. It can be proven (Gąsiorowski and Kamiński 1999) that with the coordinate converging norm, for any n it is possible to build n layer neural network that is an uniform approximator of function $T:\mathbf{R}^r \rightarrow \mathbf{R}^d$.

Above mentioned properties allow for usage of neural networks also for the identification of mathematical optimization problems. The optimization model formulated with neural networks can be solved with non-linear solvers.

5. Example - one criteria bank loan portfolio optimization.

The problem of optimization the bank loan portfolio lays in finding such loan portfolio structure that induces proper income and acceptable risk. The banks have to consider governmental safety regulations and use their equity efficiently. The regulations are expressed in form of financial ratios. In this example we will analyze two groups of loans: corporate loans and private loans. The ratios for analysis would be: share of irregular loans in net assets of the bank (ILR), income ratio (IR), the reserve coverage of irregular loans (RC), the Cook's ratio (CR), the coverage of loan portfolio with the equity (EC), the share of groups of loans in net assets of the bank. The definitions of ratios are given in Table 1.

Ratio	Definition
Income ratio	$IR = \dfrac{\text{Interest revenues}}{\text{NetAssets}}$
Irregular Loans Ratio	$ILR = \dfrac{\text{Irregula loans}}{\text{Net Assests}}$
Cook's ratio	$CR = \dfrac{\text{Banks own funds}}{\text{Weighted sum of assets}}$
Equity coverage	$PKKW = \dfrac{\text{Equity}}{\text{Loans}}$
Reserves coverage	$WRR = \dfrac{\text{Reserves for arrears}}{\text{Irregular loans}}$

Table 1. Optimization ratios

The literature discusses required levels of above mentioned ratios. Following (Misińska 1995; Boffey et. al., 1995) and the Polish Banking Law this can be described as the following set of inequalities RC≤0.7; 8≤CR≤17; EC≤0.11; x_1+x_2≤0.6; x_1≥0.1; x_2≥0.05, where x_1 is the share of corporate loans in bank's net assets and x_2 is the share of private loans in bank's net assets. As the optimization criteria we can take maximization of IR or minimization of ILR.

Let us assume that the relationship between the loan portfolio structures and values of the ratios can be written as: $IR(x)=y_1=f_1(x)$; $ILR(x)=y_2=f_2(x)$; $RC(x)=g_1(x)$; $CR(x)=g_2(x)$; $EC(x)=g_3(x)$.

Thus the optimization model that reflects the decision problem can be written as

$$f_1(x)\rightarrow max \ (or) \ f_2(x)\rightarrow min$$

subject to:

$$\begin{cases} g_1(\mathbf{x}) \geq 0.7 \\ 8 \leq g_2(\mathbf{x}) \leq 17 \\ g_3(\mathbf{x}) \geq 0.11 \\ x_1 + x_2 \leq 0.6 \\ x_1 \geq 0.1 \\ x_2 \geq 0.05 \end{cases}$$

The neural network that should approximate mappings f*i and gi* is assumed to be the multi layer neural network with three hidden layers (see Figure 2). The activation function is a squashing function that makes mapping according to

formula $y = \dfrac{x}{|x|} \ln(1+|x|)$

5.1. Approximation of the relationships

The computations were made with Neural Network Development Tool ver. 1.40. The software uses Levenberg - Marquardt method for the network training. Learning process was started with randomly generated initial weights. The example is based on the monthly data (years 1994-1995) taken from one of the Polish banks. The maximum number of iterations was constrained to 1000. The errors for approximation are shown on Figure 8 and Figure 9.

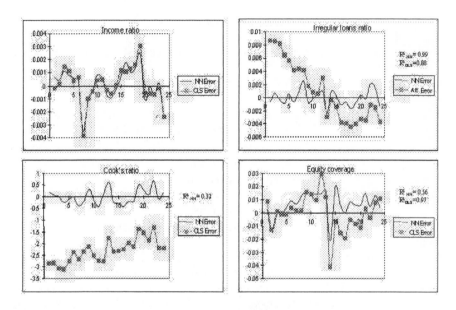

Figure 8. Approximation errors for selected ratios. The errors were calculated for the neural network (NN), analysis of regression (OLS) and average estimation (AE).

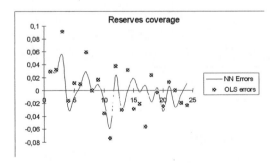

Figure 9. Approximation errors for reserve coverage ratio. The errors were calculated for the neural network (NN) and analysis of regression (OLS).

As it can be seen from the above figures the errors that were made by neural network are much smaller than the errors made by for example Ordinary Least Squares Method. There was one case when the regression analysis did not give relevant estimations e.g. for Cook's ratio. In this case neural network approximation was much better than the approximation with regression analysis. In cases where regression analysis gave good results, approximation with neural networks was more accurate.

5.2   Solution of the decision problem.

When the form and parameters of functional relationships are found we can write the optimization problem as:

$$f_1^*(x) -> max \text{ or } f_2^*(x) -> min$$

subject to:

$$x \in X \subset \mathbf{R}^n$$
$$g_1^*(x) \le b_1$$
$$g_2^*(x) \le b_2$$
$$g_3^*(x) \le b_3$$
$$x_1 + x_2 \le 0.6$$
$$x_1 \ge 0.1$$
$$x_2 \ge 0.05$$

where f_1^*, f_2^*, g_1^*, g_2^*, g_3^* stand for mappings realized by multi layer functionals.

Optimization problem was solved with non linear Solver for MsExcel. Some optimization scenarios were considered: minimization of irregular loans in bank net assets, maximization of income ratio and minimization of irregular loans in net assets with the constraint on income ratio to be equal 0.3. Table 2 shows results for those optimizations.

Objective	x_1	x_2	f_1^* IR	f_2^* ILR	g_1^* RC	g_2^* CR	g_3^* EC
min NN	23%	9%	0.046	0.057	0.728	9.226	0.110
max WP	18%	25%	0.675	0.147	0.700	9.237	0.113
min NN, WP = 0.3	18%	11%	0.300	0.059	2.254	9.229	0.110

Table 2. Optimization results

6.   Concluding remarks

In the paper we showed assumptions and theorems for formulation of the optimization model with neural networks. The neural networks proved to be successful in formulation of the difficult problem of bank's loan portfolio structure optimization and showed better approximation performance than statistical methods. The optimal structure could be found with spreadsheet Solver. The mappings found with neural networks were generalizing tendencies of historical data. Those nonlinear mappings were found without the tedious search of many functional forms of relationships.

One of the possible problems connected with application of this method is the lack of interpretation of network weights what implies difficulties in interpretation of resulting mapping. This difficulty implies that till now there is no methodology of estimation of network forecast or extrapolation error *ex-ante*.

A challenge for future research is application of neural methodology for solving of multicriteria optimization problems and the choice of optimization method capable of solving the model formulated with neural networks. Such a method should not converge to the local extreme of optimized functions.

References

1. Bierman, Bonini, Hausman, Quantitative Analysis for Business Decisions, IRWIN, Homewood, 1986
2. Boffey R., Robson G.; Bank Credit Risk Management; Managerial Finance November 1995
3. Charemza W., Deadman D; New Econometrics; PWE; Warszawa; 1997 (*in Polish*)
4. Galas Z., Nykowski I., Żółkiewski Z.; Multicirteria programming; PWE; Warsaw; 1987 (*in Polish*)
5. Gąsiorowski P.; Application of Neural Networks as functionals approximators on the example of bank loan portfolio optimization; Badania statutowe 03/S/0070/98 Institute of Econometrics; Warsaw School of Economics; 1998 (*in Polish*)
6. Gąsiorwoski P.; Bi-Referential evaluation of bank loan portfolio with neural networks; Proceedings of the Econometrics Workshop Conference, Warsaw School of Economics Press, Forthcoming, (*in Polish*)
7. Gąsiorowski P., Kamiński B.; On application of neural networks in identification of approximation problem; Badania statutowe 03/S/0016/99 Institute of Econometrics; Warsaw School of Economics; 1999 (*in Polish*)
8. Grabowski W.; Mathematical programming; PWE; Warszawa; 1980 (*in Polish*)
9. Hartman E., Keeler J., Kowalski J.; Layered Neural Networks with Gaussian Hidden Units as Universal Approximations; Neural Computation; 2, 1990; p. 210-215
10. Hornik K.; Approximation Capabilities of Multilayer Feedforward Networks; Neural Networks; vol 4, 1991; p. 251-257
11. Hornik K., Stinchcombe M., White H.; Multilayer feedforward networks are universal approximators; Neural Networks, vol 2., p. 359-366; 1989
12. Knowles T., Management Science Building and Using Models, Irwin 1989
13. Krajewski, Ritzman, Operations Management, Strategy and Analysis,

Addison Wesley Publishing Company, 1996, Reading
14. Masters T.; Neural Networks in practice; WNT; Warszawa; 1996 (*in Polish*)
15. McCulloch W.S, Pitt W.; A logical calculus of ideas immanent in nervous activity; Bulletin of Mathematical Biophysics 5; p 115-123; 1943
16. Misińska D. Commercial bank accounting, Fundacja Rozwoju Rachunkowości w Polsce, 1995, Warszawa (*in Polish*)
17. Modha D.S., Hecht-Nielsen R.; Multilayer Functionals, article in Taylor J.G; Mathematical Approaches to Neural Netowrks; North Holland; Amsterdam; 1993
18. Poggio T., Girosi F.; Networks for approximation and learning; Proc. IEEE; 78, nr 9, 1481-1497; 1990
19. Powell T.; Approximation Theory; ITP.;1980
20. Schroeder R.,Operations Management, Decision Making in the Operations Function, Mc Graw-Hill 1993 New York
21. Tadeusiewicz R.; Neural networks; Akademicka Oficyna Wydawnicza RM; Warszawa; 1993 (*in Polish*)
22. Żurada J., Barski M., Jędruch W.; Artificial neural networks; PWN; Warszawa; 1996 (*in Polish*)

The Design of the Physical Distribution System with the Application of the Multiple Objective Mathematical Programming. Case Study

Maciej Hapke[1], Andrzej Jaszkiewicz[1], Jacek Żak[2]

[1]Institute of Computing Science
Poznań University of Technology
ul. Piotrowo 3a, 60-965 Poznań, Poland
{Jaszkiewicz|Hapke}@cs.put.poznan.pl
www-idss.cs.put.poznan.pl/{~jaszkiewicz|~hapke}

[2]Institute of Working Machines & Vehicles
Poznań University of Technology
ul. Piotrowo 3, 60-965 Poznań, Poland,
jacekzak@put.poznan.pl

Abstract

The paper presents the multiobjective optimization of the all-Polish physical distribution system of cosmetics, detergents and washing articles. The research report refers to a real life case. The optimization process is focused on minimization of both total distribution cost and the delivery time within the distribution system. The primary concern of the project is to define the number and the location of the warehouses in the distribution network. The optimization process leads to the redesign of the existing distribution system. The problem is formulated in terms of bi-criteria mathematical mixed-integer programming. It has been solved with the application of an extended version of MS Excel Solver - Premium Solver Plus. A set of Pareto-optimal distribution systems has been generated. The number of Regional Distribution Centers (RDC-s) ranges from 7 to 23 in Pareto-optimal solutions. The results of the experiment are promising.

Introduction

Planning and designing of the distribution system in real life situations is a very complex and comprehensive task [6]. The whole process can be divided into the following stages [6], [7], [8]:

- designing of the distribution network, which primarily concentrates on the definition of the warehouses location,
- definition of routes and assignment of vehicles and crews to the routes,
- assignment of duties to specific crews.

The whole task involves solving a sequence of vehicle routing and scheduling problems. Those problems have been extensively considered in the last 20 years [2], [10]. Many comprehensive problems referring to the physical distribution are presented in the works of A. McKinnon [5] and D. Ross [6]. Some authors [1], [4] present concepts focused on designing and redesigning of the distribution systems.

The objective of this research is to redesign the distribution network (first stage of the whole process). The primary concern of the project is to define the number and the location of the warehouses as well as the service area of each warehouse.

The distribution network is designed for an international company based in Warsaw, Poland. The company entered Polish market at the beginning of 90's and acquired two production plants located in two large Polish cities. The company focuses on the production and sales of cosmetics, detergents and washing articles. The annual turnover of the company is roughly $100 million (400 million Polish zloty – PLN). 85% of the turnover is generated at the Polish local market and the remaining 15% is an export to Eastern European countries. At the Polish market the company's products are mainly sold to wholesalers (60% of sales) and the chains of large retailers (hipermarkets, supermarkets) – 20% of sales.

The company belongs to 6 major players at the Polish detergent/cosmetic market. It's market share equals to 15%. Compared to its competitors the company has a low net profit margin   (-4.0% of sales). Due to this fact it is very much concerned about it's costs, including distribution cost, which amount to 2.5% of sales.

The company objective, however, is to increase the market share and make the company's products available at each retail shop. In the company's top management opinion this goal can be obtained through the redesign of the distribution system, which should be more reliable and more flexible. The target for the distribution system in 2000 is to fulfill each customer's order and deliver the required products within 24 hours. Delivery time should be further decreased in the next years, reaching the level of 4-6 hours in the 2003. This should satisfy customers' expectations and requirements and make the company's slogan: "Our products in each Polish home", rational.

The Existing Distribution System

The existing distribution system is based on two production plants and two warehouses located in cities A and B (see Figure 1). Both are located next to the production facilities.

Due to the fact that the production profile and the product portfolio are different in the production plants in A and B trunking between warehouses is required. It amounts to 45% of the total number of tkm covered by the distribution system.

The order fulfillment process is managed from location B, where all the customers' orders are collected and processed. Warehousing and material handling is carried out by the company itself while the transportation service (including loading, delivery and unloading) is outsourced. The transportation service provider is located in A, where all the vehicle routes are planned and designed every day. Specialized vehicle routing software is used to this end. The transportation fleet is available both in A and B and the customers are served from both locations. Each warehouse has a certain area to cover, which corresponds to a concrete number of customers C_{1A}, C_{2A}, ..., C_{nA}, and C_{1B}, C_{2B}, ..., C_{nB} served (see fig. 1). The total number of customers is about 400. The products are delivered by 24 tractor – semi trailer units with a capacity of 33 Europallets each.

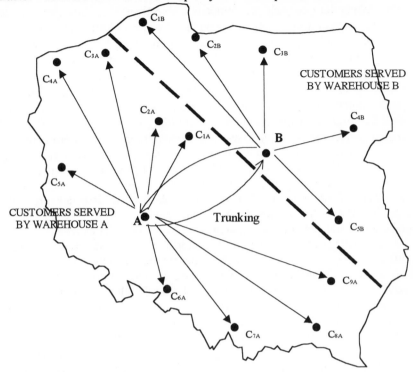

Figure 1.   The existing distribution system

Three major business processes can be distinguished in the distribution system, including order fulfillment process, inventory management process and transportation process. The most costly is the transportation process that amounts to 80% of the total distribution cost. Order fulfillment and inventory cost are equal to 5% and 15% of the total distribution cost, respectively. The overall annual distribution cost are equal to $2.5 million (10 million PLN).

As far as delivery time is concerned, the existing distribution system guarantees 48-hour deliveries in the majority of cases. The customer service level (defined as a product availability percentage) is 95%. High percentage of customer service requires a substantial level of inventory in the whole distribution system that amounts to 4% of annual sales. Based on the customers' inquiries one can also conclude that customers are not satisfied with timeliness and frequency of deliveries.

Formulation of the Problem

The goal of the project described in this paper is to redesign the distribution system taking into account the company's objectives. The first objective is to minimize the total distribution cost including the warehousing, transportation and locked-up locked-up capital costs. The second objective is to minimize the delivery time. The delivery time is defined as a period between the order receiving and order fulfillment. The delivery time may be reduced by many actions influencing on different stages of the order fulfillment process. The actions considered in this study may influence on riding time. Thus, the authors decided to use as the direct objective minimization of riding time. The company may then calculate delivery time adding to the riding time duration of other processes.

As mentioned above the company is interested in a significant reduction of the delivery time. On the other hand, it is likely that not all of the customers will need such a quick response. Thus, we decided to take into account riding time to the first customer on a route. The customers demanding fast delivery will be scheduled first in the vehicles routes. As in majority of cases 1 - 3 customers are served on a route, about 64% of customers can be served in this way.

As previously described, the transportation service provider uses a commercial vehicle routing system to optimize the routes on the operational level. The system was introduced about 18 months ago and resulted in reasonable savings. In this study, we assume the same operational level of vehicle routing in the new distribution system. In particular, it is assumed that many parameters of the routes, e.g. average load of vehicle, remain on a similar level. Due to this fact, the data about more than 6000 routes performed within last 12 months is used to calculate such parameters of the routes as: average vehicle load (vehicle capacity utilization), average number of customers served on a route and average distance between customers on a route.

The reduction of the riding time may be achieved by an introduction of a number of new warehouses serving some sub-areas of the country. In fact, the new warehouses may also reduce transportation cost. One of the elements influencing on cost of the transport is the vehicles' capacity utilization. Presently when the products are delivered directly to customers, the capacity utilization index is at the level of 66%. The deliveries to warehouses should be planned efficiently and thus the capacity utilization can be close to 100%. On the other hand, introduction of the new warehouses will increase warehousing cost and cost of locked-up capital.

In this study, 39 potential locations of the warehouses are considered. Two of them correspond to the locations of the existing warehouses. Such actions as closing one or two of the existing warehouses are also taken into account. It is assumed that each of the warehouses will distribute products of both production plants. Each of the warehouses should maintain an inventory level that would satisfy 95% of customers' orders. The two existing warehouses are owned by the company, so, their warehousing costs result from financial analysis of the order fulfillment process. It is assumed that in order to introduce new warehouses the company will rent additional warehousing space at the selected locations and it will outsource most of the warehousing services. The company, however, will manage the new warehouses. The warehousing costs of the new warehouses will in general be higher than warehousing costs in the existing warehouses. The costs were estimated taking into account market prices of warehouse space and services.

In the case of small warehouses, the products from the production plants will not be delivered every day. This will increase the products rotation time and thus, the cost of locked-up capital. A simulation model implemented under TAYLOR simulation package has been used to estimate the influence of this fact on the rotation time. It has been observed that the average rotation time increases by the average headway between deliveries from production plants.

In order to define areas served by the warehouses the whole country is divided into 49 regions corresponding to the old voivodships. It is assumed that all customers in a given voivodship will be served from a single warehouse. For each of the voivodships, its demands for the products of production plant A and B were estimated. The estimates were based on sales data from the last 18 months as well as on company's forecasts of sales increase in the next few years.

In order to calculate the transportation cost the average market prices of transportation services are used. Two kinds of vehicles are considered: tractor – semi trailer units with capacity of 33 palettes and medium sized trucks with capacity of 18 palettes. The vehicles differ by their vehicle-kilometer costs. In addition, the prices of transportation services depend on the length of the routes. In general, long routes are cheaper per vehicle-kilometer than the short routes. Finally, for each pair of region and potential location of warehouse, the average transportation cost per palette is estimated. The cost is estimated taking into account the market prices of transportation services, the distance between potential location of warehouse and the region and the average parameters of the routes in the region. In the same way the average transportation cost per palette from each production plant, to each potential location of warehouse is estimated.

Furthermore, for each pair of region and potential location of warehouse, the average riding time to the first customer on a route is estimated. This estimation takes into account the distance and quality of roads between the potential location of warehouse and the region.

Mathematical Model

The problem is formulated in terms of multiple objective mathematical programming with binary and continuous variables.

Data

The following data are used in the model:

I - the number of potential locations of warehouses,

J - the number of regions that have to be assigned to the warehouses,

DA_j - annual demand of region j for products of production plant A in [pallets], $j = 1,...,J$,

DB_j - annual demand of region j for products of production plant B in [pallets], $j = 1,...,J$,

TC_{ij} - average transportation cost from warehouse at location i to region j in [PLN/pallet], $i = 1,...,J, j = 1,...,J$,

TCA_i - average transportation cost from production plant A to warehouse at location i in [PLN/pallet], $i = 1,...,J$,

TCB_i - average transportation cost from production plant B to warehouse at location i in [PLN/pallet], $i = 1,...,J$,

TT_{ij} - average travel time from warehouse at location i to the first customer in region j in [min], $i = 1,...,J, j = 1,...,J$,

PHC_i - cost of pallet handling in warehouse at location i, $i = 1,...,J$,

CRT - current average pallet rotation time in [days], i.e. the average number of days that a pallet spends in the current distribution system,

CCA - average daily cost of locked-up capital per pallet produced in production plant A in [PLN/day],

CCB - average daily cost of locked-up capital per pallet produced in production plant B in [PLN/day],

MCC_i - minimum annual cost of locked-up capital in warehouse at location i related to the safety stock of pallets,

ML - capacity of vehicles used for transportation from production plants to warehouses,

DY - average number of working days in a year.

Decision variables

Two groups of decision variables are considered:

$y_i \in \{0, 1\}$, $i = 1,...,J$, equals to one if warehouse at location i is included in the plan, and 0 otherwise.

$x_{ij} \in \{0, 1\}$, $i = 1,...,J, j = 1,...,J$, equals to one if region j is assigned to warehouse at location i, and 0 otherwise.

Constraints

The first group of constraints assures that regions are assigned only to warehouses included in the plan:

$$x_{ij} \le y_i, \qquad i = 1,...,J, j = 1,...,J. \tag{1}$$

The second group of constraints assures that each region is assigned to exactly one warehouse:

$$\sum_{i=1}^{I} x_{ij} = 1, \qquad j = 1,...,J. \tag{2}$$

Some additional constraints are included in order to obtain a linear model. They are described in the next subsection.

Objective functions

Two objectives are considered in the model:
- TDC - total annual cost of distribution,
- MRT - maximum riding time to the first customer on a route.

Both objectives are minimized.

The first objective is defined in the following way:

$$TDC = TTC + TPHC + TCC, \tag{3}$$

where TTC denotes total annual transportation cost, $TPHC$ denotes total annual cost of pallets handling in the warehouses, and TCC denotes total annual cost of locked-up capital.

Total annual transportation cost takes into account transportation from production plants to warehouses and transportation from warehouses to the customers in the regions. It is defined in the following way:

$$TTC = \sum_{i=1}^{I} \left(TCA_i \sum_{j=1}^{J} x_{ij} DA_j + TCB_i \sum_{j=1}^{J} x_{ij} DB_j \right) + \sum_{i=1}^{I} \sum_{j=1}^{J} x_{ij} TC_{ij} (DA_j + DB_j) \tag{4}$$

Total annual cost of pallets handling in the warehouses is defined in the following way:

$$TPHC = \sum_{i=1}^{I} y_i PHC_i \left(\sum_{j=1}^{J} x_{ij} DA_j + \sum_{j=1}^{J} x_{ij} DB_j \right) \tag{5}$$

Total annual cost of locked-up capital is defined in the following way:

$$TCC = \sum_{i=1}^{I} \max \left\{ y_i MCC_i, \begin{array}{l} \sum_{j=1}^{J} x_{ij} DA_j CCA(CRT + DHA_i) + \\ \sum_{j=1}^{J} x_{ij} DB_j CCB(CRT + DHB_i) \end{array} \right\}, \tag{6}$$

where DHA_i and DHB_i are average headways of deliveries for production plants A and B, respectively. They are defined in the following way:

$$DHA_i = ML / \left(\sum_{j=1}^{J} x_{ij} DA_j / DY \right), \tag{7}$$

$$DHB_i = ML / \left(\sum_{j=1}^{J} x_{ij} DB_j / DY \right). \tag{8}$$

Total annual cost of locked-up capital is not linear as it uses max operator. In order to obtain linear model I continuos variables cc_i are added. They are interpreted as cost of locked-up capital in warehouse at location i. Furthermore, two groups of constraints are added:

$$cc_i \geq \quad y_i MCC_i, \qquad i = 1,...,I, \tag{9}$$

$$cc_i \geq \quad \sum_{j=1}^{J} x_{ij} DA_j CCA(CRT + DHA_i) +$$
$$\qquad\qquad\qquad\qquad\qquad\qquad , i = 1,...,I. \tag{10}$$
$$\sum_{j=1}^{J} x_{ij} DB_j CCB(CRT + DHB_i)$$

Total annual cost of locked-up capital is defined as follows:

$$TCC = \sum_{i=1}^{I} cc_i \tag{11}$$

Maximum riding time to the first customer on a route is defined in the following way:

$$MRT = \max\{x_{ij} TT_{ij} \tag{12}$$

Again, this objective is not linear. In order to obtain linear model a continuos variable mrt is added and the following group of constraints is constructed:

$$mrt \geq x_{ij} TT_{ij}, \quad i = 1,...,I, j = 1,...,J. \tag{13}$$

Maximum riding time to the first customer on a route is then equal to the new variable:

$$MRT = mrt. \tag{14}$$

As s result, a mixed binary bi-objective mathematical programming problem with $I \times J + I$ binary variables and $I + 1$ continuous variables is obtained. The problem can be stated in the following way:

$$\text{minimize: } TCC = \sum_{i=1}^{I} cc_i \tag{P1}$$

$$\text{minimize: } MRT = mrt$$

subject to:

$$x_{ij} \leq y_i, \qquad i = 1,...,I, j = 1,...,J$$

$$\sum_{i=1}^{I} x_{ij} = 1, \qquad j = 1,...,J$$

$$cc_i \geq \quad y_i MCC_i, \qquad i = 1,...,I$$

$$cc_i \geq \quad \sum_{j=1}^{J} x_{ij} DA_j CCA(CRT + DHA_i) +$$
$$\qquad\qquad\qquad\qquad\qquad\qquad , i = 1,...,I$$
$$\sum_{j=1}^{J} x_{ij} DB_j CCB(CRT + DHB_i)$$

$$mrt \geq x_{ij} TT_{ij}, \quad i = 1,...,I, j = 1,...,J$$

$$y_i \in \{0, 1\}, i = 1,...,I$$

$$x_{ij} \in \{0, 1\}, i = 1,...,I, j = 1,...,J$$

The second objective is similar to the objective of the p-center problem, which is known to be NP-hard [1].

In this case $J = 39$, $I = 49$, thus the problem has 1900 binary variables and 50 continuous variables.

Solution Methodology

The optimization of the distribution system has been performed with the application of the extended version of MS Excel Solver – Premium Solver Plus by Frontline Systems. It solves linear problems composed of up to 2000 variables.

The analysis has been carried out in two steps. The first step consists in single objective optimization in which the total distribution cost is minimized.

Single objective optimization of the distribution system

In the first phase, one objective - the total distribution cost is used. The aim of a single objective optimization of the distribution system is to present to the decision maker the comparison between the current and the cost-optimal distribution systems. Table 1 compares two distribution systems.

Table 1. Comparison of two distribution systems

Distribution system	Number of warehouses	Total annual distribution cost [PLN]	Riding time [h:mm]
Current	2	9 924 300	9:22
Optimal	7	9 357 784	6:09

The interesting observation is that single objective optimization results in reducing both total distribution cost (566 516 PLN annual savings) and the riding time (3h 13min shorter). Thus, from the multiple objective point of view the optimal distribution system dominates the current one. Figure 2 presents the optimal distribution system, in which 49 regions (old Polish voivodships) are assigned to 7 warehouses.

Figure 2. **Optimal allocation of 49 regions to 7 warehouses**

Since the current distribution system is composed of two warehouses and the optimal distribution system is composed of seven warehouses, the natural question is in which order the warehouses should be introduced. To answer this question we have run the optimization four more times constraining the maximum number of warehouses to 3, 4, 5 and 6. Number of introduced warehouses and the corresponding total distribution cost are presented in Figure 3.

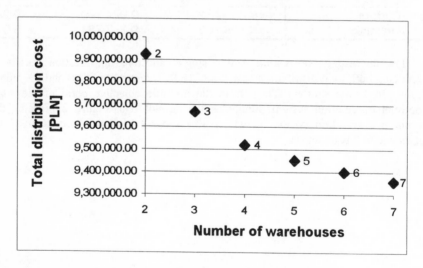

Figure 3. **Optimal order of introducing new warehouses**

It has been observed, that each solution with $K > 2$ warehouses contains all the warehouses contained in solution with $K - 1$ warehouses. In particular, the existing warehouses are included in all the solutions. This allows the company to schedule introduction of the new warehouses that assures that at each step it achieves the lowest cost possible with a given number of warehouses.

Bi-objective optimization of the distribution system

In bi-objective optimization e-constraints method ([7], ch. 8.5) has been used to generate a representative sample of Pareto-optimal solutions. Each Pareto-optimal solution has been obtained in two steps. In the first step, an upper bound on maximum riding time has been set. Then, total annual cost of distribution has been optimized. This approach may give, however, weakly Pareto-optimal solutions. Thus, in the second step, maximum riding time has been optimized with an additional constraint limiting the total annual cost of distribution to the optimum value found in the first step.

In the solution procedure, the riding time has been being constrained from 6 to 2 hours. The result of the bi-objective optimization is a set of Pareto-optimal distribution systems presented in Table 2 and a corresponding Figure 4. Calculations have been stopped when riding time reached 2h 41min, since there is no feasible solution for shorter times. The distribution system in which maximum riding time to the first customer on the route is 2 h 41min is composed of 23 warehouses. The results are interesting for the company's management since they show possible cost-time trade-offs. For instance the riding time reduction from 6h 9min to 5h 23min (46 min) results in 2 additional warehouses and generates additional cost of 186 000 PLN. The reduction of the riding time from 2h 44min to 2h 41min (3 min) also results in 2 additional warehouses but increases the total distribution cost by 548 000 PLN.

Table 2. Pareto-optimal set of distribution systems

Riding time [h:mm]	Total distribution cost [PLN]	No. of warehouses
2:41	12 972 507	23
2:44	12 424 210	21
2:59	11 653 423	18
3:28	10 813 246	15
4:00	10 090 964	12
4:20	9 802 832	10
4:35	9 746 413	10
5:23	9 543 711	9
6:09	9 357 784	7

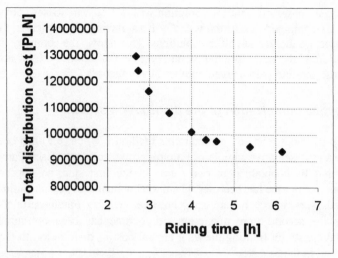

Figure 4. Pareto-optimal distribution systems

Another interesting observation originates from the comparison of the current distribution system (see Table 2) and to the set of Pareto-optimal distribution systems. As mentioned above the current distribution system is not a Pareto-optimal one. For example, with approximately the same total distribution cost equal about 9 900 000 PLN it is possible to redesign distribution system and shorten the riding time from 9h 22min to less then 4h 20min.

Conclusions

The whole project has been focused on the redesign of the existing distribution system for an international company based in Poland. As a result several Pareto-optmal variants of a new distribution system have been generated. Each optimal variant guarantees either the reduction of the distribution cost and/or the decrease of the delivery time. All the solutions suggest a certain number of Regional Distribution Centers, ranging from 7 to 23.

The results of the computational experiment let the company's management understand the trade-offs between the delivery time and the distribution cost. The application of the multiple objective approach resulted in the generation of several interesting solutions for a new distribution system. Surprisingly to the decision makers, it made possible the comparison between the existing distribution system with 2 RDC-s and the Pareto-optimal distribution systems with 7 to 23 RDC-s.

The results of the multiple objective optimization prove that the current distribution system is not a Pareto-optimal one from the point of view of the considered objectives. For example, with no increase of the distribution cost the company can reduce the riding time by 5 hours to about 4 hours 20 minutes. This can be achieved by introduction of eight new warehouses. Further reduction of riding time results, however, in a significant increase of costs.

Acknowledgment

The work of the first two authors was supported by DS grant no. 43-345.

References

[1] Arthur Andersen & Co. (1992). *Facing the forces of change 2000: The new realities in wholesale Distribution*, Washington DC, Distribution Research and Education Foundation.

[2] Bodin L., Golden B., Assad A., Ball M. (1981). *The state of the art in the routing and scheduling of vehicles and crews*, Final Report, Univ. Research for U.S. Dept. of Transportation, National Technical Information Service, Springfield.

[3] Fowler R.J., Paterson M.S., Tanimoto S.L., Optimal packing and covering in the plane are NP-hard. *Information Processing Letters*, **12**, 133-137, 1987.

[4] Gopal Ch., Gypress H. (1993). *Integrated distribution management*, Business One Inwin.

[5] McKinnon A. (1989). *Physical distribution systems*, Routledge, New York.

[6] Ross D. (1996). Distribution. *Planning and Control*, Kluwer Academic Publishers, Boston-Dordrecht, London.

[7] Solomon M. (1997). Algorithms for the vehicle routing and scheduling problems with time window constraints. *Operations Research*, **55**.

[8] Sousa J. (1991). A computer based interactive approach to crew scheduling, *EJOR*, **55/3**, 233-258.

[9] Steuer R.E. (1986). *Multiple criteria optimization - theory, computation and application*, Wiley, New York.

[10] Tzeng G.-H., Tu S.-W. (1992). Multiobjective and fuzzy time-window heuristic method in vehicle routing problems, *Proceedings of the Tenth International Conference on Multiple Criteria Decision Making*, Taipei 19-24.07.93, vol. 4, 217-227.

Integer Goal Programming Applications Using Modelling Systems and Excel

Josef Jablonský

University of Economics, W. Churchill Sq. 4, 130 67 Praha 3, Czech Republic, jablon@vse.cz, http://nb.vse.cz/~jablon

Abstract. The paper presents an integer goal programming model with several-sided penalty function and discusses its utilisation in solving several classes of decisions problems. The special attention is given to nutrition problems and scheduling of nutrition components to hospital patients with respect to the requirements of physicians. The model minimises either the weighted sum of deviations or maximum penalty deviation. The results given by both the approaches are compared. A simple support system for prescribing the patient nutrition based on the goal programming model is presented. The system is designed as an add-in application in MS Excel and uses the modelling system LINGO for model definition and solving.

Keywords. Goal programming, modelling systems, spreadsheets, nutrition problem

1 Introduction

The aim of the paper is to describe a simple decision support system for effective managing of intravenous nutrition of patients based on goal programming methodology. Patients who need intravenous nutrition are usually critically ill and require individual infusion calculation and prescribing. The nutrition is realised by available infusion solutions of different composition with respect to nutritional components taking into account. The main objective is to propose the daily nutrition mix getting near to the individually specified requirements by physician.

Let us suppose that the decision maker (physician) wants to propose a daily nutritional mix of a patient and takes into account r nutritional components (the number of components is usually between 10 and 20 in real situations). The most important among them are content of water, total energy, nitrogen, sodium, potassium, etc. The process of building nutritional proposal can be divided into several steps:

1. Specification of requirements all of the nutritional components with respect to the patient's current condition by physician.
2. Selection of the appropriate infusion solutions in order to ensure very close fulfilment of the requirements specified in the first step.
3. Time scheduling of the application of the selected infusion solutions within the day.

An expert physician can hardly be replaced by a decision support system in the first and third step presented above. But the second phase offers a field for building mathematical models for solutions selection and prescribing. In this step the decision maker has available n infusion solutions (usually several tens) that can be prescribed to the patient. It is almost impossible to find the solution of the problem (e.g. solution that minimises the sum of weighted deviations from nutritional requirements) without any support system. The computer-aided selection of infusion solutions has many advantages – it can prevent undesirable over- or under- achievement of specified requirements, save physician's time, reduce volumes of discarded solutions, make intravenous feeding cost effective, etc.

One of the possible methodological approaches for modelling nutritional problems is the application of goal programming models. The goal programming formulation of the nutrition problem is presented in the next section of the paper.

2 Goal programming formulation

The goal programming model presented below uses four-sided penalty function (Fig. 1). The positive and negative deviations in this function are normalised by their dividing by goals values (nutritional requirements) for goal values greater than 0. In this way the normalised value 1 means 100% fulfilling of the goal, the value less than 1 indicates underachievement of the goal and the value greater than 1 indicates overachievement of the goal. The decision maker must specify bounds $p_i^{min} < 1$ and $p_i^{max} > 1$ for the first level of the over- and under-achievement of the goal g_i. The values of p_i^{min} and p_i^{max} are usually from 0.80 to 0.95 and 1.05 to 1.20 respectively. The relative deviations from the goals within the interval $<p_i^{min}, p_i^{max}>$ are penalised by marginal value $s_1 w_i$, where w_i is the relative importance of the achievement of the goal g_i and s_1 is the penalty coefficient for the first level of under- or over-achievement of the goal. Similarly the marginal penalty for the under- or over- achievement exceeding the inner bounds $<p_i^{min}, p_i^{max}>$ is $s_2 w_i$. The value s_2 is is usually several times (5 to 10) greater than s_1.

The goal programming model for solving nutrition problem based on minimisation of the maximum relative penalty deviation δ can be formulated as follows:

minimise $z = \delta$, (1)

s.t. $\sum_{j=1}^{n} c_{ij}x_j + d_{i1}^- + d_{i2}^- - d_{i1}^+ - d_{i2}^+ = g_i,$ $i = 1,2,...,r, g_i \neq 0,$ (2)

$\sum_{j=1}^{n} c_{ij}x_j = g_i,$ $i = 1,2,...,r, g_i = 0,$ (3)

$\frac{w_i}{g_i}\left((d_{i1}^- + d_{i1}^+)s_1 + (d_{i2}^- + d_{i2}^+)s_2\right) - \delta \leq 0,$ $i = 1,2,...,r, g_i \neq 0,$ (4)

$\sum_{j=1}^{n} a_{ij}x_j \leq b_i,$ $i = 1,2,...,m,$ (5)

$d_{i1}^- \leq g_i - p_i^{min} g_i,$
$d_{i1}^+ \leq p_i^{max} g_i - g_i,$ $i = 1,2,...,r,$ (6)

$l_j \leq x_j \leq u_j,$
$x_j - $ integer, $j = 1,2,...,n,$ (7)

$d_{i1}^-, d_{i2}^-, d_{i1}^+, d_{i2}^+ \geq 0,$ $i = 1,2,...,r,$ (8)

where
n is the number of available infusion solutions,
r is the number of nutritional components taking into account,
m is the number of inflexible goals,
c_{ij} i=1,2,...,r, j=1,2,...,n is the coefficient expressing the volume of the i-th nutritional component in the one unit of the j-th solution,
g_i i=1,2,...,r is the daily individual requirement (goal) of i-th nutritional component,
$d_{i1}^-, d_{i2}^-, (d_{i1}^+, d_{i2}^+)$, i=1,2,...,r are negative (positive) deviation variables indicating under- (over-) achievement of the goal g_i,
w_i i=1,2,...,r is the weight expressing the importance of achieving of the i-th goal,
$p_i^{min} < 1$, $p_i^{max} > 1$, i=1,2,...,r are parameters of the penalty function of the i-th component (see Fig.1),
x_j j=1,2,...,n is the number of units of j-th solution in the daily nutritional mix,
l_j, u_j, j=1,2,...,n is the lower and upper bound for variables x_j,
s_1, s_2 are penalty coefficient for both levels of under- or over- achievement of the goals.

The constraints (2) are balance constraints for the goals greater than 0. The condition that the zero nutritional requirements must be fulfilled without any deviations is contained in (3). (4) are auxiliary constraints that make it possible to minimise the maximal deviation δ. The inflexible goals (e.g. price limitations) are represented by constraints (5) and (6) is the definition of the first level of under- and over- achievement of the goals. The constraints (7) are lower and upper bounds for number of prescribed solution units and integer conditions because of the need to prescribe the solutions as an integer multiplies of the minimum specified units (200 ml for most of the solutions).

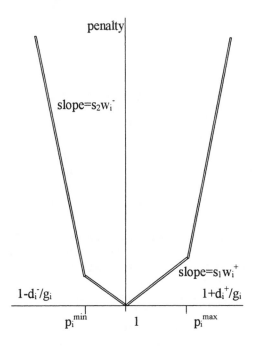

Fig.1 - Penalty function.

The goal programming model that minimises the weighted sum of relative deviations is as follows:

$$\text{minimise} \quad z = s_1 \sum_{\substack{i=1, \\ g_i \neq 0}}^{r} w_i \frac{(d_{i1}^- + d_{i1}^+)}{g_i} + s_2 \sum_{\substack{i=1, \\ g_i \neq 0}}^{r} w_i \frac{(d_{i1}^- + d_{i1}^+)}{g_i} \qquad (9)$$

s.t.   (2), (3), (5)-(8)

The above presented models represent two alternate approaches in solving goal programming problems. The paper [8] offers their interesting generalisation. The generalised model contains a new parameter λ whose value 0 leads to the minimisation of the weighted sum of deviations and value 1 to the minimisation of the maximum relative penalty deviation. The parameter $\lambda \in (0,1)$ can lead to the computation of the results between the two alternate traditional approaches. The generalised model for our application can be formulated as follows:

$$minimise \quad z = \lambda\delta + (1-\lambda)\left[s_1 \sum_{\substack{i=1, \\ g_i \neq 0}}^{r} w_i \frac{(d_{il}^- + d_{il}^+)}{g_i} + s_2 \sum_{\substack{i=1, \\ g_i \neq 0}}^{r} w_i \frac{(d_{il}^- + d_{il}^+)}{g_i} \right], \quad (10)$$

$$\lambda \in <0,1>,$$

s.t. $\quad$ (2)-(8).

3 Software support for goal programming models

The implementation of the presented goal programming models is based on solving integer liner programming optimisation problems. That is why the software support for solving such problems must contain a high quality optimisation solver because of the computational requirements connecting with solving integer problems in order to receive an acceptable solution in a reasonable time. Our software support is built in MS Excel environment and it is based on the co-operation of the professional LINGO solver with MS Excel spreadsheet.

LINGO belongs among modelling support systems. This kind of software products contains a special modelling language that makes it possible to write a mathematical model of a problem in a very close way to its standard mathematical formulation. The decision maker also can prepare general models by means of this language. These general models can be linked with appropriate data sets and then the optimisation run can start. LINGO contains linear, integer and non-linear solver which makes it possible to work with a variety of models from different operational research fields. It is suitable for solving linear and non-linear programming problems, multicriteria decision making, inventory management problems, queuing problems, etc.

The current version of the LINGO system includes tools that make it possible to control computations by means of simple software procedures. One of the possibilities for controlling the computations is a co-operation of the LINGO system with MS Excel or other spreadsheets. There are available macros and @OLE function that make it possible to run a LINGO model written directly in a named range of the spreadsheet. This feature enables to call LINGO step by step with a modified model or set of data directly from MS Excel. Modifications of the model can be simply done by using Visual Basic for Applications (VBA) implemented in MS Excel. This property of the LINGO system offers a possibility to build in MS Excel a library of models. They can be solved by LINGO but the decision maker need not know anything about the solving process because the proposed environment will be based on the decision maker communication with MS Excel only.

Our goal programming system contains generalised model (2)-(8),(10). By changing the parameter λ and other parameters of the model (e.g. solving problems with or without integer conditions) the decision maker can experiment with the formulated model. The model cannot be necessarily formulated as a nutrition problem but it was the primary aim of our study. The generalised goal programming model written in LINGO can look as follows:

```
MODEL:
SETS:
var/@OLE('nutrition.xls','solution')/:x,lo,up;
constr/price/:b;
obj/@OLE('nutrition.xls','comp')/:w,goal,dplus1,dplus2,dminus1,dminus2,opt,pmi
nus,pplus;
mata(constr,var):A;
matc(obj,var):C;
ENDSETS
min = delta*lambda + (1-lambda)*(s1*@SUM(obj(i)|goal(i)#NE#0:
      w(i)*(dminus1(i)+dplus1(i))/goal(i))+s2*@SUM(obj(i)|goal(i)#NE#0:
      w(i)*(dminus2(i)+dplus2(i))/goal(i)));
@FOR(obj(i)|goal(i)#NE#0: s1*w(i)*(dminus1(i)+dplus1(i))/goal(i) +
      s2*w(i)*(dminus2(i)+dplus2(i))/goal(i) - lambda <= 0);
@FOR(constr(i): @sum(var(j):a(i,j)*x(j)) <= b(i));
@FOR(obj(i)|goal(i)#NE#0: @sum(var(j):c(i,j)*x(j))+dminus1(i)+dminus2(i)-
      dplus1(i)-dplus2(i)=goal(i));
@FOR(obj(i)|goal(i)#NE#0: dminus1(i) <= goal(i)-pminus(i)*goal(i);
                          dplus1(i) <= pplus(i)*goal(i)-goal(i));
@FOR(obj(i)|goal(i)#EQ#0: @sum(var(j):c(i,j)*x(j))=0);
@FOR(var:@GIN(x));
@FOR(var:@BND(lo,x,up));
@FOR(obj(i): opt(i)= @sum(var(j):c(i,j)*x(j)));
DATA:
s1=1; s2=10;
lo=@OLE('nutrition.xls'); up=@OLE('nutrition.xls');
lambda=@OLE('nutrition.xls');
A = @OLE('nutrition.xls'); b = @OLE('nutrition.xls');
C = @OLE('nutrition.xls','CM');
goal = @OLE('nutrition.xls');
pminus = @OLE('nutrition.xls'); pplus = @OLE('nutrition.xls');
w = @OLE('nutrition.xls');
@OLE('nutrition.xls')=opt;
@OLE('nutrition.xls')=x;
ENDDATA
END
```

The LINGO model contains three basic sections as presented below:

1. Definition of sets (introduced by keyword SETS). This section defines sets, the number of their elements and their attributes. The number of elements of defined sets is specified by means of the @OLE function in our model. This function enable to link the data sets placed in named ranges in the spreadsheet file with the

LINGO model. E.g. the set VAR has elements that are placed in the range named SOLUTION in the file NUTRITION.XLS in our case. Each of these elements has the attribute X (the number of prescribed units of solutions), LO and UP (lower and upper bound).

2. The logic (body) of the model corresponds to its mathematical formulation. It is possible to compare the original mathematical formulation of the generalised goal programming (2)-(8), (10) with the model written in LINGO language. The first row in the body of the model is the definition of the objective function. Similarly the other rows correspond to the mathematical formulation (2)-(8).

3. The DATA section (introduced by keyword DATA) contains links to the named ranges in the appropriate spreadsheet file. E.g. the goals (attribute GOAL) of the model are read from the named range GOAL in the file NUTRITION.XLS. The results of the optimisation (if the optimal solution is found) are sent to the ranges in a spreadsheet file. It can be performed by means of the @OLE function too. The command @OLE("file.xls")= name_of _the_attribute sends the values of the appropriate attribute to the range of the spreadsheet file. The name of this range corresponds with the name of the attribute in this case. The results of the optimisation placed in spreadsheet ranges are processed by the VBA procedures and presented to the decision maker in the modified and more understandable form.

The decision maker (physician) works with the system by means of the pull-down menus and dialogue boxes. The process of building of nutritional mix starts by specifying the following important input information (it is supposed that the set of solutions and their composition with respect to the nutritional components is known and included as the basic information in the system):

- the daily nutritional requirements (goals),
- lower and upper bounds for definition of the first penalty level of under- and over- achievement,
- weights coefficients describing the importance of the goals,
- lower and upper bounds for decision variables (the number of units of solutions),
- λ parameter for selection of the goal programming model.

The results computed by LINGO solver are placed back to the spreadsheet sheet. They contain the following basic information:

- values of decision variables (the number of units of solutions),
- information about the fulfilling of goals in natural units and in the form of relative deviations,
- penalty caused by under- or over- achievement of goals for each nutritional component,
- the sum of weighted penalty deviations and the maximum penalty deviation.

4 Computational experiments

Computational experiments with the presented models were performed with a real data set containing 36 infusion solutions and 10 nutritional components. The nutritional components are listed together with their relative importance coefficients and a real set of goals in Table 1. The most important components in our experiments are water, total energy and nitrogen (weight equal to 10), the second group of components contains energy derived from fat, potassium and sodium (8) and the least important are chloride, calcium, phosphorus and magnesium (5). Table 1 does not contain the information about the bounds for definition of the first penalty level (p_i^{min}, p_i^{max}). The closest interval is usually set for the most important components – e.g. the interval for water is (0.95, 1.05) and for nitrogen (0.9, 1.05). In the contrary the interval for the least important components is relatively wide – e.g. the interval for chloride, calcium, phosphorus and magnesium is (0.85, 1.15). The weights and the intervals for the first penalty level of under- or over- prescribing can be subject for modifications during the real running of the system.

Computational results for the real set of goals and different values of parameter λ are presented in Table 1. This table contains achievement of goals in the natural and relative form for each set of parameter λ, penalty as the product of the weight and the relative deviation, the total penalty deviation and the maximum penalty deviation. The parameter space splits into three subsets in our example. The first one leads to the solution that minimises the sum of penalty deviations and the last one to the solution that minimises the maximum penalty deviation.

The support system for nutrition management is built as an open system that enables easy modifications of the set of solutions and nutritional components and all of the parameters of the model. At the present time the utilisation of the system is being verified in the clinical practice.

Component	w_i	Goal	Opt.	[%]	Penalty
			$\lambda \in <0, 0.581>$		
Water [ml]	10	2800	2931	104.68	46.79
TE [kJ]	10	10800	10726	99.32	6.80
Fat [kJ]	8	0	0	100.00	0.00
N [g]	10	8	7.8	97.50	25.00
Na [mmol]	8	200	201	100.50	4.00
K [mmol]	8	60	59.4	99.00	8.00
Cl [mmol]	5	220	218.8	99.45	2.75
Ca [mmol]	5	5	5	100.00	0.00
P [mmol]	5	15	15	100.00	0.00
Mg [mmol]	5	5	5	100.00	0.00
Sum of penalty deviations					**93.34**
Max. penalty deviation					**46.79**

Comp.	Opt. [%] Penalty $\lambda \in <0.582, 0.977>$			Opt. [%] Penalty $\lambda \in <0.978, 1>$		
Water [ml]	2896	103.43	34.29	2901	103.61	36.07
TE [kJ]	10392	96.22	37.81	10726	99.32	6.81
Fat [kJ]	0	100.00	0.00	0	100.00	0.00
N [g]	7.8	97.50	25.00	7.8	97.50	25.00
Na [mmol]	200	100.00	0.00	191	95.50	36.00
K [mmol]	59.4	99.00	8.00	59.4	99.00	8.00
Cl [mmol]	220.3	100.14	0.70	203.8	92.64	36.92
Ca [mmol]	5	100.00	0.00	5	100.00	0.00
P [mmol]	15	100.00	0.00	14	93.33	33.33
Mg [mmol]	5	100.00	0.00	5	100.00	0.00
Sum			105.80			182.13
Max			37.81			36.82

Table 1 – Computational results.

Acknowledgements

The paper is supported by the Grant Agency of Czech Republic – grant no. 402/98/1488 and corresponds to the research programme of the Faculty of Informatics and Statistics no. CEZ:J18/98:311401001.

References

[1] Jablonský J.: Decision Support System for Prescribing of Patient Nutrition: An Interactive AHP/Goal Programming Approach. In: Goicoechea,A., Duckstein,L., Zionts,S.: Multiple Criteria Decision Making: Proceedings of the 9th International Conference: Theory and Applications in Business, Industry and Government, Springer-Verlag, New York 1992, s.135-148.

[2] Jablonský,J.: Multicriteria Modelling by Means of the LINGO System. In: Metody i zastosowania badań operacyjnych II, Katowice 1998, s. 63-71.

[3] Jablonský,J,: Systems for Mathematical Modelling: a Comparative Study. In: Proceedings of the 16th Conference MME'98, Cheb 1998, p. 61-67.

[4] Lee,S.M.: Goal Programming for Decision Analysis. Auerbach Publ., Philadelphia 1972.

[5] Rehman,T., Romero,C.: Goal Programming with Penalty Functions and Livestock Ratio Formulation. Agricultural Systems 23 (1987), 117-132.

[6] Schrage,L.: Optimization Modelling with *LINGO*. Lindo Systems Inc., Chicago 1999.

[7] Steuer,R.: Sausage Blending Using Multiple Objective Linear Programming. Management Science 30 (1984), 11, pp. 1376-1384.

[8] Vitoriano, B., Romero, C.: Extended Interval Goal Programming. Journal of the Operational Research Society (1999) 50, pp. 1280-1284.

On Shaping Multi Criteria Marketing Strategy of a Pension Fund

Anna Jędryka
Commercial Union PTE BPH CU WBK S.A.
Division of Marketing
Jana Pawła II Av. 23
00-854 Warsaw, Poland
anna_jedryka@cu.com.pl

Tomasz Szapiro
Warsaw School of Economics
Division of Decision Analysis and Support
Institute of Econometrics
Niepodległości Str. 162
02-554 Warsaw, Poland
tszapiro@sgh.waw.pl

Abstract

In the paper the case study concerning multi criteria optimization of promotion campaign in a pension fund is considered. The significance of the problem is implied by the decisive role of marketing activities of firm which attempts to effectively compete in market environment. The impressive costs of TV campaign forces to focus on optimization of promotion. The specificity of pension fund is reflected in natural definition of the target group, in the structure of options and criteria and in evaluation procedures. Without loss of generality these procedures are simplified (the number of variables and criteria was left enough numerous to show multi criteria nature of the problem but restricted in order to clarify the presentation). The set of assumptions on a procedure supporting decision-makers was identified based on experience. It appears that the problem has a natural mathematical description which allows to formulate strictly the problem and to determine the set of solutions. The review of the set of solutions requires additional information. A procedure was presented which allows to collect the information needed. In order to collect this information the user is not forced to use any technical terminology but natural language. Collected data can be used to control the process of learning and elicitation of preferences. Randomly generated data illustrate this methodology which can be used for the real data as well.

The procedure can be further expanded firstly including neglected factors (e.g. length of a campaign and its variability) and then use benchmarking information to support the process of evaluation of trial solutions. For example, one can recommend the equalization strategy which, by definition, assumes that decisions are targeted on improving levels of these criteria which are below the average in the group of competitors. Another, satisfactory, strategy is defined by the requirement of exceeding a pre-defined threshold – reservation outcome. The software allows to use also other strategies focused on strengths or weaknesses or copying strategies of other competitors.

1. Introduction

It is believed that quality of product (service) is one of the most important tools to create competitive advantage of a firm. However the concept of quality has been rapidly changing during last half the century. While in fifties, quality was company and customer driven, later – in sixties – quality was standard and usage driven, from seventies – quality was oriented towards cost and hidden expectations of a consumer. It is nowadays accepted that in principle quality is related to expectations of a consumer[1]. He or she may be satisfied with a product of relatively low technical parameters if the product meets expectations. Quality and consumer satisfaction became milestones of each strategy.

---

[1] American Society for Quality Control – ASQC - define quality as the set of elements and features of a product or a service capable do satisfy defined needs (Evans and Lindsay, 1996).

It is impossible to meet consumers' expectations if he or she does not know the product. If a customer meets a new product and does not understand the purpose for which the product is designed then he or she is subjected to mechanisms of cognitive dissonance. These mechanisms create very strong and unpleasant feeling. This feeling results from contradiction between – usually high - self-evaluation of a person and the fact that recognition of usage of a product appears too difficult. In consequence, the consumer rejects the product. The cognitive bias can be here extremely strong – from unconscious forgetting about the product to implicit or explicit suppositions that the product is bad, ugly, unnecessary etc. This leads to reinterpretation of data and redefinition of problem, which strongly influences the decision making process, (Tversky and Kahneman, 1985). As it can be seen e.g. from inspection of the Deming Cycle, the implication of this mechanism seriously threatens the producer, (Deming, 1986).

Traditionally marketing strategy starts with identification of a target group. Target group, by definition, consists of persons who should be reached by an advertising message; the target group may be formed by different criteria, e.g. by sex, purchasing power or specific interests. As we will see, in the situation of pension fund the target group is identified in a natural way. To this end let us define the following two situations. In the first we deal with a customer, which knows the product of firm, and in the second – with new customers.

It is believed that even in case if a producer is concerned only with a target group of old customers who know the brand, he or she cannot resign from launching new products. Even in case if current production sells well, competitors who follow copying strategy will soon lead to decrease in sales, see also (Porter, 1980). Another important factor forcing design of new products is related to the fact that new technologies shorten the life cycle of products. In such situation crucial role is to be played by promotion aimed at information on a new product and teaching potential customers about destination of the product in order to eliminate cognitive dissonance.

The second situation happens when a group of new customers enters the market. With exception of initial period of the pension reform in Poland, this situation occurs in case of pensions fund. New generation enter the labor market and start to interest in pensions. In this way they create a target group for pension fund promotion activities. Then, from point of view of a pension fund, i.e. producer of specific service, the fund copes with challenge to effectively inform and teach about a product, which is new to the potential customer. Since the product is in Poland identified with brand rather then its specific features, thus one of most important issues in pension fund strategy is related with brand awareness. This is optimization problem – one can get satisfactory brand awareness on several ways related with different cost. One is interested in this situation with the lowest cost.

These remarks suggest that the objective of marketing strategy is to reach desired level of brand or product awareness on minimal costs. This solution of the problem analyzed in the paper is based assumptions, which were derived from practical experience. In order to present this solution the following assumptions were introduced:

- the satisfactory brand awareness and level of knowledge of the product can be achieved through proper promotion campaign,
- without a loss of generality the considerations of optimality can be restricted to the TV promotion campaign,
- practical routines, criteria and references forming experience of pension funds analysts, as well as availability of existing data bases are to be taken into account in the phase of optimization model construction,
- subjectivity of evaluation of uncertainty cannot be neglected in the model,
- the solution of the problem is to involve scenario in which decision maker co-operates with an expert/analyst who is assisted by a computer equipped with a Decision Support System.

These assumptions attract the attention to multiple criteria methods with on line articulation of preferences, see (Evans, 1984;.Słowiński, 1984a,b) for reviews. This approach proposed by Zeleny (1980) and in mature shape presented e.g. by Steuer (1996) and Yu (1985) enables to support decision maker in situations where subjectivity and imprecise description of uncertainty influence strict solution provided by mathematical methods[2].

---

[2] As useful readings (Goicoechea *et al.*, 1982) and (Galas *et al*, 1987) can be recommended.

As the particular method used to determine the final solution we propose the discrete version of the Bireference Interactive Procedure (BIP) to support decision makers introduced by Michałowski and Szapiro (1991). The procedure determines trial solutions using the reference frame. The reference is composed of the ideal point and the point of pessimistic expectation (externally defined by an user evaluation levels to be improved). The BIP was used in managerial training, also in the context of promotion policy optimization (Ochocki, 1996). The Bireference Interactive Procedure was implemented of the discrete case – the package dBIP works in Windows environment on standard PCs (Ożdżeński, 1996).

The paper is organized as follows. The Introduction is followed by a Chapter 2, where the Promotion Campaign Efficiency Optimization Problem is formulated. Then in Chapter 3 short description of a procedure and the package dBIP is presented. A simulation of decision-making process in the assumed scenario is reported in Chapter 4. Concluding Remarks and References complete the paper.

2. The Promotion Campaign Efficiency Optimization Problem

2.1. The Decision Space

As stated earlier the objective of marketing strategy is to reach desired level of brand or product awareness on minimal costs. There are several actions that can be undertaken in order to achieve this goal, (Beliczyński, 1999; Surmanek, 1996). Therefore we start with definition of a decision space. This space is defined by the set of feasible actions among which the final solution is to be selected. To this end let us consider the following three sets:

$X_{TV} = \{t_1, t_2, t_3, t_4, t_5, t_6, t_7, t_8, t_9, {}_{10}, t_{11}, t_{12}, t_{13}\}$,

$X_{BANDS} = \{b_1, b_2, b_3, b_4, b_5\}$,

$X_{SPOT} = \{s_0, s_1, s_2, s_3\}$,

Here t_1 denotes the TV station TV1, t_2 - TV2, t_3 - TV4[3], t_4 - TVN , t_5 - Polsat, t_6 - RTL7, t_7 - Polsat 2, t_8 - TV Polonia, t_9 - Polonia 1, t_{10} - Canal+, t_{11} - HBO, t_{12} - Wizja TV, t_{13} - Cyfra +, Similarly, b_1 denotes the early morning time band (02:00 – 10:59), b_2 – early afternoon time band (11:00 – 16:44), b_3 – late afternoon (16:45 – 19:14), b_4 – early evening time band (19:15 – 21:54) and b_5 – late evening time band (21:55 – 01:59)[4]. Similarly s_i denote spots: s_1=15 seconds, s_2=30 seconds and s_3=45 seconds spots[5] and s_0 is artificial notation for decision on rejecting the possibility to buy a spot.

Let us consider the set

$$T=X_{TV} \times X_{BANDS} = \{(t_i, b_j) : t_i \in X_{TV}, b_j \in X_{BANDS}\},$$

The set T is composed of pairs $\tau_p = \left(t_{i_p}, b_{i_p} \right)$, $p=\{1,\ldots,13 \cdot 5\}=\{1,\ldots,65\}$. Each pair describes the TV station and the band. It is known that the price of spot depends on these two characteristics and therefore the pair $\tau_p = \left(t_{i_p}, b_{i_p} \right)$ will be called a *type of the spot*. The decision maker is expected to determine for each TV station the number of spots in each band (this number may be equal to zero). We will resign from description of buying multiple spots of the same type[6]. With this interpretation the decision can be described as follows as an element of the Cartesian product $X=X_{SPOT} \times \ldots \times X_{SPOT}$, where the product is   composed of 65 copies[7] of X_{SPOT}. An element $x \in X$, $x = \left(s_{i_1}, \cdots, s_{i_{65}} \right)$ is described as the ordered

---

[3] The successor of Nasza TV.

[4] Without loss of generality we restrict the set X_{BANDS} is restricted to five elements. However the (Advertising…, 1999) identifies about 40 bands daily (different bands are defined for different days of week).

[5] Again we do not lose generality when we restrict the set X_{SPOT} to three elements. The (Advertising Pricelist, 1999) identifies 8 types of spots which can be repeated during all bands, see also (Banaszkiewicz- Zygmunt, 2000).

[6] This assumption is not restricting since multiple choices can be described through introduction of artificial spots which are sums of spots defined in a pricelist – e.g. the 45 spot represents decision on buying two spots of duration 15 and 30 seconds.

[7] The number 65 counts for number of different types of spots and in our case it is equal to the result of multiplication card $X_{TV} \times$ card X_{BANDS}.

collection of 65 decisions on the length of a spot of each type. Thus the coordinate s_{i_p} in the sequence $x=\left(s_{i_1},\cdots,s_{i_{65}}\right)$ corresponds to the type $\left(t_{i_p},b_{i_p}\right)$ and represents the length of spot in the time band b_{i_p} bought in TV station t_{i_p}. The coordinate s_{i_p} will be shortly described s_{ij} if it describes a spot of type t_i in the band b_j. E.g. if a firm decides to buy 30 second spot on TV1 between 11:00 – 16:44. Then this decision is represented by the 65-tuple $(0,\ldots,30,\ldots,0)$ in which 30 is located on the place corresponding to the type describing the pair $(t_1,b_2)=(TV1,"11:00 – 16:44")$, This interpretation justifies the following definition.

<u>Definition</u> 1. The space $X=X_{SPOT}\times\ldots\times X_{SPOT}$ described above is said to be the *set of promotion campaigns* or a *decision space*. The element of X is said to be a *promotion campaign*.

Let us consider the criteria space in the next sub-section.

2.2. The Criteria Space

Let us denote by p_{ij} the *price* $C(x)$ of one second of the spot s_{ij} of type (t_i,b_j). Consequently the cost of the promotion campaign x is obtained as the result of multiplication of prices of a spot of given type times the length of spots bought by a company and by summing the resultant amounts, i.e..

$$C(x)=\sum_{i=1}^{13}\sum_{j=1}^{5}p_{ij}s_{ij}$$

The cost $C(x)$ is a variable, which will be minimized.

Let us denote by e_{ij} the number $TVR(x)$ of points, which measure the *exposure* of promotion campaign. It is assumed that efficiency of a campaign is directly proportional to the exposure. Thus exposure is a feature of a campaign, which is to be maximized. The exposure of the promotion campaign x is obtained as the result of multiplication of rating points e_{ij} of a spot of given type times the length of spots bought by a company and by summing the resultant amounts, i.e.

$$TVR(x) = \sum_{i=1}^{13} \sum_{j=1}^{5} e_{ij} s_{ij}$$

The cost TVR(x) is a variable, which will be maximized.

The cost C(x) of a spot is set up using rating points TVR – the higher is exposure the more expensive is a campaign. Thus we have a conflict requirement of simultaneous maximization of exposure and minimization of cost. Since a promotion campaign x is composed of different spots we may consider different campaigns with different structure of spots with the same cost and different exposures and of the same exposure at different costs. This observation shows that there is also need to optimize both criteria.

It is worth to mention that theoretical analysis proves that aggregate objective built from all criteria F could be found in two ways. Firstly, in analogy to classical approach of von Neumann and Morgenstern (1947), one can define a set of axioms which are to be satisfied by aggregate objective function. Secondly, one can estimate coefficients in a postulated formula for a group utility using econometric techniques for observed data. There is no aggregate objective function for a set of natural axioms, moreover axioms are hardly likely to be credible descriptions in the real life decision problems. On the other hand, it is hard to justify the shape of the group utility used in econometric estimations as well as its time independence.

For given promotion campaign x let us consider the number GRP(x)[8], which measures the designation for the *promotion print*. This number is identified on the basis of historical date from marketing research on the coverage[9], share[10] and the average frequency of exposure of promotion campaign and its elements. The

---

[8] GRPs - Gross Rating Points serve to compare different media strategies.

[9] Coverage is a concept serving to describe geographically the region where a TV station can be received. For the purpose of market research the coverage can be measured using the number of single customers or households equipped with appropriate TV set.

[10] Share is a concept serving to describe preferences of audience in a region where a TV station is received. In desired time periods, it is measured using telemetrics.

GRP(x) is a variable, which will be maximized. In the sequel we will assume that GRP(x) is given[11].

In order to simplify the presentation we will not consider other criteria used in evaluation of a promotion campaign. For the sake of completeness of problem description let us only mention the most commonly used criteria. Managers want to maximize the *Reach*, i.e. the audience reached by a promotion campaign. It is measured as a percentage of target group reached once in a given time period. Next important criterion subjected to maximization is *Effective reach* reflecting percentage description of audience reached with pre-defined frequency level. Next criterion to be maximized is the number of OTS points - *Opportunities to see* - reflecting the average number of impacts during a promotion campaign. There are also supplementary cost criteria subjected to minimization: *Cost per point* – average cost of a single reaching 1% of a target group, and *Cost per thousand* - average cost of a single reaching 1000 person from the target group.

Let us denote by $y_1=-C(x)$, where C(x) is defined above, similarly let $y_2=TVR(x)$ and $y_3=GRP(x)$. The multi criteria evaluation of the campaign x is therefore given as the vector **y**,

$$y(x) = \begin{bmatrix} -C(x) \\ TVR(x) \\ GRP(x) \end{bmatrix} = \begin{bmatrix} -\sum_{i=1}^{13}\sum_{j=1}^{5} p_{ij}s_{ij} \\ \sum_{i=1}^{13}\sum_{j=1}^{5} p_{ij}e_{ij} \\ \text{given externally} \end{bmatrix}.$$

As it results from the earlier remarks, all criteria are to be maximized. The formula for evaluation of the campaign defines the mapping $y:X \rightarrow \mathbf{R}^3$.

Definition 2. The evaluation **y'** of the campaign x' *dominates* (*in the set* Y=y(X)) the evaluation **y''** of the campaign x'' iff

C(x')≤C(x''), TVR(x')≥TVR(x'') and GPR(x')≥GPR(x'') and **y'**≠**y''**.

---

[11] This is important restriction since marketing surveys increase the costs of every promotion campaign. We assume here that the campaign is based on the data available in the firm.

The set of evaluations, which are not dominated in the set $Y=\mathbf{y}(X)$ will be denoted Y^{ND} and its elements are called non-dominated evaluations.

Generally speaking, the definition introduces a partial order is in $\mathbf{R}^3$ using the cone (in fact: the orthant defined by -x, y and z axis). Thus only for minor class of subsets of $\mathbf{R}^3$ there exists the maximal element with respect to this partial order.

<u>Definition 3</u>. The campaign x' *is preferred to* the campaign x" iff the evaluation $\mathbf{y}'(x')$ dominates the evaluation $\mathbf{y}''(x'')$. The set of campaigns with non-dominated evaluations is said to be the *efficient frontier* or the *efficient set* of the set X, (Steuer, 1986).

Let us observe that an feasible decision is efficient if it cannot be improved simultaneously with respect to all partial evaluations.

<u>Definition 4</u>. The Promotion Campaign Efficiency Optimization Pre-Problem (PCEO Pre-Problem) is to find the campaign x in the decision space X which is preferred to all other promotion campaigns.

<u>Definition 5</u>. Given the number B>0 (interpreted as the budget for the promotion campaign), the subspace X_B of the decision space $X=X_{SPOT}\times\ldots\times X_{SPOT}$ given by the formula:

$$X_B = \{x\in X : C(x)\leq B\}$$

is said to be the *set of feasible promotion campaigns* or simply - *the feasible set*. The element of X_B is said to be a *feasible promotion campaign*.

<u>Definition 6</u>. The point $\mathbf{y}^l=(y_1^l,y_2^l,y_3^l)$ is said to be the ideal point for the set Y, if

$$y_k^l=\max\ \{y\in R : y=y_k \wedge y=(y_1,y_2,y_3)\in Y\},\ k=1,2,3.$$

<u>Definition 7</u>. The feasible set is said to *trivial if* the ideal point for the set of evaluation of feasible campaigns is included in $\mathbf{y}(X_B)$. This case corresponds to situations where one can afford the ideal solution.

<u>Corollary</u>. In nontrivial cases there is no solution of the PCEO Pre-Problem.

<u>Definition 8</u>. The *Promotion Campaign Efficiency Optimization Problem* (*PCEO Problem*) is to find the set of *efficient* feasible promotion campaigns x, i.e. such feasible promotion companies, which have non-dominated evaluation $\mathbf{y}(x)$ in the set $\mathbf{y}(X_B)$.

In the sequel, the PCEO Problem will be denoted by (n,m,B,X_B,y), where n denotes the number of options (promotion campaigns in our case), m is the number of criteria (m=3 in the case under consideration), B corresponds to the promotion budget, the set X_B is the collection of feasible options, and y is a mapping $y:X_B \to \mathbf{R}^m$ describing evaluations.

In non-trivial case the set Y_B^{ND} of non-dominated evaluations contains more then one element. This means that there is no unique solution of the PCEO Problem. Let us consider the procedure of reviewing and solving non-dominated evaluation in the Section 3.

3. The *dBIP* procedure

The *dBIP* procedure is designed to support multiple criteria problems with a finite set of options and given a partial order defined by an orthant. The early version of the Bireference Interactive Procedure was introduced by (Michałowski, 1988) for the continuous, linearly constrained case with linear objective functions. The full version was presented in (Michałowski and Szapiro, 1991) and (Szapiro, 1991, 93). In (Ożdżeński and Szapiro, 1997) computer implementation was presented. Ożdżeński (1996) worked out a version of BIP with a finite set of options. The PCEO Problem (n,m,B,X_B,y) fits requirements of the *dBIP* methodology and it can be treated using this tool.

Following the Bi-Reference Procedure a decision-maker starts from edition of the model (data input) and from pessimistic evaluation definition. Improvement direction is determined and the trial solution determined then. Trial solution is evaluated resulting in halting the procedure or in displacement of reference points and modifications of improvement direction.

The following steps create the algorithm of the procedure:

1.1. The feasible set X_B is entered
1.2. The evaluation of feasible options from set X_B are entered:
    dBIP admits keyboard input as well as spreadsheet data - in MsExcel format. The data are collected in tables designed in a manner to which typical users are used to.

1.3. The components of the ideal point $\mathbf{y}^l$ of the set $\mathbf{Y_B}=\mathbf{y(X_B)}$ are determined following the formula from the Definition 6,

1.4. The user inputs his/her pessimistic evaluation $\mathbf{y}^W$,

2.1. Under assumption that $\mathbf{y}^W$ is feasible, the improvement direction d is determined:
$\mathbf{d}=\mathbf{y}^l-\mathbf{y}^W$. The trial solution $\mathbf{y}^T$ is given as $\mathbf{y}^T=\mathbf{y}^W+t^*\mathbf{d}$, where t* is the solution of the problem [12] max $\{t\in\mathbf{R} \mid \mathbf{y}^W+t\mathbf{d}\in\mathbf{Y_B}\}$.

3.1. The user accepts the trial solution $\mathbf{y}^T$ recommended by the system, otherwise goes to 3.2.

3.2. User decides which partial evaluations y_i^T of the trial solution $\mathbf{y}^T$ are to be:
- improved ($I^+(r)$ denotes the corresponding set of indices),
- preserved ($i\in I^0(r)$) or
- worsened ($i\in I^-(r)$). [13]

4.1. The following formula [13] rules the displacement of pessimistic evaluation in each iteration (denoted in formulae by r):

$$y_i(r)^W = \begin{cases} y_i(r-1)^T & dla \ i \in I^0(r)\cup I^+(r) \\ y_i(0)^W & dla \ i \in I^-(r) \end{cases}$$

The ideal point $\mathbf{y}^l$ of the set of feasible evaluations $\mathbf{Y_B}$ is displaced to the point $\mathbf{y}^l(r)$ following the assumption on preserved evaluations $i\in I^0(r)$. This requirement results in new set of evaluation of feasible options $\mathbf{Y_B}(r)$. The new set of evaluations $\mathbf{Y_B}(r)$ of feasible options is in fact the section of the initial set $\mathbf{Y_B}$ of feasible evaluations. The section is obtained from the requirement on keeping constant variables y_i for $i\in I^0(r)$. The new ideal point $\mathbf{y}^l(r)$ for the set $\mathbf{Y_B}(r)$ is determined from the formula in the Definition 6

4.2. Modified reference points are used in the step 2.1.

Figure 1. The flowchart of the Bireference Procedure.

---

[12] For the sake of simplicity it is assumed here that $\mathbf{y}^T$ is non-dominated. Otherwise a procedure of further improvement is defined.

[13] The coefficient r stands for negotiation round number (r=0 describes the initial situation, with pessimistic evaluation equal to the initial trial solution).

The Bireference Interactive Procedure uses the dual reference frame (the ideal point and the pessimistic evaluation). This frame is displaced during a decision process. The displacement follows restructuring of the problem (including options, the ideal point and pessimistic evaluation). The restructuring process is qualitatively controlled by subjective evaluations of the trial solutions, which are successively provided by the procedure. These features decrease random influence of the structure of a problem. The procedure admits preference reversal and imprecise determination of evaluations.

In the next Section *dBIP* is described in simple simulation of Promotion Campaign Effective Multiple Criteria Optimization.

48;1	Cost	Exposure	Promotion pri
Typ kryt.	Min	Max	Max
Option 1	9.00	49.00	27.00
Option 2	44.00	51.00	78.00
Option 3	78.00	22.00	95.00
Option 4	19.00	88.00	8.00
Option 5	42.00	47.00	32.00
Option 6	50.00	12.00	82.00
Option 7	19.00	69.00	98.00
Option 8	37.00	34.00	46.00
Option 9	67.00	89.00	17.00
Option 10	85.00	26.00	55.00
Option 11	74.00	25.00	85.00
Option 12	83.00	56.00	8.00
Option 13	72.00	62.00	96.00
Option 14	11.00	92.00	3.00
Option 15	91.00	68.00	70.00
Option 16	81.00	1.00	93.00
Option 17	33.00	13.00	85.00
Option 18	7.00	14.00	46.00
Option 19	89.00	45.00	20.00
Option 20	7.00	83.00	14.00
Option 21	79.00	69.00	97.00
Option 22	38.00	15.00	9.00
Option 23	27.00	91.00	43.00
Option 24	57.00	92.00	86.00
Option 25	65.00	54.00	37.00
Option 26	21.00	62.00	23.00
Option 27	72.00	50.00	86.00
Option 28	13.00	21.00	23.00

Figure 2. The dBIP main screen for the PCEO Problem described in the section 2.

The Discrete Decision Support System *dBIP* was implemented by Ożdżeński (1996) *dBIP* assists a decision maker who follows the Bireference Interactive Procedure. The package is especially useful for large data sets. The user is provided with the main screen split into two parts – the upper belt and spreadsheet notebook. The upper belt serves to manage the model in edition functions. The central part, designed as a spreadsheet notebook, serves for communication on a decision problem. The sheets (see the Figure 2) serve to edit the problem (and during the decision process - to restructure it). The data on constraints, preferences, (pessimistic) expectations and tolerances are entered as in typical spreadsheet.

The Figure 2 presents the spreadsheet filled with data for the PCEO Problem considered in the Section 2. In the first colon in table (on the screen in the Figure 2), only part of options can be visible – using scroll bars on the right hand side of the screen we may see other options. Subsequent campaigns are labeled as *Options* with ordering number added. Other columns correspond to the criteria (Cost, Exposure, Promotion Print).

The data visible in the sheet on the Figure 2 were randomly generated. In real application they can be manually input from the keyboard or transferred from MsExcel. Clicking the icon with the bulb on the upper belt one fires the solving procedure. The result of solving - trial solution - appears in a window. This window is supplied with possibility to input evaluation of trial solution using natural language. User is expected to select which components of trial solution are to be improved, preserved and/or worsened (this is required if an efficient option is to be changed).

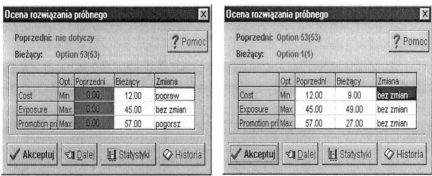

Figure 3. Two screen presenting subsequent trial solutions for the PCEO Problem.

The Figure 3 presents two subsequent trial solutions. Trial solutions presented in the Figure 3 recommend the Option (1) and Option (33) as subsequent solutions of the problem.

dBIP supports sensitivity analysis showing the current trial solution and presents the history of a decision making process. The history is composed of all displaced ideal points, pessimistic evaluations and trial solutions. Thus decision maker can review his choices and compare the new solution with previous ones. If he or she is satisfied with the solution he can accept the solution – otherwise an extensive restructuring of the problem is allowed. *dBIP* offers several additional tools to analyze the problem – it enables to analyze conflict matrices, to group variants[14], and perform other operations useful in sensitivity analysis.

The work with the *dBIP* assumes therefore the scenario described by the algorithm from the Section 3. The user, presumably an analyst from the Marketing Research Department of the Pension Fund, is assumed to work out a series of versions of promotion campaigns for his or her superiors from the Board. The first step requires to collect (or update) and input the data in order to prepare *dBIP* to assist in the decision making process. Then, he or she introduces initial preferences concerning pessimistic expectations. Pessimistic expectations represent the evaluations of a campaign that cannot satisfy the superior (the firm goals). Then the program computes auxiliary objects needed to get the trial solution and the trial solution itself. This solution is then presented to the user. User can accept this solution and save it (print). If he or she is not satisfied with the *dBIP* recommendation, then his evaluation is input. As mentioned earlier the evaluation is to be formulated in natural language using three-word vocabulary (improve, preserve, worsen). One cannot require improvement or preservation of all partial evaluations if something is to be changed – at least one evaluation is to be worsened in order that other evaluation could be improved.

The evaluation leads to restructuring of mathematical model (fired by clicking the button with bulb icon). The restructuring is done by a computer and the decision maker is not charged with any technicalities. His or her next intervention is evaluation of the next trial solution. If, after a series of restructuring, he is satisfied with the solution he accepts the solution and saves (prints) this. Thus *dBIP* offers a

---

[14] Technical description of the software is presented in (Ożdżeński, 1996).

possibility to shape the promotion strategy through simulation of desired improvements of auxiliary, trial recommendations for the decision.

5. Concluding Remarks

In the paper the case study concerning multi criteria optimization of promotion campaign in a pension fund is considered. The significance of the problem is implied by the decisive role of marketing activities of firm which attemps to effectively compete in market environment. The impressive costs of TV campaign forces to focus on optimization of promotion. The specificity of pension fund is reflected in natural definition of the target group, in the structure of options and criteria and in evaluation procedures. Without loss of generality these procedures were simplified (the number of variables and criteria was left enough numerous to show multi criteria nature of the problem but restricted in order to clarify the presentation). The set of assumptions on a procedure supporting decision makers was identified based on experience. It appeared that the problem has a natural mathematical description which allows to formulate strictly the problem and to determine the set of solutions. The review of the set of solutions requires additional information. A procedure was presented which allows to collect the information needed. In order to collect this information, the user was not forced to use any technical terminology but natural language. Collected data can be used to control the process of learning and elicitation of preferences. Randomly generated data illustrated this methodology which can be used for the real data as well.

The procedure can be further expanded firstly including neglected factors (e.g. length of a campaign and its variability) and then using benchmarking information to support the process of evaluation of trial solutions. For example, one can recommend the equalization strategy which, by definition, assumes decisions which are targeted on improving levels of these criteria which are below the average in the group of competitors. Another, satisfactory, strategy is defined by the requirement of exceeding a pre-defined threshold – reservation evaluation. The software allows to use also other strategies focused on strengths or weaknesses or copying strategies of other competitors.

The model suggests further research directions which seem interesting. Here, a design of neural networks capable to learn from records of own decisions and decisions of competitors, are to be mentioned at especially interesting project. Another interesting field of investigation is related with digital marketing in Internet (Goban-Klas, 1999).

References

Advertising Pricelist. National and regional TV stations, in Polish, Press Ltd, Poznań, 1999.

Banaszkiewicz-Zygmunt E., (ed.), Media, in Polish, PWN, Warszawa, 2000.

Beliczyński J., Media planning in Advertising Management, Antykwa Press, Kraków 1999.

Deming W.E., Out of Crisis, MIT Centre for Advanced Engineering Study, Cambridge, MA, 1986.

Evans G.W., *An Overview of Techniques for Solving Multiobjective Mathematical Programs*, Management Science, t. 30, nr 11, pp. 1268-1282, 1984).

Evans J.R., W.M.Lindsay, The Management and Control of Quality, West Publ. Cy, 1996)

Galas Z., Nykowski I., Żółkiewski Z., *Programowanie wielokryterialne*, PWE, Warszawa (1987).

Goban-Klas T., Media i Mass Communiction: Theories and Press, Broadcasting, Televison and Internet Analyses, in Polish, PWN, Kraków, 1999.

Goicoechea A., D.R.Hansen, L.Duckstein, Multiobjective Analysis with Engineering and Business Applications, Wiley, New York, 1982.

Michałowski W, T.Szapiro, *A Bi-Reference Procedure for Interactive Multiple Criteria Programming*, Operations Research, t. 40, nr 1, pp. 247-258 (1992).

von Neumann J., O.Morgenstern, "Theory of Games and Economic Behavior", Pr\inceton University Press, New Jersey, 1947.

Ochocki M., A Selection of Promotion Channels, Master Dissertation, in Polish, Warsaw School of Economics, Warszawa, 1996.

Ożdżeński W., Bireference Procedure in a Discrete Decision Problem, in Polish, Technical Report 03/S/0045/96, Warsaw School of Economics, Warszawa, 1996.

Ożdżeński W., T.Szapiro, BIP 4W v 2.02 – Computer Implementation of the Bireference Procedure, in Polish, in: Proceedings of the Conference "Operations Research Application", T.Trzaskalik (ed.), Absolwent Press, Łódź, 1997

Porter M., Competitive Strategy. Techniques for Analysing Industries and Competitors, Macmillan, 1980.

Słowiński R., Przegląd metod wielokryterialnego programowania liniowego, cz. I, Przegląd Statystyczny, t. 31, nr 1/2, str. 47-64 (1984a).

Słowiński R., Przegląd metod wielokryterialnego programowania liniowego, cz. II, Przegląd Statystyczny, t. 31, nr 3/4, s. 303-317 (1984b).

Steuer R.E., Multiple Criteria Optimization: theory, computation and application", Wiley, New York, 1986.

Surmanek J., Media planning: a practical guide, NTC Business Books, Lincolnwood 1996.

Szapiro T., Interactive Approach in Decision Making Support (in Polish), Monographs and Reports Series, vol. 338, 1991, WSE Press, Warsaw.

Szapiro T., Convergence of the Bi-Reference Procedure in Multiple Criteria Decision Making, Ricerca Operativa, 1993, vol. 23, nr 66, pp. 65-86.

Tversky A., Kahneman D., *The framing decisions and the psychology of choice*, in: „Behavioral Decision Making", G.Wright (ed.), Plenum Press, New York, pp. 25-40, 1985.

Yu P.-L., Multiple-Criteria Decision Making. Concepts, Techniques and Extensions, 1985, Plenum Press, New York.

Zeleny M., Multiple Criteria Decision Making, McGraw-Hill, New York, 1980.

Multiple Criteria Company Benchmarking Using the BIPOLAR Method

Ewa Konarzewska-Gubała

Department of Operations Research, Wrocław University of Economics
Komandorska 118/120, 53-345 Wrocław, Poland
ewakg@credit.ae.wroc.pl

Abstract. The paper presents the multiple criteria analysis approach to the company benchmarking measurement and analysis. The key phases of benchmarking process are identified according to the current theoretical and practical experience related to benchmarking method. For comparisons and analysis phase of benchmarking process the use of MCDA method BIPOLAR is suggested. It helps to measure the company performance improvement against the performance levels considered as the standard of excellence for a specific business process and against company own standard from the beginning of the self-assessment process. The evaluation criteria and weight coefficients are given by the requirements of European Business Excellence Model.

Keywords. Company Benchmarking, EFQM Business Excellence Model, BIPOLAR method

1. Introduction

Benchmarking is one of the last words to be introduced into the lexicon of modern management. Benchmarking as it is known today – i.e. *the continuous process of comparing an organisation's products, services and processes (not just ratios) against those of its competitors or those of organisations renowned as world class or industry leaders* – is a part of the Total Quality Management concept and was developed in the USA in the second half of the 70s (Camp, 1994). However the benchmarking concept is not new. The studies performed by Frederick Taylor on the scientific methods for work organisation based on the comparisons of processes may be seen as a starting use of this concept.

After the World War II, Japanese were considered the masters of copying. However they used these benchmarking tools to develop products and processes more efficiently in terms of time and money. The development of the *just-in-time* technique by Toyota was based on the analyses and the adaptation of the supply methods used by the big super market distribution chains, during the II World War. Although some companies, such as Xerox and Motorola began benchmarking as early as 1980, there has been dramatic increase in benchmarking practices in the recent past (Boxwell, 1994). Leading companies in USA from most industries are involved in benchmarking processes and 90% of benchmarks have active TQM programmes under way (Trybus, Kumar, 1998). A great number of benchmarking applications, composed of 27 cases from manufacturing, service educational institutions, and non-profit organisations is presented by Camp (1998).

Benchmarking was "invented" by many organisations and that process seems to be ongoing, since benchmarking is only slowly beginning to become know in Europe. The European Commission has adopted on April 16 1997 a Communication on *"Benchmarking: implementation of an instrument available to economic actors and public authorities" (COM(97)153 of 16 April 1997)* which presents a series of initiatives aimed at promoting the use of benchmarking, at three levels: company benchmarking, sectoral benchmarking and benchmarking of framework conditions or systems.

To identify best practices and for collecting and sharing information on benchmarks in the European Company Benchmarking Network, the use of quality models, such as the European Business Excellence Model (i.e. the European Quality Award Model) was considered to be very useful. Applying this TQM model, an organisation tries to describe itself on the basis of 9 criteria of performance, which are divided into a total of 33 or 22 elements (sub-criteria).Using this model in the self-assessment procedure, comparisons with other organisation are repeatedly requested.

In this paper we suggest a multiple criteria analysis approach for comparisons and analysis phase of benchmarking process. Besides such tools as spider diagram we will use the BIPOLAR model (Konarzewska (1989), Konarzewska (1996) to measure the company performance improvement against the performance levels considered as the standard of excellence for a specific business process and against company own standard from the beginning of the self-assessment process. The evaluation criteria and weight coefficients are accepted according to the requirements of European Business Excellence Model. The large number of criteria and possibility of considering more than one benchmarking partner are the decisive factors for development the methodology of comparisons based on BIPOLAR method.

In the first two sections we will present the basic issues in the benchmarking process and benchmarking methodology and the main elements of the European Business Excellence Model. In section four the conceptual model of benchmarking analysis is developed in the framework of multiple criteria analysis with bipolar reference performance standards. Section five concludes the paper.

2. Company Benchmarking Process

In order to cope with growing competition, organisations continuously have to acquire new abilities and have to realise new ideas. That implies that they have to change and improve their performance. Change and improvement in turn are directly connected with learning. Learning from the others – this is the subject area of benchmarking in a managerial environment. The purpose of benchmarking is to become aware how other organisations achieve their benchmarks and which processes they use (EC Quality Series no 7, 1998).

If a benchmarking project is to have a quick and positive impact on the company it must focus on areas which are critical to the success of business Irrespectively of the fields of application we can distinguish three main types of company benchmarking projects (Watson, 1992, p. 10)

1. Strategic: the analysis of world class companies in non-competitive industries to determine opportunities for strategic change initiatives in core business processes.

2. Performance: the analysis of relative business performance among direct or indirect competitors.

3. Process: the analysis of performance in key business processes among identified best-practice companies selected without regard to industry affiliation.

More specifically benchmarking means a measured excellent performance of a company; a reference point or a unit of measurement for making comparisons – a performance level considered as the standard of excellence for a specific business process or goal.

Particularly, if the business goal has been stated as "to be lowest price producer" the typical benchmarks supporting this goal could be cost related: materials cost per product, labour cost per product, overheads per unit of production, cost of distribution channels etc. The goal "to maintain or to increase customer loyalty" can be supported by the following benchmarks concerning the customer service: volumes if repeat business, levels of customer complaint, delivery performance complaints procedure etc.

The real benefit of using benchmarking tools can only be attained by analysis of processes the comparison of your own performance against that of the partner as well as by the final decision on steps how to close the performance gap.
Four fundamental questions should be raised (EC Quality Series no. 7, p.20):

1. What do we want to benchmark?
2. Who should be our benchmarking partner? Who has excellent processes in the area where we are looking for a solution?
3. How are we doing it? How well are our processes performing?
4. How well do the processes of others perform?

In the course of time, various methodologies were developed. The most popular is that using, with reference to the four phases of the Deeming Wheel (Plan-Do-Check-Act), four phases for benchmarking process. These are: Plan-Collect-Analyse-Adapt or Plan-Analyse-Integrate-Act (**Figure 1**). This benchmarking model has been accepted by the American Productivity and Quality Centre and the International Benchmarking Clearinghouse (a service of the APQC) as well as by European Foundation for Quality Management (EFQM).

3. The EFQM Business Excellence Model and its criteria

One of principles of Total Quality Management is the continuous improvement process. The Excellence Model of EFQM expresses this requirement by constantly demanding comparisons with other organisations in the scoring tables.

The EFQM Model is a non-prescriptive framework based on nine criteria. Five of them are *Enablers* and four are *Results* (**Figure 2.**). The *Enabler* criteria cover what organisation does. The *Result* criteria cover what an organisation achieves. The EFQM Model attempts to portray the salient elements of the TQM concept. It is based on apparently sound and logical assumption that the end results are the by-product of managerial competence, policies and processes. There is little empirical evidence to support this proposition, although logically it is an attractive and acceptable suggestion (Ghubadian and Woo,1996).

Applying this TQM model, an organisation tries to asses its progress towards excellence. Each of the nine criteria has a definition, which explains the high level meaning of that criterion. To develop the high level meaning further each criterion is supported by a number of sub-criteria (22 or 33 elements). Sub-criteria pose a number of questions that should be considered in the course of an assessment.

The EFQM Excellence Model can be used for a number of activities: self-assessment, third party assessment, benchmarking and as a basis for applying for The European Quality Award.

To assist users of the model in assessment and scoring, EFQM created two evaluation tools: The Pathfinder card and the RADAR scoring matrix.

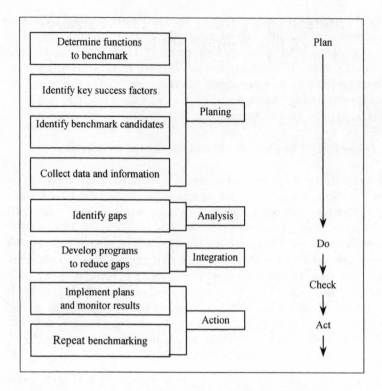

Figure 1. The phases of benchmarking process

Source: *Adapted from Camp* 1998, p. 20.

The Pathfinder card is a self-assessment tool for identifying opportunities for improvement. For the purpose of benchmarking the RADAR scoring matrix can be used. In such cases weights are given to each of nine criteria, as shown in the **Figure 2.**, to calculate the number of points awarded. These weights were established in 1991 as the result of a wide consultation exercise across Europe. Generally each sub-criterion is allocated equal weight within the criterion (there are three exceptions).

The first step to scoring is to use scoring matrix to allocate a percentage score to each sub-criterion. Then the score is awarded for each of nine criteria as the arithmetic average of the percentage scores awarded for the sub-criteria. Finally the scoring summary sheet is used to combine the percentage scores awarded to sub-criteria and weighting factors to give an overall score on a scale of 0–1000 points.

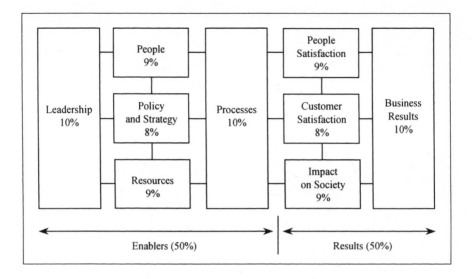

Figure 2. The European Business Excellence Model

Using these scoring results, comparisons with competitors and/or best practices organisations are repeatedly requested. Since the empirical evidences show that no one company is best in every category the multiple comparisons are required.

4. Bipolar approach to benchmarking analysis

4.1. Purpose and elements of BIPOLAR model

The typical benchmarking analysis phase consists usually of following tasks (see Camp, 1998):
− measure performance of benchmark partners,
− measure your own performance,
− determine current performance gap,
− project future performance levels.

It was just presented (in section 3) how to measure own and others performance using the EFQM Model and scoring matrix as a tool of multiple criteria evaluation. The supportive tool is also needed to show the benchmarking results: gaps and projected performance levels, particularly when the benchmarking comparisons are repeated for monitoring the progress.

Taking in consideration the multiple criteria and multiple benchmarking partners as a base of comparisons, the spider diagram is used sometimes as a presentation tool of benchmarking results (**Figure 3.**).

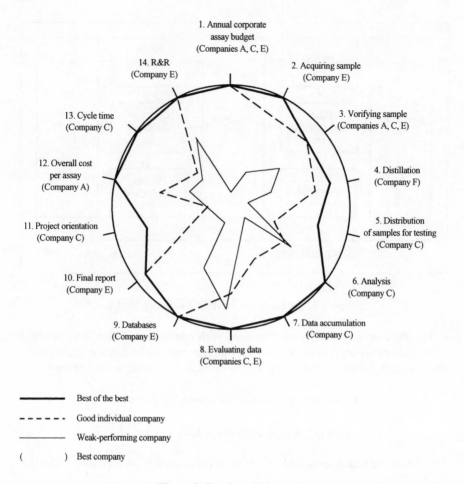

Figure 3. Benchmarking results

Source: *Camp*, 1998, p. 25.

A spider diagram for all benchmarking partners is very complicated. For illustration included in **Figure 3** are the highest scores achieved in all 14 categories (the best of the best), together with the results from the good performer (company E) and a weak performer. This again illustrates that no one company is best in every criterion.

As the analytical tool for the determination the current gap and projected future performance levels the BIPOLAR (see Konarzewska 1989, 1996; Konarzewska, Trybus 1999) method is suggested. In this method, formulated originally as multiple criteria decision aid model the benchmarking comparisons form a crucial concept of searching the recommended decision.

The BIPOLAR model distinctive feature is that users of benchmarking analysis must define two sets (poles) of real reference performance profiles: desirable and non-acceptable. Both reference poles reflect the management`s aspirations, goals and organisational objectives. One set is composed of profiles best in the class, while the second is the set of weak performance profiles that management will try to avoid.

For the company benchmarking purposes we suggest to use gradually industry standards, industry leaders and world class performing companies (see **Figure 4**.) to define the positive pole. Negative pole can be composed of the weak-performing companies or/and our own performance profiles reached from the be-ginning quality improvement movement and self-assessment process. Comparing current performance with previous ones we can monitor the progress done.

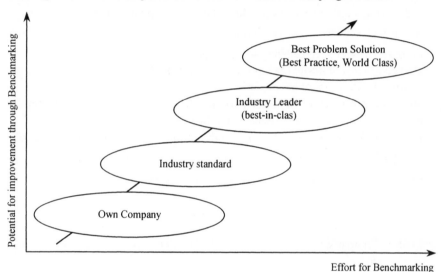

Figure 4. Relationship between standard of comparisons, improvement potential and effort for benchmarking.

Source: EC Quality Series no. 7, p.17

The purpose of the analytical tool we propose below is to compare current and projected performance of organization to the bipolar reference performers: good and week benchmarking partners. Introducing the outrankig relation (Konarzew-ska 1989) among all compared elements the bipolar approach allows to answer three questions:
1. How good or/and how bad is our current performance with regard to the benchmarking partners?

2. What progress has been done in comparison to the former result of self-assessment?
3. Which projected performance profile is closest to the good performers' standard?

The **BIPOLAR model** requires to identify the following elements of benchmarking analysis:
– **finite set of evaluated profiles**: $O = \{o_i\}$; it will include first of all the current own performance and alternative future performance profiles,
– **evaluation criteria** (performance dimensions): $K = \{f_j\}, f_j(o_i): O \rightarrow E_j$ where E_j is cardinal or ordinal or binary scale; they can be oriented for a specific industry or product or process as well as generic like EFQM Model criteria and scoring matrix just suggested for company benchmarking purposes,
– **weights of relative criterion importance**: $P = \{p_j\}, \Sigma p_j = 1$; the weights of European Model of Excellence are suggested,
– **characteristics of desirable values of criteria**: in the case of using the scoring matrix all criteria are to be maximised,
– **outranking threshold value (or accordance level)** z; it sets what fraction of all criteria is necessary to establish the final evaluation and
– **bipolar reference system** $R = \{r_t\}$ in the form of two sets of profiles: "good" $D = \{d_h\}$ and "bad" $Z = \{z_k\}$ such that $D \cup Z = R$, $D \cap Z = \varnothing$ (of performance settings: positive and negative poles, just discussed above).

4.2. Phases of analysis

PHASE I: Comparison of the objects o_i to the elements r_t of reference system $R = D \cup Z$.
A. Establishing outranking indicators. The comparison is made between the elements of set $O = \{o_i\}$ and elements of reference set $R = \{r_t\}$; we do not consider the relations in O and R. For each pair (o_i, r_t) we verify the hypothesis "o_i outranks r_t" (analogously, for pair (r_t, o_i) we verify the hypothesis "r_t outranks o_i"). According to the ELECTRE II method, the hypothesis is accepted if two tests are fulfilled: concordance test and non-discordance test (see Roy 1985). For this reason, for each pair (o_i, r_t) we calculate three numbers as follows:

$$P^+(o_i, r_t) = \sum_{j+} p_{j+}, \quad j^+ \in \{j : f_j(o_i) > f_j(r_t)\},$$

$$P^-(o_i, r_t) = \sum_{j-} p_{j-}, \quad j^- \in \{j : f_j(o_i) < f_j(r_t)\},$$

$$P^= \left(o_i, r_t \right) = \sum_{j=} p_{j=}, \quad j^= \in \left\{ j : f_j \left(o_i \right) = f_j \left(r_t \right) \right\}.$$

The concordance test is fulfilled for $\left(o_i, r_t \right)$ if

$$P^+ \left(o_i, r_t \right) + \min_j p_j > P^- \left(o_i, r_t \right).$$

The non-discordance test is fulfilled for $\left(o_i, r_t \right)$ if

$$\left(f_j \left(o_i \right), f_j \left(r_t \right) \right) \notin N_j \quad \forall j \in J^-,$$

where $N_j \subset E_j \times E_j$ is a set of non-admissible discordance's for any j-th criterion.

If both tests are fulfilled for pair $\left(o_i, r_t \right)$ the outranking indicator d_{it}^+ of profile o_i with regard to reference profile r_t is calculated as follows:

$$d_{it}^+ = P^+ + P^= \quad \text{(in this case } d_{it}^- = 0 \text{)}.$$

B. Establishing preference structure. Let us assume that $s = z - \min p_j$. Now, we compare the outranking indicators with the threshold values and for any pair $\left(o_i, r_t \right)$ we define the following binary relations:

− preference "$\succ$"

$$o_i \succ r_t \Leftrightarrow d_{it}^+ > s \wedge d_{it}^- = 0,$$

$$r_t \succ o_i \Leftrightarrow d_{it}^+ = 0 \wedge d_{it}^- > s,$$

− indifference "$\simeq$"

$$o_i \simeq r_t \Leftrightarrow d_{it}^+ > s \wedge d_{it}^- > s,$$

− incomparability "!"

$$o_i ! r_t \Leftrightarrow \left(d_{it}^+ < s \wedge d_{it}^- < s \right) \vee \left(d_{it}^+ < s \wedge d_{it}^- = 0 \right) \vee$$
$$\left(d_{it}^+ = 0 \wedge d_{it}^- < s \right) \vee \left(d_{it}^+ = 0 \wedge d_{it}^- = 0 \right).$$

PHASE II: Comparison of the profiles o_i to the set of "good" ones D and to the set of "bad" ones Z.

A. Comparison of o_i **to the set of "good" profiles** $D = \{d_h\}$ **(Figure 5)** we establish the degree of reaching the success d_s as follows:

1) If $\exists h : o_i \succ d_h \vee o_i \simeq d_h$, then $d_s = d_{iD}^+ = \max_{h^*} d_{ih}$,

where $h^* = \{h : o_i \succ d_h \vee o_i \simeq d_h\}$.

2) If $\sim \exists h : o_i \succ d_h \vee o_i \simeq d_h$ and $\exists h : d_h \succ o_i$, then $d_s = d_{iD}^- = \min_h d_{ih}^-$.

3) Otherwise $d_s = d_{iD}^+ = d_{iD}^- = 0$ ("o_i is incomparable to set D").

348

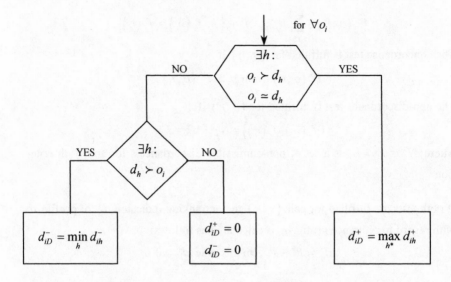

Figure 5. Phase II: Comparison of the profiles o_i to the set of "good" ones $D = \{d_h\}$. Flowchart for the degree of reaching the success for $\forall o_i$

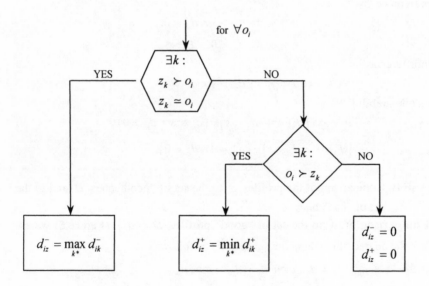

Figure 6. Phase II: Comparison of the profiles o_i to the set of "bad" ones $Z = \{z_k\}$. Flowchart for the degree of avoiding the failure for $\forall o_i$

B. Comparison of o_i to the set of "bad" profiles $Z = \{z_k\}$ (Figure 3). For any
object o_i we establish the degree of avoiding the failure d_N as follows:

1) If $\exists k : z_k \succ o_i \vee z_k \simeq o_i$ then $d_N = d_{iz}^- = \max_{k^*} d_{ik}^-$,

    where $k^* = \{k : z_k \succ o_i \vee z_k \simeq o_i\}$.

2) If $\sim \exists k : z_k \succ o_i \vee z_k \simeq o_i$ and $\exists k : o_i \succ z_k$, then $d_N = d_{iz}^+ = \min_k d_{ik}^+$.

3) Otherwise $d_N = d_{iz}^- = d_{iz}^+ = 0$ ("o_i is incomparable to set Z").

PHASE III: Establishing the position of profile o_i with regard to the bipolar refer-
        ence system (D, Z) .

As a result of phases I and II, any evaluated performance profile o_i is described
by vector $[d_S, d_N]$. Let us combine the possible states of the prifile o_i :

d_N \ d_S	$d_{iD}^+ > 0$	$d_{iD}^- > 0$	$d_{iD}^+ = d_{iD}^- = 0$
$d_{iz}^- > 0$	(0)	(1)	(2)
$d_{iz}^+ > 0$	(3)	(4)	(5)
$d_{iz}^- = d_{iz}^+ = 0$	(6)	(7)	(8)

The possible states of o_i are: (1), (2), (3), (4), (5), (6), (7), (8). Since $D \cap Z = \varnothing$
the state (0) cannot occur.

As a result of this confrontation any current and projected performance is described by two indicators calculated by BIPOLAR method:
– the degree of reaching the success (d_S) and
– the degree of avoiding the failure (d_N).
This information is communicated to users in numerical and visual way. It can be
immediately interpreted in terms of present and future gaps.
The indicator d_S informs what is the gap between own company and all considered good performers. The indicator d_F measures the progress (if any) made in
performance in respect to the beginning of self – assessment process.

5. Conclusion

The paper presents some results of a research project conducted in the field of
Total Quality Management and its tools (grant H02 D02312). The special attention
has been paid to the company benchmarking methodology and self-assessment

procedure based upon the European Business Excellence Model. We have focused first:
- on the phases of benchmarking process and
- on the multiple criteria evaluation in EFQM Excellence Model.

To improve the multiple comparisons and analysis phase of the benchmarking process we have designed the method of company benchmarking against the industry leaders. It adopts the BIPOLAR methodology developed by Author primarly as the Multiple Criteria Decision Aid tool. The BIPOLAR benchmarking procedure can support the organization to answer the question how good or/and how bad is its current performance with regard to the benchmarking partners.

References

Boxwell R.J. (1994) Benchmarking for competitive Advantage, McGraw-Hill

Camp R. C. (1994) Benchmarking, Carl Hanser Verlag, Munchen

Camp R. C. (1995) Best Practice Benchmarking, ASQC Quality Press, Milwaukee

Camp R. C. (1998) Global Cases in Benchmarking: The Best Practices from Organizations Around the World. ASQC Quality Press, Milwaukee

GhubadianA., H.S. Woo (1996) Characteristics, benefits and short comings of four major quality awards. *Intern. Jour. of Quality and Reliability Management, Vol. 13, No 2,* pp. 10-44

Konarzewska-Gubała E. (1989) BIPOLAR: multiple criteria decision aid using bipolar reference system. Document du LAMSADE, 56, Universite de Paris-Dauphine, Paris

Konarzewska-Gubała E. (1996) Suporting an effective performance appraisal system. *Argumenta Oeconomica, vol. 1,* pp. 123, 135

Konarzewska-Gubała E., E. Trybus (1999) Benchmarking, Multi-Criteria Evaluation Model, and ISO 9000 Registration. Proceedings of the International Conference on „Technology and Innovation Management", Portland, 24-29 July

Roy B. (1985) Méthodologie Multicritère d'Aide à la Décision, Editions Economica, Paris

Trybus E. Kumar A. (1998) Critical success factors for ISOO 9000 registration. *Jour. of the Academy of Business Administration, vol. 3.* pp. 17-26 Spring

The Benchmarking Management Guide, Productivity Press, Portland 1993

The European Quality Promotion Policy, EC Quality Series nr 7, January 1998

Watson G.H. (1992) The Benchmarking Workbook. Productivity Press, Cambridge, MA

Multiobjective Analysis of a Financial Plan in a Bank

Jerzy Michnik
Department of Operations Research
The Karol Adamiecki University of Economics in Katowice
ul. 1 Maja 50, 40-287 Katowice, Poland
e-mail: jmichnik@ae.katowice.pl

Abstract

Financial planning in a modern commercial bank comprises several issues like profitability, risk profile and market competition. There are many subjects engaged what makes the whole process even more complex. In this paper the multiobjective linear programming model is presented. It is designed to help choosing strategic directions in bank's financial plan.
The numerical example is performed with the use of data from financial statement of one of the largest Polish commercial banks. The model is solved with the aid of Steuer's ADBASE method. Relatively large number of non-dominated vertices makes useful the method of filtering the solutions during the interactive-like procedure.

1. Introduction

Commercial banks are intermediaries providing financial services to individuals and institutions. The management of the complicated process of drawing funds and allocation of them to a number of uses is one of the most important elements of a bank's strategic planning process.

An overview of uses of operations research techniques in bank management presented by Cheng [4] states that banks have been quite willing to adopt various sophisticated methods in an effort to improve the efficiency of operations. Two main factors affect the frequency with which a particular technique is adopted:
- simplicity of the technique, which means the ease of understanding by non-technical managers of how solution can be obtained,
- applicability of the technique. This refers to the real-life usefulness of the technique in the day-to-day banking operations.

A number of programming models has been developed to assist the banks in solving the financial planning problem[2, 3, 5-7, 9]. The most common types of model structure so far were linear programming and linear goal programming. Booth and Dash [3] considered implications of different model structures: linear programming, two-stage linear programming, linear goal programming and two stage linear goal programming. Two-stage model expands the linear programming approach by explicitly incorporating uncertainty into the model, while goal programming permits more than one goal in the model objective function. The authors considered four objectives: minimisation of the excess cash holdings, maximisation of loan's volume, minimisation of excess of loans to deposit ratio and maximisation of profitability.

The extended model [2] examined the normative effect of changing interest rates on the rearrangements of depository bank balance sheet and profits. In a two-stage linear goal programming model authors include on- and off-the-balance-sheet decision variables. The goal of the bank was to stated to obtain the status-quo profits for both periods in every state of nature (three scenarios were considered).

Giokas and Vassiloglou [5] discussed construction and application of a linear goal programming model, which had a hierarchical structure. Among objectives there were: gross revenues, capital adequacy, liquidity, increase of deposits and loans.

The other practical application of linear goal programming model was presented by Korhonen [6]. The model considered three one-year planning periods and a number of alternative scenarios were used to describe uncertainty. The model comprised several goals with different priorities, for instance expected profits, liquidity, capital adequacy, deposit growth, unsatisfied loans demand, minimum loan demand.

It is now clear that the conventional linear programming is unable to comprise all kinds of managerial objectives at the same time. The complexity of the problem can only be addressed by the multiobjective decision models. This paper discusses the multiobjective linear programming model constructed to solve the problem of strategic directions of financial planning in a large commercial Polish bank. The aim of the work was to contain all important features of the financial planning process avoiding unnecessary complexities which lead to large scale models. In such models the important issues are frequently screened by the huge number of details. The use of explicit multiobjective solving procedure gives many nondominated solutions. This enables the use of interactive-like procedure during which the decision maker has the opportunity to analyse nondominated solutions and reveal his/her hidden preferences.

2. Presentation Of The Model

2.1. Decision variables

Decision variables are chosen to represent all main activities of a Polish commercial bank. Assets positions are described by ten and liabilities by eight decision variables. The last four variables measure the income and expenses of the bank.

The fixed model parameters and beginning values are taken from the financial statement published by one of the largest Polish commercial banks. Interest rates simulate the market values of considered period.

The variables and parameters are as follows:

x_1 – Cash and accounts in the Central Bank

x_2 – Loans to financial institutions

x_3 – Loans to financial institutions (On demand)

x_4 – Loans to financial institutions (Deposits)

x_5 – Due from customers and budget sector

x_6 – Due from customers

x_7 – Due from budget sector

x_8 – Debt securities (treasury bills and bonds)

x_9 – Shares

x_{10} – Fixed assets

x_{11} – Liabilities to customers

x_{12} – Liabilities to customers (On demand)

x_{13} – Liabilities to customers (Term deposits)

x_{14} – Liabilities to budget sector

x_{15} – Liabilities to budget sector (On demand)

x_{16} – Liabilities to budget sector (Term deposits)

x_{17} – Liabilities to financial institutions

x_{18} – Liabilities due to securities issued

x_{19} – Interest income

x_{20} – Commission income

x_{21} – Interest expense

x_{22} – Commission expense

Share capital = 150.00
General reserves = 100.00
Liabilities to the Central Bank = 808.45
Cash and accounts in the Central Bank = 515.03
Loans to financial institutions (On demand) = 384.17
Loans to financial institutions (Deposits) = 4,319.95
Due from customers = 1,657.95

Due from budget sector = 1.16

Debt securities = 8,966.05

Shares = 446.6
Fixed assets = 505.69
Liabilities to customers (On demand) = 4,980.73
Liabilities to customers (Term deposits) = 8,187.04
Liabilities to budget sector (On demand) = 40.98
Liabilities to budget sector (Term deposits = 20.49
Liabilities to financial institutions = 1,447.54
Liabilities due to securities issued = 4.87

2.2. Solid constraints

The first group contains constraints imposed by technical and market limitations. On the one hand they represent limited ability of development of branches' net and consequent top limits on the volume of financial services. On the other hand it is not possible for the bank to quit any of its main activities what results in the several bottom limits on decision variables.

$$x_2 \geq 1,000.00 \qquad\qquad 2,000.00 \leq x_{12} \leq 6,000.00$$

$$x_3 \geq 400.00 \qquad\qquad 5,000.00 \leq x_{13} \leq 10,000.00$$

$$x_4 \geq 1,300.00 \qquad\qquad 40.00 \leq x_{15} \leq 125.00$$

$$x_6 \geq 1,700.00 \qquad\qquad 30.00 \leq x_{16} \leq 65.00$$

$$x_7 \geq 1.50 \qquad\qquad 500.00 \leq x_{17} \leq 1,400.00$$

$$x_9 \geq 350.00 \qquad\qquad 10.00 \leq x_{18} \leq 1,400.00$$

$$x_{10} \geq 500.00$$

The following equations present the formal relationships between decision variables.

$$x_1 + x_2 + x_5 + x_8 + x_9 + x_{10} = x_{11} + x_{14} + x_{17} + x_{18} + 1058.45$$

(Balance sheet equation)

$$x_2 = x_3 + x_4$$

(Loans to financial institutions = (On demand) + (Deposits))

$$x_5 = x_6 + x_7$$

(Due from customers and budget sector = Due from customers + Due from budget sector)

$$x_{11} = x_{12} + x_{13}$$

(Liabilities to customers = (On demand)+ (Term deposits))

$$x_{14} = x_{15} + x_{16}$$

(Liabilities to budget sector = (On demand)+ (Term deposits))

The next two inequalities represent the external conditions imposed by the banking supervision. The first establishes the bottom limit on capital adequacy ratio to be 8 %, the second the – bottom limit on obligatory reserves.

$0,04x_2 + 0,08\ x_6 + 0,008x_8 \le 250.00$

(Capital Adequacy Ratio $\ge$ 8%)

$x_1 \ge 20\%\ (x_{12} + x_{15}) + 11\%\ (x_{13} + x_{16})$

(Obligatory reserves)

The role of the following constrains is to reflect managerial view of the relations between balance sheet positions. The first establishes the relation between credit volumes of two main groups of clients. The second limits the volume of shares portfolio. The third gives some prudent limit on the ratio of credits to deposits. The last one limits the risk of wholesale deposits, whose volatility can be dangerous for liquidity of the bank.

$x_6 \ge 70\%\ x_5$

(Due from customers $\ge$ 70% Due from customers and budget sector)

$x_9 \le 20\%\ (x_1 + x_2 + x_5 + x_8 + x_{10})$

(Shares $\le$ 20% Total assets)

$x_5 \le 40\%\ x_{11}$

(Due from customers and budget sector $\le$ 40% Liabilities to customers)

$x_{17} \le 15\%\ x_{11}$

(Liabilities to financial institutions $\le$ 15% Liabilities to customers)

At last, the following equalities calculate the income statement positions.

$$
\begin{aligned}
x_{19} = {} & 0.5\times23.75\%\ (384.17 + x_3) + 0.5\times24\%\ (4{,}319.95 + x_4) + \\
& + 0.5\times25\%\ (1{,}657.95 + x_6) + 0.5\times25\%\ (1.16 + x_7) + \\
& + 0.5\times23.5\%\ (8{,}966.05 + x_8)
\end{aligned}
$$

(Interest income)

$$
\begin{aligned}
x_{20} = {} & 0.5\times0.25\%\ (384.17 + x_3) + 0.5\times0.25\%\ (4{,}319.95 + x_4) + \\
& + 0.5\times0.75\%\ (1{,}657.95 + x_6) + 0.5\times0.75\%\ (1.16 + x_7) + \\
& + 0.5\times1.25\%\ (8{,}966.05 + x_8)
\end{aligned}
$$

(Commission income)

$$
\begin{aligned}
x_{21} = {} & 0.5\times18.5\%\ (4{,}980.73 + x_{12}) + 0.5\times21.5\%\ (8{,}187.04 + x_{13}) + \\
& + 0.5\times15.5\%\ (40.98 + x_{15}) + 0.5\times21.5\%\ (20.49 + x_{16}) + \\
& + 0.5\times20.5\%\ (1{,}447.54 + x_{17}) + 0.5\times11.5\%\ (4.87 + x_{18})
\end{aligned}
$$

(Interest expense)

$$
\begin{aligned}
x_{22} = {} & 0.5\times1.8\%\ (4{,}980.73 + x_{12}) + 0.5\times1.05\%\ (8{,}187.04 + x_{13}) + \\
& + 0.5\times0.75\%\ (40.98 + x_{15}) + 0.5\times0.85\%\ (20.49 + x_{16}) + \\
& + 0.5\times0.25\%\ (1{,}447.54 + x_{17}) + 0.5\times0.75\%\ (4.87 + x_{18}).
\end{aligned}
$$

(Commission expense)

2.3. Criteria

In the model we maximise:

1. net income,
2. loans balance,
3. treasury bills and bonds balance,
4. liabilities to customers (on demand) balance,

$$\left[\begin{array}{l} F_1(x) = x_{19} + x_{20} - x_{21} - x_{22} \\ F_2(x) = x_5 \\ F_3(x) = x_8 \\ F_4(x) = x_{12} \end{array}\right] \rightarrow max$$

The first criterion is obvious. The second and the last one represent the managerial attitude towards market position of the bank. The second means that the bank tries to meet the clients' demand for credits at the maximum level. The fourth criterion maximises the clients' current accounts. However they are not profitable to the bank at the moment, the bank expects the future profits provided it keeps many clients with it.

The model belongs to the class of multiple objective linear programming models and can be solved by any available algorithm.

3. Numerical Results

To help the decision maker with the analysis, the solutions presented to him/her will be supplemented with the set of commonly used bank performance ratios. We choose the following ratios for the presentation[1]:

General Condition Ratios

1) Loan to Asset Ratio (LA):

$$LA = \frac{Total\ Loans}{Total\ Assets} \times 100\%,$$

2) Loan to Deposit Ratio (LD):

$$LD = \frac{Total\ Loans}{Total\ Deposits} \times 100\%$$

Profitability Ratios

1) Return on Equity (ROE)

$$ROE = \frac{Net\ Income}{Average\ Total\ Equity}$$

2) Return on Assets (ROA)

$$ROA = \frac{\text{Net Income}}{\text{Average Total Assets}}$$

3) Effectiveness Ratio (E)

$$E = \frac{\text{Interest Income} + \text{Commision Income}}{\text{Interest Expense} + \text{Commision Expence}} \times 100\%$$

Capital Adequacy Ratio (R)

$$R = \frac{\text{Total Equity}}{\text{Risk Weighted Assets and Off Balance Sheet Items}} \times 100\%$$

The model was solved with aid of ADBASE [8], which is the procedure for enumerating efficient points and unbounded efficient edges. The size of the model makes the vector-maximum approach reasonable. We also assume that the decision maker, by reviewing the list of nondominated criterion vectors, would be able to identify his/her efficient extreme point of greatest utility. It is hoped this extreme point would be optimal, or close enough to being optimal.

The list of all nondominated extreme points of the model is presented in Table 1.

We observe some degeneracy in our problem. However there is a reason for keeping all solutions to the very end of the procedure. During the final analysis of the group of similar solutions the decision maker can reveal his/her hidden preferences towards the decision variables values, which are, of course, not the same for degenerated solutions. As the number of solutions is relatively large, we use a technique of interactive search through the set of nondominated solutions. This technique consists of two phases of filtering [8].

The phase of forward filtering gives the P vectors that are most different from one another. This is accomplished by finding the P vectors that are furthest apart from one another according to a given metric. The filtered P vectors are presented to the decision maker. When he/she chooses the most preferred one from them, the second phase starts.

During the second phase of reverse filtering we choose the set of R vectors that are the most similar to the one chosen by the decision maker at the end of the first phase. This is accomplished by finding R-1 vectors closed to the chosen one according to a given metric.

To perform the forward and reverse filtering we use the program FILTER [8]. The FILTER enables to perform filtering with the use of the family of L_p metrics defined as follows:

$$L_p(\mathbf{x}_a, \mathbf{x}_b) = \left[\sum_{i=1}^{n} |x_{ai} - x_{bi}|^p \right]^{\frac{1}{p}},$$

$$L_{\infty}(\mathbf{x}_a, \mathbf{x}_b) = max_i |x_{ai} - x_{bi}| \quad \text{(Tschebycheff metrics)}$$

Table 1. Nondominated solutions

	F1	F2	F3	F4
Sol. no.	net income	loans balance	TB balance	current acc. bal.
1	435	2602	4533	2000
2	435	2429	5750	3098
3	424	2694	3891	2000
4	418	2429	5750	3992
5	423	2705	3812	2000
6	416	2429	5750	4077
7	388	2800	3150	2000
8	325	2429	5750	5814
9	336	2903	2430	2257
10	306	2429	5750	6000
11	306	2429	5750	6000
12	306	2429	5750	6000
13	-8	3250	0	3125
14	188	3052	1385	2631
15	-8	3250	0	3125
16	-299	3250	0	6000
17	109	2697	3874	6000
18	-299	3250	0	6000
19	-8	3250	0	3125
20	-8	3250	0	3125
21	-299	3250	0	6000
22	-299	3250	0	6000

For all calculations with FILTER we used the method called "furthest point out-side the neighbourhoods". For both forward and reverse filtering we can use more then one vector as the initial set for the filtering. These vectors are called "seed vectors".

If we analyse the content of Table 1 from the economic point of view, we see that the better achievement of the TB balance and current account balance (criteria F3 and F4) is accompanied usually by the worse result for the income and loans bal-ance (criteria F1 and F2). Some solutions (no. 13,15, 16, 18-22) have not accept-able level of liquidity (TB balance is zero) and negative income. They all are not supposed to be really considered as the desired solutions. Some of the solutions represent satisfactory level of achievement of all criteria. among them we have chosen solutions no. 2 and 8 for the purpose of further analysis.

In the process of forward filtering we have experimented with three types of the above metrics: $p = 1,2$ and ∞. In every case we have chosen the number of filtered solutions (P) to be 5 and two seed vectors: solutions no. 2 and 8. As the result (in addition to seed vectors) we received: for $p = 1$: solutions 7, 14, 16; for $p = 2$ solutions 5, 14, 16; for $p = \infty$, solutions 9, 13, 16. The complete list of forward filtered solutions is given in Table 2.

Table 2 Forward filtered solutions

Sol. no.	F1 net income	F2 Loans balance	F3 TB balance	F4 current acc. bal.
2	435	2429	5750	3098
8	325	2429	5750	5814
5	423	2705	3812	2000
7	388	2800	3150	2000
9	336	2903	2430	2257
13	-8	3250	0	3125
14	188	3052	1385	2631
16	-299	3250	0	6000

Let assume that the decision maker chose the solution no. 8 as the most preferred one from the set of forward filtered solutions. Next we perform the reverse filtering with the sol. 8 as a seed vector and the number of filtered vectors R=3. For different metrics ($p = 1,2, \infty$) we received the same set of solutions: no. 8, 10, 11. They are presented in Table 3 accompanied by the values of all decision variables and calculated ratios. This set of solutions can be considered as a base for the final decision.

Table 3 Reverse filtered solutions

Solution no.	8	10	11
F1 - net income	325	306	306
F2 - loans balance	2429	2429	2429
F3 - TB balance	5750	5750	5750
F4 - current acc. bal.	5814	6000	6000
Capital Adequacy Ratio	8.00%	8.00%	8.00%
Loan to Deposit	36.27%	35.68%	35.68%
Loan to Asset	33.15%	32.67%	32.67%
Effectiveness Ratio	111.62%	110.88%	110.88%
ROE	113.07%	110.13%	110.13%
ROA	2.55%	2.37%	2.37%
X(1)	1724	1910	1761
X(2)	1700	1700	1700

X(3)	400	400	400
X(4)	1300	1300	1300
X(5)	2429	2429	2429
X(6)	1700	1700	1700
X(7)	729	729	729
X(8)	5750	5750	5750
X(9)	350	350	499
X(10)	500	500	500
X(11)	10814	11000	11000
X(12)	5814	6000	6000
X(13)	5000	5000	5000
X(14)	70	70	70
X(15)	40	40	40
X(16)	30	30	30
X(17)	500	500	500
X(18)	10	10	10
X(19)	3008	3008	3008
X(20)	115	115	115
X(21)	2628	2646	2646
X(22)	169	171	171

4. Summary

The presented model is more universal and realistic than classic linear methods. It allows to consider various sets of criterion functions which can represent different objectives of importance for bank's management. The limited size of the model is enough for strategic analysis of bank's financial plan. On the other hand it enables the use of quasi-interactive method with enumerating and filtering all nondominated solutions of a problem.

References

1. *Banking Terminology*. Third Edition (1989) American Bankers Association, Washington D.C.

2. Booth G.G., Bessler W., Foote W.G. (1989). Managing interest-rate risk in banking institutions. European Journal of Operational Research 41, pp. 302-313.

3. Booth G.G., Dash G.H., Jr. (1979). Alternate programming structures for bank portfolios. Journal of Banking and Finance 3, pp. 67-82.

4. Cheng T.C.E. (1990). An Overview of Uses of OR Techniques in Bank Management. Managerial Finance Vol. 16, No. 1.

5. Giokas D., Vassiloglou M. (1991). A goal programming model for bank assets and liabilities management. European Journal of Operational Research 50, pp. 48-60.

6. Korhonen A. (1987). A dynamic bank portfolio planning model with multiple scenarios, multiple goals and changing priorities. European Journal of Operational Research 30, pp. 13-23.

7. Langen D. (1989). An (Interactive) Decision Support System for Bank Asset Liability Management. Decision Support Systems 5, pp. 389-401.

8. Steuer R. E.(1986). Multiple Criteria Optimization: Theory, computation and Application, Wiley, New York.

9. Telgen J. (1985) MCDM Problems in Rabobank Nederland. W: *Multiple Criteria Decision Methods and Applications*. Edited by Gunter Fandel and Jaap Spronk in collaboration with Benedetto Matarazzo, Springer Verlag, pp. 307-316.

Inverse Stochastic Dominance and its Application in Production Process Control

**Maciej Nowak[1], Tadeusz Trzaskalik[2],
Grażyna Trzpiot[3], Kazimierz Zaraś[4]**

[1,2,3] The Karol Adamiecki University of Economics in Katowice,
ul. 1 Maja 50, 40-287 Katowice, Poland
[1,2] Department of Operations Research
[3] Department of Statistics
[1] nomac@ae.katowice.pl, [2] ttrzaska@ae.katowice.pl,
[3] trzpiot@ae.katowice.pl
[4] Université du Québec en Abitibi-Temiscamingue,
Rouyn-Noranda, Québec, Canada
Kazimierz.Zaras@uqat.uquebec.ca

Abstract

We are considering the problem of production process control in a firm, where a point to point type of production organisation is applied and production process control is held according to the Just-in-Time rule. In our paper we propose to solve the problem of production process control as a multiattribute problem. The algorithm, which we are proposing is built on a concept of outranking relation and inverse stochastic dominance. The multiattribute analysis, based on stochastic dominance, applies the utility theory to individual attributes in order to determinate a concordance level among them.

1. Introduction

Decision aid is possible if we are able to model preferences of the decision-maker. In the American approach there is no place for incomparability between decision alternatives. Keeney'a i Raiffa (1976), founders of multiattribute utility theory and representatives of this approach, reduced the multicriteria problem to one-attribute problem by using synthesis function. They assumed that:

1. Decision-maker preferences are clear and give order of alternatives with respect to attributes,

2. There is a global utility function allowing us a priori to set the complete order of alternatives.

The simplest "additive" global utility function enables to measure utility of each alternative with respect to each attribute and then to aggregate partial utilities to global utility.

European (or French) approach based on the outranking relation proposed by B. Roy (1985) is in opposition to the American approach. Application of stochastic dominance in multiattribute analysis enables to take advantage of both approaches. We base on expected utility with respect to each attribute separately and then seek concordance by multiattribute aggregation.

The paper deals with solving the problem of production process control as a multicriteria problem. The problem is formulated in Section 2. Section 3 contains definitions of inverse stochastic dominance. The algorithm is described in Section 4. The last Section of the paper gives an example.

2. Production process control as a multiattribute problem

We consider a problem of production process control in job-shop environment, where machines are grouped together according to type. Machines are not devoted exclusively to one operation. An operation may be carried out by any of the machines from a work centre. In a job-shop products have different processing sequences through the shop, and parts may return to the same work centres at several stages in the process. As a lot of products may be simultaneously produced in the work centre, many operations may wait to be performed on each machine.

We assume that Kanban method is used for control of production. This method was initially designed for volume production. Gravel and Price (1988, 1991) showed that it could also be used in a job-shop system. Production orders are then broken into split-lots that are treated individually. They are processed only if the next stage of production process indicates that this work is required. By using Kanban method significant reduction of work-in-progress can be obtained. The work flow is controlled by Kanban cards. In a job-shop, Kanban card is associated with an operation instead of a machine or a workstation. The operation can be performed if the appropriate card is free. Decision rules are used to determine which of the sets of waiting operations should be executed on a given machine.

Production may proceed differently according to a lot size, number of Kanban cards used, and the decision rule for choosing the waiting job to process. Smaller lot-sizes will usually reduce work-in-progress, but can also enlarge the number of machine set-ups. Larger number of cards improves machine utilisation, but also may increase average stock size. The choice of the best triplet involving the Kanban lot size, the decision rule and the number of Kanban cards constitute a multicriterion problem. Gravel et al. (1992) used stochastic dominance to solve this problem. They have assumed that the decision-maker is risk-averse. Nowak et al. (1997) proposed a modification of this method assuming that decision-maker is risk-prone in relation to the attributes expressed as cost or loss.

In a problem considered below the set of alternatives includes all triplets – the lot size, the number of cards and the decision rule. The set of attributes includes:

- makespan,
- average stock (work-in-progress) level,
- the number of set-ups.

Performances of each alternative with respect to the attributes are evaluated by distribution functions. The knowledge base used for construction of these functions may be obtained by using simulation model of the process. A set of simulations is carried out for each triplet. For each alternative with respect to each attribute we have a sequence of observations that can be used for construction of distribution functions. In references the production of each product was simulated separately. In a job-shop usually several products are manufactured simultaneously. We have decided to simulate such a process.

Our problem can be represented as "A, A, E model" - Alternatives, Attributes, Evaluations (Zaraś, Martel 1994). We consider:

1. A finite set of alternatives:

$A = \{a_1, a_2,..., a_i,..., a_m\}$, where: m - the number of alternatives,

2. A set of attributes:

$X = \{ X_1, X_2,..., X_k,..., X_n \}$ where: n - the number of attributes,

3. A set of evaluations of alternatives with respect to attributes:

$E = \{ X_{ik} \}_{mxn}$ where: X_{ik} - random variable with probability function $f_i(x_{ik})$

We assume that attributes are probabilistically independent and also satisfy the independence conditions allowing us to use additive utility function.

When stochastic dominance is being used, it is not necessary to state explicitly a decision-maker's utility function. Decision under risk involves selection between two alternatives, a_j and a_j', for attribute X_i in a closed interval $[x_0, x^0]$, where:

$$x_o = \min [\min\{x_{ij}\}, \min\{x_{ij}'\}]$$
$$x^o = \max [\max\{x_{ij}\}, \max\{x_{ij}'\}]$$
$$x_{ij} \in X_{ij}, x_{ij}' \in X_{ij}'$$

The attributes are defined in such a way that a larger value is preferred to a smaller one ("more is better") and probability functions are known. The comparison between two alternatives, a_j, $a_j' \in A$ leads to a comparison of two vectors of probability distributions. Taking into account the hypothesis of independence we assume that the multiattribute comparison can be decomposed into n one-attribute comparisons. As these comparisons are obtained from the stochastic dominance, they are expressed in terms of "a_j is at least as good as a_j'" in relation to each attribute and for all pairs $(a_j, a_j') \in A \times A$. We use concordance analysis, based on Roy's Preference Aggregation Rule (1985), to conclude on the global outranking relation.

3. Types of stochastic dominance established for all pairs of alternatives.

Stochastic dominance is used to compare alternatives with respect to the attributes. Decision-maker's goal is to minimize values of all attributes. Kahneman and Tversky (1979) and Zaraś and Martel (1994) showed that a decision-maker is risk-prone with reference to the attributes involving loss or cost. We assume that decision-maker's utility function is convex utility function of INARA type (Increasing Absolute Risk Aversion). The comparison of alternatives can be conducted by means of First Degree Stochastic Dominance

(FSD), Second Degree Inverse Stochastic Dominance (SISD) and Third Degree Inverse Stochastic Dominance (TISD1, TISD2).

Let F_i and F_j are cumulative distribution functions and $\overline{F}_i$ and $\overline{F}_j$ are decumulative distribution functions:

$$\int_{x_0}^{x^0} f(x)dx = \int_{x_0}^{x^0} dF_i(x) = \int_{x_0}^{x^0} d\overline{F}_i(x) = 1$$

$$\overline{F}_i(x) = 1 - F_i(x)$$

F_i FSD F_j if: $\quad F_i \neq F_j \quad$ and $\quad H_1(x) = F_i(x) - F_j(x) \leq 0 \quad$ for all $x \in \left[x_0, x^0\right]$

F_i SISD F_j if: $\quad F_i \neq F_j \quad$ and $\quad \overline{H}_2(x) = \int_x^{x_0} H_1(y)dy \geq 0 \quad$ for all $x \in \left[x_0, x^0\right]$

F_i TISD1 F_j if: $\quad F_i \neq F_j \quad$ and $\quad \hat{H}_3(x) = \int_{x_0}^{x} \overline{H}_2(y)dy \geq 0 \quad$ for all $x \in \left[x_0, x^0\right]$

F_i TISD2 F_j if: $\quad F_i \neq F_j \quad$ and $\quad \overline{H}_3(x) = \int_x^{x^0} \overline{H}_2(y)dy \geq 0 \quad$ for all $x \in \left[x_0, x^0\right]$

SISD and TISD2 were defined by Goovaerts (1984) and TISD1 was defined by Zaraś (1989). Trzpiot and Zaraś proposed algorithm for TSD if empirical distributions were known. We propose modification of this algorithm for inverse stochastic dominance.

The first step of the algorithm is to calculate of decumulative distribution functions for two compared alternatives with probability functions $f_i(x)$ i $f_j(x)$ according to the following formulas:

$$\overline{F}_i(x_n) = \sum_{k=N}^{N-n+1} f_i(x_k), \quad n = 1,2,...,N$$

$$\overline{F}_j(x_n) = \sum_{k=N}^{N-n+1} f_j(x_k), \quad n = 1,2,...,N$$

The random variable with probability function $f_i(x)$ dominates the random variable with probability function $f_j(x)$ according to SISD rule if, and only if $F_i^{SISD}(x_n) \geq F_j^{SISD}(x_n)$ for all n (n=1, 2, ..., N) and $F_i^{SISD}(x_n) > F_j^{SISD}(x_n)$ for at least one n where:

$$F_i^{SISD}(x_n) = \sum_{k=N}^{N-n+1} \overline{F}_i(x_{k+1})(x_k - x_{k+1}), \quad \text{for } n = 2,3,\dots,N$$

$$F_i^{SISD}(x_n) = 0 \quad \text{for } n = N$$

$$F_j^{SISD}(x_n) = \sum_{k=N}^{N-n+1} \overline{F}_j(x_{k+1})(x_k - x_{k+1}), \quad \text{for } n = 2,3,\dots,N$$

$$F_j^{SISD}(x_n) = 0 \quad \text{for } n = N$$

The random variable with probability function $f_i(x)$ dominates the random variable with probability function $f_j(x)$ according to TISD1 rule if, and only if $F_i^{TISD1}(x_n) \geq F_j^{TISD1}(x_n)$ for all n ($n=1, 2, \dots, N$) i $F_i^{TISD1}(x_n) > F_j^{TISD1}(x_n)$ for at least one n where:

$$F_i^{TISD1}(x_n) = \frac{1}{2} \sum_{k=2}^{N} \left[F_i^{SISD}(x_k) + F_i^{SISD}(x_{k-1}) \right](x_k - x_{k-1}), \quad \text{for } n = 2,3,\dots,N$$

$$F_i^{TIDS1}(x_1) = F_i^{SISD}(x_1)$$

$$F_j^{TISD1}(x_n) = \frac{1}{2} \sum_{k=2}^{N} \left[F_j^{SISD}(x_k) + F_j^{SISD}(x_{k-1}) \right](x_k - x_{k-1}), \quad \text{for } n = 2,3,\dots,N$$

$$F_j^{TIDS1}(x_1) = F_j^{SISD}(x_1)$$

The random variable with probability function $f_i(x)$ dominates the random variable with probability function $f_j(x)$ according to TISD2 rule if, and only if $F_i^{TISD2}(x_n) \geq F_j^{TISD2}(x_n)$ for all n ($n=1, 2, \dots, N$) i $F_i^{TISD2}(x_n) > F_j^{TISD2}(x_n)$ for at least one n where:

$$F_i^{TISD2}(x_n) = \frac{1}{2} \sum_{k=N}^{N-n+1} \left[F_i^{SISD}(x_k) + F_i^{SISD}(x_{k+1}) \right](x_k - x_{k+1}), \quad \text{for } n = 2,3,\dots,N$$

$$F_i^{TIDS2}(x_n) = 0 \quad \text{for } n = N$$

$$F_j^{TISD2}(x_n) = \frac{1}{2} \sum_{k=2}^{N-n+1} \left[F_j^{SISD}(x_k) + F_j^{SISD}(x_{k+1}) \right](x_k - x_{k+1}), \quad \text{for } n = 2,3,\dots,N$$

$$F_j^{TIDS2}(x_1) = 0 \quad \text{for } n = N$$

The algorithm may be used for any empirical distributions. Values of observed variables are the points that generate distances between compared points.

4. Description of the method[1]

Two complexity levels are distinguished in the expression of decision-maker's pairwise alternative preferences with respect to attribute X_i:

1. Clear - if SD are consistent with decision-maker's utility function ("transparent" stochastic dominance - SD_T)
2. Unclear - if SD are not consistent with decision-maker's utility function ("non-transparent" stochastic dominance - SD_{NT})

Explicable concordance results from cases in which the expression of the decision-maker's preferences is clear:

$$C_E(a_j, a'_j) = \sum_{i=1}^{n} w_i d_i^E(a_j, a'_j)$$

where $\quad d_i^E(a_j, a'_j) = \begin{cases} 1 & \text{if } F_{ij} \, SD_T \, F'_{ij} \\ 0 & \text{otherwise} \end{cases}$

w_i - relative importance accorded to the i-th attribute with $\quad \sum_{i=1}^{n} w_i = 1$

Non-explicable concordance corresponds to the potential value of the cases in which the expression of the decision-maker's preferences is unclear:

$$C_N(a_j, a'_j) = \sum_{i=1}^{n} w_i d_i^N(a_j, a'_j)$$

where $\quad d_i^N(a_j, a_j') = \begin{cases} 1 & \text{if } (F_{ij} \, SD_{NT} \, F'_{ij} \text{ and not } F'_{ij} \, SD_T \, F_{ij}) \\ & \text{or } (F'_{ij} \, SD_{NT} \, F_{ij} \text{ and not } F_{ij} \, SD_T \, F'_{ij}) \\ 0 & \text{otherwise} \end{cases}$

The following question arises: is it always necessary to clarify all the situations where decision-maker's preferences are unclear in order to make use of a multicriterion decision aid for the statement on alternative ranking. It depends on the level of concordance threshold p required by decision-maker in the construction of the outranking relations according to Roy's rule.

If $C_E(a_j, a'_j) \geq p$ then it is unnecessary to explain unclear relations.

If $C_E(a_j, a'_j) \geq p$, then $a_j \, S \, a'_j$ (i.e. $(a_j, a'_j) \in S(p)$) where $S(p)$ is a set of alternative pairs $(a_j, a'_j) \in A \times A$ such that an outranking relation on the concordance threshold level p is verified. In particular if $p = 1$, then Multiattribute Stochastic Dominance MSD_n is fulfilled.

---

[1] See: Zaraś, Martel (1994)

The explanation of the unclear cases may be beneficial if the following two conditions are verified:

$$C_E(a_j, a_j') < p \quad \text{and} \quad C_E(a_j, a_j') + C_N(a_j, a_j') \geq p$$

If we wish to obtain a more complete network of relations between alternative pairs, we can decrease the value of the concordance threshold. If we order the relative importance accorded to each attribute in the following manner:

$$w_1 \leq w_2 \leq, ..., w_n$$

then for $p = 1 - w_1$ we have that $a_j \, MSD_{n-1} \, a_j'$ if $F_{ij} \, SD_T \, F'_{ij}, \, \forall \, X_j \in A \backslash X_1$.

Then we obtain a partial Multiattribute Stochastic Dominance for all attributes, except the attribute whose relative importance is minimal. Then we can build the global outranking relation based on partial Multiattribute Stochastic Dominance for n and n-1 attributes.

$$MSD_n \cup MSD_{n-1} \subseteq S(1-w_1)$$

This procedure can be continued for n-2 attributes if the decision-maker agrees to do so.

5. An application of multicriteria decision aid in production process control

The "Omega" company is a producer of sports equipment. The firm is a manufacturer of 25 products such as tents, rucksacks, various bags and covers for sports equipment. The production process of each product includes a number of operations made on different machines. The number and type of operations are different for each product. Parts may return to the same machining centre in the process. 24 devices are installed in the work centre: 6 machines of M1 type, 6 machines of M2 type, 4 machines of M3 type, 4 machines of M4 type, 2 machines of M5 type and 2 machines of M6 type.

The production planning and control are organised according to the "Just-in-Time" rules. Production orders are broken into small Kanban lots that are treated individually. The firm uses Kanban cards in order to control the work flow. Each operation has its Kanban. One or more Kanbans may be used for each operation.

Before starting his work an operator has to choose one of the waiting operations. Four decision rules can be used:

1. FIFO - first in, last out;

2. LIFO - last in, first out;

3. SPT - shortest processing time;

4. LPT - longest processing time.

The problem is to choose the best triplet of the Kanban lot size, the decision rule and the number of Kanban cards. For managers it is most important to achieve three goals:

1. To shorten the time needed for realising production orders;

2. Reduction of average stock size;

3. Reduction of machine set-ups.

The solution of the problem proceeds as follows:

1. Simulation of the production of selected products for each triplet of parameters;

2. Construction of distribution functions for each triplet with respect to each attribute;

3. Identification of stochastic dominance between triplets of parameters in relation to each attribute;

4. Multiattribute analysis.

The production program involves 12 products and the acceptable values of parameters are as follows:

1. Kanban lot-size: 5 or 10;

2. Decision rule: FIFO, LIFO, SPT, LPT.

3. The number of Kanbans for each operation: 2 or 4.

In our case the set of alternatives includes 16 triplets (table 1)

Table 1

The set of alternatives

Alter-native	Lot-size	Decision rule	Number of cards	Alter-native	Lot-size	Decision rule	Number of cards
a_1	5	FIFO	4	a_9	5	FIFO	2
a_2	5	LIFO	4	a_{10}	5	LIFO	2
a_3	5	SPT	4	a_{11}	5	SPT	2
a_4	5	LPT	4	a_{12}	5	LPT	2
a_5	10	FIFO	4	a_{13}	10	FIFO	2
a_6	10	LIFO	4	a_{14}	10	LIFO	2
a_7	10	SPT	4	a_{15}	10	SPT	2
a_8	10	LPT	4	a_{16}	10	LPT	2

The simulation model of the process was constructed to study the behaviour of the system under different conditions including:

- the time that is needed for manufacturing products included in current production plan - X_1;
- the number of machine set-ups on all machines - X_2;
- the average stock size (the average number of waiting details) - X_3.

The sequences of 100 simulations were conducted for each triplet. Their results were used to construct distribution function. We can use stochastic dominance if we assume that larger values of attributes are preferred to smaller values. If we want to minimize values of attributes we have to change the sign of obtained values. Other distribution functions were obtained in a similar way. Next we start to identify types of SD between alternatives with respect to attributes. We assume that the decision-maker is risk-prone with reference to attributes of cost or loss type and so we use FSD, SISD, TISD1 and TISD2 to explain relations between alternatives. Tables 2, 3 and 4 show the relations between all alternative pairs explained by stochastic dominance.

Table 2

Stochastic dominance for attribute X_1 (makespan)

X_1	a_1	a_2	a_3	a_4	a_5	a_6	a_7	a_8	a_9	a_{10}	a_{11}	a_{12}	a_{13}	a_{14}	a_{15}	a_{16}
a_1				FSD	FSD			FSD				FSD	FSD			FSD
a_2	FSD		FSD	FSD	FSD	FSD	FSD	FSD	FSD	TISD1	SISD	FSD	FSD	FSD	FSD	FSD
a_3	FSD			FSD	FSD		FSD	FSD	TISD1			FSD	FSD	TISD1	TISD1	FSD
a_4					SISD			FSD				FSD				FSD
a_5								FSD				FSD				TISD1
a_6	FSD		TISD2	FSD	FSD		SISD	FSD	SISD			FSD	FSD	TISD1	SISD	FSD
a_7	FSD			FSD	FSD			FSD				FSD	FSD			FSD
a_8											TISD1					
a_9	FSD			FSD	FSD		FSD	FSD				FSD	FSD	TISD1		FSD
a_{10}	FSD		SISD	FSD	FSD	SISD	FSD	FSD	SISD		TISD2	FSD	FSD	FSD	SISD	FSD
a_{11}	FSD		FSD	FSD	FSD	TISD1	FSD	FSD	FSD			FSD	FSD	TISD1	FSD	FSD
a_{12}																
a_{13}				FSD	FSD			FSD				FSD				FSD
a_{14}	SISD			FSD	FSD		SISD	FSD				FSD	FSD			FSD
a_{15}	FSD			FSD	FSD		FSD	FSD	TISD2			FSD	FSD	TISD1		FSD
a_{16}							SISD					FSD				

Table 3

Stochastic dominance for attribute X_2 (the number of set-ups)

X_2	a_1	a_2	a_3	a_4	a_5	a_6	a_7	a_8	a_9	a_{10}	a_{11}	a_{12}	a_{13}	a_{14}	a_{15}	a_{16}
a_1		FSD							FSD	FSD						
a_2									FSD							
a_3	FSD	FSD							FSD	FSD	FSD	FSD				
a_4	FSD	FSD	FSD						FSD	FSD	FSD	FSD				
a_5	FSD	FSD	FSD	FSD		FSD			FSD	FSD	FSD	FSD	FSD	FSD		
a_6	FSD	FSD	FSD	FSD					FSD	FSD	FSD	FSD		TISD1		
a_7	FSD	FSD	FSD	FSD	FSD	FSD			FSD	FSD	FSD	FSD	FSD	FSD	FSD	FSD
a_8	FSD	FSD	FSD	FSD	FSD	FSD	FSD		FSD	FSD	FSD	FSD	FSD	FSD	FSD	FSD
a_9																
a_{10}		FSD							FSD							
a_{11}	FSD	FSD							FSD	FSD						
a_{12}	FSD	FSD							FSD	FSD	FSD					
a_{13}	FSD	FSD	FSD	FSD		SISD			FSD	FSD	FSD	FSD		FSD		
a_{14}	FSD	FSD	FSD	FSD					FSD	FSD	FSD	FSD				
a_{15}	FSD	FSD	FSD	FSD	SISD	FSD			FSD	FSD	FSD	FSD	FSD	FSD		
a_{16}	FSD	FSD	FSD	FSD	FSD	FSD			FSD	FSD	FSD	FSD	FSD	FSD	FSD	

Table 4

Stochastic dominance for attribute X_3 (average stock)

X_3	a_1	a_2	a_3	a_4	a_5	a_6	a_7	a_8	a_9	a_{10}	a_{11}	a_{12}	a_{13}	a_{14}	a_{15}	a_{16}
a_1					FSD											
a_2	FSD		FSD	FSD	FSD	TISD1	FSD	FSD	FSD		FSD	FSD	FSD		FSD	FSD
a_3	FSD				FSD		FSD	FSD	FSD				FSD			
a_4	FSD		SISD		FSD		SISD	FSD	SISD				FSD			
a_5																
a_6	FSD		FSD	FSD	FSD		FSD	FSD	FSD		FSD	FSD	FSD		FSD	FSD
a_7	FSD				FSD			TISD1	SISD				FSD			
a_8	FSD				FSD				TISD2				FSD			
a_9	FSD				FSD								FSD			
a_{10}	FSD	FSD	FSD	FSD	FSD	FSD	FSD	FSD	FSD		FSD	FSD	FSD	FSD	FSD	FSD
a_{11}	FSD		FSD	FSD	FSD		FSD	FSD	FSD			FSD	FSD		FSD	FSD
a_{12}	FSD		FSD	FSD	FSD		FSD	FSD	FSD				FSD		FSD	FSD
a_{13}	FSD				FSD											
a_{14}	FSD	SISD	FSD	FSD	FSD	FSD	FSD	FSD	FSD		FSD	FSD	FSD		FSD	FSD
a_{15}	FSD		FSD	FSD	FSD		FSD	FSD	FSD				FSD			
a_{16}	FSD		SISD	FSD	FSD		FSD	FSD	FSD				FSD		SISD	

The last step of our procedure is the multicriteria aggregation, which proceeds as follows:

1. We set the importance of each attribute w_k, such that:

$$\sum_{k=1}^{n} w_k = 1$$

2. We calculate explicable concordances for each pair of alternatives:

$$C_E(a_i, a_i') = \sum_{j=1}^{3} w_j d_j^E(a_i, a_i')$$

where:

$d_j^E(a_i, a_i') = 1$ if the alternative a_i dominates a_i' with respect to attribute j according to SD rule,

$d_j^E(a_i, a_i') = 0$ otherwise.

3. We compare the values of calculated indexes with the concordance threshold p. If $C_E(a_i, a_i') \geq p$, then we assume that there is outranking relation between alternative a_i and a_i'.

4. We build the graph that shows the relations between alternatives.

Table 5

Explicable concordances

	a_1	a_2	a_3	a_4	a_5	a_6	a_7	a_8	a_9	a_{10}	a_{11}	a_{12}	a_{13}	a_{14}	a_{15}	a_{16}
a_1	0,00	0,15	0,00	0,50	0,85	0,00	0,00	0,50	0,15	0,15	0,00	0,50	0,50	0,00	0,00	0,50
a_2	0,85	0,00	0,85	0,85	0,85	0,85	0,85	0,85	1,00	0,50	0,85	0,85	0,85	0,50	0,85	0,85
a_3	1,00	0,15	0,00	0,50	0,85	0,00	0,85	0,85	1,00	0,15	0,15	0,65	0,85	0,50	0,50	0,50
a_4	0,50	0,15	0,50	0,00	0,85	0,00	0,35	0,85	0,50	0,15	0,15	0,65	0,35	0,00	0,00	0,50
a_5	0,15	0,15	0,15	0,15	0,00	0,15	0,00	0,50	0,15	0,15	0,15	0,65	0,15	0,15	0,00	0,50
a_6	1,00	0,15	1,00	1,00	0,85	0,00	0,85	0,85	1,00	0,15	0,50	1,00	0,85	0,65	0,85	0,85
a_7	1,00	0,15	0,15	0,65	1,00	0,15	0,00	0,85	0,50	0,15	0,15	0,65	1,00	0,15	0,15	0,65
a_8	0,50	0,15	0,15	0,15	0,50	0,15	0,15	0,00	0,50	0,15	0,15	0,65	0,50	0,15	0,15	0,15
a_9	0,85	0,00	0,00	0,50	0,85	0,00	0,50	0,50	0,00	0,00	0,00	0,50	0,85	0,50	0,00	0,50
a_{10}	0,85	0,50	0,85	0,85	0,85	0,85	0,85	0,85	1,00	0,00	0,85	0,85	0,85	0,85	0,85	0,85
a_{11}	1,00	0,15	0,85	0,85	0,85	0,50	0,85	0,85	1,00	0,15	0,00	0,85	0,85	0,50	0,85	0,85
a_{12}	0,50	0,15	0,35	0,35	0,35	0,00	0,35	0,35	0,50	0,15	0,15	0,00	0,35	0,00	0,35	0,35
a_{13}	0,50	0,15	0,15	0,65	0,85	0,15	0,00	0,50	0,15	0,15	0,15	0,65	0,00	0,15	0,00	0,50
a_{14}	1,00	0,50	0,50	1,00	0,85	0,35	0,85	0,85	0,50	0,15	0,50	1,00	0,85	0,00	0,35	0,85
a_{15}	1,00	0,15	0,50	1,00	1,00	0,15	0,85	0,85	1,00	0,15	0,15	0,65	1,00	0,65	0,00	0,50
a_{16}	0,50	0,15	0,50	0,50	0,50	0,15	0,35	0,85	0,50	0,15	0,15	0,65	0,50	0,15	0,50	0,00

In our paper we present only a simple example involving a small number of alternatives. Usually, when we search for the best combination of parameters of production control we have to examine many alternatives. Considering this we resign calculation of non-explicable concordance indexes and explanation of the cases where decision-maker's preferences are unclear. Moreover in our situation the decision-maker is interested rather in finding the best alternative then in identification relations between all alternatives.

Assuming, that $w_1=0.5$, $w_2=0.15$, $w_3=0.35$. The values of explicable concordances are shown in table 5.

If we assume, that the concordance threshold $p=1$, then the best alternatives are: a_2, a_6, a_7, a_8, a_{10}, a_{11}, a_{14}, a_{15}, a_{16}. To obtain a more detailed ranking we can reduce the value of concordance threshold. The next value that can be analysed is $p=0.85$. In this case the best alternatives are a_2 and a_{10} (see Fig. 1). If the value of concordance threshold is reduced to $p=0.65$, then the best alternatives are still a_2 and a_{10}. Therefore the best triplets of parameters are:

- the Kanban lot size = 5; decision rule = LIFO, the number of Kanbans = 4;
- the Kanban lot size = 5; decision rule = LIFO, the number of Kanbans = 2.

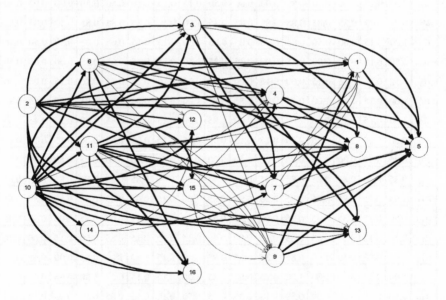

Fig. 1. Concordance threshold $p=0.85$.

6. Conclusion

The procedure given in this paper constitutes a dynamic decision aid in the production process control. It can be adapted to other production environments by changing parameters (alternatives) and attributes. Decision aid based on the rules that have been shown is necessary in modern company, as decision-maker is able to schedule intuitively only a very simple process. Production control in a company that fulfils simultaneously many different orders is only possible under automatic control.

References

1. Arrow K. (1951). Social Choice and Individual Values. John Wiley and Sons, New York.
2. Arrow K. (1965). Aspects of the Theory of Risk Bearing. Yrjö Jahnssonin Säätio, Helsinki.
3. Bawa V.S., Linderberg E.B., Rafsky L.C. (1979). An Efficient Algorithm to Determine Stochastic Dominance Admissible Sets. Management Science, vol. 25, no. 7.
4. Goovaerts M.J. (1984). Insurance Premium. Elsevier Science. Publishers B.V.
5. Gravel M., Martel J.M., Nadeau R., Price W., Tremblay R. (1992). A multicriterion view of optimal resource allocation in job-shop production. European Journal of Operational Research 61, 230-244.
6. Gravel M., Price W.L. (1988). Using the Kanban in job shop environment. International Journal of Production Research 26/6, 1105-1118.
7. Huang C.C., Kira D., Vertinsky I. (1978). Stochastic Dominance Rules for Multiattribute Utility Functions, Review of Economic Studies, vol. 41, 611-616.
8. Kahneman D., Tversky A. (1979). Prospect theory: an analysis of decisions under risk. Econometrica 47, 262-291.
9. Keeney R.L., Raiffa H. (1976). Decisions with Multiple Objectives: Preferences and Value Tradeoffs. Wiley.
10. Martel J.M., Zaraś K. (1995). Une methode multicitere de rangement de projects face au risque. MS/OR Division, vol. 16, no. 2, 135-144.

11. Nowak M (1998) Wielokryterialna optymalizacja rozbudowy parku maszynowego. In: Modelowanie preferencji a ryzyko '98. AE Katowice.

12. Nowak M., Trzaskalik T., Zaraś K. (1997). Dominacje stochastyczne i ich zastosowanie w analizie sterowania procesem produkcyjnym. In: Zarządzanie przedsiębiorstwem XXI wieku. WSZMiJO Katowice, 255-264.

13. Roy B. (1985). Methodologie Multicriterie d'Aide à la Décision. Economica, Paris.

14. Simon H.A. (1955). A Behaviour Model of Rational Choice. Quarterly Journal of Economics, 69, 99-118.

15. Trzaskalik T., Trzpiot G., Zaraś K (1998). Modelowanie preferencji z wykorzystaniem dominacji stochastycznych. AE Katowice

16. Trzpiot G. (1997). Odwrotne dominacje stochastyczne. In: Zastosowania Badań Operacyjnych. Absolwent. Łódź, 435-448.

17. Trzpiot G., Zaraś K. (1999). Algorytm wyznaczania dominacji stochastycznych stopnia trzeciego. Badania Operacyjne i Decyzje 2/1999, 75-85.

18. Whitemore G. (1970). Third Stochastic Dominance. American Economic Review, no. 60.

19. Zaraś K. (1989). Dominance stochastique pour deux classes de fonctions d'utille: concaves et convexes. Rairo: Recherche operationnelle, no. 23.

20. Zaraś K., Martel J.M. (1994). Multiattribute Analysis based on Stochastic Dominance. In: Models and Experiments in Risk and Rationality. Kluwer Academic Publishers, 225-248.

Multi Criteria Multilevel Transshipment Problem and its Software Support

Tomas Šubrt and Ludmila Domeová

Department of Operations Research and System Analysis
Faculty of Economics and Management
Czech University of Agriculture In Prague
Czech Republic
(subrt@pef.czu.cz, domeova@pef.czu.cz)

Abstract

The paper deals with problematic of solving of multilevel transshipment problem with more than one criteria function. There are two levels of such problem. First of them refers to a conversion of a multilevel transshipment model to a standard optimization transportation problem. For such purpose we use a special form of mathematical model, which is here described. Following problem deals with possibilities of solving the converted model using interactive multi criteria optimization methods, specially methods based on ALOP. Another part of our paper is oriented in software realization of such problem on a spreadsheet. For this purpose a special add in Excel module was developed. It includes as well conversion of a multilevel problem to a standard one as its interactive solving using ALOP method. Up to 5 levels transshipment problem with up to 4 criteria functions can be solved.

1. Introduction

A classical topic in transport optimization is a simple transportation problem as formulated in [1]. Usually it is used for minimizing total cost of material transfer between a set of sources and a set of destinations. Each source has a capacity and each destination has a demand which must be satisfied. Simple transportation problem can be used for minimizing the time needed for satisfying consumer's demands or for minimizing the number of kilometers needed for transfer realization. We can assume that the cost of transport closely depends on the distance between both sets and on the time needed for transport realization. Practical experiences especially from the urban transport do not converse to such assumptions. The time needed for transport realization depends more on the daytime when it is realized and on the transport direction then on the distance between source and destination. Sometimes may be cheaper to realize longer journey from the distance point of view but shorter from the duration point of view [2].

To be able to respect these dependences three kinds of optimization techniques can be used

- techniques for stochastic optimization
- techniques for optimization in multi dimensional transportation problems
- techniques for solving multi criteria transportation problem i.e. transportation problem with more then one criteria function.

Only the third kind of technique will be mentioned in further text.

By defining a multi criteria transportation problem we must consider a special character of criteria functions. In contrast to a standard linear multi criteria optimization model the criteria functions are usually not antagonistic. According to the most powerful criterion one solution mostly dominates the others. This domination is typical for a classic transportation problem (Fig. 1) i.e. for the problem, where no transshipment points between sources and destination are defined. To derive meaningful results in multi criteria transport optimization we must consider either large transportation problems or a transshipment problem.

$$\sum_{i=1}^{m}\sum_{j=1}^{n} c_{tij} x_{ij} \to \min; \quad t=1,2,...,s \quad (1)$$	**where** m ... number of sources n ... number of destinations
$$\sum_{j=1}^{n} x_{ij} \le a_i; \quad i=1,2,...,m \quad (2)$$	s ... number of objective functions a_i ... capacity of i-th source
$$\sum_{i=1}^{m} x_{ij} = b_j; \quad j=1,2,...,n \quad (3)$$	b_j ... demand of j-th destination
$x_{ij} \ge 0 \quad (4)$	c_{tij} ... cost coefficient of the t-th criteria function x_{ij} ... amount of material transported between i-th source and j-th destination

Fig. 1: Mathematical Model of Multi Criteria Transportation Problem

2. Multi Criteria Transshipment Problem

Transportation problems with one or more sets of transshipment points (TS points) between a set of sources and a set of destinations will be called a transshipment problem (TSP) as defined in [1,7]. The two level TSP is defined to have one set of sources, one set of transshipment points and one set of destinations. Each material unit transported from a source point to a destination point must pass exactly one TS point. The r level TSP is defined to have $(r-1)$ sets of TS points. Each material unit transported from a source point to a destination point must pass exactly one TS point from each set of TS points. The k-th level of TSP determines a transport between outgoing TS points (from level $k-1$) and incoming TS point (current level k). The term k-th level TS point refers to an incoming TS point for k-th level of TSP. The 0-th level of TS point refers to a source, the r-th level of TSP refers to a destination.

Applying more than one criteria function on the r level TSP we obtain following mathematical model:

$$\sum_{k=1}^{r}\sum_{i=1}^{n^{k-1}}\sum_{j=1}^{n^{k}} c_{tij}^{k} x_{ij}^{k} \rightarrow \min; \quad t=1,2,...,s \tag{5}$$

$$\sum_{j=1}^{n^{k}} x_{ij}^{k} + y_{i}^{k-1} = a_{i}^{k-1}; \quad i=1,2,...,n^{k-1}; \quad k=1,2,...,r \tag{6}$$

$$\sum_{i=1}^{n^{k-1}} x_{ij}^{k} + y_{j}^{k} = a_{j}^{k}; \quad j=1,2,...,n^{k}; \quad k=1,2,...,r \tag{7}$$

$$x_{ij}^{k} \geq 0, \ y_{i}^{k-1} \geq 0, \ y_{i}^{r} = 0; \quad i=1,2,...,n^{k-1}; \ j=1,2,...,n^{k}; \quad k=1,2,...,r \tag{8}$$

$$\min_{k=1,2,...,(r-1)} (\sum_{i=1}^{n^{k}} a_{i}^{k}) \geq \sum_{i=1}^{n^{0}} a_{i}^{0} \geq \sum_{i=1}^{n^{r}} a_{i}^{r} \tag{9}$$

where:
s ... number of criteria functions
r ... number of TSP levels
k ... current level of TSP or level of TS point
n^{k} ... number of TS points of k-th level
... capacity of i-th TS point of k-th level

... capacity slack of i-th TS point of k-th level

$_{ti}$ ... cost coefficients of the t-th criteria function in k-th level of TSP (between i-th TS point of $(k-1)$-th level and j-th TS point of k-th level)

$_{j}$ ... amount of material transported in k-th level of TSP (between i-th TS point of $(k-1)$-th level and j-th TS point of k-th level)

The set of feasible solution Ω is defined by conditions (5), (6), (7).

Fig. 2: Mathematical Model of Multi Criteria r-level Transshipment Problem

This problem can be converted to a classic transportation model [7] under following steps

1) The capacity slack of *i-th* TS point of *k –th* level y_i^k is defined as an amount of transported material within a single transshipment point. These slack variables have zero costs.

2) The amount of material transported on prohibited routs (e.g. on routs among transshipment points of the same level or routs among transshipment points of non adjoining levels) is defined using artificial variables. These artificial variables have penalty costs to be eliminated from the optimal solution.

3) Each TS point from the *0 –th* level up to *(r-1) -th* level represents a source

4) Each TS point from the *1 –st* level up to *r -th* level represents a destination

5) Each *t –th* criteria function coefficients are ordered into a matrix $\mathbf{C}^t$ where three types of submatrixes are defined
   a) $\mathbf{C}^t_k$ ... submatrixes of real cost coefficients of *k –th* TSP level
   b) $\mathbf{P}$ ... submatrixes of penalty costs coefficients among non adjoining TS point levels
   c) $\mathbf{F}$ ... submatrixes of penalty costs and zero cost coefficients between transshipment points of the same level. These matrixes have zero elements on main diagonals and penalty elements besides it.

$$\mathbf{C}^t = \begin{pmatrix} C^t_1 & P & & \cdots & & P \\ F & C^t_2 & & & & \\ P & F & \cdots & & & \\ \cdots & P & \cdots & C^t_k & & \\ & & & F & \cdots & P \\ P & & \cdots & P & F & C^t_r \end{pmatrix}$$

Fig. 3: Cost Coefficient Matrix of One of Criteria Functions

3. Interactive Solving of Multi Criteria Transshipment Problem

A variety of multiple criteria optimization methods can be used for solving multi criteria transshipment problem (MCTSP). Some of them are less suitable then the others because of specific type of constraints in TSP. We decided to modify a standard interactive method ALOP [8] for transshipment problem purposes. The modified method we call TransALOP.

ALOP – Aspiration Levels Oriented Procedure – is an interactive procedure for multi criteria linear programming problems, where the decision space is determined by linear constraints and linear objective functions. The decision maker states aspiration levels for each criteria value. Depending on aspiration levels values the problem can have a unique nondominated solution or can be feasible or infeasible.

In case feasibility the decision maker can either accept found solution or can make changes in his aspiration levels by which a nondominated solution is obtained in the next step. In case of infeasibility the decision maker must make necessary changes in his aspiration levels by which the nearest nondominated solution can be found.

In the first step of the TransALOP algorithm a goal programming model (Fig.4 - Model A) derived from the model mentioned in Fig. 2 is solved.

	where:
$$\sum_{k=1}^{r}\sum_{i=1}^{n^{k-1}}\sum_{j=1}^{n^k} c_{tij}^k x_{ij}^k - p_t = g_t; \quad (10)$$	$c_{tij}^k, x_{ij}^k, n^k,$ ... see Fig. 2
$t = 1, 2..., s$	g_t ... t -th criterion aspiration levels
$$v = \sum_{t=1}^{s}\frac{1}{|\overline{z}_t|}p_t \to \max \quad (11)$$	p_t ... t -th aspiration level overachievement
$x_{ij}^k \in \Omega \quad (12)$	v ... subsidiary objective function
$i = 1, 2, ..., n^{k-1}; j = 1, 2, ..., n^k;$	$\overline{z}_t$ ... optimal value of t-th objective
$k = 1, 2, ..., r$	function of the model in Fig.2

Fig. 4: Mathematical Model A for TransALOP Method

In case of model A (Fig.4) feasibility either a nondominated solution is obtained (all $p_t = 0$, $v = 0$) or p_t values show aspiration levels proposed changes to obtain a nondominated solution.

In case of model A (Fig.4) infeasibility current aspiration levels could not be reached. In the next step of TransALOP method a model B (Fig. 5) is derived.

In the solution of Model B (Fig. 5) necessary changes of t -th aspiration level is denoted by the difference of $(p_t - n_t)$.

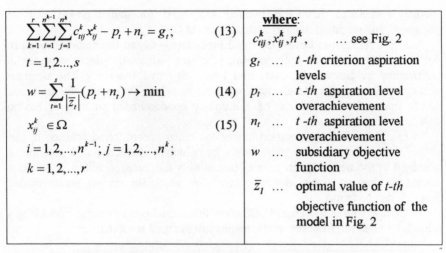

$$\sum_{k=1}^{r}\sum_{i=1}^{n^{k-1}}\sum_{j=1}^{n^k} c_{tij}^k x_{ij}^k - p_t + n_t = g_t;$$ (13)	**where**:
$t = 1, 2..., s$	$c_{tij}^k, x_{ij}^k, n^k,$ ... see Fig. 2
	g_t ... t-th criterion aspiration levels
$$w = \sum_{t=1}^{s}\frac{1}{|\overline{z}_t|}(p_t + n_t) \to \min$$ (14)	p_t ... t-th aspiration level overachievement
$x_{ij}^k \in \Omega$ (15)	n_t ... t-th aspiration level overachievement
$i = 1, 2,..., n^{k-1}; \; j = 1, 2,..., n^k;$	w ... subsidiary objective function
$k = 1, 2,..., r$	$\overline{z}_1$ ... optimal value of t-th objective function of the model in Fig. 2

Fig. 5: Mathematical Model B for TransALOP Method

4. Software Support of TransALOP Method

As a starting point of TransALOP software support we took two modules from our previously created and published system for mathematical modeling in spreadsheets [4], [5], i.e. the module for interactive multi objective programming (Alokosa.xla) and the module for single objective transport optimization (Dumkosa.xla). These modules are directly applicable on a spreadsheet table. They operate according to world standard and contain widely used mathematical functions. All their inputs and outputs are provided only using a standard sheet in Excel. These modules communicate via input dialog boxes mostly with cells and arrays addresses where a model components are stored. They are constructed as Add In Tools for Excel and their use corresponds with all other standard Excel Add Ins. Adapting the module Dumkosa for multilevel problems and connecting it with the module for interactive multi objective programming a new module called TRANSALOP.XLA arose.

With this module we can work in three following steps.

1) Sheet preparation for converting a multilevel TSP to a standard transportation problem. Each sheet contains just one criteria function (decomposed cost matrix – see Fig. 3). First of them additionally contains names of sources, names of transshipment points, names of targets and the amounts of their capacities and supplies. (Theoretically all matrixes can be located on a single sheet but because of a large dimensions of converted cost matrixes this type of model location is unpractical.)

2) Interactive solving of a problem using TransALOP method until acceptable nondominated solution is found. In this step only current values of objective functions, aspiration levels and aspiration levels under (over) achievement are displayed.

3) Displaying a final solution tableau – one of nondominated transport schedule – on a separated sheet.

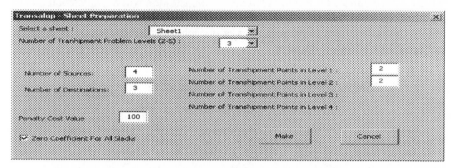

Picture 1: TRANSALOP.XLA - Dialog for Input Sheet Preparation

Criteria Function 1 – Distances (km)								
	T 1(1)	T 1(2)	T 2(1)	T 2(2)	D 1	D 2	D 3	Fictive	Capacities
S 1	12	15						0	500
S 2	13	10						0	150
S 3	11	8						0	300
S 4	6	20						0	120
T 1(1)	0		15	10					500
T 1(2)		0	9	9					600
T 2(1)			0		4	1	2		550
T 2(2)				0	1	2	2		580
Capacities	500	600	550	580	400	350	300	20	

Picture 2: First Criteria Function Cost Matrix on a Prepared Sheet ("Sheet 1")

Picture 3: TRANSALOP.XLA - Dialog for Model Parameters Input (each criteria function on a separate sheet)

Using TRANSALOP.XLA module a model with up to 5 levels, 4 criteria functions, 50 sources, 50 targets and 50 transshipment points in each level can be solved. The example for program features demonstration will be very small due to a limited space in this article. We shall solve 3 level problem with three criteria minimization functions in the meanings of distance, pessimistic transport duration and optimistic transport duration.

Aspiration levels - model Example MOPGP00

				Nadir	Ideal	Nadir Proposed Changes	Nondom. Solution Values
Distance	21980	24330	22080	24330	21980	-2350	21980
Optimistic Duration	19150	19050	19450	19450	19050	-300	19150
Pessimistic Duration	32750	36100	32750	36100	32750	-3350	32750

Feasible	New Levels 1	Proposed Changes	Nondom. Solution Values
Distance	23000	-970	22030
Optimistic Duration	19100	0	19100
Pessimistic Duration	35000	-2150	32850

Nondominated	New Levels 2
Distance	22030
Optimistic Duration	19100
Pessimistic Duration	32850

Picture 4: TRANSALOP.XLA - Sheet with Nadir and Ideal Values of Criteria Functions and with Inputs of User Requested Aspiration Levels (Interactive)

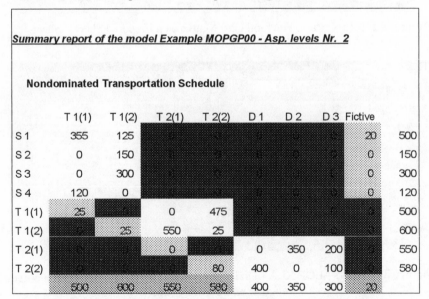

Summary report of the model Example MOPGP00 - Asp. levels Nr. 2

Nondominated Transportation Schedule

	T 1(1)	T 1(2)	T 2(1)	T 2(2)	D 1	D 2	D 3	Fictive	
S 1	355	125						20	500
S 2	0	150						0	150
S 3	0	300						0	300
S 4	120	0						0	120
T 1(1)	25		0	475					500
T 1(2)		25	550	25					600
T 2(1)			0		0	350	200		550
T 2(2)				80	400	0	100		580
	500	600	550	580	400	350	300	20	

Picture 5: Nondominated Solution (Transportation Schedule - Amount of Transported Material) Reached for Aspiration Levels 2

Conclusion

While solving a multi criteria transshipment problem the first step can be represented by its transformation to a multi criteria transportation problem. In this paper an algorithm of such transformation has been described.

Because of a special non antagonistic character of criteria functions in most multi criteria transshipment problems it is hard to use some standard non interactive methods. An interactive goal programming method primary based on the ALOP method has been proposed, verified and called TransALOP.

Modern software support makes possible to model and solve large problems on the field of transport optimization. According to the standard of mathematical modeling on a spreadsheet a new Add In module for solving multi criteria multi level transshipment problem using TransALOP method has been developed.

References

[1] Anderson DR, Sweeney DJ, Williams TA, Loucks J (1999): An Introduction to Management Science : Quantitative Approaches to Decision Making. Southwestern Pub Co.

[2] Belenky AS (1998): Operations Research in Transportation Systems - Ideas and Schemes of Optimization Methods for Strategic Planning. Kluwer Academic Publishers

[3] Bell GHM, Yasunori L, Yasunori A, Yasunori I (1997): Transportation Network Analysis, John Wiley and Sons, Inc., New York.

[4] Brožová H., Marangon, F. (1997) Uno strumento informatico in ambiente MS Excel per l'analisi a molti objectivi. La gestione delle risorse agro-ambientali, working paper University of Udine, Udine.

[5] Brožová H., Šubrt T., Houška M.(1999) : Software Support of Multi Criteria Decision Making in Spreadsheets. In: Proceedings of the Mathematical Methods in Economics Symposium, VŠE Praha, Jindřichův Hradec.

[6] Cohon, J.L., Multiobjective Programming and Planning (1978), Academic Press, New York San Francisco London.

[7] Daskin MS (1995): Network and Discrete Location: Models, Algorithms, and Applications, John Wiley and Sons, Inc., New York.

[8] Fiala P. (1991): Problem Solving Methods in Multicriteria analysis, Diskusionsbeitrag Nr. 181, Feruniversitaet Hagen, Hagen

On Ranking of Economic Educational Institutions in Poland

T. Szapiro, M. Knauff

Division of Decision Analysis and Support,
Warsaw School of Economics,
Al. Niepodległości 162,
02-554 Warsaw Poland;
E-Mail: mknauff@sgh.waw.pl, tszapiro@sgh.waw.pl

Abstract

The problem of ranking of educational institutions is discussed in the paper. Using the Polish case, there is presented a conceptual framework enabling analyses of information and decision processes related to functioning of the educational system. The main actors are university management, future students (households) and government. General concepts are illustrated based on results of recent Polish educational rankings.

Ranking is introduced as a tool that leads to decline uncertainty connected with continuous changes and lack of transparency of the educational system. The paper focuses on economic analysis of rankings and identification of principles, which lead to correct use of these tools. Producer's perspective is used here - the decision-maker is management of university. Then the other actors are discussed as consumers of the output of education. We consider separately decisions of government representing society and decisions of individuals (households). This allows considering a scenario for correct ranking application. Case study providing results of ranking with comments on possibility of decision support is reported.

1. Introduction

Managing an economic organization displays in deciding. Decisions are taking to realize mission of the organization and to meet goals of the organization. Process of the decision making is multistage, sequential and has both informational and decisional consequences. Krzyżanowski (1994) distinguished tree stages of the process: a) getting, collecting and processing information; b) assessment of the information and preparing decision in form of alternatives and c) choice. Information is crucial from the point of view of the management of any organization.

Bittel (1989) pointed out that one of the sources of difficulties of objective analysis in decision making is existing a variety of alternatives, when the economic environment is continuously changing. In such circumstances improvement of the decisions result can be expected when data is used, rather then the decision basing on intuition or guess. According to Krzakiewicz (1993) systematic approach to decision making forces decision-maker to characterize clearly constraints of decision variants and criteria, which are used to evaluate and compare them. Ranking is an important technique supporting decision-makers in her or his task.

The main actors on educational market are university management, future students (households) and government. In any systematic approach to educational decisions goals, tasks, tools and criteria requirements of actors need to be identified. Not all relevant circumstances are known to decision-makers. The uncertainty calls for techniques to cope with this problem.

Ranking is a tool to get, structure and process information also in educational system. Information collected from the participants of the market of educational services is to be processed according to a certain methodology (compare illustration in Section 4). Carefully worked-out ranking allows observing the market environment as complex construction, distinguish participants and characterize them in abovementioned categories of goals, tasks, tools and criteria requirements (compare also Table 3 in Section 3).

The problem of ranking of higher education institution is discussed in the paper which is organized as follows. After this Introduction, in Section 2 the educational system and market of higher education services in Poland is described. This allows illustrating the general conclusions and complexity of the educational system. The data shows clearly needs of using tools supporting educational decision-making. Section 2 starts with the producer perspective (i.e. the need for ranking from point of view of management of university is considered here). Then in Section 3 other actors are discussed. They are consumers of the output of education called here *educational services*. We consider separately decisions of government representing society and the decisions of individuals (households) in Section 4 dealing with case study (the Polish weekly *Polityka* ranking). The paper is concluded with short sections on the final remarks and references. Here a scenario for correct ranking applications and formulating directions for further research is commented.

2. Socio-economic perspective - the data

During last decade one observes in Poland radical revolution at economical education institutions, as a response to demand for new elite and new type of professionals. In background one witnesses violent escape from state employer (e.g. in 1994 employment at private sector have amounted 46.9% in industry and 92% in commerce). The reorientation of economic system was accompanied with reengineering of education system, see also (Szapiro, 1998c). Outdated and ideologically oriented programs, bureaucratic management, insufficient budgeting of institutions and people caused that the former system could not answer market calls. New situation was related with legal changes in 1990. The new Act on Higher Education from September 12, 1990 introduced a possibility to establish non-state or private university[1]. Due to the Act creation of a private university became legally feasible. The Act provides clear definition of requirements for creation of a university and the formal procedures for its founding.

Thus from 1990 universities in Poland may be divided into two categories of so called public and private universities, as far as the legal status is concerned.

Private universities, as well as any others, fulfill tasks specified in the law. Universities are expected to: educate students in the respective field of knowledge and prepare them to perform specific professions; to carry out scientific research; to prepare candidates for individual and didactic work; to organize post-graduate studies; to popularize the national culture and to propagate knowledge in the society (Szapiro, 1998a).

This change of law launched unusually dynamic change of educational system in its part related with economic education. These is respected and graphed in Figures 1, 2 and 3.

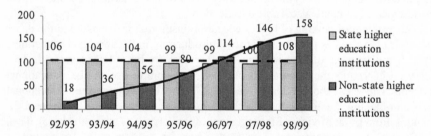

Figure 1. Number of Polish private universities grows fast.

During the last decade the number of students has doubled. This appeared possible mainly due to extramural studies offered by public universities. But input of private universities cannot be neglected - it exceeds 25% of total number of students and 50% of the increase.

---

[1] The higher education institution is said to be a private university if it is owned by individual, company, cooperative, vocational or scientific or religious association, and if it enjoys full economic autonomy.

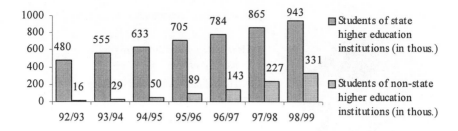

Figure 2.Number of students in Poland.

As it is illustrated in the Figure 4, almost 40% of Polish universities offer economic education.

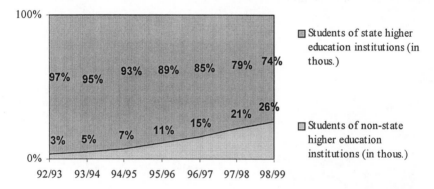

Figure 3. Proportions of students in Poland.

In the group of private universities the domination of economic institutions is even greater (Figure 5) and reaches 60%. Among Polish universities, technical schools (engineering) have a modest representation. Academies of medicine almost disappear from statistics since similarly to technical universities these disciplines need heavy investment to initiate educational activities and this delays monetary return for owners and decreases salaries.

390

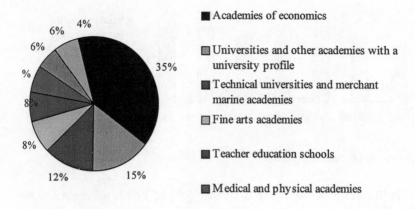

Figure 4: Educational profiles (1998/99).

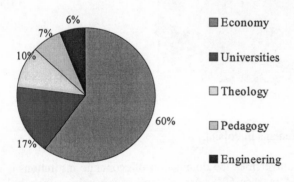

Figure 5: Profiles of private universities in 1997/98.

There are data, which lead to the conclusion that the Polish educational system still has not exhausted its capability to grow. Firstly this is seen from comparisons with other countries. As an example let us consider the reference frame created from the data for three reference countries: France - the West European country with stronger than Polish economy, Romania - an European country with weaker but comparable to Polish economy i.e., and US. All data were collected in 1996 from Central Statistical Office.

	Population (mln)	GNP (bln US$)	GNP per capita (US$)	Salaries (US$)
Poland	38.6	134.6	3484	201.2[a]
France	58.4	1548.2	26624	1200[c]
Rumania	22.6	35.5[a]	1567[a]	7[b]
US	266.5	7263.2	27248	1830[a]

a - 1995; b - 1994; c- 1993; d - 1993/1994.

Table 1. The starting point. General reference data (1996):

Poland with medium population and low GNP per capita reflected in salaries has low potential to finance further growth of educational system. The educational share of the state budget remained during the last decade practically constant. The increase of number of universities and students was financed from private pocket of students. However for the first time, after the decade, Polish universities created the satisfactory number of places for future students - the number of places at Polish universities had exceeded the number of pupils who completed the high school education. Also the number of students is closer to the level of developed western countries then in 1996 (Table 2).

	Students in secondary schools (#/1000)	Students at universities (#/10000)	Graduates in law, social sciences and economy (% of all graduates)
Poland	17	195[d]	25.5%[b]
France	78[d]	362[d]	28.3%[b]
Rumania	65	109[d]	16.1%[b]
US	80[d]	555[d]	37.7%[c]

a - 1995; b - 1994; c- 1993; d - 1993/1994.

Table 2. Selected data on educational systems.

Thus from the socio-economic point of view, the situation of Polish educational system enters the phase of maturity: private universities have to compete for students, if they want to survive on market. Similarly, public universities, which are co-financed by extramural students and state budget depend on income, which is directly related to number of students registered at the university. Thus all universities entered the phase of competition, (Szapiro, 1999, 1998b).

Important fact in this competition is related to benchmarking - reliable comparison of selected evaluations of other universities. Traditionally, in mature market economies educational benchmarking results from accreditation procedures and from rankings. Rankings help university in building a competitive strategy.

On the market of educational services there are however also other actors - households and government.

3. Economy and education

By *education* we understand here a system of institutions in country, which provides citizens with *educational services*. The individual interest in education is obvious. This can be explained using concept of human capital, (Domański, 1993), utility theory and the private rate of return from investment in human capital. This point of view advocates market approach to education management. Following this reasoning, the individual demand for education creates stimuli to offer educational services. For the sake of simplicity, one can briefly argue that since services have to be produced, there arises a cost and market price of this service is assumed to cover this cost. In this model the consumer is charged for the service. However things appear not that simple, since the consumer of educational service is not the only subject profiting from his or her education, see also (Mas-Colell, Whinston, Green, 1995; Varian, 1993).

Psacharopoulos (1987) reports on the research proving that a minimal level of education is indispensable for the state to achieve appropriate rate of economic growth. Increase in the level of education leads to profits for the whole society. Citizens who live in educated society face lower criminality and higher life standard (Czapiński, 1995) in comparison to less educated societies.

This remark suggests that - being in a sense a co-consumer of educational service - the society should share pay charges related to this service, see also (Appelton, 1997; Blaug, 1987; Cohn, 1997; Psacharopoulos, 1987). But being a co-investor, the society is justified to intervene in the process of service production. Thus education cannot be administered basing simply on market mechanisms.

There are also other reasons justifying state intervention in the education system. Firstly, the risk related to future outcome from individual investment in education and the lack of return of the invested funds makes this investment too expensive for individuals and too risky for creditors. State intervention enables to get funds for those who cannot afford education payments. Secondly, outcomes of the decision on education are delayed decades. There is a cognitive gap which disturbs the decision making process - parents can decide being unconsciously influenced by their profit or other factors[2]. The state is hence expected to assist individual educational decisions. Thirdly, the state intervention in educational system is necessary to achieve socially optimal level of educational services. Social optimality is related with external effects of individual economic decisions see also (Knauff, Szapiro, 1998). As examples may serve the ability to absorb and distribute new technologies, health, social and political activities which influence

---

[2] Appelton (1997) reports cases where parents believed the education of son pays more off then education of a daughter.

quality of management processes. In these cases, maximization of individual utilities needs not to lead to socially optimal results. However market mechanism cannot be completely eliminated from provision of educational services, see also (Knauff, Szapiro, 1999). It appears that the state may not be able to optimize the educational policy since the information needed to fulfill this task is not in the state disposition. Also the bureaucracy may deviate the intentions of state partner.

It is not therefore strange that in almost all countries education is co-financed by state and private sector (Cohn, 1997). Thus both subjects influence strategic decisions concerning education. There are the following fundamental issues related with this respect. Firstly, the content and quantity of educational services should be identified. Secondly, the allocation of educational services should be effective; finally distribution of educational services should satisfy equality principle (Stiglitz, 1988).

Thus we need to ponder three actors who are involved in the process of management in educational system: university management, candidates (households) and government. While the first subject is directly involved in management, other two influence the management indirectly since they co-finance the educational offer and thus can exert pressures on decisions. Let us review their objectives and threats to their achievement.

The government is interested in socially optimal outcomes of education. To this end the government is expected to provide the society with reasonably funding and allocation of this funding. Another task is to inform individuals who are not capable to decide on their education. Finally the state is expected to participate in control of universities. The decision on allocation of funds, on informing households and control require evaluation of elements of educational system. One of form of such evaluation is ranking of educational institutions. This ranking is to be based on the criteria reflecting social preferences. As an example, one can consider a ranking used as a tool to create a scheme for allocation of public funds addressed for universities. The decision will be correct if criteria for the ranking reflect correctly social objectives.

Households make decisions on the choice of the economic service. This service is nowadays strongly linked with the economic institution, which provides the service. Utility of these decisions depends on many factors, which create criteria for evaluation of these institutions. The detailed information on all economic institutions is uncertain, hardly available and difficult to process. Thus households are interested in rankings of education institutions. Ranking provides household with aggregated information. If it based on appropriate criteria it is sufficient tool to make decisions on a choice of educational program.

University management objective is related with efficient administration of the university. University subjected - at least in part - to market mechanisms has to include market orientation into managerial operation. One of the most important tools needed to make decisions is benchmarking and this can be supported by comparative analyses underlying ranking preparation. The benchmarking requires taking into account university mission as well as current policy objectives as criteria for comparisons.

	Government	Households	Universities
Goal	Socially optimal outcomes of education.	Optimal choice of the economic service.	Efficient administration
Tasks	to provide funding to allocate it to inform to participate in control.	to elicit preferences to collect the data to process information.	to include market orientation into managerial operation. to perform the comparative analyses
Tool	Ranking of educational institutions.	Ranking of relevant universities	Ranking of competitors
Criteria requirements	to reflect social preferences to create a scheme for allocation of public funds addressed for universities.	to involve utility of a household to aggregate the date clarity of criteria and results.	to serve as reference in curricula design to serve as reference in pricing programs to identify competitive (external) threats

Table 3. The differences of goals result in different tasks and different measures of preferences

Rankings play important role for all subjects in educational system if they are based on proper criteria. Since the criteria of our actors are different there is small chance that a single unique ranking can be useful for all of them simultaneously. The differences are significant as well from point of view of content as formal feature of a ranking, see Table 3.

The Table 3 shows that there is no possibility to built a common, unique ranking meeting goals of government, household and university. Rankings use for comparison of universities and their offers rather complex then sophisticated techniques worked out by different groups of authors.

Internal university rankings are not communicated and cannot be commented here. The government substitutes a ranking in the task of allocation of funds (for public universities) using the *Algorithm* - the procedure to determine the amount of funding addressed to each university. From conceptual point of view, the algorithm is based on a rigid scoring procedure[3]. The rigidity is important since it guaranties stable economic rules. Stability of rules results in predictable behaviors and thus allows to construct effective mechanisms[4]. However the Algorithm is widely criticized. Although it provides the tool to allocate funding, it is not

---

[3] The Algorithm is created in Poland by the Ministry of National Education.

[4] E.g. inclusion of number of Ph.D. students as a factor influencing (increasing) university score (and funding) resulted in increase of Doctoral Programs offered by universities.

effective in information policy and inadequate to perform control functions. In the next Section, the ranking created to assist household in educational decision is reported.

4. Case study

Let us consider a ranking of economic institutions prepared in spring 2000 by a nationwide Polish periodical *Polityka*. The ranking was worked out by a group of anonymous experts appointed by the periodical. The ranking provided readers of *Polityka* with list of Polish universities which offer programs in Economy, Management and Law (the most popular education areas; compare Section 2). The editorial recalls that for inexperienced person, the comparison in this area is really difficult since new schools use similar names and their offer is difficult to distinguish and to evaluate. The same editorial clearly states that the ranking is created to help households in selection of university close to household expectations.

Eighty institutions were ranked, eleven others refused to participate in ranking and to provide experts with relevant information. Information sources were: Ministry of National Education, National Research Committee and own surveys conducted by professional institution.

Public and private universities were investigated if they offer at least programs for the Bachelor degree. It appeared necessary to present results in two groups. The first one grouped these institutions for which economic education is a primary concern. In the second group institution which offer economic programs as a supplementary activity were reported.

Ranking was prepared based on six criteria groups collecting a set of eighty sub-criteria. The following groups of sub-criteria were identified. The *academic position* (weight 25) reflected e.g. the rank assigned to universities by the National Research Committee, share of students at Bachelor, Master and Doctoral programs. The *academic staff potential* (weight 20) reflected e.g. share of fulltime faculties, different faculty-students ratios, scientific promotions. The *pro-student orientation* (weight 20) reflected e.g. degree of flexibility, assistance, role of student evaluation. The *environmental contacts* (weight 15) reflected e.g. international contacts, extramural programs, career tracing. The *selectivity* (weight 10) measured ratio of candidates and registered fulltime students who passed the entering exams, formal exam requirements. Finally the *infrastructure* (weight 10) reflected assets (books, computers, etc.) in disposition of university. Each group consisted of sub-criteria The sub-criteria were weighted using percentage point (the minimal weight was 2 and the maximal - 25).

The results of ranking were published as a cover story in the supplement bulletin attached to the regular edition of the periodical. A net version of report was simultaneously presented on the Internet. The list of criteria and main group weights was published. The newspaper encouraged readers to manipulate with numbers order to get better fit with own evaluation of importance of criteria with respect to subjective goals. This can be easily done using spreadsheet. Standard functions allow then manipulate with weights and rank alternatives with respect to each criterion and their weighted sums.

The results of ranking (top ten institutions) are presented also in the Figure 6 as a printscreen from package $dBIP^5$. The data were imputed to the computer program $dBIP$ a designed to interactively support multicriteria optimization problems.

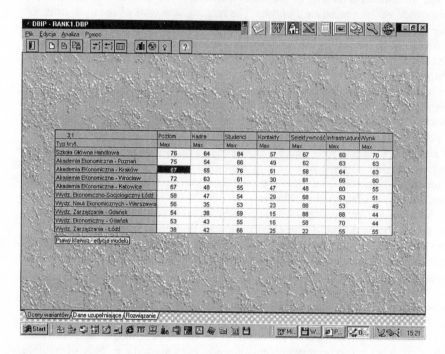

Figure 6. $dBIP$ enables registration of evaluations of educational institutions and determines the best one. Provided with new qualitative information, $dBIP$ modifies initial results.

The simulated results of multicriteria optimization is presented in communication window (see Figure 7) which allows introducing qualitative information on requested direction of modification of the solution.

---

5 The Bireference Interactive Procedure (Michałowski and Szapiro, 1992) and its implementation $dBIP$ by Ożdżeński (1996) is described in (Jędryka and Szapiro, 2000) in the Materials for this Conference.

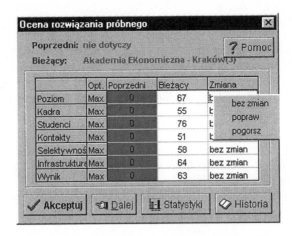

Figure 7. Communication window presents top ranked institution and invites to accept or modify the result.

The software performs functions of the Decision Support Systems significantly enriching user of ranking in his information needs. Expanding the database, this tool can effectively support also other actors described in the Table 3.

5.   Concluding remarks

In the paper an attempt to identify elements of market structure, which influence educational decisions. All actors on the educational market act in uncertainty and therefore need a methodology to process information. After characterizing structure of the market and examining dynamic of educational decision process, the case study providing results of a ranking with comments on possibility of decision support was reported.

Basic dilemma arising in the problem educational decision support is related with need to take into account preferences of a variety of participants with their different goals, criteria and expectations. The next – political - challenge is to built a synergic system of evaluation of universities. This task calls for answers to many methodological questions. They are related to collecting reliable data and decreasing uncontrollable biases resulting from accepting of data structures.

Also a problem of construction of efficient (may be Internet-based) routines is to be mentioned. Opportunities connected with development of computer technology can be used to build a database and to implement the ranking methodology for interactive net-based use.

Next, let us also mention that the mechanisms of educational market should probably intervene in formal construction of ranking procedures. This issue is not investigated in deep and thus there is lack of theory allowing to create general prescriptions for educational case.

Acknowledgements

We are indebted to Danuta Deręgowska from Division of Decision Analysis and Support, Warsaw School of Economics, for providing us data related to educational system in Poland. We are also grateful to all our colleagues from Division of Decision Analysis and Support for helpful comments and suggestions.

References

1. Act on Higher Education from September 12, Journal of Laws, No. 65, pos. 385 (in Polish), 1990;
2. Appelton S.; User Fees, Expenditure Restructuring and Voucher System in Education, The United Nation University, Working Papers No. 134, May 1997;
3. Bittel Lester, R.; Business in action: an introduction to businesses, New York: McGraw-Hill Book, 1989;
4. Blaug M.; The Economics of Education and the Education of an Economists, New York University Press, 1987;
5. Cohn E.; Market Approaches to Education: Vouchers and School Choice, Pergamon 1997;
6. Czapiński Janusz, Cywilizacyjna rola edukacji: dlaczego warto inwestować w wykształcenie, (in Polish) Wydział Psychologii: Instytut Studiów Społecznych Uniwersytetu Warszawskiego, Warszawa 1995;
7. Domański S., R.; Kapitał ludzki a wzrost gospodarczy, PWN, Warszawa 1993;
8. Knauff M., T. Szapiro; Educational Vouchers in Higher Education, (in Polish) TR, No. 03/E/0009/99, WSE, 1999;
9. Knauff M., T. Szapiro; Higher Education as a Public Good – Regulation Dilemma, (in Polish) TR, No. 03/E/0004/98, WSE, 1998;
10. Krzakiewicz K.; Podejmowanie decyzji kierowniczych, (in Polish) Wydawnictwo Akademii Ekonomicznej, Poznań 1993;
11. Krzyżanowski L.; Podstawy nauk o organizacji i zarządzaniu, (in Polish) PWN Warszawa, 1994;
12. Mas-Colell A., M. Whinston, J. Green; Microeconomic Theory, New York: Oxford University Press, 1995;
13. Michałowski W, T.Szapiro, A Bi-Reference Procedure for Interactive Multiple Criteria Programming, Operations Research, t. 40, nr 1, pp. 247-258 1992;
14. Ożdżeński W., Bireference Procedure in a Discrete Decision Problem, in Polish, Technical Report 03/S/0045/96, Warsaw School of Economics, Warszawa, 1996.
15. Psacharopoulos G.; Economics of Education: research and studies, Oxford 1987;

16. Stiglitz J.; Economics of the Public Sector, New York 1988;
17. Szapiro T., "Liberal Arts, Case – Based Skills Formation and Procedural Treatment", notes for the IIIrd Academic Conference of the Community of European Management Schools, Louvain–la–Neuve, 1998c;
18. Szapiro T., „Barriers to Transforming Economic Institutions and How to Overcome Them", in Proceedings of the Fulbright Alumni Association Conference „Education for Transition to Market Economy", Warsaw 1998a;
19. Szapiro T., „Managerial mechanisms and education quality", in Proceedings of the International Conference "Economic and Managerial Studies Quality", Łódź, 1998b;
20. Szapiro T., „Remarks on university management" (in Polish), Nauka i Szkolnictwo Wyższe, nr 12/98, 1999;
21. Varian H.; Microeconomics Analysis, W.W.Norton&Company Inc., 1993.

Multicriterion Analysis Based on Marginal Conditional Stochastic Dominance in Financial Analysis

Grażyna Trzpiot

Department of Statistics, University of Economics, Katowice
ul. 1- Maja 50, 40-287 Katowice, Poland,
trzpiot@figaro.ae.katowice.pl

Abstract. Multicriterion formulation of a decision situation can be defined as a model of three components: the set of attributes, the set of actions and the set of evaluations. In multicriterion financial analysis we apply such a model using Stochastic Dominance for all risk averters. Next we add to analysis Marginal Conditional Stochastic Dominance for help in the decision making process.

Key words: multicriterion analysis, Stochastic Dominance, Marginal Conditional Stochastic Dominance

1. Introduction

Marginal Conditional Stochastic Dominance states the condition under which risk-averse individuals, when presented with a given portfolio, prefer to increase the share of one risky asset over that of another (Shalit, Yitzhaki). Marginal Conditional Stochastic Dominance states rules also the question of whether risk-averse individuals include a new asset when returns of assets are correlated. Marginal Conditional Stochastic Dominance criteria are expressed in terms of the probability distributions of the assets.

In terminology introduced by Vansnik, the multicriterion formulation of decision situation can be defined as a model of three components: the set of attributes, the set of actions and the set of evaluations. Each pair (attribute, action) is described by vector of evaluation. In multicriterion analysis under uncertainty we apply MCAP procedures (Martel, Zaras) which we combine with Marginal Conditional Stochastic Dominance, for help in the decision making process. An empirical application of proposed method is provided using stocks traded on the Warsaw Stock Exchange.

2. Multicriterion Analysis Based on Stochastic Dominance

Multicriterion problem can be defined as a model A, X, E (the set of alternatives, the set of attributes and the set of evaluations) (Zaraś, Martel, 1994).

We have:

1) the set of alternatives $A = \{a_1, a_2, ..., a_m\}$;
2) the set of attributes $X = \{X_1, X_2, ..., X_n\}$, which are independent
3) the set of evaluations $E = \{X_{ij}\}_{mxn}$, where X_{ij} is a random variable with probability function $f_{ij}(x)$. If the interval of variation of the random variables associated with the attribute X_i is represented by $[x_{io}, x_i^o]$ where x_{io}, is the worst value of the attribute X_i, and x_i^o - is the best value of this attribute.

Value of each alternatives according to each attributes can be noticed as a random variable:

Table 1

Model (A, X, E)

Attributes Alternatives	X_1	X_2	... X_j	... X_n
a_1	$f_1(x_{11})$	$f_1(x_{12})$	$f_1(x_{1j})$	$f_1(x_{1n})$
a_2	$f_2(x_{21})$	$f_2(x_{22})$	$f_2(x_{2j})$	$f_2(x_{2n})$
....	....	....	....	....
a_m	$f_m(x_{m1})$	$f_m(x_{m2})$	$f_m(x_{mj})$	$f_m(x_{mn})$

Using stochastic dominance, it is unnecessary to make completely explicit the decision maker's utility function. A decision is made to choose between to alternatives a_i and a_i' on attribute X_i in a close interval $[x_o, x^o]$ where :

$$x_o = min [min\{x_{ij}\}, min\{x_{ij}'\}]$$
$$x^o = max [max\{x_{ij}\}, max\{x_{ij}'\}]$$
$$x_{ij} \in X_{ij}, x_{ij}' \in X_{ij}'$$

Attributes are defined in this way that we know the probability function and the higher value of each attribute is better than lower. We compared pair alternatives $a_i, a_i' \in A$, by comparing two random variables using stochastic dominance. ON one hand we have assumption of independence and we can decompose multiattribute comparing for n one attribute comparing. On the other hand, we use stochastic dominance and we have conclusion „a_i is at least as good as a_i'" for each attributes and form all pair par $(a_i, a_i') \in A \times A$. We use Roy's Preference Aggregation Rule (1985) for building a global outranking relation.

We have two different levels in the expression of the decision-maker's pair wise alternatives preferences with respect to each attribute:

1) Clear - if SD is transparent (SD_T).
2) Unclear - if SD are non- transparent (SD_{NT}).

Given the level of concordance threshold desired by decision maker, the value of concordance index (according to Roy's Preference Aggregation Rule) can be decomposed into two parts:

Explicable concordance

This results from the case in which the expression of the decision maker is clear:

$$C_E\left(a_i, a_i'\right) = \sum_{i=1}^{n} w_j d_j^E\left(a_i, a_i'\right),$$

where $d_i^E(a_i, a_i') = \begin{cases} 1 & \text{if } F_{ij} \, SD_T \, F_{ij}' \\ 0 & \text{otherwise} \end{cases}$

w_j - relative importance accorded the j-th attribute, with $\sum_{j=1}^{n} w_j = 1$,

F_{ij} – the distribution of the i-th alternatives.

Non-explicable concordance

This results from the case in which the expression of the decision maker is unclear:

$$C_N(a_i, a_i') = \sum_{j=1}^{n} w_j d_j^N(a_i, a_i') \quad ,$$

where $d_i^N(a_i, a_i') = \begin{cases} 1 & \text{if } ((F_{ij} \, SD_{NT} \, F_{ij}') \wedge \neg(F_{ij}' \, SD_T \, F_{ij})) \vee \\ & \quad ((F_{ij}' \, SD_{NT} \, F_{ij}) \wedge \neg(F_{ij} \, SD_T \, F_{ij}')) \\ 0 & \text{otherwise} \end{cases}$

w_j - relative importance accorded the j-th attribute, with $\sum_{j=1}^{n} w_j = 1$

The following question arises: is it always necessary to clarify all the case in which the decision maker's preferences are unclear in order to make use of a muticriterion decision aid for statement on alternatives ranking? That depends on the level of concordance threshold required by decision maker in the construction the outranking relation according to Roy's rule.

If the explained concordance index is superior or equal to the concordance threshold p, then it is unnecessary to explain the unclear relations, because we have clear preference for each attributes.

If $C_E(a_i, a_i') \geq p$ then $a_i \, S \, a_i'$,

so $(a_i, a_i') \in S(p)$,

where S(p) is a set of alternatives $(a_i, a_i') \in A \times A$, such that an outranking relation on the concordance threshold level p is verified. Moreover if the concordance threshold p is equal 1, then Multiarrtribute Stochastic Dominance MSD_n is fulfilled.

In particular for $p = 1$ we have:

$a_i \, MSD_n \, a_i'$ if $F_{ij} \, SD_T \, F_{ij}'$, $\forall \, X_j \in A, j = 1, ..., n$ and $MSD_n \subseteq S(1)$

The explanation of the unclear cases may be beneficial if the following conditions are verified:

If $C_E(a_j, a_i') < p$ and $\quad C_E(a_j, a_i') + C_N(a_j, a_i') \geq p$,

where p is a concordance threshold.

If we wish to obtain a more complete network relations between alternative pairs, we can decrease the value of the concordance threshold. If we order the relative importance accorded to each attribute in the following manner:

$w_1 \leq w_2 \leq ,..., w_n$

then for $p = 1 - w_1$ we have that :

$$a_i\, MSD_{n-1}\, a_i' \text{ if } F_{ij}\, SD_T\, F_{ij}', \; \forall\, X_j \in A\backslash X_1$$

Then we obtain a partial Multiarrtribute Stochastic Dominance for all attributes, except the attribute whose relative importance is minimal. Then we can built the global outranking relation based on partial Multiarrtribute Stochastic Dominance for n and n-1 attributes.

$$MSD_n \cup MSD_{n-1} \subseteq S(1-w_1)$$

We can continue this procedure for n-2 attributes, if the decision maker agrees to do so.

3. Marginal Conditional Stochastic Dominance

Marginal Conditional Stochastic Dominance (MSCD) states the probabilistic conditions under which all risk averse individuals, given a portfolio assets, prefer to increase the share of one risky asset over that of another. MSCD is a more confining concept than SSD because it considers only marginal changes in holding risky assets in a given portfolio.

We define MCSD as follows (Shalit, Yitzhaki, 1994): Given a portfolio of risky assets, under what conditions do all risk − averse investors prefer marginally increasing the share of one asset to another? MCSD is not an alternative to SSD; it is an instrument used to reach SSD.

Assume that we analyse the portfolio of an expected utility-maximising individual who holds a portfolio of risky assets and has the opportunity to invest in a new asset. Let's assume that the share of one asset is marginally increased at the expense of an alternative asset, keeping the initial wealth constant.

Consider an investor with a concave utility function, $U(.)$, who holds a portfolio of n assets. Let K_0 be the initial wealth, K final wealth and r_i the rate of return on asset i. The portfolio $\{w\}$ is defined such that $\sum_{i=1}^{n} w_i = 1$, while final wealth is defined by $K = K_0(1 + \sum_{i=1}^{n} w_i r_i)$.

Given portfolio {w} is there an asset k that, if increased the share of it by reducing asset j, will lead to change that will prefer by risk – averse investor? The answer to this question determines the MCSD criterion.

Let dw_k be the marginal change in holding asset k. From $\sum_{i=1}^{n} w_i = 1$ we have

$dw_k + dw_j = 0$.

Hence the marginal change in expected utility is

$$dE(u(K)) = E(u'(K))dK = E_r(u'(K))K_0(c)$$

where E_r is the expectation with respect to all assets return. Inserting $dw_k + dw_j = 0$ and assuming that dw_k is positive, yields

$$dE(u(K))/\, dw_k = E_r(u'(K))K_0(r_k - r_j).$$

Asset k said to dominance asset j, given portfolio {w}, if last equation is positive for all risk – averse investor. MCSD theorem presents the necessary and sufficient condition for dominance in terms of Absolute Concentration Curves (ACC). Let R be the portfolio's rate of return:

$$R = \sum_{i=1}^{n} w_i r_i \, .$$

We define $E(r_i | R=R_0)$ the conditional expected rate of return on asset i when the portfolio's return equals R_0. In a sample of discrete observations, one estimates the conditional expected return $E(r_i | R=R_0)$ by following steps:
1) one finds the set of assets' return that yield a return R_0 on the given portfolio
2) one averages all the realisations of asset i in that set. ACC of asset i with respect to portfolio w is defined as the cumulative conditional expected return on asset i as a function of the cumulative distribution of the portfolio.

Formally:

$$ACC_i(F) = \int_{-\infty}^{R_0} E(r_i | R = t) f_w(t) dt$$

Theorem 1. (Shalit, Yitzhaki 1994). Given portfolio w asset k dominates asset j for all concave u and K if and only if $ACC_k(F) \geq ACC_j(F)$.

This theorem distinguishes between the wealth level of the portfolio and the rates of return on single assets.

4. An Empirical Application of Proposed Method Using Stocks Traded on the Warsaw Stock Exchange

We apply the multicriterion analysis and MCSD in financial analysis as follows: as a set of alternatives we have set of assets, as a set of attribute we have a rate of return, P/E, P/C, and empirical distribution of empirical data (9 assets trade on April 1999) from the Warsaw Stock Exchange.

We solve the Warsaw problem of building efficient portfolio in tree steps:

1) we establish a set of efficient assets by stochastic dominance and multicriterion analysis
2) we create initial conditional portfolio for initial wealth K_0,
3) we test the efficiency of portfolio using MCSD method

Table 2. Observed dominance

Attribute 1	X1	X2	X3	X4	X5	X6	X7	X8	X9
X1	X	SISD	SISD	SISD	SISD	SISD	SISD	SISD	SISD
X2		X							
X3		FSD	X	TSD	TSD			SISD	
X4	TSD	SISD		X	SISD			SISD	SISD
X5	SSD		TSD		X				
X6	FSD	SISD	SSD	SISD		X		SISD	SISD
X7	FSD	SISD	TISD1	SISD	TISD1		X	SISD	SISD
X8	FSD		TSD	TSD				X	
X9		SISD	TISD1		SISD			TISD1	X

Attribute 2	X1	X2	X3	X4	X5	X6	X7	X8	X9
X1	X	SISD	TISD2		SISD			FSD	
X2		X			TISD2			FSD	
X3	SSD	SSD	X		FSD			FSD	
X4	SSD	SSD	FSD	X	FSD			FSD	
X5	TSD	SSD			X			FSD	
X6	FSD	FSD	FSD	FSD	FSD	X	FSD	FSD	FSD
X7	SSD	SISD	SISD	SISD	SISD		X	FSD	SISD
X8								X	
X9	SSD	SSD	FSD	SSD	FSD		TSD	FSD	X

Attribute 3	X1	X2	X3	X4	X5	X6	X7	X8	X9
X1	X	FSD	FSD	FSD	FSD	FSD	FSD	FSD	TISD2
X2		X	FSD	FSD	FSD	FSD		FSD	
X3			X	FSD	FSD	FSD		FSD	
X4				X	FSD	FSD		FSD	
X5					X			FSD	
X6					FSD	X		FSD	
X7		SISD	SISD	SISD	FSD	FSD	X	FSD	
X8								X	
X9	SSD	FSD	FSD	FSD	FSD	FSD	FSD	FSD	X

We started by comparing each of the two random variables on each attribute using stochastic dominance (table 2, we can observe that X2 FSD X3) according to attribute 1) and next we count an explicable concordance index and a non-explicable concordance index (table 3).

Table 3. Explicable concordance and a non-explicable concordance CE and CN

CE/CN	1	2	3	4	5	6	7	8	9
1	X	0,05	0,05	0,05	0,05	0,05	0,05	0,2	-
	X	0,95	0,8	0,8	0,8	0,8	0,8	0,8	0,8
2	-	X	0,05	0,05	0,05	0,05	-	0,2	-
	0,95	X	-	-	-	-	0,2	-	08,
3	0,15	0,95	X	0,85	1	0,05	-	0,2	-
	0,8	-	X	-	-	0,8	1	0,8	0,8
4	0,15	0,95	0,15	X	0,2	0,05	-	0,2	-
	0,8	-	-	X	-	-	1	-	0,8
5	0,15	0,95	-	0,8	X	-	-	0,2	-
	0,8	-	-	-	X	0,8	0,95	-	0,8
6	0,15	0,95	0,15	0,95	0,2	X	0,15	0,2	0,15
	0,8	-	0,8	-	0,8	X	0,8	0,8	0,8
7	0,15	0,8	-	-	0,05	0,05	X	0,2	-
	0,8	0,2	1	1	0,95	0,8	X	0,8	0,8
8	-	0,8	-	0,8	0,8	-	-	X	-
	0,8	-	0,8	-	-	0,8	0,8	X	0,8
9	0,2	0,2	0,2	0,2	0,2	0,05	0,2	0,2	X
	0,8	0,8	0,8	0,8	0,8	0,8	0,8	0,8	X

We use Roy's Preference Aggregation Rule (1985) to build a global outranking relation (figure1, we read graph from left to right, first level is the best asset).

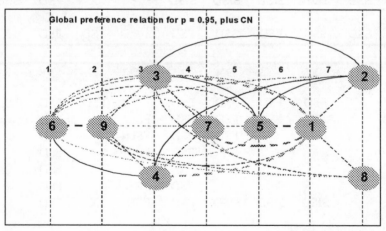

Figure 1.

When we try to choose portfolio we can see from this graph that the best assets are number 6 and number 9, but we can not distinguish between number 3 and 4. We add to procedure MCSD. We count Absolute Concentration Curves (ACC) and Absolute Lorenz Curves (ALC) to compare different portfolio, we use different triple of assets with two different sets of weight.

Table 4.

	ACC			ALC	
Cumulative probability	HANDLOWY 6	WBK 9	BPH 4	ALC1	ALC2
0,07	-0,21	-0,36	-0,21	-0,26	-0,27
0,14	-0,36	-0,43	-0,43	-0,39	-0,39
0,21	-0,50	-0,50	-0,64	-0,53	-0,51
0,29	-0,50	-0,43	-0,79	-0,54	-0,50
0,36	-0,50	-0,36	-0,93	-0,54	-0,49
0,43	-0,50	-0,29	-1,00	-0,54	-0,46
0,50	-0,43	-0,21	-1,07	-0,49	-0,41
0,57	-0,36	-0,14	-1,00	-0,42	-0,34
0,64	-0,21	0,00	-0,86	-0,28	-0,19
0,71	-0,07	0,14	-0,71	-0,14	-0,05
0,77	0,14	0,29	-0,57	0,04	0,13
0,86	0,36	0,50	-0,36	0,26	0,34
0,93	1,00	0,79	0,21	0,78	0,84
1,00	1,86	1,21	1,36	1,56	1,55

weight
ALC1		0,5	0,3	0,2
ALC2		0,5	0,4	0,1

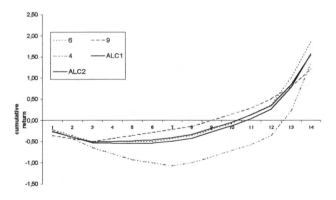

Assets ACCs and Portfolio ALC

Figure 2.

Table 5

Cumulative probability	ACC			ALC	
	HANDLOWY 6	WBK 9	BPH 3	ALC1	ALC2
0,07	-0,21	-0,36	-0,14	-0,24	-0,26
0,14	-0,36	-0,43	-0,29	-0,36	-0,38
0,21	-0,50	-0,50	-0,36	-0,47	-0,49
0,29	-0,50	-0,43	-0,43	-0,46	-0,46
0,36	-0,50	-0,36	-0,50	-0,46	-0,44
0,43	-0,50	-0,29	-0,50	-0,44	-0,41
0,50	-0,43	-0,21	-0,50	-0,38	-0,35
0,57	-0,36	-0,14	-0,43	-0,31	-0,28
0,64	-0,21	0,00	-0,36	-0,18	-0,14
0,71	-0,07	0,14	-0,21	-0,04	0,00
0,77	0,14	0,29	-0,07	0,14	0,18
0,86	0,36	0,50	0,14	0,36	0,39
0,93	1,00	0,79	0,57	0,85	0,87
1,00	1,86	1,21	1,29	1,55	1,54

weight
ALC1   0,5   0,3   0,2
ALC2   0,5   0,4   0,1

Assets ACCs and Portfolio ALC

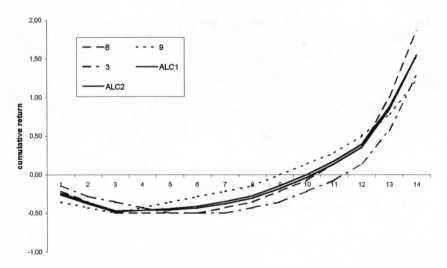

Figure 3.

409

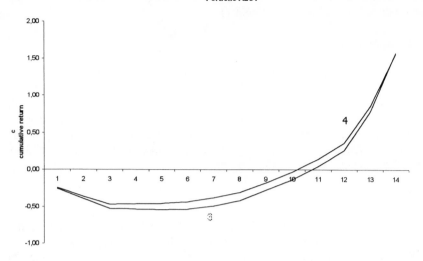

Figure 4.

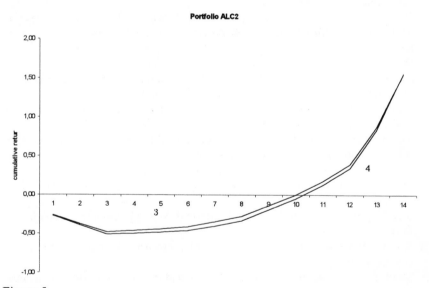

Figure 5.

From this result we can see which portfolio we can choose, which is best according to cumulative return for chosen weight for each assets. Figure 4 informs that for weight as in ALC1 we had better choose asset 4. In case of ALC2 had asset 3 will be better decision (theorem 1).

5. Conclusion

The multicriterion decision situation was defined as a model of three components: the set of attributes, the set of actions and the set of evaluations. In multicriterion analysis under uncertainty we apply MCAP procedures which we combine with Marginal Conditional Stochastic Dominance, for help in the decision making process. An empirical application of proposed method is provided using stocks traded on the Warsaw Stock Exchange. Using the Warsaw Stock Exchange data, we test the efficiency of the market portfolio.

References

1. D'Avignon G.R., Vincke Ph. (1988). An Outranking Method Under Uncertainty. European Journal of Operational Research, 36, 311-321.
2. Fishburn P.C. (1965). Analysis of Decisions with Incomplete Knowledge of Probabilities. Operations Research, 13, 2, 217-237.
3. Hadar J., Russel W. (1969). Rules for Ordering Uncertain Prospect. American Economic Review, 58, 25-34.
4. Huang C.C., Kira D., Vertinsky I. (1978). Stochastic Dominance Rules for Multiattribute Utility Functions. Review of Economic Studies, 41, 611-616.
5. Keeney R.L., Raiffa H. (1976). Decisions with Multiple Objectives: Preferences and Value Tradeoffs. Wiley, New York.
6. Mareschal B. (1986). Stochastic Multicriteria Decision Making and Uncertainty. European Journal of Operational Research, 26, 58-64.
7. Martel J.M., Azondékon S., Zaras K. (1992). Preference Relations in Multicriterion Analysis under Risk. JORBEL, 31, 3-4, 55-83.
8. Martel J.M., Zaras K, (1995). Stochastic Dominance in Multicriterion Analysis under Risk. Theory and Decision, 39, 31-49.
9. Martel J.M., Zaras K. (1997). Modeling Preferences Using Stochastic and Probabilistic Dominances. Doc. de travail 1997-011, Fac. des sc. de l'adm., U. Laval.
10. Roy B. (1985). Methodologie Multicriterie d'Aide à la Décision. Economica, Paris.
11. Roy B., Bouyssou D. (1993). Aide multicritère à la décision : méthodes et cas. Économica, Paris.
12. Shalit H., Yitzhaki S. (1994). Marginal Conditional Stochastic Dominance, Managemant Science, 40, 5, 670 – 684.
13. Trzaskalik T., Trzpiot G., Zaras K. (1998). Modelowanie preferencji z wykorzystaniem dominacji stochastycznych. AE Katowice.
14. Trzpiot G. (1997). Odwrotne dominacje stochastyczne. W: Zastosowania badań operacyjnych, 435-448, Absolwent, Łódź.
15. Trzpiot G. (1998). Stochastic Dominance Under Ambiguity in Optimal Portfolio Selection: Evidence from the Warsow Stock Exchange, Data

Science Classification and Related Methods, Short Papers from VI Conference of the International Classification Societies, Rome, 311-315.

16. Trzpiot G., Zaraś K. (1998). Stabilność dominacji stochastycznych w analizach inwestycyjnych. W: Modelownie preferencji a ryzyko'98, 371-383, AE Katowice.

17. Trzpiot G., Zaraś K. (1999). Algorytm wyznaczania dominacji stochastycznych stopnia trzeciego, Badania Operacyjne i Decyzje, 2, 75-85.

18. Vanderpooten D. (1990). The Construction of Prescriptions in Outranking Methods. In Bana e Costa (eds.). Readings in multiple criteria decision aid. Springer Verlag, Berlin, 184-215.

19. Vansnick J.C. (1990). Measurement Theory and Decision Aid. In Bana e Costa (eds.). Readings in multiple criteria decision aid. Springer Verlag, Berlin, 81-100.

20. Whitmore G.A. (1970). Third-Degree Stochastic Dominance. American Economic Review, 60, 27, 457-459.

21. Zaras K. (1989). Dominance stochastique pour deux classes de fonction d'utilité: concaves et convexes. RAIRO (Recherche opérationnelle/Operations Research), 23, 1, 57-65.

22. Zaras K., Martel J.M. (1995). Une méthode multicritère de rangement de projets face au risque. Compte-rendu ASAC 1995 – Management science/Recherche opérationnelle, 16, 2, 135 - 144.

Multicriteria Analysis Based On Stochastic and Probabilistic Dominance in Measuring Quality of Life

Michał Zawisza[1] & Grażyna Trzpiot[2]

[1]*Department of Operation Research*

[2]*Department of Statistics*

University of Economics, Katowice

ul. 1- Maja 50, 40-287 Katowice, Poland

1. Introduction

In terminology introduced by Vansnik [10], the multicriteria formulation of decision situation can be defined as a model of three components: the set of attributes, the set of alternatives and the set of evaluations. Each pair (attribute, alternatives) is described by vector of evaluation, which may be of different nature. In multicriteria analysis with uncertainty we apply MCAP procedures by Zaras and Martel [13] based on stochastic and probabilistic dominances for welfare in the decision making process.

The problem is formulated in the second section. In the third section multicriteria model based on stochastic and probabilistic dominance is described. Section four contains basic information about social welfare and in section five we have described an empirical application of MCAP in social welfare, especially in some factors as: homelessness, poverty, unemployment etc.

2. Formulation of the Problem

Multicriteria problem can be defined as a model A, X, E (the set of alternatives, the set of attributes and the set of evaluations)

We have:

the set of alternatives $A = \{a_1, a_2, ..., a_m\}$;

the set of attributes $X = \{X_1, X_2, ..., X_n\}$, which are independent

the set of evaluations $E = \{X_{ij}\}_{mxn}$, where X_{ij} is a random variable with probability function $f_{ij}(x)$. If the interval of variation of the random variables associated with the attribute X_i is represented by $[x_{io}, x_i^o]$ where x_{io}, is the worst value of the attribute X_i, and x_i^o - is the best value of this attribute.

Value of each alternative according to each attribute can be noticed as a random variable:

Table 1 Model (A, X, E)

Attributes Alternatives	X_1	X_2	... X_j	... X_n
a_1	$f_1(x_{11})$	$f_1(x_{12})$	$f_1(x_{1j})$	$f_1(x_{1n})$
a_2	$f_2(x_{21})$	$f_2(x_{22})$	$f_2(x_{2j})$	$f_2(x_{2n})$
....	....	....	....	....
a_m	$f_m(x_{m1})$	$f_m(x_{m2})$	$f_m(x_{mj})$	$f_m(x_{mn})$

Attributes are defined in this way that we know the probability function and the higher value of each attribute is better than lower.

Using stochastic dominance, it is unnecessary to make completely explicit the decision-maker's utility function. In most situations the construction of f the utility function is too difficult because the complete information about an individuals preference is difficult to obtain.

Using SD to model preferences of the DM with risk aversion (DARA utility functions $u(x_k)$ which is continuos, concave, and three times differentiable, such that

$u'(x_k) > 0$, $u''(x_k) \leq 0$ and $u'''(x_k) \geq 0$) SD means one of three Stochastic Dominances; FSD, SSD, TSD. The relation between two alternatives was unclear if Inverse Stochastic Dominance (SISD TISD1 or TISD2) was fulfilled between these alternatives and it had to be consulted with the DM [5]. The PD concept was adopted to omit that inconvenience.

3. Multicriteria Analysis Based On Stochastic and Probabilistic Dominance

When comparing two probability distributions we can be confronted with various situations. Our perception will be different if F_{ik} FSD_k F_{jk} when $P(X_{ik} > X_{jk}) = 0,9$ and different for $P(X_{ik} > X_{jk}) = 0,1$. To show the difference Zaras and Martel [13] proposed a precriteria, which discriminated between P_k (strict preference) and Q_k (weak preference) as follows

a_{ik} P_k b_{jk} if $\exists$ $x_k^\alpha \in X_{ik}$ such that $Pr(X_{jk} < x_k^\alpha) > \beta / (1-\alpha)$ i $\neg$ F_{jk} SD_k F_{ik} where $\beta \in [0,5; 1,0]$, $\alpha \in [0; 1,0)$ i $x_k^\alpha = \sup\{x_k / Pr(X_{ik} < x_k) \leq \alpha\}$,

a_{ik} Q_k b_{jk} if $\exists$ $x_k^\alpha \in X_{ik}$ such that $Pr(X_{jk} < x_k^\alpha) \leq \beta / (1-\alpha)$ i F_{ik} SD_k F_{jk},

a_{ik} R_k b_{jk} for the others

R_k are relationships of incomparability or indifference.

This precriterion combines the SD and the PD concepts. We have the strict preference when $Pr(X_{ik} > X_{jk}) \geq \beta$ and F_{ik} SD_k $F_{jk,}$ and also when SD is not verified but $\Pr(x_{ik} > X_{jk}) \geq \beta$ is verified (extention of SD concept by PD). If these two concepts are in opposition, this rule gives priority to the more restrictive condition of SD and then we have weak preference.

If these two concepts (SD i PD) are in oposition, this rule gives priority to more restrictive condition of SD, and classifies that relationship as a weak preference.

To build a global preference relationships between each alternative pair in a multiatribute problem Zaras and Martel [13]suggested the following rules:

$a_i > b_j$ if $\neg\, b_{jk}\, P_k\, a_{ik}$ for all k
and if $w^{P+} + w^{Q+} \geq w^{Q-}$,

$a_i \sim b_j$ for the others

when the two binary relations $>$ and $\sim$ are defined as large preference and no preference, and w^{P+} is the sum of weights for all k where $a_{ik}\, P_k\, b_{jk}$
w^{Q+} is the sum of weights for all k where $a_{ik}\, Q_k\, b_{jk}$
w^{Q-} is the sum of weights for all k where $b_{jk}\, Q_k\, a_{ik}$

At the end, to find the best alternative, we will use the ELECTRE I method (Roy i Bouyssou, [7]).

4. Assignments of Social Welfare

The assignments of social welfare are duties of commune and government administration. Assignments of social welfare are divided into two groups: charged and commune assignments. In both cases a Manager or another person that possess rights given by the City Board decides about acknowledgement of the subsidy.

Charged assignments are obligatory assignments. These are different kinds of allowances, which are warranted by state by the rules contained in law about social aid, paid from budget of the state. Charged assignments are: admitting and paying of stable allowances, social pensions and vested additions, admitting and paying periodic allowances, assignments as a results of government social welfare programs or other laws, which came into existence to protect standard of living of people and their families.

Commune assignments are paid by local commune and they are not obligatory. Authorities of the local commune and social service are to economise suitable money from commune budget to be able to realise payments for all people who need help. The commune assignment allowances are allocated to cover definite needs e.g. purchase of clothing, foods, fuel etc

Basic criterion, which has to be fulfilled by the person wishing to receive the allowance, is the income per one person in family; it cannot exceed a definite threshold.

Second criterion is a fact, that applying for an allowance the candidate has to be characterised by at least one dysfunction, which is called main dysfunction, the others are accompanying dysfunctions.

Total allowance depends on availability of money, which are at social welfare centre's disposal and of course on individual needs of the person who wants to get subsidy from social welfare. Qualifying the needs of customers and proposals of allowances amounts are being prepared by social workers. Final sum of allowance can be changed by Manager e.g. because of limited quantity of money available.

The own assignments are the area, which we consider in this work.

5. Application of Multicriteria Models Based On Stochastic and Probabilistic Dominance In Social Welfare

Data

Constructing the models we used real data, together 10122 records, describing the decisions undertaken in period from January 1997 to December 1998 (not including the negative decisions).

Model I

We examine the model, in which the periods of two years are the alternatives, selected dysfunctions are the attributes and probabilities of the amount acknowledgement from given section are the actions. With this model we would like to check, whether there are any dependencies between amounts of admitted allowances and the period when they were realised. In our model we didn't take into consideration the inflation.

Description of the model

1) set of alternatives A – eight quarters of 1997 and 1998years:

2) set of attributes X - dysfunction:

X_1 - unemployment

X_2 - illness

X_3 - protection of motherhood

X_4 - handicap

X_5 - helplessness in bringing the children up

X_6 – other dysfunction

3) set of evaluations of actions E which were created through qualification of probability of amount acknowledgements from given section, in given quarter for every dysfunction. Sections have ranges 1-200, 201-400, 401-600, 601- 800, 801-1000, 1001-1200, 1201-1400, 1401-1600. From the data we randomised 100 records for every attribute, together 600 from 10122 records.

Example

Using this model we will try to qualify whether amounts admitted allowances for alternative X_2 - illness, which will be the main dysfunction, with other dysfunctions as concurrent in certain quarters of two given years.

In our model we give the following weights for attributes: $w_1=2/25$, $w_2=10/25$, $w_3=5/25$, $w_4=4/25$, $w_5=1/25$, $w_6=3/25$. Results was obtained using MultiSPD software. In the first step we compute stochastic dominances using an alghoritm by Trzpiot, Trzaskalik and Zaras [9]. and the probabilistic dominances Table 1 and 2. show stochastic and probabilistic dominances for attribute X6

Table 1. Stochastic dominances for attribute X6

StochDom	X1	X2	X3	X4	X5	X6	X7	X8
X1	X							
X2	FSD	X	FSD		FSD		FSD	
X3	FSD		X					
X4	FSD	FSD	FSD	X	FSD	SSD	FSD	
X5	FSD		FSD		X		FSD	
X6	FSD	SISD	FSD		SISD	X	FSD	
X7	FSD		FSD				X	
X8	FSD	SISD	FSD	SISD	SISD	FSD	FSD	X

Table 2. Probabilistic dominances for attribute X6

ProbDom	X1	X2	X3	X4	X5	X6	X7	X8
X1	X							
X2	1,00	X	1,00		0,20	0,29	0,46	0,29
X3	1,00		X					
X4	1,00	0,38	1,00	X	0,40	0,43	0,58	0,43
X5	1,00		1,00		X		0,43	
X6	1,00		0,86		0,26	X	0,45	
X7	1,00		0,67				X	
X8	1,00		0,86		0,26	0,33	0,45	X

Then we build a precriterion by Zaras i Martel [13] for each attribute.

Table 3. Precriterion for attribute X6

Precriterion	X1	X2	X3	X4	X5	X6	X7	X8
X1	X	+	+	+	+	+	+	+
X2	P	X	P	+	Q	R	Q	R
X3	P	+	X	+	+	+	+	+
X4	P	Q	P	X	Q	Q	P	Q
X5	P	+	P	+	X	R	Q	R
X6	P	R	P	+	R	X	Q	+
X7	P	+	P	+	+	+	X	+
X8	P	R	P	+	R	Q	Q	X

At the end we build global outranking relations of preference, which are presented in the table 4.

Table 4. Global relations of preferences

Preferencje	X1	X2	X3	X4	X5	X6	X7	X8
X1	X	~	~	~	~	~	~	~
X2	~	X	~	~	~	~	>	~
X3	~	~	X	~	~	~	~	~
X4	~	>	>	X	~	>	~	>
X5	>	>	>	~	X	>	>	~
X6	~	~	>	~	~	X	>	~
X7	~	~	~	~	~	~	X	~
X8	~	>	>	~	~	>	>	X

To find the set of the best alternatives we build a graph uusing thr Electre I method [7]

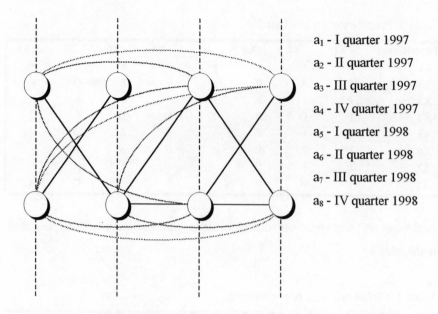

a₁ - I quarter 1997
a₂ - II quarter 1997
a₃ - III quarter 1997
a₄ - IV quarter 1997
a₅ - I quarter 1998
a₆ - II quarter 1998
a₇ - III quarter 1998
a₈ - IV quarter 1998

Fig.1 Global outranking relations for $\beta = 0,5$

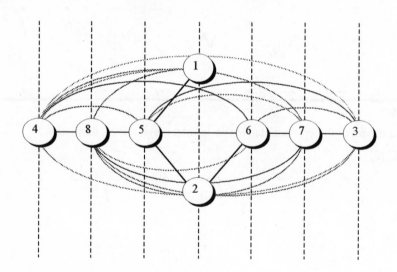

Fig.2 Global outranking relations for $\beta = 0,9$

For β=0,5 alternatives X_4, X_5 which represent and 4th quarter of 1997 and 1st quarter of 1998 remain undominated (fig. 1). As we can see these are winter 97/98 quarters. On the second level we have next two winter quarters. We can assume that during winter quarters amounts of allowances are clearly higher. For β=0,9 four winters quarters lined up themselves in the following order: IV/97, IV/98, I/98 I/97 and II/97. From such order we can infer, that inflation did not have of significant influence on height of admitted allowances. Allowances rather depend on season of the year.

6. Conclusions

We have presented an application of an approach based on the rule of precriteria built on SD and PD concepts in social welfare. We have prepared the software MultiSPD that we used to compute all the results. In the nearest future we would like to build many more models to show the usefulness of these methods and its application in the social welfare problems and other types of problems.

Definitions:

First Stochastic Dominance FSD

F_{ik} FSD F_{jk} if and only if $F_{ik} \neq F_{jk}$ and

$$F_{ik}(x_k) \leq F_{jk}(x_k) \text{ for all } x_k \in [x_{k0}, x_k^0]$$

Second Stochastic Dominance

F_{ik} SSD F_{jk} if and only if $F_{ik} \neq F_{jk}$ i

$$\int F_{ik}(x_k) \leq \int F_{jk}(x_k) \text{ for all } x_k \in [x_{k0}, x_k^0]$$

Third Stochastic Dominance TSD   Whitemore [8]

F_{ik} TSD F_{jk} if and only if $F_{ik} \neq F_{jk}$ i

$$\iint F_{ik}(x_k) \leq \iint F_{jk}(x_k) \text{ for all } x_k \in [x_{k0}, x_k^0]$$

Probabilistic Dominance PD   Wrather and Yu, [11]

F_{ik} PD_k F_{jk} if and only if $Pr(X_{ik} > X_{jk}) \geq \beta$

where $\beta \in [0,5 ; 1,0]$

References

[1] Bawa V.S., Lindberg E.B., Rafsky L.C. „An Efficient Algoritm To Determinate Stochastic Dominance Admissible Sets", Managment Science, Vol 25, No 7, July 1979, (609-622)

[2] Burr R., Porter Portfolio Applications: Empirical Studies; - Stochastic Dominnce. An Approach to Decision-Making Under Risk, Lexington Books, D.C. Heath and Company, Lexington, Massachusetts, Toronto, 1978.

[3] Hadar J., Russel W. R. „Rules of Ordering Uncertaine Prospects", American Economic Review, Vol. 59, 1969. (25 - 34)

[4] Lee Y. R., Stam A. and Yu P.L. (1984). Dominance Concepts in Random Outcomes. Proceedings of International Seminar on the Mathemathics of Multi-Objective Optimization, CISM, Udine, Italy.

[5] Martel J.M., Zaras K. (1994). Multiattribute analysis based on stochastic dominance, in Models and Experiments in Risk and Rationality. Kluwer Academic Publishers, , (225-248)

[6] Quirk P., Saposnik R. Admissibility and Measurable Utility Functions. Review of Economic Study, Vol. 29, 1962, (142 - 146)

[7] Roy B. and Bouyssou D. (1993). Aide multicritere a la decision: Methodes et cas, Economica, Paris.

[8] Whitemore A. (1970). Third Degree Stochastic Dominance. American Economic Review, Vol. 60, , (457-459)

[9] Trzaskalik T.,Zaraś K., Trzpiot G. (1996). Modelowanie preferencji z wykorzystaniem dominacji stochastycznych. Akademia Ekonomiczna w Katowicach, Katowice

[10] Trzaskalik T.,Zaraś K., Trzpiot G. (1997). Modelowanie preferencji z wykorzystaniem dominacji stochastycznych - etap II. Akademia Ekonomiczna w Katowicach, Katowice

[11] Vansnik, J.C. (1990) Measurment theory and decision aid", Readings in Multiple criteria decision aid, Springer Verlag, Berlin 81-100

[12] Wrather, c. and Yu, P.L. 1982 „Probability Dominance in Random Outcomes". Journal of Optimization Theory and Appliccation, 36, 3, 315-334.

[13] Zaraś K. (1989). Dominances stochastiques pour deux classes de fonctions d'utilite: concaves et convexes. RAIRO: Recherche Operationnelle. Vol 23, 1, (57-65)

[14] Zaras K. and Martel J. M. (1997). Modeling Preferences Using Stochastic and Probabilistic Dominances. International Conference on Methods and Applications of Multicriteria Decision Making, Mons, Belgium.

[15] Zawisza M. (1997). Dominacje stochastyczne i ich implementacja komputerowa. Praca magisterska pod kierunkiem naukowym T. Trzaskalika i G. Trzpiot, Akademia Ekonomiczna w Katowicach, Katowice.

Company Financial Multiple Attribute Evaluation under Vagueness Conditions

Zdeněk Zmeškal

VŠB - Technical University of Ostrava, Faculty of Economics,

Sokolská 33, 701 21, Czech Republic,

E-mail: Zdenek.Zmeskal@vsb.cz

Abstract. The ranking of the companies according to financial characteristics is a crucial problem of the financial decision-making. Paper describes an approach to the multiple attribute financial level evaluation. Conditions of financial decision-making are supposed to be only vaguely determined. Fuzzy methodology is applied and fuzzy simple additive weighting method type model is designed. It means financial indices, weights are fuzzy terms and the aspect of non-fixed preciousness of data is included. Fuzzy sets of T-number types, extension principle, ε-cut methodology are used. Methodology of ranking companies is suggested. The simplified illustrative example is introduced.

Keywords: financial level, financial analysis, fuzzy methodology, fuzzy multiple attribute weighting method, companies ranking.

1. Introduction

Under multiple criteria decision making (MCDM) methodology we can distinguish, (1) discrete type approach which is represented by multiple attribute decision making (MADM) models and (2) continuous type approach characterised as multiple objective decision making (MODM). The determining of financial company level is included under the first approach and the paper is dealt with.

The problem of decision making could be divided into two phases. The first phase concerns of aggregations of satisfaction for all criteria per decision alternative. The second phase determines either the ranking of alternatives or assigning alternatives to some groups.

Crisp multiple attribute decision making models formulation

Let us assume that the problem for the first phase is described by, (1) alternatives (A_i), the set of corporations, (2) criteria (C_j), each alternative is characterised by set of characteristics, in finance by financial ratios (indices), (3) utility function for every company (U_i) is an aggregation of criteria by multiple attribute utility function (MAUF),

$$U_i = U_i (C_1, C_2 \ldots\ldots C_n). \tag{1}$$

The many utility models were studied. The most applied is the composition of partial utility function u_{ij} assuming the independence of criteria and their addition. The very well known type of this function is simple additive weighting method (SAWM) where w_j are weights of criteria and numerical ratings (indices) of alternative A_i for criteria C_j are $r_{ij} = u_i (C_j)$, aggregated utility function $U_i = U_i (r_{i1}, r_{i2} ..... r_{in})$ is transformed as follows,

$$U_i = \sum_j w_j \cdot r_{ij} / \sum_j w_j \qquad (2)$$

The second phase is very simple and consists of ranking the real numbers.

Sources of vagueness of MADM financial problems

There are many aspects and reasons that MADM models applied in finance are imprecise in nature,

(1) *Precision* – the requirement for high level of precision may cause the accounting models can lose part of their relevance to the real world by ignoring some relevant items because of not precise measurement or their inclusion may increase the complexity of model.

(2) *Neglect* – many decision models are concentrated on benefits that are not difficult to measure, or improved accuracy could ignore benefits that are difficult to measure such as reduce decisional effort including mental ones. Neglect of vagueness may cause the analysis to be incomplete, unrepresentative and irrelevant.

(3) *Effectiveness* – high levels of precision required by accounting and financial models are not unwarranted, but also uncertainty for an effective analysis.

(4) *Applicability* – the call for precise measure that are difficult to obtain can hinder the applicability of financial models.

(5) *Precise data ability providing* - the demand for precise input data may represent a primary reason for the uneasiness of the potential models users. The difficulty concerns of decision-maker to provide precise data necessary for models to give reliable results. When precise data are not attainable, the decision-makers are forced to resort or enrich the data.

(6) *Fixed level of accuracy* – this assumption is often unrealistic, and may cast doubt about the usefulness of the aggregate totals. There is question whether variables estimated with different degrees of accuracy can be meaningfully aggregated.

(7) *Predictive and descriptive power* – incorporating the vagueness and ambiguity displayed in the accounting environment into financial models may improve the descriptive and predictive power of models.

(8) *Flexibility* – managers usually make decisions without having a full range of accurate measurement. The ability to deal with that situation affords them great flexibility in compare with traditional techniques.

The introduced features are basic arguments for application of indeterminacy models. Since this aspect is typical for financial decision making, it might be fruitful to apply a soft computing methodology. Fuzzy approach is one of possibilities characterised by good way of simplification, interpretability and implementation.

2. Fuzzy multiple attribute decision making models

There are possible to distinguish under fuzzy multiple attribute decision making (FMADM) methodology three basic model variants,

(1) Fuzzy variables – weights and utility functions are stated as fuzzy sets, for instance "leverage is approximately 40 % ", "return on equity is about 10 %", etc.

(2) Linguistic variable – linguistic terms are assigned fuzzy sets, for example "leverage is sufficient", "liquidity is low", etc.

(3) Real (crisp) variable – special case of fuzzy models, fuzzy sets are of singleton type, it means real numbers and the model is deterministic.

Definition 1. A *fuzzy set* (depicted with tilde) is commonly defined by a membership function (μ) as a representation from E^n (Euclid n-dimensional space,

$n > 1$) to a set of E^1 especially to the interval of $[0; 1]$, $\tilde{s} \equiv \mu_{\tilde{s}}(x)$, where $\tilde{s}$ is

fuzzy set, x is vector and $x \in X \subset E^n$, $\mu_{\tilde{s}}(x)$ is membership function.

Very fruitful and powerful instrument which might be used for calculating of a function of fuzzy sets is extension principle, see (Zadeh (1965)).

Definition 2. The *extension principle* is derived by sup min composition between fuzzy sets $\tilde{r}_1...\tilde{r}_n$ and $\tilde{s} = f(\tilde{r}_1...\tilde{r}_n)$ as follows. Let $f : E^n \to E^1$, then membership function of fuzzy set $\tilde{s} = f(\tilde{r}_1...\tilde{r}_n)$ is defined by

$$\mu_{\tilde{s}}(y) \equiv \tilde{s} = \sup_{\substack{x_1,...,x_n \\ y=f(x_1,...,x_n)}} \min[\mu_{\tilde{r}_1}(x_1)......\mu_{\tilde{r}_n}(x_n)], x_i, y \in E^1 \tag{3}$$

The fuzzy multiple attribute decision making (FMADM) model may be commonly expressed by extension principle as follows,

$$\tilde{U}_i \equiv \mu_{\tilde{U}_i}(u_i) = \sup_{v:u_i=f(y_j,x_{ij})} \min_j \left| \mu_{\tilde{w}_j}(y_j); \mu_{\tilde{r}_{ij}}(x_{ij}) \right|, \tag{4}$$

where $v = (y_1 ..... y_n; x_{i1} .....x_{in})$ and $\mu_{\tilde{U}_i}(u_i), \mu_{\tilde{w}_j}(y_j), \mu_{\tilde{r}_{ij}}(x_{ij})$ are membership functions of $\tilde{U}_i, \tilde{r}_{ij}, \tilde{w}_j$.

The solution method of the model described is not possible to get generally analytically and thus an approximate procedure is to be applied. Procedure selection depends mainly on fuzzy set types and fuzzy operation between fuzzy sets.

FSAWM under linear T-numbers and non-fixed input data preciousness

In this section we present a model methodology of fuzzy simple additive weighting method (FSAWM) type under T-numbers and non-fixed input data preciousness. The model is of SAWM version, however data are introduced vaguely by fuzzy sets of T-number type and assumption of non-fixed level of input data accuracy is considered. Partial utility function of crisp case is $U_i = \sum_j w_j \cdot r_{ij} \cdot v_{ij} / \sum_j w_j$, where parameter v_{ij} means degree of preciousness (credibility) of data. If $v_{ij} = 1$, for every j, the problem is of SAWM version. Formulation of fuzzy utility function in accordance with the extension principle (Definition 2) is following,

$$\mu_{\tilde{U}_i}(u_i) = \sup_{v: u_i = \sum_j y_j \cdot x_{ij} \cdot z_{ij} / \sum_j y_j} \min_j [\mu_{\tilde{w}_j}(y_j); \mu_{\tilde{r}_{ij}}(x_{ij}); \mu_{\tilde{v}_{ij}}(z_{ij})] \tag{5}$$

Definition 3. *T-number* is fuzzy set meeting preconditions of normality, convexity, continuity and closeness and being defined as quadruple $\tilde{s} = (s^L, s^U, s^\alpha, s^\beta)$ where $\phi(x)$ is non-decreasing function and $\psi(x)$ is non-increasing function as follows, a set of T-numbers is denoted by $F_T(E)$,

$$\tilde{s} \equiv \mu_{\tilde{s}}(x) = \begin{cases} 0 & \text{for} \quad x \le s^L - s^\alpha; \phi(x) \text{ for} \quad s^L - s^\alpha < x < s^L; \\ 1 & \text{for} \quad s^L \le x \le s^U; \psi(x) \text{ for} \quad s^U < x < s^U + s^\beta; \\ 0 & \text{for} \quad x \ge s^U + s^\beta \end{cases} \tag{6}$$

Definition 4. The *linear T-number* is defined so as T-number where functions $\phi(x)$ and $\psi(x)$ are linear, $\phi(x) = \dfrac{x - (s^L - s^\alpha)}{s^\alpha}$, $\psi(x) = \dfrac{(s^U + s^\beta) - x}{s^\beta}$, and is depicted as quadruple $\tilde{s} = (s^L, s^U, s^\alpha, s^\beta)$, the set of linear T-numbers is denoted by $F_{TL}(E)$.

Under T-numbers three approaches of solution FSAWM problem formulated by (5) might be used, (1) analytical solution by application of extension principle, (2) approximate fuzzy algebraic operations procedure, (3) approximate ε-cut procedure. Because the analytical solution is not mostly usable this approach is not explained.

Approximate fuzzy algebraic operation procedure

Under this procedure the $\tilde{U}_i$ value is computed by approximate fuzzy algebraic operations between T-numbers. Because of application aspects and paper purpose, operations are described for linear T-number. The FSAWM model (5) under suppositions said could be formulated,

$$\tilde{U}_i = (\tilde{w}_1 \otimes \tilde{r}_{i1} \otimes \tilde{v}_{i1} \oplus \tilde{w}_2 \otimes \tilde{r}_{i2} \otimes \tilde{v}_{i2} ..... \tilde{w}_n \otimes \tilde{r}_{in} \otimes \tilde{v}_{in}) \div \sum_j \tilde{w}_j \tag{7}$$

Definition 5. The operations of fuzzy addition and fuzzy multiplication are defined in accordance with Bonnisone (1982) for positive linear T-numbers as follows,

(1) *Fuzzy addition* $(\oplus, \tilde{\Sigma})$ for $\tilde{s}, \tilde{r} \in F_{TL}(E)$, for $\tilde{s}; \tilde{r} > 0$,

$$\tilde{s} \oplus \tilde{r} = (s^L; s^U; s^\alpha; s^\beta) \oplus (r^L; r^U; r^\alpha; r^\beta) = (s^L + r^L; s^U + r^U; s^\alpha + r^\alpha; s^\beta + r^\beta),$$

where fuzzy set is *positive fuzzy set* ($\tilde{s} > 0$), if for every $x \in \text{supp} \tilde{s}$, x>0, and $\text{supp} \tilde{s} = \{x \in X; \mu_{\tilde{s}}(x) > 0 \}$,

(2) *Fuzzy multiplication approximation* $(\otimes; \tilde{\Pi})$ for $\tilde{s}, \tilde{r} \in F_{TL}(E)$, for $\tilde{s}; \tilde{r} > 0$,

$$\tilde{s} \otimes \tilde{r} = \left(s^L \cdot r^L ; s^U \cdot r^U ; s^L \cdot r^\alpha + r^L \cdot s^\alpha - s^\alpha \cdot r^\alpha ; s^U \cdot r^\beta + r^U \cdot s^\beta - s^\beta \cdot r^\beta \right),$$

(3) *Fuzzy division approximation* ($\tilde{:}$) for $\tilde{s}, \tilde{r} \in F_{TL}(E)$, for $\tilde{s}; \tilde{r} > 0$,

$$\tilde{s} \tilde{:} \tilde{r} = \left(\frac{s^L}{r^U}; \frac{s^U}{r^L}; \frac{s^L \cdot r^\beta + r^U \cdot s^\alpha}{r^U \cdot \left(r^U + r^\beta \right)}; \frac{s^U \cdot r^\alpha + r^L \cdot s^\beta}{r^L \cdot \left(r^L - r^\alpha \right)} \right).$$

Remark 1: The results of operation of fuzzy addition is correct in accordance with the extension principle. Fuzzy multiplication and division are the approximate operations, because the results of multiplication and division are not linear T-numbers under the extension principle rule.

Advantage of the method described is in using a simple and few calculations, the results are in the same class of fuzzy sets. Disadvantage consists in confining approach applicability on special types of fuzzy sets, (linear) T-number (or generally fuzzy numbers) and getting only approximate results.

Approximate ε-cut procedures

Assuming a fuzzy set is of the T-number type (fuzzy number type as well) there is possible to solve function of fuzzy numbers $\tilde{s} = f(\tilde{r}_1 ... \tilde{r}_n)$ in accordance with the extension principle as the approximate procedure of ε-cuts.

Definition 6. The *ε-cut* of the fuzzy set $\tilde{s}$, depicted $\tilde{s}^\varepsilon$, is defined as follows.

$$\tilde{s}^\varepsilon = \left\{ x \in E'; \mu_{\tilde{s}}(x) \geq \varepsilon \right\} = \left[^-s^\varepsilon, {}^+s^\varepsilon \right], \tag{8}$$

where $^-s^\varepsilon = \inf \left\{ x \in E'; \mu_{\tilde{s}}(x) \geq \varepsilon \right\}$, ${}^+s^\varepsilon = \sup \left\{ x \in E'; \mu_{\tilde{s}}(x) \geq \varepsilon \right\}$.

Definition 7. *Approximate procedure of ε - cuts* for construction the T-numbers, $\mu_{\tilde{s}}(x)$, is defined as follows,

$$\mu_{\tilde{s}}(x) \equiv \tilde{s} = \bigcup_\varepsilon \varepsilon [^-s^\varepsilon, {}^+s^\varepsilon] \quad \text{for any} \quad x \in E' \text{ and any } \varepsilon \in [0;1],$$

where $\tilde{s}^\varepsilon = [^-s^\varepsilon, {}^+s^\varepsilon]$ is ε - cut. Here $\left(\varepsilon; [^-s^\varepsilon, {}^+s^\varepsilon] \right) = \begin{cases} \varepsilon \text{ if } x \in [^-s^\varepsilon, {}^+s^\varepsilon] \\ 0 \text{ if } x \notin [^-s^\varepsilon, {}^+s^\varepsilon] \end{cases}$.

Definition 8. *Approximate procedure of ε - cuts* for construction a function of T-numbers (fuzzy numbers as well),

$\mu_{\tilde{s}}(y) \equiv \tilde{s} = f[\mu_{\tilde{r}_1}(x_1) ..... \mu_{\tilde{r}_n}(x_n)]$, where $x_i, y \in E'$, is defined as follows.

$$\mu_{\tilde{s}}(y) \equiv \tilde{s} = \bigcup_\varepsilon \varepsilon [^-s^\varepsilon, {}^+s^\varepsilon], \tag{9}$$

for any $\varepsilon \in [0;1]$, where $^-s^\varepsilon = \min_{x \in \tilde{x}^\varepsilon \subset E^n} f(x)$, ${}^+s^\varepsilon = \max_{x \in \tilde{x}^\varepsilon \subset E^n} f(x)$.

Remark 2. It is apparent that applying the Definition 8 a function of T-numbers (fuzzy numbers as well) could be transformed and solved as several mathematical programming problems for ε by this way,

max (min) $s \equiv {}^+s^\varepsilon, (^-s^\varepsilon)$,

s.t. $s = f(x_1 .... x_n)$,

where $x_i \in \left[{}^-x_i^\varepsilon, {}^+x_i^\varepsilon\right]$ for $i \in \{1, 2 \ldots \ldots n\}$, and $\varepsilon \in [0;1]$.

Advantage of the approximate procedure is in generalised application possibility for T-numbers (fuzzy numbers as well). Disadvantage consists in computation difficulty.

Ranking and similarity of the fuzzy sets

Because the utility value ($\tilde{U}_i$) is fuzzy set, to solve the second problem phase means ranking of fuzzy sets or assigning them into groups. Solutions concern of binary relation types. There are many approaches, (1) binary preference relations, (2) fuzzy scoring relations, (3) fuzzy mean and spread, (4) linguistic methods, see for instance Dubois (1980), Tsukumoto (1983), Tong (1984), Ramik (1986), Lee (1988), Chen (1989), Ramik (1996).

The purpose of determining a corporate financial level is to assign the corporations into groups. The similarity measure is useful conception, which could be used, one of examples is the discrete inclusion measure $I_{ik}(\tilde{U}; \tilde{Z}_k)$:

$$I_{ik}(\tilde{U}; \tilde{Z}_k) = \left|\tilde{U} \cap \tilde{Z}_k\right| / \left|\tilde{U}\right|, \qquad (10)$$

where $\tilde{Z}_k$ is the k-th category of financial corporate level, $\tilde{U} \cap \tilde{Z}_k = \bigcup_x \min\left[\mu_{\tilde{U}_i}(x), \mu_{\tilde{Z}_K}(x)\right]$.

Further $\left|\tilde{U}\right|$ is the card of a fuzzy set, which is defined for discrete and continuous case as follows, $\left|\tilde{U}\right| = \sum_x \mu_{\tilde{U}}(x)$ or $\left|\tilde{U}\right| = \int_x \mu_{\tilde{U}}(x)\, dx$.

It is apparent that the measure $I_{ik} \in [0;1]$. If $I_{ik} = 1$, then corporation is fully a member of particular category, if $I_{ik} = 0$, then company is not.

3. Illustrative example

Now a simplified model of FWSAM type with non-fixed data preciousness (5) and under linear T-number (Definition 4), parameterised by linguistic variables, solved by approximate ε-cut procedure (Definition 8 and realisation by Remark 2) will be described and solved.

We assume of having three companies (A1, A2, A3) which might be assigned in five categories of financial level, which are articulated as follows, (1) excellent, (2) good, (3) middle, (4) bad, (5) poor.

Further we suppose that the aggregate financial level, $\tilde{U}_{ij}$, is characterised through three criteria, $\tilde{r}_{ij}$, (1) profitability, (2) liquidity, (3) leverage. Weights of criteria, $\tilde{w}_{ji}$, data preciousness, $\tilde{v}_{ij}$, are expressed linguistically and every term is equivalent with linear T-number. The particular shape is shown in Table 1 and Figure 1.

Table 1 Input linguistic parameters and linear T-number shape assigned

	Aggregated financial level	Profitability, Liquidity, Data preciousness	Leverage	Weights	linear T-number			
	$\widetilde{U}_{ij}$	$\widetilde{r}_{i1j}, \widetilde{r}_{i2}, \widetilde{v}_{ij}$	$\widetilde{r}_{i3j}$	$\widetilde{w}_{jj}$	a^L	a^U	a^α	a^β
1	excellent	high	Low	significant	0,9	1	0,1	0
2	good	rather high	rather low	-	0,7	0,8	0,1	0,1
3	middle	middle	middle	middle significant	0,4	0,6	0,1	0,1
4	bad	rather low	rather high	-	0,2	0,3	0,1	0,1
5	poor	low	high	non-significant	0	0,1	0	0,1

Figure 1 Graphical representation of linear T-numbers

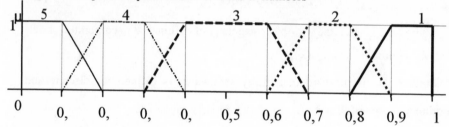

Now we suppose that a financial analyst estimates and gives for every corporation (A1, A2, A3) financial characteristics, weights and data preciousness vaguely by linear T-numbers. These data estimates show Table 2. (For the sake of simplicity the parameter of data preciousness is for every financial characteristic for particular company the same it means that $\widetilde{v}_{i1} = \widetilde{v}_{i2} = \widetilde{v}_{i3}$).

Table 2 Linguistic characteristics of companies financial level

Characteristics	Profitability	Leverage	Liquidity	Data preciousness
Weights	middle significant	significant	non-significant	-
Company A1	rather high	low	middle	rather high
Company A2	rather low	rather low	rather low	middle
Company A3	low	rather low	middle	rather low

Calculated results of fuzzy utility functions in accordance with (5) and maximum inclusion measure Iik according to (10) are shown in following Table 3 and Table 4.

Table 3 Evaluation results of companies' utility functions

Company	Utility functions	linear T-number			
		a^L	a^U	a^α	a^β
A1	$\widetilde{U}_1$	0,5556	0,7543	0,1603	0,1249
A2	$\widetilde{U}_2$	0,1925	0,3943	0,0825	0,1549
A3	$\widetilde{U}_3$	0,0837	0,0180	0,0517	0,1154

Table 4 Evaluation results of companies' financial level with the different data preciousness

Company	Inclusion – similarity measure						Evaluation
	Ii1	Ii2	Ii3	Ii4	Ii5	max Iik	
A1	0,2641	0,8338	0,5818	0,0117	0	0,8338	good
A2	0	0	0,4153	0,975	0,3	0,975	bad
A3	0	0	0	0,4884	0,6141	0,6141	poor

From the results it is possible to judge that on the FSAWM method basis including data preciousness determining, the financial level of corporation A1 is good, A2 bad and A3 poor.

It is interesting to compare these results with the same problem but without considering the data different preciousness it means $\widetilde{v}_{ij} = [1; 1; 0; 0]$ for every data. Results illustrate Table 5.

Table 5 Evaluation results of companies' financial level with the same data preciousness

Company	Inclusion – similarity measure						Evaluation
	Ii1	Ii2	Ii3	Ii4	Ii5	max Iik	
A1	0,7326	0,6186	0,0686	0	0	0,7326	excellent
A2	0	0,4615	0,8057	0,1617	0	0,8057	middle
A3	0	0,3461	0,9372	0,2059	0	0,9372	middle

The calculations show (detailed data of utility functions are not for the sake of conciseness introduced) that financial level of company A1 is excellent, A2 is middle and A3 is also middle.

This simple example illustrates the significant difference concerning the results and their sensitivity on input data preciousness.

4. Conclusion

The methodology of FMADM shows possibility to describe more realistically conditions and circumstances of decision making. There are many approaches used. From implementation point of view the FSAWM method is simple and useful. As was explained there are many aspects of vagueness. The weights, utility functions could be stated vaguely. In the paper the aspect of non-fixed preciousness input data were stressed and modelled vaguely and FSAWM model was modified. This aspect is often neglected, but in financial decision is presented and very significant and that is why it could be suitable to model and include a degree of preciousness data parameter in fuzzy multiple attribute decision models.

Acknowledgements: The research was partly supported by Grant Agency of the Czech Republic (GAČR) CEZ: J 17/98: 75100015

References

Bonissone, P.P.: A Fuzzy Sets Based Linguistic Approach, Theory and Application, In: Gupta, M.M., Sanchez, E. (1982): Approximate Reasoning in Decision Analysis. North-Holland,

Copeland, T.E, Weston, J.F. (1988), Financial theory and corporate finance, Addison - Wesley.

Dubois, D., Prade, H.,.(1980), Fuzzy sets and systems, Academic Press, New York, 9-35.

Gupta, M.M., Sanchez, E. (1982): Approximate Reasoning in Decision Analysis. North-Holland,

Chen, S.J., Hwang,C.L. (1989): Fuzzy Scoring of fuzzy number - A direct comparison index, Kansas State University

Chen, S.M.: Evaluating weapon systems using fuzzy arithmetic operations, Fuzzy Sets and Systems, 77, 1996

Lee, E.S., Li, R.L. (1988): Comparison of fuzzy numbers based on the probability measure of fuzzy events. Computer and Mathematics with Applications, 15, p.887-896

Ramík, J. (1996), „New Interpretation of the Inequality Relations in Fuzzy Goal Programming Problems", Central European Journal for Operation Research and Economics, No. 4.

Ramík, J., Římánek, J. (1986): Inequality relations between fuzzy numbers and its use in fuzzy optimization. Fuzzy Sets and Systems, 16

Ribeiro, R. A.: (1996): Fuzzy multiple attribute decision making. A review and new preference elicitation techniques. Fuzzy Sets and Systems, No. , 151-18178

Riberio, R. A., Zimmermann, H. J., Yager, R. R., Kacprzyk, J. (1999): Soft Computing in Financial Engineering, Springer Verlag

Rommelfanger, H. J. (1999): Fuzzy Logic Systems for Checking Credit Solvency of Small Business Firm. In: Riberio, R. A., Zimmermann, H. J., Yager, R. R., Kacprzyk, J. (1999): Soft Computing in Financial Engineering, Springer Verlag

Siegel, H.P., de Korvin,A., Omer, K. (1995): Application of Fuzzy Sets and the Theory of Evidence to Accouting, JAI Press Inc.

Tong, R.M., Bonissone, P.P. (1984): Linguistic solutions to fuzzy decision problems. In: TMS/Studies in the Management Science, 20, Zimmermann, H.J., Elsevier Science Publishers B.V., North-Holland, p.323-334

Tsukamoto,Y.P., Nikiforuk, N. - Gupta ,M.M. (1983): On the comparison of fuzzy sets using fuzzy chopping. In: Control Science and Technology for Progress of Society, Pergamon Press, New York, pp.46-51

Zadeh, L. A.(1965), „Fuzzy sets", Information Control, 8 (3), 338-353.

Druck: Strauss Offsetdruck, Mörlenbach
Verarbeitung: Schäffer, Grünstadt